D1568936

Japan in the World

Edited by Masao Miyoshi and
H. D. Harootunian

Duke University Press
Durham and London 1993

Second printing, 1996
© 1993 Duke University Press
All rights reserved
Printed in the United States of America
on acid-free paper ∞
Except for "Japan in the World," "Japan's Industrial Revolution in Historical Perspective,"
"Archaeology, Descent, Emergence: Japan in British/American Hegemony, 1900–1950,"
"America's Japan / Japan's Japan," and "The Invention of English Literature in Japan,"
the text of this book was originally published as volume 18, number 3 of *boundary 2: an
international journal of literature and culture.*
Library of Congress Cataloging-in-Publication Data
Miyoshi, Masao.
Japan in the world / edited by Masao Miyoshi, and H. D.
Harootunian.
p.   cm.
Includes bibliographical references and index.
ISBN 0-8223-1350-2 (alk. paper) —ISBN 0-8223-1368-5
(pbk. : alk paper)
1. Japan—Relations—Foreign countries.   2. Japan—Foreign
economic relations—United States.   3. United States—Foreign
economic relations—Japan.   4. Japan—Civilization—1945–
I. Harootunian, Harry D.
DS845.M56   1993
952.04'9—dc20   93-2399

Contents

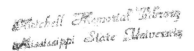

Note on Japanese Names

Japanese names throughout this issue, except those of Japanese-Americans (and Japanese-Europeans), are written in Japanese order—surname first. This can still present confusion, however: In Oe Kenzaburo, Oe is the author's surname, and Kenzaburo is his given name; but in Kazuo Ishiguro, Ishiguro is the author's surname, and Kazuo is his given name. In Japan, writers are sometimes known by their surnames and sometimes by their given names. For example, Natsume Soseki is known as Soseki (not as Natsume), while Watsuji Tetsuro is known as Watsuji.

We have decided against the use of macrons to indicate long vowels in anglicizing Japanese names. Those who know the language have no difficulty in differentiation, and such symbols are of little use to those unfamiliar with the language.

Japan in the World

Masao Miyoshi
H. D. Harootunian

During the Cold War the two superpowers were forced to compete for the allegiance of the Third World countries. As could be expected, they reacted by manipulating the bipolar tension to their own economic advantages. With the end of the Cold War, dramatically marked by the U.S. invasion of Iraq, this situation was irretrievably altered. Since neither the United States nor the Soviet Union required the support of the Third World countries any longer, they radically reduced the material assistance they had provided during the previous four decades. The collapse of the Soviet Union exacerbated this process of abandonment. Left alone, several nonindustrial nations slipped into uncontrolled and, possibly, irreversible balkanization and fragmentation, if not famine and starvation. Thus the end of the Cold War deprived many Third World nations of even the illusion of an opportunity for industrial development. With the decline of bipolarism, the world now seems to be heading toward some sort of division among powerful economic powers. The United States and its North American neighbors, the European Community, and Japan with its NIEs now present the possibility of tripartite regionalism. The Second World—with the possible exceptions of the People's Republic of China and Cuba—are virtually being absorbed into the ranks of the Third World.

In the new global paradigm, Japan is being compelled to define its position in the world for the first time since the end of World War II. And yet, as its conduct during the Gulf War demonstrates, it has not been forthcoming with a clear enunciation of its political role in the shaping of a new world system. During the Gulf War, Japan was regarded as an ally of the "U.N. forces," making contributions of well over ten billion dollars for the war expenses, but refused to send ground troops because its postwar constitution explicitly prohibits the use of armed forces, as further explained below. A mere two years later, however, Japan grudgingly yielded to international pressure toward participation in the U.N. peace-keeping organization and embarked upon a different course of action. Without full debate or resolution of the issues concerning the dictates of the constitution, the ruling Liberal Democratic Party (LDP) passed a bill authorizing the dispatch of peace-keeping forces to Cambodia. Although the deployment is officially claimed to be only for noncombative purposes, the fundamental change in Japan's military policy since the Gulf War is indisputable, and the reversal seems unalterable. This ambiguity surrounding Japan's foreign policy, including its military planning, is also evident in the U.S.-Japan agreement regarding the stationing of U.S. troops in Japanese territories. Now that the obvious threat of a hostile superpower no longer exists, the maintenance of a large-scale U.S. military presence for the protection of Japan is simply inexplicable. The Japanese government, however, shows no sign of raising this issue any time soon.

One possible explanation of this persistent ambivalence derives from Japan's postwar relationship with the United States. Since the war, Japan has been wholly under the political, economic, and cultural hegemony of the United States. As a result of this relationship, Japan has not yet been able to achieve true independence and autonomy, even though by all agreement American occupation ended long ago and the Japanese have declared an end to the postwar era. The American occupation early imposed a constitutional framework on the defeated population of Japan. This constitution, specifically its Article 9, prohibited the Japanese from future remilitarization. A consequence of this clause was to divide Japanese thinking into two quite distinct camps: those who were fully convinced that Japan's total defeat resulted in the imposition of an alien principle and the loss of national autonomy; and those who believed that the renunciation of arms was absolutely vital to the maintenance of a peaceful world order, despite the foreign origins of the principle embodied in the constitution. In a sense, the Japanese commitment to peace was seen by the latter group as a uniquely enlightened example for the rest of the world to follow.

The same constitution also redefined the nature of political authority by recoding the Japanese emperor as a "symbol of the State and of the unity of the people," whereas before the war he had been the sole authority, sacred and inviolable. Yet this effort to retain an archaic imperial institution, while weakening it by removing its original source of divine legitimation, created still another ambiguity in Japan's national consciousness. Nobody foresaw in 1946 what now appears as an inherent disposition to continue the myths employed by the prewar Japanese order. The consequences of establishing a symbolic emperorship have proved to be far more pervasive and serious than anyone suspected at the time. Ramifications have touched every aspect of Japanese society. As Japanese prosperity began to invite closer attention from the world, it became evident that one of the enabling factors of this economic order was the recycling of the older elements in the national myth of racial homogeneity and familial consensuality, symbolized by the imperial family, that were capable of eliminating opposition and criticism and allowing claims to cultural uniqueness. These ideologies have combined to establish a society marked by a network of tight social relationships modeled after the patriarchal household. From the academic world to industrial and financial organizations to political parties and government structures, there are no relations unmarked by this patriarchal/familial principle. It should be reiterated that the reification of this model of social relationships was fundamentally legitimated by the machinery of neo-emperorism. While it is undeniable that this network of relationships has resulted in guaranteeing minimal security and welfare for every Japanese by incorporating all into a national program, this very hegemonism has also severely inhibited the spirit of criticism and opposition within all areas of Japanese society. This effort to make the Japanese appear as members of the vast "middle stratum" has been reinforced immeasurably by an ideology of cultural exceptionalism that has sought to construct a national subjectivity devoid of class and gender divisions (*Nihonjin-ron*). Furthermore, it has enabled Japanese society to resist all outside intervention and interference, which invariably means that any view expressed or articulated by foreigners will be dismissed as uninformed, inaccurate, and thus invalid. Yet the Japanese, by the same measure, have too often appropriated foreign views and analyses, especially to answer critics when it was convenient or when the views were capable of affirming more indigenous pieties.

It is not an accident that Japanese social relationships are condensed into a form of "gangsterism" (*yakuza*), in which behavior is codified and ritualized. It is an institution that, though often dismissed as marginal, is in fact a vast shadowy organization of political power and economic influence. The *yakuza* is closely affiliated with the ruling conservative party at many levels, serving to bridge the once again increasingly forceful right-wing elements with corporate entities. This was dramatically shown in the summer of 1992 with revelations of collusion between the LDP and the *yakuza*. The case against the LDP kingmaker, Kanemaru Shin, for accepting a four-million-dollar bribe and using *yakuza* assistance was initially allowed to end with his payment of a fine of less than $2,000, without any further penalty. No government agency was willing to investigate or prosecute the scandal further. The government's inability to determine the nature of what might be regarded elsewhere as a criminal conspiracy unmistakably proves that those occupying the seat of power in Japan are invulnerable. Such an arrangement has been made possible at least in part by the uninterrupted monopoly of power by the LDP since 1955 and the installation of what has been called single-party democracy. This systemic immunity is a reflection of the deeper logic of structural exemptionism and metalegality that can be explained only in relation to emperorism. The possibility of rooting out the system of gangsterism seems remote as long as emperorism is permitted to persist in Japanese society.

That the *yakuza* does not often display bloody traces of destruction means little; gangsterism manipulates with the invisible but ever-present threat of violence. The media and social analysts are intimidated, bowing to the pervasive paradigm of taboo and self-censorship. In the spring of 1992, Itami Juzo, the noted film director, was stabbed by *yakuza* thugs as a warning against making anti–organized crime movies. While the event was reported even in the American media, no widespread outrage was expressed in Japan. Furthermore, gangsterism structurally enacts the rule of unity and conformity: One either accepts what he or she is told or becomes ostracized. This same principle of exclusion and inclusion, which is governed not so much by argument and contestation as by consent and consensus, works to a surprising degree in every segment of Japanese society. In the academic and intellectual precincts, for instance, the spirit of hierarchic order and tribal loyalty persists to discourage free exchange of criticism and opinion. Ironically, the Japanese intellectual and academic world functions much like an industry to produce probably more formal oral exchanges than any other society. These exchanges are regularly transcribed and published in opinion magazines that attest not to the existence of criticism but to mutual agreement. Graduate students seldom express disagreement with professors; book reviewers rarely do more than register approval of a book's content; discussion in the Diet is always perfunctory.

Fear is not the only instrument of the rulers: nostalgia is used, too, with surprising efficacy. The idea of reifying a tradition of village life on the basis of a pastoral model has been important in reinforcing the principle of social cohesion by appealing to historical continuity and identification of the past with the present. In recent years, for instance, the government has made an immense number of grants to village communities for any project devoted to the resuscitation of village life, ranging from the construction of a village archive to the reenactment of a traditional festival.

As discussed earlier, Japan's desire to present itself as a player among the leading First World nations has led to the establishment with Europe and the United States of a trilateral hegemony, which at the same time has resulted in distancing Japan from the Third World. This alienation from the non-West is based on Japan's refusal to articulate its relationship to the non-West, especially Asia, both in the past and in the present. To this day Japan has not accepted the responsibility of accurately accounting for its actions during World War II. It might be pointed out that early in the postwar years Japan began to conceal its wartime role as the victimizer of Asia under the new guise of Japan as the victim of the inhumane U.S. atom bombings of Hiroshima and Nagasaki as well as of the earlier Western imperial hegemonism. This displacing of roles has resulted in historical forgetfulness and revisionism. History has become merely an arena for national politics. For example, the Japanese have been embroiled in a controversy with the Chinese and Koreans over the textbook representations of the imperial atrocities committed on the continent during the war. The officially approved history textbooks have consistently denied the savage acts of the imperial forces, from the rape of Nanjin to biological experimentation and chemical warfare. As another example, cases of Korean women forced to serve as prostitutes in government sponsored "comfort stations" for the Japanese troops recently came to light despite repeated attempts to suppress evidence and deny official complicity. It should be pointed out that while memories of wartime brutalities are still vivid among members of the older generations, there is a younger generation of Asians willing to forget Japan's dark past in lieu of the promises of capital, technology, and consumer goods. Nevertheless, unskilled "guest laborers" from South Asia and elsewhere, like Koreans and outcast populations long residing in the country, have been subject to what can only be described as racial discrimination.

Japan's foreign aid is now impressively higher than any other country's, yet it has been intimately tied to Japan's industrial trading agenda. One might view in a similar light the policy of internationalization recently enunciated by the Japanese government. The policy was prompted in part by the long-standing foreign complaint that Japan plays no responsible political or diplomatic role in the world commensurate with its economic presence. Thus the program has called for a greater involvement of the kind that might show Japan as a responsible member of the First World bloc. This program of so-called internationalization, however, has resulted only in the expansion of tourism and trade, which in turn necessitates importation of cheap foreign labor. While it is true that there is a genuine aspiration to flee from insular provincialism, and public and private institutions in Japan have invited numerous foreign artists and writers and sponsored countless international conferences, they have not as yet produced any serious exchange. Moreover, internationalization has often been used to mask Japan's further penetration of foreign markets and acquisition of technologies. The funding of academic institutions and the media abroad must be mentioned in this connection. The leading business and engineering schools in the United States regularly receive a large number of Japanese students who are sponsored by their firms for advanced graduate training. In addition, an increasing number of small, financially suffering schools in the United States are being purchased by prosperous Japanese institutions.

• • • •

For Japan, the world is the United States. World War II, of course, created grounds for this perception and its persistence. Europe, on the other hand, has been adamant in refusing to recognize Japan as either a significant culture or a politically important state. Serious studies of Japan have been principally concentrated in the United States since the end of the war. In Europe—and Britain to some degree—any interest in Japan still takes the form of Oriental studies.

All is not well in the United States, however. Today a fairly large number of U.S. colleges and universities offer courses in Japanese language, culture, literature, history, and politics. This incorporation of Japan into the general curriculum and its virtual disciplinization attest to both the intellectual importance of Japan-related subjects and a commitment by American institutions of higher learning to study foreign areas. At one level, however, the study of Japan derives from the earlier focus on such areas in the Pacific as objects of U.S. commercial and military policies—a viewpoint that remains unchanged in putative Pacific Rim programs. With the expansion of Japan's economy, however, the scope of interest in the country has widened considerably. Despite this increased interest in the study of Japan, the disciplinization has paradoxically isolated scholars concerned with Japan. Across disciplines scholars all too readily assemble as Japan specialists rather than as members of distinct intellectual constituencies. One possible reason for this ghettoization has been a widely held view that the Japanese language is very difficult for Westerners. While this is true in part, it is all too often employed merely as an excuse to exclude participation by those who are not deemed specialists. The isolation of Japanese studies is also due to a curious specular relationship between the two groups of scholars— those in the United States and those in Japan. At an earlier time, Americans seized the initiative for constructing an image of Japan and portrayed the country as a model of peaceful modernization (in a contest with the Soviet Union for "unaligned" nations) based upon the presumed continuity of traditional values. Later on, the Japanese incorporated the self-same image into their own scholarly considerations to explain their success in modernization. Hence, this image was exported back to the United States, where it has become an orthodoxy vociferously defended by a number of committed specialists and experts on Japan.

More recently, as Japan's economic challenge has become crucial to industrial and economic life in the United States and Europe, many experts have revised their perceptions. Some have emerged as custodians of American national interests within the context of change in the U.S.-Japan relationship. These specialists in "Japanology" have put their expertise into the service of defending American industrial hegemony. Their characteristic strategy has been to see all the shortcomings and failures in Japan without ever reflecting on comparable experiences and conditions in their own society. Often called "bashing," it is a desperate bullyism in the hands of those who are fearful of America's declining domination. As described above, Japanese society has suffered profound ills brought on by vast socioeconomic changes; Western society has also failed gravely in its encounter with accelerated social and technological transformations. We need only call attention to symptoms such as chronic unemployment, the widening gap between the rich and the poor, the general deterioration of the infrastructure, the intensification of racial conflict, the failure of primary and secondary education, increased violence, the weakening of the fundamental political structure, the disappearance of genuine intellectual and political analysis, the general indifference to the Third World, the vast waste of human and natural resources for so-called defense programs, and, finally, the nearly complete failure of national leadership in moral vision and practical administration. In short, the United States in particular, but Europe as well, is faced with failures and crises on an immense scale. Obviously, the West suffers from deficiencies usually reserved for Japan alone. The attempt by Japanologists to differentiate Japan from the hegemonic West cannot be described in any other term but ethnocentrism.

Other experts employ their knowledge to represent Japan as a model of rational efficiency, management, and order. This group sees contemporary Japanese achievements as an exemplar for a failing American economic and social order, without ever acknowledging the great differences marking the two countries. Even the area of interest seems to have changed. An earlier appreciation of Japanese literature and arts has noticeably declined in recent years and has been replaced by a preoccupation with political economy. Most Americans still know Japan only through commodities or occasional newspaper or TV reports, which too often call attention to the trade imbalance and investment figures. Assuming the existence of genuine interest in Japanese history, literature, and culture among college students today, we see too few places where such curiosity can be satisfied, given the current agenda dominating Japanology.

We have already remarked that the familiar binarism that sustained a whole set of oppositions in the Cold War no longer adequately explains how states relate to each other. In such a heretofore unimagined world incorporation, colonialism will recognize neither color of skin nor geographic divisions. It will absorb any place, any people, that promises production, consumption, and profit. Under these circumstances, national borders and narratives that have been constructed by colonialism during the past two centuries are no longer viable units. Japan in the world as an isolated national entity is no more meaningful than any other claim to a unique national identity. Global hegemony knows no nationalities but prevails everywhere, uniting the rich with the rich, regardless of geographic borders. Thus, new lines will be drawn, constructing an intricate pattern of suppression and segregation across the world, while vast portions of the world—the Second World and the Third World—will be left in hopeless poverty and sickness. In order to form an alliance of resistance and opposition to such an overwhelming global incorporation, a radically new accountability will have to be devised for differences that are no longer dictated by the will to dominate. Whatever the ultimate outcome of the post–Cold War realignment may be, the task of cultural critics in Japan and the world over is likely to be immense.

It may be that the only real link between the rich and the poor on earth today is the imminent threat of extinction due to environmental degradation. Although the rich, as of now, seem more protected than the poor (in using their influence to divert pollutants and nuclear wastes to the impoverished regions of the world), the oceans, atmosphere, ozone, and smog are inescapably around everyone, both weak and strong, both poor and rich. Ultimately affecting all human populations without exception, the health of the planet may be the final guarantor for co-survival, if only humanity finally recognizes the absolute limits to its capacity for greed and consumption and acknowledges the common bond of all.

• • • •

Most of the papers in this collection were presented initially on two occasions: at an international conference, "Japan in the World: Today and Tomorrow," held at the University of California, San Diego, in January 1990; and at the University of California Humanities Research Institute as part of a collaborative research project, "Representations of Otherness: Japan and the United States," in the spring of 1990. We are deeply grateful to the University of California, San Diego, the University of California Humanities Research Institute, and the University of California, San Diego, Organized Research Project in the Humanities for their sponsorships and assistance.

The World

Japan's Industrial Revolution in Historical Perspective

Tetsuo Najita

I shall address this essay to the general pedagogical problem of constructing and teaching Japan's industrial revolution in historical perspective. An event of pivotal importance in modern East Asian and international histories, the industrial revolution continues to inform every facet of intellectual and cultural life in Japan.

Let me first explain my reason for attempting this. Partly it is because as students and teachers of East Asian Studies, we need to focus our attention on constructing and teaching something or other of great significance about our field. But it is also because I have been concerned of late with what I read about Japanese political economy that de-historicizes the industrial revolution and, in extreme cases, frames that experience in prejudicial, culturalist terms. A recent example warns of the severity of Japan's economic challenge because Japan is unlike any other nation-state known, as its people are "creatures of an ageless, amoral, manipulative and controlling culture . . . suited only to this race, in this place"[1] While the language

This essay is based on a lecture presented at Rutgers University at a symposium, "The Construction and Presentation of Asia" (1 April 1992).

1. Andrew J. Dougherty, "Japan 2000" (Unpublished summary account of a 1990 project at the University of Rochester funded by the Central Intelligence Agency), 151.

is admittedly excessive, there is here a sentiment that is often expressed in more moderate terms about Japan (or perhaps more broadly, Asia) as the new, post–Cold War enemy.

One of the important contributions we can make as teachers of Asian Studies, it seems to me, is to try to ensure the historical autonomy of our respective fields and to keep them from being simplified and stripped of their historicity. We need, in this regard, to readdress and teach subjects in our fields that we sometimes take for granted, or, for that matter, find boring and uninteresting, such as Japan's industrial revolution, which is mistakenly seen as being only about concrete and dusty things and not about thought and conceptualization.

I should like, in this spirit, to discuss Japan's industrial revolution, by walking over a terrain that is generally familiar to students in the field. Since my main interest is intellectual rather than economic history, the perspective that I shape will reflect the particular orientation I take to historical study.

In doing so, I draw encouragement, ironically, from an economist, Kenneth E. Boulding, who called on his scientific colleagues, twenty-some years ago, in a presidential address to the American Association of Economics, to think about "Economics as a Moral Science." As he put it: "The myth that science is simply discovering knowledge about an objectively unchangeable world may have had some validity in the early stages of science, but as the sciences develop this myth becomes less and less valid."[2] Economics, he observed, is about epistemological preferences, the ordering of choices that are entwined with culture and subculture. It is part of social process, and hence, is akin to what Clifford Geertz observed about interpreting "culture"—of its being, finally, about "thought."

From my perspective as an intellectual historian, this means studying the following kinds of processes in regard to economic history: How do human beings think economically to order the world and make decisions, to choose and agree on strategies?; How might economic knowledge be seen as integral with a social system so as to reveal a consistent pattern of commercial practice over time?; What kinds of economic intelligence grounded in a history persist in fragmented forms as legacies of the past? It would seem that economists by and large have ignored this perspective, and, to be fair, humanists and intellectual historians have shown little interest in economic history.

2. Kenneth E. Boulding, "Economics as a Moral Science," *American Economic Review* 3 (1969): 1–12.

Let me take a belated turn at addressing this problem of the epistemological question as regards the Japanese industrial revolution and thereby bring thought and history back into the teaching of this transformational event.

I shall begin with the obvious: Our construction should identify clearly what elements about that event were specifically Asian—what features were grounded in a particular Asian history, Tokugawa Japan in this instance. Alternatively, we also need to know what things were Western. The essential components as I have organized them are as follows: 1) the epistemological legacies of the Old Tokugawa Regime; 2) the enabling ideologies produced during Japan's modern revolution, the Meiji Ishin of the 1860s; 3) the strategic choices made from the Western experience, underscoring here the word "choices," as these might resonate with received epistemologies; 4) the nature of commoner participation in the economic history of that time, and, in particular, the structure and process of social capitalism; 5) the social, ecological, and cultural consequences and their probable significances, especially regarding aesthetic production and the re-production, or the re-invention, of culture in the twentieth century; 6) the swirl of imperialist rivalries, first between Britain, Russia, and France and, later, the United States, that challenged stabilities in Asia and infused the industrial transformation with a powerful sense of tension and urgency.

Obviously, it will not be possible to address all of these parts in this brief presentation, for each could be singled out for full and extended treatment. Given the constraint of space, I will not discuss the context of international history or the cultural consequences—I shall defer these to later efforts. I should like, however, to comment on the other items, especially the intertextual relationship of Asian and Western ideas, beginning first with a focus on the epistemological legacies of the old regime.

• • • •

In eighteenth-century Osaka, merchants did not greet one another by saying "Good morning," or "*Ohayogozaimasu.*" They said, "*Mokarimakka?,*" which is like our casual way of saying, "How're you doing?" but meaning specifically, "How are your profits of late?" or "Your earnings are okay, yes?" This salutation was indicative of the ethicality of everyday commerce in Osaka and castle towns and cities throughout the country. That world of commerce, moreover, was a diverse field of practices, all bearing long-term significance: gauging supply and price in the rice market; calculating the exchange rates between copper, silver, and gold; balancing bullion deposits in bank houses with the use of paper currency in regional domains; drafting bank certificates and contracts for large-scale trade transactions; and so forth.

Now these were not simply mechanical practices but rather were informed by an economic epistemology about numerical accuracy that was articulated with an identifiable vocabulary. This was conveyed in the everyday world with the phrase *me no ko zan,* meaning "attending to small details," as a woman watching over a child. The term *me* here was written with the ideograph for "woman," but it is also homophonic with the word for the human "eye"; the ideograph for *ko* was written as "child," which is homophonic with "small," meaning "details"; and *zan,* one of the root ideographs for "mathematics," simply means "the mental act of calculation." Put together, *me no ko zan* meant "the mental ability to make a quick and precise reading of numerical figures." Education for commoners, it was often said, consisted of "reading, writing, and abacus"—"*yomi, kaki, soroban.*" The abacus is the concrete physical image of the metaphor of the woman's swift watchful eye for precise details.

The language and practices of commoners engaged in everyday commerce meshed with, and indeed injected new meanings into the more formal vocabulary widely used in the surrounding intellectual world. A few familiar terms will serve by way of example.

One is the idea of the "mean." Traceable textually to the Doctrine of the Mean in ancient China, the "mean" in eighteenth-century Japan served as a focus of debate regarding the possibility of objectivity outside the knowing self: Was the "mean" stable or was it simply a subjective choice between limits that were arbitrarily set? We find the "mean" being confirmed in the following modified way. The "mean" is not reliable as a stable philosophical norm that confirms the moral centeredness of the subject; it is valid, however, if interpreted instead as a theory of relative accuracy in which the "mean" is never totally arbitrary and is always dependent on human knowledge and action. The emphasis on action rather than identity suggests a sharp turn in the understanding of the "mean" from a noun to a verb. And, indeed, we often find in merchant writings the ideograph for the "mean" being specifically read as the active verb, "to strike"—*ataru*—and not as a noun indicating a stable moral norm with which the self identifies. (I might add appropriate to this discussion that the given name of Chu [mean] is sometimes read as Ataru [to strike], as in Kobayashi Ataru, one of the principal architects of Japan's high-growth economics of the 1950s and 1960s.)

To the idea that human action referenced to the "mean" was relative, but never totally arbitrary, was added the dimension of time. The "mean" was an idea of the reenactment of relative accuracy over time, which meant for merchants, year in and year out, one generation into the long and indefinite future. The "mean" was a way to project the long-term and open-ended future, connected by the reenactment of relatively accurate practice over time. The "mean" may indeed be abstractly thought of as a series of closely connected points on a linear graph. The "mean" clearly was not a static target to be aimed and shot at, as might be understood in the military arts.

The linking of the idea of the mean to accurate human action over time was reinforced by another familiar ethical concept, that of "righteousness"—*gi*. In our context this concept came to include arithmetic, or the careful study and control of numbers. Righteousness referred, more generally, to an intellectual resource or capacity within all human beings to know things outside the self, to discriminate between one thing and another, and to make moral or political judgments about them. In the eighteenth century, this power of discrimination took on the significance of being able to consistently minimize error through numerical calculation. I think we may locate in this epistemology of "righteousness" the theoretical orientation toward the minimization of risk, extended as a "mean" over the long haul (rather than maximization of profit over a short term), that has persisted into modern times.

Let me cite an example of how numbers were used. The Osaka financial house of Konoike compiled a handbook that served as a guide to investment in the rice market. This handbook documented the fluctuation in the supply and price of rice relative to the value of silver over a 100-year period, ca. 1720 to 1820. This macro-longitudinal analysis of production and price yielded a provocative political analysis. The information showed that over a 100–year period, the price of rice had steadily decreased relative to the production of rice, which had steadily increased. This overall pattern was unequivocal, even when corrected for fluctuations due to weather conditions. Merchants drew from this pattern the inevitable conclusion that the existing regime was doomed to bankruptcy. Since the entire ruling aristocracy relied on cash income from rice, the argument went, increased production simply drove prices downward, requiring the aristocracy to remove more rice from the countryside (aggravating famine conditions there) to maintain the same level of income as in previous years, a pattern that was not sustainable as prices increased.

The prescription offered by merchant intellectuals is worthy of note, as it marks a turn from the use of numbers for investment to issues of public policy. The alternative to production as a solution to the economic crisis was distribution through trade. The regime must institute, under merchant supervision, a strategy of large-scale, inter-regional, indeed, international trade through contracts that would be certified with the resources of banking houses in the cities.

This linking here of the argument for trade with the reformulation of public policy was a major breakthrough in thinking about political economy. Here again, we are able to identify a key epistemology; this being the "risk-taking" idea known as "independent authority," or *ken,* that was familiar in private as well as public arenas. Traditionally, the ideograph for ken meant "arbitrary power," meaning autonomous authority to be used only in the most unusual emergency circumstances. From the late eighteenth century onward, ken came to mean a form of authority that must be used constantly in the course of normal history, which was a way of saying the state of affairs was in a chronic state of crisis, requiring the use of emergency authority even if, theoretically, this meant departing from traditional and conventional practices.

The idea of ken was taught to merchants to mean, conservatively, that even the best of plans may be altered if a completely new set of reliable information called for it. Independent authority or ken should be exercised to choose a more effective alternative. This risk-taking philosophy did not displace the theories of accuracy that I noted earlier. It was, rather, an additional authorization to be used with care, but to be used if need be, such as merchants thought with regard to a new policy of inter-regional trade.

The importance of the idea of ken can be seen in its uses in the modern era to translate Western political theory into Japanese. It served as a key ideographic construct mediating between the discourses on reason in the old regime and the new: rights (*kenri*); individual rights (*jinken*); people's rights (*minken*); sovereignty (*shuken*); national sovereignty (*kokken*); political power (*kenryoku*). In all of these potent concepts, which range from individual autonomy to national sovereignty, the root ideograph of ken is conspicuously present.

• • • •

This ideographic linkage between two discursive universes marks a good point for me to turn to the second part of my construction, namely the

Meiji Ishin. Our awareness of the deep intertextual relationship between one discourse and the other should not lead us to the conclusion often made that the latter, or the new discourse, is merely traditional thought warmed over. Intervening between discourses is the event, the Meiji Ishin, that produced enabling ideologies and the authorization to translate from a wide variety of sources and to create a new vocabulary about political economy. The Ishin facilitated the interfacing of old regime epistemologies with the new modes of doing economics. Yet as we conceptualize this interfacing, we should remind ourselves that those who did the translating, and those who sifted through the new epistemologies and made those strategic choices that would come to be identified with the industrial revolution were, in fact, educated in the old regime. They did not possess modern-day degrees in economics or business science.

To come to grips with this relationship between "Asian" (a metaphor that may be taken here to mean "non-Western") epistemology and Western economic theory, we need to make two suppositions. One is that the epistemologies and commercial practices that evolved in the old order, while substantial and truly necessary for an industrial revolution, were also not sufficient for such a transformation. The other is that a revolutionary event such as the Meiji Ishin was essential to generate the empowering ideologies to turn previous epistemologies toward the making of grand risk-taking choices unconstrained by previous moral precepts and institutional arrangements. .

One of the difficulties we face in teaching the industrial revolution is that the Ishin as the pivotal event authorizing that economic revolution is called a "restoration." It is, in terms of rhetoric, and in some sense, therefore, of logic, incongruous to speak of a "restoration" producing a "revolution." The explanation for this incongruence is often sought, as we all know, in distinct or peculiar "culture." It seems to me that if the economic transformation is unproblematically understood to be an industrial "revolution," the event that enabled it cannot be a "restoration." Our teaching of this subject should be clear on this point, which E. H. Norman went through great pains to argue in his study, *Japan's Emergence as a Modern State*.[3] The resistance to this simple truism is astonishing, and seems to reflect a continuing social-scientific thematizing of modern societies outside the West, such as

---

3. E. H. Norman, *Japan's Emergence as a Modern State* (New York: Institute of Pacific Relations, 1940).

Japan, as being, in the words of Wlad Godzich, "a potential same-to-be yet-not-same."[4]

In all of our narratives, however, including, I must confess, my own, the Meiji Ishin appears as the Meiji Restoration. We will probably never know who supplied this translation or why, although a variety of suggestions are possible, especially as regards the ideography of "revolution"—*kakumei*—and "restoration"—*chuko*—and their probable relevance to the Ishin. The ideograph *kakumei* stands for the changing of mandate between one imperial dynasty and the next, and *chuko* for restoring a faltering dynasty somewhere midway in its cycle.

In one of my works, *Intellectual Foundations of Modern Japanese Politics*,[5] I used the term *restorationism* to incorporate the meaning of the Ishin as the idealistic commitment to resist and challenge the old order. As my translator would inform me, there is in fact no Japanese equivalent for *restorationism* that conveys the action theory of idealistic resistance. In short, the term *restoration* could not be translated back into Japanese with any kind of dynamic meaning with reference to the Ishin. Although we settled on something like *ishin-ism,* this too is ordinarily not used in Japanese.[6]

It is fairly certain that the term *restoration* was introduced after the Ishin itself; it seems to have been part of the "counter-revolutionary" process of political consolidation, when it was in the best interest of the new regime to discourage further radical upheavals. Another possibility is that the industrial state in the twentieth century favored *restoration* because of the use of *revolution* in socialist theories of history. And finally, *restoration* served nicely within modernization theory to reinforce the idea of a relatively smooth evolution from traditional to modern.

Historians and commentators of the immediate post-Ishin era did not use the term *restoration.* The influential historian of liberal persuasion, Takekoshi Yosaburo, writing shortly after the Ishin, characterized the Ishin as "revolution"—*Ishin kakumei* and as "anarchical revolution"—*anakiitaki reboryushon.*[7] Also from a liberal stance, Ernest Satow, who served in the British Foreign Service during the Ishin (and later became ambassador to

4. Introduction to Michel de Certeau, *Heterologies,* ed. Wlad Godzich (Minneapolis: University of Minnesota Press, 1986), xiii.
5. Tetsuo Najita, *Intellectual Foundations of Modern Japanese Politics* (Chicago: University of Chicago Press, 1974).
6. Tetsuo Najita, *Meiji Ishin no isan* (Tokyo: Chuokoronsha, 1979).
7. Takekoshi Yosaburo, *Shin Nihon shi* (Tokyo: Meijishironshu, 1965), 3–225, esp. 3–28.

Japan) would recall, "To the lips of those of us who were eyewitnesses of what went on, the word 'revolution' came spontaneously, never the other (restoration)."[8]

The Russian anarchist Lev Ilyich Metnikov, who taught mathematics in the School for Foreign Language Study in Tokyo in the mid-1870s, reported on the Ishin in similar terms. A follower of Bakunin, Metnikov gained fluency in Japanese studying with Ishin activists turned students in Paris. Metnikov secured a teaching appointment through the good offices of Oyama Iwao (later admiral) and Kido Koin (then the leading figure in the new government), and taught students who would introduce Russian "realism" to the literary world, the best-known figure in this development being Futabatei Shimei. To Metnikov, the Ishin was the "most complete and radical revolution" known at that time. The "civilized nations," he observed, could no longer ignore Japan, for what it had realized and would continue to realize in the future.[9]

Despite these testimonies, the term *restoration* came to be accepted as the translation for the Ishin as a transforming event. This definition is somewhat problematic in the attempt to make sense of the industrial revolution. Literally, "Ishin" means "the constructing of something new," or the pledge or vision of doing so. On the heels of a civil war, in which the old regime went down to defeat, the Ishin set the basic, general terms for Japan, in the wording of Metnikov, in the passage just cited, "to move away from its foundation" and to "sever organic connections with its historical past" and to set out on an irreversible course containing a totally new "logic of inevitability"—a national future that would be drastically different from previous history.[10]

The term *restoration* carries none of the sense of radical potential that Metnikov saw. We are reminded of just how powerful and problematic translations are in providing us with the "names" that serve as conceptual references in our teaching of deep historical events.

Even the transference of authority to the monarchy is not a restoration, since the monarchy had little or no power to restore, as the term was used in Chinese history to indicate the rehabilitation of a declining dy-

---

8. Letter to F. V. Dickens, 1 June 1895. Ernest Satow Papers, Public Record Office, London. Courtesy of Hagihara Nobutoshi. See also Ogura Takekazu, *Can Japanese Agriculture Survive?* (Tokyo: Agricultural Research Center, 1979), 646.
9. Watanabe Masaji, *Bomei Roshiajin no mita Meiji Ishin* (Tokyo: Kodansha, 1982), 16–18.
10. Ibid.

nasty midway in its life cycle. Indeed, the transference should more properly be seen as redefining the "sovereign" to being central to the "sovereign" nation-state, a move compatible with the Western theory of national sovereignty identified with monarchy as independent agency—as *kokken.*

My point, in any event, is that we need to teach the Ishin as a real break and not a restoration. The event set the general terms for a society setting out in a drastically different direction that would lead to the industrial revolution. The Ishin is best seen as the pivotal event between the old order and the new regime that created vastly expanded fields of choices far beyond anything that the semi-centralized Tokugawa order could have provided. It was within these new fields of choices that old regime epistemologies gained a new expansive capacity and range.

The Meiji Ishin, in short, provided ideological empowerment for the quest for a new industrial order and thereby dramatically reoriented previous epistemologies toward a new discourse on political economy. In the old order, discussions of political economy were framed within the ideographic phraseology "ordering society and saving the people"—*keisei saimin.* In the new regime, the old ideography was elided into *keizai,* which, while still containing the meaning of ordering and saving, came more forcefully to signify "economics" as understood in "modern economics," a specialized science undergirding the "wealth and strength" of autonomous nation-states. By 1900, the term *keizai* had lost its association with the Tokugawa discourse on political economy and had come to be identified without equivocation with the political objective of achieving national independence through wealth and strength. The Ishin is the event that transformed *keizai* from one discursive meaning to another, from the political ethic of saving others to the science of national power.

The general terms for the new discourse are outlined in the five-point pledge or oath of the Meiji Ishin itself. The terms of the pledge are well known and need not be discussed in their entirety here. An item or two might be underscored, however, to highlight the ideological shift accompanying the Ishin. For example, the second pledge announced the end of the old aristocracy through the union of high and low, indicating that there would be broad social participation in the building of the new future. We may also take this to mean the right of all to acquire knowledge as well as the likelihood that all would be subject to mobilization—as in *levée en masse*—in the unspecified struggles in the future. Item four says that traditional customs and practices that are not useful to the building of the new order will be abandoned, and this is followed with the statement that knowledge would be sought from throughout the world, signifying here quite certainly scientific knowledge from the West and prefiguring Japan's severance from Asia as the primary intellectual resource—a view that would come to be expressed as "leaving Asia" or *Datsu-A,* a vision containing far-reaching diplomatic and cultural consequences.

What I wish to emphasize about the language of the Ishin is the distinction being made between "custom" or "culture" on the one hand and "science" on the other. Culture is specific to time and place; a society may choose what it appreciates as having particular cultural value and may abandon that which it does not value. Science, however, does not involve choice; a society does not have the leeway to pick and choose from within the scientific body of knowledge, as might be done with culture. Being "universal," science is inclusive of all the parts, but precisely because it is "universal," it is not the prerogative of any particular region of the globe. No area or nation has a special privilege to that body of knowledge. Science, therefore, will be sought from the "World," not from the "West." The language in the Ishin in this regard is crucial to the empowering of absorbing new fields of scientific knowledge.[11]

There is no neat narrative to describe the specific choices that led to the Japanese industrial revolution. Between 1868 and 1880 there was considerable chaos and uncertainty. Indeed, from the time of Perry's arrival in 1853 until the 1880s some thirty years later, every indication seemed to point to political and economic failure. Civil wars and rebellions continued to disrupt the political landscape well into the early 1880s, and the regime, semi-colonized by the unequal treaties, was also on the verge of bankruptcy. Warlordism was not an unlikely scenario for the future.

As there were no blueprints to follow, the new choices to be made were hardly self-evident. It is only in retrospect that we discern those choices that made the difference and brought knowledge from the past into a discursive relationship with new strategies drawn from the West. I shall briefly list a few (other than the more obvious ones, such as a unified currency and a system of taxation) that I regard as pivotal to our epistemological perspective.

First, and most comprehensive, is the commitment to a theory of

11. H. D. Harootunian, *Toward Restoration* (Berkeley: University of California Press, 1970). See especially chapters 3 and 6 on Yokoi Shonan and Sakuma Shozan, respectively.

planning and public policy as the responsibility of the nation-state. The idea that comprehensive policy should be drawn up under crisis conditions was not new: It was debated in the Tokugawa era, as I have already indicated in the previous discussion of trade and the concept of ken. That such a policy should be designed to nourish and protect infant industries *was* a new idea.

Broadly conceived, these ideas may be identified with Friedrich List (1789–1846), who observed and drew lessons, quite ironically from today's perspective, from the United States when it protected its new industries. List studied the ideas developed by a group of scholars, such as Matthew Carey, Charles Ingersoll, and especially Daniel Raymond, whose ideas about "public economics" (as contrasted with Adam Smith's "individual economics") gained considerable influence as they came also to be identified with the policies proposed by Alexander Hamilton, for example, large-scale banking.

The main point here is that "wealth" was defined by these political economists not as a relationship between individual and market, but in terms of social productivity—what the Japanese would ideologize as national "wealth and power." Proposing comparable policies for continental Europe, List wrote first his *Outlines of American Political Economy,* [12] from which he developed his influential work *The National System of Political Economy.* [13] The argument for free trade through comparative advantage, List argued, was a luxury that could be afforded only by Great Britain as "the predominant manufacturing, commercial, and naval power." The United States could not afford this luxury, and neither could the nations of continental Europe. The theory of free trade through comparative advantage would lead to the indefinite subjugation by Great Britain of the less advanced nations (colonial possessions, in the wording of Marx and Lenin, who drew from List). Such a conclusion, from List's point of view, was indisputable. The proper corrective to this projection was the exercise of the "right of each nation"—*kokken,* in Japanese—to shape and execute a national economic policy that would organize a system of manufacturing for competitive international trade.

12. Friedrich List, *Outlines of American Political Economy*, trans. Sampson S. Lloyd (London, 1885). See Friedrich List, *The National System of Political Economy*, trans. and ed. W. O. Henderson (London: Frank Cass, 1983).
13. Friedrich List, *The National System of Political Economy* (1841). Reprinted in Margaret E. Hirst, *Life of Friedrich List* (1909), 147–272.

This particular Listian perception of international economics can be discerned in such modern works as Alexander Gerschenkron's classic collection of essays *Economic Backwardness in Historical Perspective,* [14] in which, echoing List, Gerschenkron argued that, historically, every country was relatively backward in relation to England, with some, such as Russia, being much more so than others. This Gerschenkronian perspective, in turn, served as the operating premise in Henry Rosovsky's seminal work, *Capital Formation in Modern Japan.* [15]

Although List was translated along with a lot of other authors in the 1880s, it is certain that individuals such as Matsukata, Shibusawa, Inoue, and Ito imbibed Listian ideas much earlier during their study tours in the 1870s, especially in France and Germany. Being advanced or backward was relative, all these men agreed, and that much would depend on the choice of public policy, for which the nation-state must assume responsibility.

The specific long-term policy choice centered on the problem of controlling inflation. Large multi-regional national banks, such as those established in France, could set interest rates, control the available supply of money in the economy, and, hence, also regulate price levels. While the old regime provided plenty of know-how regarding money and banking and trade—a know-how that sustained the commercial economy of the old order well into the early 1880s—controlling inflation through the Bank of Japan was a new institutional breakthrough.

In what is known as the Matsukata Policy of the early 1880s, the pattern of profit over inflation that had persisted in the old commerce over the previous one hundred years was brought to an abrupt halt in the early 1880s, marking the pivotal turning point from a commercial to an industrial economy. By controlling interest rates, money, and prices, the value of fiscal intake was stabilized, thereby combatting the erosion caused by inflation, and allowing, in turn, for capital savings for long-term investments in new, high-risk, industrial ventures. The classic strategy that I am describing here was learned from the West; the minds that chose that strategy, Matsukata and his colleagues, were Tokugawa minds that organized and made sense of reality with old regime epistemologies about numerical accu-

14. Alexander Gerschenkron, *Economic Backwardness in Historical Perspective* (Chicago: University of Chicago Press, 1952).
15. Henry Rosovsky, *Capital Formation in Modern Japan* (New York: Free Press, 1961).

racy and consistency over time and macro policy as necessary in times of crisis.

The additional policy of allocating capital savings rested on the discovery that technology could be organized into production. This was also new. In the old regime, technology was focused on medical technology, such as might be involved in combatting cholera, as in the epidemics of the 1840s, and on engineering sciences, such as gunnery. But the idea of organizing technology for purposes of trade was a conscious choice specific to early Meiji. The strategy of trade was not a new idea, as I have already noted; however, the connection between trade and the organization of technology *was* new. One of the key figures behind this movement was Shibusawa Eiichi, who observed this in Europe and went on to organize more than a hundred new ventures. Shibusawa, it should be emphasized, was a peasant country merchant, raised in the interstices of the old regime.

A third example is also well known, and in some ways the most fundamental. Knowledge would be distributed throughout society. Again, the idea of general education for commoners was not new, as it had been discussed widely in the late Tokugawa period as a necessity. However, the structuring of universal education was new; fateful choices—some remain controversial even today—were made leading to education from elementary through university levels. Especially important with regard to the industrial revolution was the belief (put into practice) that the sciences—mathematics, physics, and so forth—need not be taught to youngsters in Western languages but in Japanese. Universal knowledge could be taught in the language of a particular culture. Prodigious efforts were made at producing translations. While in the old order translations were limited mainly to Dutch medical works on anatomy and diseases, now the fields were vastly expanded to include all the branches of the sciences. Ideographs from the past were taken out of historical context and used to translate abstract concepts in the sciences and the social and human sciences, infusing new meanings into the old ideographs. Out of this a new vocabulary was produced that has become part of the intellectual property of modern East Asia.

The agreement that science could be translated and taught in Japanese and not in the language of foreign texts resulted in translations not only of the leading intellectual works of the time but also of important standard textbooks and manuals. This agreement, moreover, was based on the Asian idea, nourished in the eighteenth century, that the virtue of "righteousness," the power to discriminate and know things objectively, was a universal human possession, and not the monopoly of the aristocracy. The decision that emerged from the Meiji Ishin to translate all forms of knowledge for purposes of general instruction went well beyond anything conceivable in the old order.

• • • •

Let me now quickly turn to the place of the population as a whole in this history. The policy choices that I have touched on, while far-reaching, were also limited in range. They did not include social policy, a feature of most Western societies at that time. What then were the common people doing anyway? What sort of a social history might we construct here? The view often advanced that the populace was inert, responsive only to commands from above, is inaccurate and misleading. That the Matsukata deflationary policy weighed heavily on the populace cannot be doubted, since capital was not recycled into society as a whole. Much resentment against the state ensued paralleling the emergence of the so-called differential structure separating the commercial and industrial sectors of the economy. The participation of commoners should be properly assessed and not deleted from this history through which they suffered. Without a social history of capitalism among commoners, the industrial experiments would surely have failed.

The key perspective for me, once again, is the epistemological one. The various epistemologies that I mentioned earlier in my lecture were not a possession of the upper classes but broadly distributed throughout society. They are part and parcel of the widespread practices of commerce in Tokugawa town and country.

We get a sense of this in the observation of the Russian Orthodox missionary Nicholai. Commenting on the impressive levels of literacy among the peasantry in Japanese villages in the late Tokugawa era, Nicholai said that in terms of the level of education, Japan was unlike any other Asian society. He saw Japan as being on par with most European nations and vastly superior to Russia.[16]

Metnikov, again from the work cited earlier, adds confirmation from his teaching. The mathematical knowledge his students had inherited from

16. Nakamura Kennosuke, *Nicholai no mita bakumatsu Nihon* (Tokyo: Kodansha, 1979), 13–15.

the old order had not advanced to the level of algebra, he would note. But their understanding of the importance of mathematics and their ability in the subject was astonishing—*tadatada odoroku bakari de aru.*[17]

It is instructive, in this regard, to interface the samurai Matsukata, who directed the deflationary policy, and Shibusawa, the peasant merchant, both of whom agreed on what the nation had to do economically. Although from different social strata, they shared a common economic intelligence. Epistemologies cannot be contained within social boundaries; it would not be surprising, therefore, to find peasants using them for their own purposes.

In my own recent work on commoner discourse and practice in the late Tokugawa and Meiji eras, I have found considerable evidence to confirm this view. There is a broad sense of defiance against the ruling elite when that elite talks down to commoners in pronouncements on why and how they should save scarce resources. There is general agreement that commoners ought not rely on politics from above to save them or provide benevolent welfare. There is, as James Nakamura argued in his work *Agricultural Production and the Economic Development of Japan,*[18] the self-conscious distortion of local evidences in order to assure protection against the state's land tax. In a positive light, we see commoners organizing themselves into risk-taking ventures along a broad front, such as in agricultural co-ops, savings and loans groups, new commercial ventures, insurance co-ops, and so forth.

All of these activities were undertaken beyond the public order, without direction from the state. Health care among commoners during the industrial revolution, especially during some devastating cholera and measles epidemics, was provided for the most part by local insurance and medical co-ops. Perhaps most significant with reference to the industrial revolution, contract co-ops (*keiyaku ko*) were organized into large associations and called "companies"—literally, "unlimited resource companies" (*mujin kaisha*). Although not formally recognized by public law until 1915, these "companies" functioned as credit and loan banks in the regions and countryside. Many of them remain today as powerful credit resources in the regions, some of them flying under the proud banner of a "mutual trust bank" (*sogo ginko*), or simply "bank". Although these banks are extensions of the discourse and practices of the old regime, they are also commoner

17. Masaji, *Bomei Roshiajin,* 157.
18. James Nakamura, *Agricultural Production and the Economic Development of Japan* (New Jersey: Princeton University Press, 1966).

inventions that are grounded in the social history of the industrial revolution. They are not so much "traditional" as they are simultaneous with and part and parcel of the shared process of economic transformation.

. . . .

My purpose has not been to rush through a lot of material or to cover a broad time period; it has been rather to isolate the major components that we might consider in constructing and teaching the Japanese industrial revolution. Because it is one of the pivotal events in modern Asian history, we need to maintain a clear historical perspective of it, especially in light of the ease with which it is dehistoricized with culturalist vocabulary.

The perspective that I have outlined reveals this industrial revolution to contain specific Asian qualities. Indeed, the controlling epistemologies early in the industrial revolution may be located within the old regime. The minds making choices were educated in the Tokugawa era. The epistemologies of the Tokugawa order and the civil wars that produced the Meiji Ishin, Japan's modern revolution, are grounded in an Asian historical reality. That reality, let me also add, is not an incipient cultural propensity buried deep in an archaic past. They draw on traditional ethical ideography, but as forms of economic intelligence they were produced in the context of commercial practices and debates over the meaning of commerce that were specific to the eighteenth-century Tokugawa order. These epistemologies, sprung loose, or liberated, by the revolutionary Ishin, led to the making of specific choices from the Western experience, such as of macro-level economic public policy that should be entirely familiar to the economic histories of Western Europe. In short, the Japanese industrial revolution, including the economic history of commoners, should be historicized in terms of its specificity in time. Both its differences—what I have termed its Asian dimension—and its similarities with other nation-states then become plausible as historical experience.

Given the limitation of space, I have not discussed international history, the swirl of imperialist rivalries that injected a powerful sense of tension and urgency into Japan's industrial revolution. And I have not gone into the important subject of the severe ecological and cultural consequences of that revolution. The industrial revolution in Japan did not produce a stable, organically well-tempered order. Quite the contrary, the twentieth century reveals a destabilized society, one that energized, in turn, yet another discourse about identity, aesthetic production, and the reinvention of culture—

the articulate and often angry search for "difference" in a cosmopolitan universe.[19]

These issues, too, must obviously be included in any thorough discussion of our historical perspective. My aim in this essay has been more modestly to bring history back into our understanding of Japan's industrial revolution and to invest it with thought, the intellectuality it deserves. As humanists we need to address this history as an epistemological event.

19. H. D. Harootunian and Tetsuo Najita, "Japanese Revolt against the West: Political and Cultural Criticism in the Twentieth Century," in vol. 6 of the *Cambridge History of Japan* (New York: Cambridge University Press, 1988), 711–74.

The Prussia of the East?

Perry Anderson

I would like to look not only at the broad similarities in the historical experiences of Japan and Germany but also at some significant contrasts. The parallelism between the two was, of course, noted very early on. Already in the 1890s, observers in England were calling Japan the "Prussia of the East," some of them urging—even then—the need for the British to emulate Japanese values if they were to maintain their position in the world. Japan, like Germany, was a latecomer to industrialization. Both countries had been unified, within a few years of each other, in the 1860s, under the leadership of regional agrarian elites—Prussian junkers and Sat-Cho samurai, for example. In both, national reconstruction produced imperial states that intervened actively to promote industrialization in the interests of military expansion. The Meiji oligarchs, indeed, used the Second Reich as their model when they framed an authoritarian constitution and legal code for Japan. Whereas Bismarck had reduced Denmark and vanquished France, Japan seized Korea and defeated Russia. The two states fought on opposite sides in the First World War, but each emerged as a dissatisfied power from it—Germany humiliated and impoverished at Versailles, Japan cheated of spoils and isolated at Washington. In the twenties, a shaky parliamentary order was established in each country, with party competition and much popular unrest. Weimar and Taisho democracies alike then collapsed under the impact of the depression, giving way to fascist regimes mobilizing forces of social reaction from below and above.

Each dictatorship, having crushed opposition at home, launched on an escalating path of aggression abroad—Japan taking the lead in Manchuria, Germany following in Bohemia—which detonated the Pacific and European conflicts that merged into the Second World War; the two powers were formally bound to each other as partners in the Axis Pact. After spectacular initial gains brought a lightning mastery of continental Europe and Southeast Asia, each was rolled back by the Allies in a long, grinding process that ended in massive physical destruction of their economies and complete political defeat. Devastated and occupied, their postwar states were set up by the occupying powers amidst widespread social misery and dislocation. Twenty years later, West Germany and Japan were stabilized capitalist democracies and had the fastest growing economies in the advanced industrial world. Today, another twenty years on, each appears the colossus of its region—the threat of Japanese trade and financial hegemony obsesses America, while a reunified Germany looms ahead as the dominant power of a federated Europe, to the alarm of its neighbors. In this uncanny series of symmetries, we seem to witness the movement through the heavens of the Castor and Pollux of renascent capitalism.

But what then are the portents of their current constellation? The chain of connections and resemblances linking them needs to be examined before we suggest any answers, for along with the striking sequence of similarities is a set of significant contrasts that are less frequently noted. The history of their correspondences can be divided into four main episodes— construction of the Imperial State, abortive democratization, fascism, and the rise toward global economic ascendancy. In each of these episodes, critical distinctions can be made. Let me indicate a few of them.

1. Although the Meiji Restoration represented an even more deliberate and sweeping revolution from above than Bismarckian unification, it occurred in a qualitatively more backward social context. There was a relationship between these two facets and Japan's initial modernization. In both Germany and Japan, the forced march toward industry and empire was led by aristocratic elites. In Japan, however, there was no counterpart

to the German industrial bourgeoisie, which was based along the Rhine and the Ruhr and with which Bismarck had to come to terms in the North German Confederation, even if these terms left it subordinate in the new unitary state. There had been nothing like the experience of liberal upheaval in 1848—the failed revolution from below that prepared the successful revolution from above. The merchant class lacked any political autonomy or initiative. Nor was there any urban culture comparable to the German Enlightenment or the Hegelian flowering that followed it. The memory of the tragic Osaka uprising of 1837, isolated and doomed, had been confiscated by the *bakumatsu* period. In the countryside, on the other hand, where the Prussian Reform Era had, over time, converted the junker class into capitalist landowners managing estates run with wage-labor, the Meiji reforms stripped away the feudal integument of *daimyo* rule but left in place a parasitic village landlordism that had grown up beneath it, exploiting an often desperate peasantry. The samurai class, unlike any European nobility or gentry, had long been divorced from the land by the castle-town and rice stipend, a separation that was the condition of its administered dissolution in the 1870s. These were the circumstances that gave exceptional decisional leeway to the Meiji oligarchs, who had to confront neither a consolidated bourgeoisie in the towns nor an entrenched aristocracy in the countryside, let alone an organized working class or an independent peasantry. The result was an institutional program much more radical in scope than anything dreamt of by Bismarck. But the price of the same conditions was a far more regressive model of accumulation, one not to be lightly assimilated under the rubric of a "labor-repressive" road common to the two countries, as Barrington Moore may have suggested. Where the investment capital for German industrialization was, after 1830, largely generated in the growth of manufacturing itself, the surplus in Japan was relentlessly squeezed from the agrarian sector, at the cost of the peasantry. On this social basis, no *Rechtsstaat,* public life, or mass parties of the kind that marked the politics of the Wilhelmine epoch, within the framework of the imperial constitution, could grow.

2. Participation on the winning side in the First World War saved Japan from the aftershock of defeat, which toppled the Hohenzollern monarchy and brought universal suffrage, as well as revolutionary pressures from the Left, to Germany. When democratization came to Japan, it was belated and halting. Not until 1925 was the electoral system broadened, and then only to male suffrage. For seven years, half as many voters as in Germany were essentially given a choice between two conservative parties

financed by rival *zaibatsu*—rather as if Weimar politics had been confined to two variants of the National party, one funded by Krupp and the other by Thyssen. No Social-Democratic movement emerged, Labour never got as much as a tenth of the vote, and the small Communist party was wiped out by the police under parliamentary rule. Parliamentary rule itself succumbed to the Fascist uprising of 1932, which put Japan on the road to the regimes that plunged it toward the Pacific War.

3. Japanese fascism was to draw direct inspiration from Nazism for a number of key institutional features of its rule: above all, the creation of the Imperial Rule Assistance Association to mobilize the population behind the state and the organization of the Patriotic Industrial Associations to incorporate and subjugate labor. It is also the case that the final rush to war was set off by the wave of excitement—and envy—in the Japanese army at Hitler's successes in Europe, as Operation Barbarossa neared Moscow. Such elements of imitation, however, were of less significance than in the Restoration period. Fundamentally, the dynamic of Japanese fascism was very different from the German. The main domestic pressure to which it was a response lay not in the challenge of an insurgent working class but in the distress of a peasantry wracked by the world slump in rice and silk prices. It was village misery, not factory militancy, that concerned the ideologues of the Showa Restoration. On the other hand, this determinant was of lesser moment in the overall slide toward fascism than the external pressure from Japan's exposed position within the inter-imperialist rivalries of the time. For Japan was not just industrially and socially less developed, it was also more dependent economically on the outside world than Germany—indeed than any other major power—because of its lack of numerous raw materials. It was thus no accident that Japan led the way in overseas expansion between the wars, with the seizure of Manchuria in 1931, the forward role of the Kwantung Army providing a marked contrast to the reticence of the German High Command in the Czech crisis, nor that the incident at Mukden should have been the trigger for the collapse of the parliamentary order at home. In social origin, the Japanese officer corps was more like the activists of the Nazi party than the Wehrmacht elite and played the leading role in the buildup of Japanese fascism, but the sequence of crises that brought it about was unlike anything in the experience of European fascism. The most striking consequence of this difference was the singular character of Japanese colonial rule itself. Unlike any European imperialism, whether Anglo-French in Africa and Asia, or German in Europe itself, Japan invested massively in the industrialization of its conquests in Manchuria,

and Korea as well, to create a modern economic complex for the exploitation of natural resources in the service of its war machine. This was not enough, however. By 1940, Japan had to import nearly half of its supplies of the two main sinews of war—oil and iron—from the power that was its principal Pacific rival, the United States. Such structural dependence of one imperial state on industrial inputs from another that was its major adversary had no precedent; this was the reason, more than any other, for the countdown to Pearl Harbor. Whereas the originating impulse in Nazism had been counterrevolution, with expansion coming later, expansion was always the dominant in Japan. There, the German adage—so often misapplied to Germany itself—came true: There was a *Primat der Aussenpolitik* in the swing into a Japanese fascism.

4. The war itself, however, separated the destinies of the two countries more sharply than these variations in the regimes that led to it. The Nazi dictatorship was fully constructed, its competing institutions in position, before the outbreak of hostilities. It was then leveled to the ground in defeat, leaving nothing behind. The Japanese dictatorship, by contrast, achieved institutional consummation only during the war itself, when it created the mass organizations that had marked Hitler's state from the start. The crucial difference, however, was that military defeat led not to the razing of this political edifice but rather to a partial dismantling of it within a wider reconstruction of state and society that actually extended or renewed certain key wartime instruments of social control. The occupations of Japan and Germany were, in this respect, quite distinct historical processes, and there are a number of reasons for this. Germany was invaded by a four-power coalition still held together by the common experience of the war for Europe. Truncated and divided by the Allies, its postwar shape reflected the diversity of their outlooks and goals. In the East, the junker class was eliminated at a stroke by the USSR, with the annexations of East Prussia and the creation of the DDR, which destroyed the traditional basis of agrarian reaction in Germany. In the West, the trade union movement was resurrected by British authorities in the spirit of the Labour regime in London, while the long-term connections of the political architect of postwar stability, Konrad Adenauer, were with France. The role of the United States was naturally dominant in the creation of the Federal Republic, but it was never unmitigated. In Japan, on the other hand, the United States exercised power alone, excluding its allies from the start. Moreover, by the time Japan surrendered, Washington had a new administration more hostile to Moscow—and all it appeared to stand for—than its predecessor, so that

from the start American goals in the Far East were more conservative than in Europe, as the preservation of the imperial dynasty made clear.

Capitalist democracy was to be brought to Japan, and one decisive measure was taken to safeguard it: the agrarian reform that abolished traditional landlordism in the countryside. Labor insurgency, after brief toleration, had been ruthlessly crushed by the end of the forties. On the other hand, the bureaucracy forged under fascism was never seriously purged and returned in force as the collective organizer of what became, in due course, a de facto, one-party state. The leading cadres of the Liberal Democratic Party (LDP)—and of the Keidanren that put it together—were heavily recruited, in particular, from the Manchurian colonial complex that had been the proving ground of military expansion and bureaucratic rationalization in the Co-Prosperity Sphere. After the Korean conflict made Japan an American command post in a Hot War with communism (not just the Cold War, as was West Germany), these functionaries and fixers became the chosen partners of the Security Pact. Yet, although U.S. policies were a powerful and calculated determinant of this outcome, it could not have occurred if the social landscape had resembled that of the Federal Republic, which was coming into being at the same time. There, a competitive parliamentary system emerged without further ado, based on parties that were re-creations of major forces in the Weimar period—a transformed *Zentrum* becoming the Christian Democratic Union (CDU) and the Social Democratic Party of Germany (SPD) reviving with no break in its identity. In Japan, there was scarcely any legacy or continuity with Taisho traditions at all; at most, the LDP, it might be said, performed the functions once divided between the two equally venal business parties of the prewar Diets—Minseito and Seiyukai. For all the repression and manipulation that was the work of the Occupation, the underlying balance of forces in Japan was itself much less advanced, politically and culturally, than in Germany and provided more natural terrain for the construction of a *Rechtsstaat* structurally interlocked with what amounts to a *Geldstaat*.

In other words, the traditional sociopolitical "lag" of Japan behind Germany persisted through postwar reconstruction. Paradoxically—or should one say predictably?—it was precisely this lag that facilitated faster and more innovative economic growth from the sixties onward. Today, Japan's GNP is twice that of West Germany, nominal per capita incomes are about 10 percent higher, its trade surplus is some 30 percent greater, and in American eyes—at any rate those of the media—it is the only serious economic rival to the United States. Chalmers Johnson has provided a classic description of how much of this was achieved, in what he calls the capitalist developmental state. There were three fundamental ingredients of the Japanese growth machine. The first was a state capable of a unique degree of market-conforming intervention and coordination, largely effected through directives of the central bank to the major commercial banks. The second ingredient to the Japanese growth machine was a corporate structure of extraordinary concentration, dominated by the *keiretsu*—massive, diversified consortia that were the much more sophisticated and supple successors to the prewar *zaibatsu,* forming the necessary partners for ministerial monitoring. The resultant cooperation between bureaucracy and big business made Japan, in effect, the most successfully planned economy in the world. The final ingredient was a labor force domesticated and divided as in no other advanced capitalist country: One-third of it was muzzled in company unions with high wage rates and lifetime employment; two-thirds of it sweated at far cheaper rates in a vast undergrowth of petty enterprises subcontracting from giant firms. The social overheads of this model were minimal: little social security or medicare, wretched infrastructures, and an average pittance of ten days' holiday a year. Its political condition was, of course, the absence of opposition to the monopoly of the LDP.

Meanwhile, West German growth was impressive enough by any other standards, if slowing down significantly in the eighties, but it was based on a very different configuration. The three great private banks, controlling one-third of the equity of major industrial companies, provided a central nervous system to the economy, but one with less capacity for strategic steerage than the Ministry of International Trade and Industry (MITI) or the Ministry of Finance in Japan, above all in the financing of long-range investments and rapid alterations in product lines. Business itself was characterized not by the overwhelming dominance of huge groups but rather by the striking efficiency and vitality of modern medium and small firms, with companies employing fewer than five hundred workers accounting for half of the GDP and generating the majority of annual patents. Labor, in turn, was organized in powerful industrial unions, assembled in a single national federation linked to a Social-Democratic party with long periods in government. The results were a far more homogeneous wage structure, much higher levels of vocational training, greater work-force say in management decisions, and an extensive welfare state. The difference in the position of labor is fundamental. Two figures will suffice: While in Japan annual working time is one-third longer than in the Federal Republic, the share of earnings in value added in manufacturing is one-third lower. The cultural and political contrast of the German model with the Japanese is perhaps deeper than at any time in the history of the two countries over the past century. Civically, who could doubt that the German pattern is preferable? Economically, however, can it be judged competitive against the superior rates of accumulation steadily achieved, through greater centralization of capital and exploitation of labor, in Japan?

Prognostications would be hazardous, but two fundamental changes are now going to alter Germany's position in the world and the basic terms of any future comparison with Japan. One is the advent of a unified German state, with a population of eighty million, a qualitatively larger critical mass than that of any neighboring power in Europe, and what might, in principle, be thought a natural sociological majority for the Left, once the traumas of reunification are over. The second alteration will be the European Community's acceleration toward a federal structure, with a common currency and central bank, that will make Western Europe the largest integrated zone of the world economy. West Germany is already tightly embedded within this zone, which its monetary policy dictates and to which over half its exports go. One possible prospect during the next decade, then, is something that has never been seen before—a social-democratic *Grossmacht,* within a continental *Zollverein.*

What, then, of Japan? Two diametrically opposite forecasts are currently on offer. One is best represented by Karel van Wolferen's *Enigma of Japanese Power*, which ends its savage survey of the present order—one-party rule, structural corruption, manipulated law, submissive media, conformist education, officialized crime, mendacious ideology, amnesiac culture—with the bleak conclusion that "the wonderful alternative of turning the System into a genuine constitutionalist state" (a modest enough objective, please note—not even an ordinary welfare state!) "would require realignments of power akin to those of present revolution": an outcome his own account renders unthinkable.[1] The other prognosis, egregiously displayed in Bill Emmott's *Sun Also Sets*, is eupeptic. Here, Japan, far from being a threat to the United States or itself, is becoming just like us—a nation of hedonistic consumers, tireless travelers, comfortable pensioners, joyful speculators, reveling in its newfound wealth, which will conveniently run down its trade surplus as savings fall, investments migrate, tourism expands, the yen rises, and the best of all worlds comes happily and promptly to pass. As Emmott puts it, "Japan is, despite all that has been written and

---

1. Karel van Wolferen, *The Enigma of Japanese Power* (London: Macmillan, 1989), 433.

said to the contrary, a country that, just like any other, is affected by human nature and market forces."[2] Between these two extremes, Chalmers Johnson's paper, stressing the novelty of the political crisis of 1989, strikes a more balanced and realistic note. If one can concur that the result of last year's elections "opened up the possibility that Japan might resume its development towards democracy," it is more difficult to agree that it "broke the grip of vested interests on the Japanese political system."[3] That clammy grasp is a tenacious one, and there is little sign that it has really been broken. For that to occur, a unified and modernized Japanese left would be necessary, one capable of advancing a credible alternative to LDP management of the country. In other words, what is needed is something Japan has never possessed—a Pacific variant, perhaps, of social democracy. There seems a good way to go before anything like this emerges: ample time for the ruling system to recover its confidence and restore normal control. On the other hand, Japan is rather regionally isolated, and relations with its nearest capitalist neighbor, South Korea, are rife with suspicion. It is even more trade dependent than before the war on its major Pacific rival, the United States, to which it sends no less than 40 percent of its exports. This proportion is comparable to West Germany's trade with the European Community, but the structural reality of it is quite different, since Germany possesses political rights in the community itself and, hence, has a capacity to codetermine its economic environment, something Japan lacks in its increasingly tense relationship with the United States. What Japan possesses instead, of course, is an immense potential for financial leverage, but that is a high-risk advantage, given the adversarial character of Japanese trade practices and the growing foreign resentment of them. Single-party rule at home and sacred-nation egoism abroad have served Japanese capitalism well until now. It remains to be seen whether this combination—modern descendants of long Japanese traditions of bureaucratism and isolationism— will prove optimal in the years ahead.

2. Bill Emmott, *The Sun Also Sets* (New York: Simon & Schuster, 1989), 132.
3. Chalmers Johnson, "Japan: The Politics of Late Development," unpublished manuscript. A longer version of this paper was published under the title "The People Who Invented the Mechanical Nightingale," *Daedalus: Journal of the American Academy of Arts and Sciences* 119, no. 3 (Summer 1990): 71–90.

Racism and the State: The Coming Crisis of U.S.-Japanese Relations

Eqbal Ahmad

1

International relations are in the process of transformation. The uncertainties over the shape of things to come are greater today than they were at the end of World War II. Then, we knew the salients of the world in the making: There were the victors who would shape the world order and the vanquished who would adapt to it. Decolonization was a predictable occurrence; the only question was the ease and pace with which it would be accomplished. The war foreshadowed the emergence of the United States and the USSR as superpowers; the limits of armed conflict among nations would be defined by the existence of nuclear weapons. Today, there are no answers to these basic questions: What is the future of the arms race? of the Soviet Union? of the Atlantic Alliance? What is the role of Japan in the world?

In recent years, observers have noted a marked shift in U.S.-Japanese relations. They describe the primary cause of the shift in American attitude, especially the government's and the media's, toward Japan as being rooted in two interrelated phenomena: (1) the rise of Japan as the world's major, and the most competitive, industrial power; and (2) the relative decline of American economic capabilities. This is a topic of much discussion and analysis, and we need not recapitulate it here. This essay argues that the bases of American-Japanese tensions, which have been growing steadily since the early seventies, are broader than the emphasis on U.S. economic decline and unfavorable trade balances suggests. The roots of the tension lie in a preoccupation with the general decline of American power and the failure to reverse this perceived trend. The importance of imbalances in Japanese-American trade is exaggerated because American anxieties focus on it as the pivotal factor in that decline.

The United States's post–World War II pride and paternalism over the American role in Japan's economic reconstruction and political democratization have been yielding to envy, anxiety, and, not infrequently, outright hostility. Many Japanese, and at least some non-Japanese, commentators have suspected at least an element of racial and ethnic prejudices in the emerging American mood. As their responses to Akio Morita and Shintaro Ishihara's *The Japan That Can Say No* suggested, members of the American establishment bitterly deny the charge. These denials notwithstanding, there is more than an element of racism in U.S. attitude toward Japan, and it is likely to augment as the contradictions between the capitalist giants become greater.

As a result of the multinationalization of Japanese capital, there is a growing dichotomy of Japanese and American global power that is unique in the history of international relations. Many Third World countries are already experiencing a dyarchy (i.e., Japanese and American) of commercial and strategic domination. Since the trend toward Japanese multinationalization is likely to continue, and the United States appears determined to expand its strategic and political hold globally, the dichotomous pattern is likely to grow. It is an inherently unstable situation. If Japan and the United States do not work out an arrangement for exercising condominium over much of the Third World, then Japan may feel compelled to rearm and develop its own national security apparatus. Another sort of Cold War may then commence.

Some kind of condominium of economic and political power is not without risk for both partners. Postwar Japan has so far escaped being the target of Third World nationalism and liberation movements; this privilege may not last once Japan becomes an overt partner in America's global enterprise. Similarly, an arrangement of shared domination may not help restore the ailing American economy; it may render the United States a Sparta in the service of Japan—a prospect the United States will not welcome. In fact, such a development would present the temptation of reoccupying Japan. European countries, including Germany, are unlikely to upset these equations, because in the coming decades their energies shall probably be focused on Eastern Europe, the USSR, and, to a lesser extent, the Middle East.

The alternative to these unpleasant scenarios is for Japan to continue to forgo military buildup, which does not preclude a posture of active, and global, diplomacy. The goal of Japanese policy could be to foster a world without domination. It alone can serve the interests of a commercial, island nation. The development of such an international order requires economic and technological growth on a world scale, and a fostering of trade and technology transfers on as even a scale as the resources and skills of given regions will permit. The United States has not quite reconciled itself to a world without American paramountcy. It would undoubtedly pressure Japan to apply political criteria in commercial dealings. This would be harmful to Japan and to the future of world peace if Japan continues to buckle under such pressures of a still-powerful ally.

2

The perception of American decline preceded the emergence of what is now described as "America's Japan Problem." The first intimations of decline in the United States appeared in the mid-sixties and were related either to strategic or subjective factors—the nuclear arms race or the debacle in Vietnam. In the last days of Lyndon Johnson, Washington had been flooded by warnings of decline by strategic planners and congressional and corporate leaders. The popular image of the American Century was replaced by the Crippled Giant. In the first Nixon administration, this perception of decline produced a new global design. Clark Clifford and Henry Kissinger preceded David Calleo and Paul Kennedy. It was only after Kissinger's strategic design had fizzled out in the mid-seventies that attention focused on economics and, specifically, on Japan.

It is widely recognized that the United States's attainment of paramountcy as a world power was a function of the exhausting war between the colonial haves and have-nots. World War II ravaged the European powers that had created and dominated the world system of market capitalism and colonialism. The United States alone among the industrialized nations had remained intact and profited from the war. Its supremacy was at first assured merely by the exhaustion of others. However, in the subsequent decades, the structure of American power rested on four pillars:

1. The United States had strategic superiority over any other power or group of powers. For two decades, it alone had the capability to strike any country in the world with nuclear weapons.

2. The United States had the will and capacity to intervene by military or paramilitary means against any government or party that Washington wished to eliminate. These interventions, undertaken by some calculation at the rate of once every eighteen months, were possible and broadly accepted because they were "limited" in their consequences for the United States. As postwar equivalents of "showing the flag," they defined the global reach of American power.

3. The United States had strategic and economic dominance over Western Europe and Japan. This allowed it not merely economic influence but an enormous leverage as the leader of the "free world."

4. The United States had a national consensus on an activist foreign policy that allowed the U.S. government to conduct policy aggressively and without accountability and that held until the movement against the war in Vietnam.

Before the end of the sixties, all four pillars of American power had collapsed or were in the process of collapsing. The notion of strategic superiority became meaningless after the Soviets, too, deployed intercontinental ballistic missiles. The resulting nuclear parity also reduced America's leverage over allies. The economic leverage over Europe and Japan was similarly diminished as their economies recovered and became competitive with that of the United States. The Vietnam War destroyed the presumptions of the interventionist doctrine of limited and invisible wars. Reaction to it also ended the consensus behind a forward foreign policy. As the American Century seemed to be ending in its third decade, decline became an obsession; nearly every American weekly carried cover stories on it, and media pundits frequently prescribed recipes to prevent the deterioration. Japan rarely figured in the debate.

The first organized response to the perceived decline of American power came with the accession to power of Richard Nixon. Although Kissinger and Nixon employed the rhetoric of reform and reconstruction, their strategic design was restorationist. They sought to restore strategic superiority by seeking a first-strike nuclear capability and through a counterforce strategy that included MX missiles, B-1 bombers, and, later, research into the SDI; similarly, there was a doctrinal change from Mutual Assured De-

struction to Flexible Targeting Options. To police the Third World, they
cooked up the Nixon Doctrine of dividing it among "regional influentials"—
U.S.-armed neo-fascist regimes of which only a few have survived popular
opposition. As a means to acquire new leverage over old allies, a reassertion of American power in the oil-producing Middle East was attempted with
partial success. To regain the fractured national consensus, new slogans
were employed—of a structure of peace, of human rights, and of peace
through strength.

Until Mikhail Gorbachev monopolized world attention to himself and
his "bloc" and injected an unhealthy dose of triumphalism in the American
psyche, nothing seemed to work for the United States, unless one counts
the intervention in tiny, faction-ridden Grenada. Nuclear manipulations had
frightened even the normally sedate Europeans into activism. The recalci-
trant spirits in the Third World were not being tamed. Troubles mounted,
with allies more than with adversaries; so did the trade deficit, with Germany
no less than with Japan. Through their competitiveness—and not, I think,
by "adversarial trade," as Professor Peter Drucker alleges—the Japanese
have undoubtedly contributed their share to America's predicament. They
are, nevertheless, taking more blame than seems warranted.

At this point, I should admit the possibility of a certain bias, for I tend
to judge Japan's commercial behavior by the standards that the Western
nations, including the United States, have set in relation to the Third World.
Japan's "unfair" trade practices come nowhere near the thuggery that the
United States, Britain, France, and other Western countries have practiced
and continue to practice in South America, Asia, and Africa. On reading the
dire prescriptions for "disciplining" Japan that policy experts of the West are
making, I could not help thinking that if Third World intellectuals made similar recommendations in worse situations of unfair capitalist behavior, they
would be given bad names; and if there were a government that heeded
them, it might suffer a fate as tragic as Salvador Allende's.[1]

1. See, for example, Karel G. van Wolferen, "The Japan Problem," Foreign Affairs (Winter
1986–1987). "The Japanese political-economic system fosters inward looking attitudes.
It is incapable of selfless gestures, but it can react with alacrity once it is imbued with
a pervasive sense of crisis. In the growing conflict with America, no significant Japanese
adjustment can be expected until the entire establishment has been thoroughly imbued
with the idea that there is a new reality to which it must adjust, like the reality created by
OPEC. No verbal threats serve this purpose, because for many years they have proved
quite empty" (302; my emphasis). Note especially the analogy with OPEC, an organization of raw material–producing countries, in calling for a cartel of industrialized Western

3

Throughout history, there has existed a coincidence of economic, military, and political power in world politics; the rise of Japan and Germany as global economic giants who do not enjoy concomitant military and political power is a unique phenomenon. It progressively becomes a striking feature of international politics as Japan and, to a lesser extent, Germany go multinational. In Pakistan, for example, the United States has become so powerful that almost all citizens assume an American hand in every major political event in the country. Americans apparently enjoy becoming heirs to Britain's colonial tradition; for the hauteur with which he apparently comports himself, the American ambassador is widely known as Lord Oakley. Yet Japan, diplomatically and militarily invisible, is the most ubiquitous economic presence in Pakistan; Suzukis and Hondas occupy its streets. Contemporary international politics is fraught with irony and, I imagine, instability. Dual power, Lenin wrote, cannot last.

Powerful American interests and individuals remain convinced, nevertheless, that continued U.S.-Japanese collaboration is an essential condition of American power and prosperity. Since Commodore Perry's days, there is also a section of interested opinion in this country that would rather declare the Japanese white and get on with business. But the divide remains, and as interests diverge and the ideological cement of anticommunism dissolves, the United States and Japan may enter us into an era in which race, not ideology, shall define international relations.

Racial and cultural divides are more easily crossed in relationships of inequality and subservience than in situations that require antagonistic collaboration between equals. As a new generation of postwar Japanese has come of age, the paternalistic bases of ties between America and Japan have eroded. Japan would now seek partnership, not patronage, and this is one privilege the United States may be reluctant to grant Japan.

Partnership is a popular word in Washington, but its practice will prove hard, if not impossible, in these confusing times of insecurity, as-

---

nations to create "a pervasive sense of crisis" among the Japanese. Lest this appear a case of misinterpretation on my part, Mr. Wolferen, Tokyo correspondent for the Dutch daily *NRC Handesblad*, clarifies the point on the next page: "When the Japanese system has become fully alerted to the new reality, a modus vivendi must be arranged with it. One part of the new set of conditions could be direct fixed commitments *between Western and Japanese* economic institutions for an international division of labor" (my emphasis).

sertion, and triumphalism. Race has long conditioned Japanese-American relations. The internment during World War II of Americans of Japanese origin, the bombing of Hiroshima and Nagasaki, perhaps even the postwar absence of a Pacific Community analogous to the Atlantic Community are examples of how race has conditioned American behavior toward Japan. It is possible that in response to heightened tensions, racism shall augment and become again an integral part of the culture of world politics, a legitimizing and motivational force in international relations. There are a variety of reasons for fearing this development.

Modern imperialism is distinguishable from its ancient and medieval predecessors in many respects. One of its distinct features has been that power and material benefits have not served sufficiently to justify its existence. Historically, the development of capitalism, imperialism, and liberal democratic institutions have been organically linked; therefore, imperialism has needed popular justifications. The language of realpolitik offers a poor basis for constructing popular consensus behind the imperialist enterprise. A policy that responds to the interests of the few but needs the support of the many must, in order to legitimate itself, necessarily mobilize a people's sense of fear and idealism. Power is, of course, congenial to any people, but its exercise becomes morally acceptable when it is employed in behalf of a noble cause and against an alien, unprincipled, and devious enemy.

Modern imperialism has needed, therefore, a ghost and a mission, a more or less credible threat and a moral epistemology, to legitimate itself and feel virtuous about the enterprise that normally involves violent domination and exploitation of other people. The British carried the White Man's Burden; the French had a *Mission Civilisatrice;* and America of Manifest Destiny, in its latest phase of expansion, stood watch on the walls of world freedom. Each was threatened by the forces of evil—the black, brown, yellow, or red peril. At this juncture in history, neither the Communist menace nor the defense of the free world are likely to serve the American national purpose. It is significant, perhaps, that for the first time in its postwar history of interventions, Washington did not invoke either the Communist threat or the defense of the free world as justification for the invasion of Panama.

The United States may already have lost what Henry Kissinger has accurately described as the legitimizing instrument of social repression. Mr. Lawrence Eagleburger, under secretary of state and a Kissinger associate, has eloquently described American concerns over the demise of the Free World/Communism divide. Although neither he nor any other official would say so explicitly, America needs a credible enemy, and Japan may eventually prove the best candidate around. Gore Vidal had earlier signaled, in what seems in retrospect to have been a seminal article, that American anxieties may feed on racial sentiments and solidarities.

Racism is an ideology of difference and superiority; devaluation of the humanity, history, and culture of the Other is integral to it. All capitalist-imperial powers, including Japan, have practiced it. But post-Enlightenment settler-states internalize racist values and express them in ways that others do not. Pioneering colonialism seeks to exclude, if not altogether eliminate, the native inhabitants, not merely exploit them. The settler-state, being committed to permanent occupation and to dispossessing the native population, propagates racial values intensively. It not only assumes the inferiority of the natives but demonizes them in complex and multiple ways. It develops a moral and social epistemology uniquely its own, involving almost total negation of native history no less than needs. It creates myths, magical, though far too deadly, of empty lands, swamps reclaimed, and deserts being brought to bloom, myths that reassure and make society righteous about the unpleasant pursuit of inhumane objectives. As an entity that is founded on another's back and perpetuated at another's cost, the settler-state produces a paranoid strain in the colonizing culture, an instrumentalist attitude toward violence, and a certain disregard of rules and agreements with adversaries, especially when the adversary is the Other. South Africa and Israel are extreme contemporary examples of this phenomenon.

American racism and the state's sanction of it were further reinforced by the institutions of slavery and, after emancipation, the practice of discrimination. Yet, over time it has mellowed. The abolitionist movement, a civil war, then waves of new immigrants, two world wars, the civil rights movement, and the exercise of global power in the era of decolonization have had a universalizing effect on it. Much of the old instinct remains, however, and the settler culture still constitutes the core of American society. Modern education and the media have tended to reinforce it. It is only understandable that in times of perceived decline, the country yearns for old virtues, responds to restorationist promises, and votes right-wing governments into power.

The rhetoric of civil rights and gestures of affirmative action notwithstanding, socialization into the settler culture continues in educational institutions and the media. As a newcomer in this country, I was struck by the thematic consistency of films on America's colonization and the audience's reaction to them. In the typical western, the whites are a human grouping in all their diversities, emotions, and failings. There is a hero among them, a heroine, and also villains who usually have foreign accents. Tension builds up around the pioneer group, united by a common enterprise and threatened by an invisible, elemental enemy. The Indians are outsiders and dehumanized. One does not learn of their family life, hopes, fears, or grievances. These screaming primitives attack in hordes. White guns, strategically placed and expertly fired, wipe them out. The Indians fall in stylized movements that elicit oohs and aahs from the audience. Wondering if this view of history could be repeated in school textbooks, I examined a fairly representative sample for a college term paper. The texts conformed, by and large, to the image presented on screen. The Indians' "humble reality"— I paraphrase Edward Said writing in the context of Zionist colonization of Palestine—is subordinated to America's "higher mission."

As revolutionary changes occur throughout the world, the American mood remains clearly revivalist. In religion, fundamentalism is on the rise; in politics, the values and promises of the Right; in society at large, antiblack racism is returning, and the size of the underclass has enlarged; in international relations, an increasingly interventionist posture is evident, and there is but marginal domestic opposition to it. As for culture, it does seem to me that after the angry, energetic, and creative outbursts of the sixties and early seventies, we have hit stagnation. How else could an essay like Francis Fukuyama's on the "end of history" become a cause célèbre?[2] And why else would *Daedalus* help complete the American circle from X to Z? For the last three years, my return journeys to the United States have felt like journeys to the past. That is one reason perhaps for this pessimistic prognosis on the future of Japanese-U.S. relations.

2. Francis Fukuyama, "End of History," *National Interest* 16 (Summer 1989): 3–18.

"Past Experience, If Not Forgotten, Is a Guide to the Future"; or, What Is in a Text? The Politics of History in Chinese-Japanese Relations

Arif Dirlik

The quotation in the title above is taken from a statement made by Zhou Enlai in September 1972 on the occasion of the Zhou-Tanaka Communiqué, which normalized relations between China and Japan. I use it here not only because it has been a staple over the past decade of Chinese criticism of Japanese endeavors to rewrite the history of World War II in Asia but also because it points to an aspect of the relationship between Japan and China (and Asian countries in general) that seems to me to be peculiar to that relationship: the issue of history. Since 1982, when the Japanese Ministry of Education approved a major revision to textbooks, the issue of history has remained in the forefront of Chinese thinking over China's relationship to Japan. The history of World War II is the most visible

I gratefully acknowledge the help of Professor Lu Zhe (Nanjing University) and Ms. Rebecca Karl in acquiring the materials that proved to be indispensable to the argument I present here. This essay was originally presented as a paper at the workshop on "Japan and Otherness" (Humanities Research Institute, University of California, Irvine, Spring 1990). I thank Masao Miyoshi, Harry Harootunian, Rob Wilson, and other participants in this workshop for their comments and suggestions.

aspect of the controversy, but by extension this has invoked recollections of a more distant past and, perhaps more importantly, speculation over the future that may have something to tell us about the disruptive elements that lie barely beneath the surface of an otherwise amicable relationship.

Two observations may underline the significance of the issue. The legacy of World War II may be a factor in Japan's relationship with all the countries involved in the Pacific War, including the United States. But it has a special immediacy (and poignancy) in an Asian perspective that it does not have in the case of the United States (though from a *Japanese* perspective, the United States may be equally important, and I will discuss this more below). The textbook issue (and related historical issues) created barely a ripple in the United States, and even some Japan experts have found it possible to dismiss it as an "unfortunate" issue arising from marginal ideological conflicts within the Japanese education establishment.[1]

Secondly, the emphasis on the past should not be taken to mean that the past is to be divorced from contemporary issues; indeed, it is arguable that the concern with history takes the present (and the future) as its point of departure. For all their claims to an *objective truth* of the past, the Chinese themselves have chosen to interpret the past within a framework established by present needs. The issue of history on either side is bound up with the two countries' efforts to define their places in the contemporary world as well as their relationship to one another, which also entails different conceptions of history.

Memories of the past have an autonomy of their own. For both the Chinese and the Japanese, World War II is too recent to be easily forgotten. As the head of the Chinese Education Society put it in 1982, "The Japanese aggression against China is still in the memory of the Chinese people, especially the old and the middle-aged. No one can erase these historical facts of blood."[2] Much the same could probably be said of the old and middle-aged Japanese. These memories have played a significant part in shaping the attitudes that underlie the relationship between the two countries. Nevertheless, these memories must be viewed within a contemporary context, which is essential to understanding how the issue of history

---

1. Chalmers Johnson, "The Patterns of Japanese Relations with China, 1952–1982," *Pacific Affairs* 59, no. 3 (Fall 1986): 402–28. In particular, see 419–25.
2. Xinhua (New China News Agency) report, 23 July 1982. In *Foreign Broadcast Information Service* (hereafter cited in my text and notes as *FBIS*), 26 July 1982, sec. D, p. 1.

has been phrased and, more practically, how the two sides have sought to contain the problems to which it gave rise.

Since the Zhou-Tanaka Communiqué of 1972, but especially since the signing of the Treaty of Peace and Friendship in 1978, China and Japan have had an amicable and close relationship. To be sure, there has been a series of problems and controversies, including those over the status of the Diaoyutai Islands in the early seventies; the "anti-hegemony clause" to be included in the Treaty of Peace and Friendship in the mid-seventies; Chinese cancellation of contracts in 1981; historical issues in 1982, 1985, and 1986; the problem of the trade deficit since the early eighties; and the question of Taiwan (or "two Chinas") on several occasions, most importantly in the Kokario Dormitory Incident of 1987, which led to a serious crisis for a while.[3] Nevertheless, the two countries have been able to weather all these difficulties because of a mutual recognition of common interests. In most instances the Japanese government gave in to Chinese demands in order to preserve a good relationship, in which decision considerations of economic benefit loomed large.[4] Compromise and declarations of closeness, reaffirmed by both the frequent exchange of visits by top leaders and by joint economic and cultural activities, yield an impression of constant improvement in relations in spite of the continuing friction.

The problems raised by the issue of history have also been contained by this overall relationship. The past has entered the making of this relationship in two important, albeit contradictory, ways. First, it is the basis for a *special* relationship—the basis, in Chalmers Johnson's words, for "a warm reunion among people who shared *dobun doshu* (a common script and a common race)."[5] Secondly, the past serves as a disruptive element that has perpetuated mutual suspicion and disdain underneath all the declarations of a common history.

3. For discussions of these various problems, see Johnson, "The Patterns of Japanese Relations"; Yung H. Park, "The 'Anti-hegemony' Controversy in Sino-Japanese Relations," *Pacific Affairs* 49, no. 3 (Fall 1976): 476–90; Wang Jianwei, "A Clash of Asymmetric National Powers: Sino-Japanese Relations in 1987," *Spring-Autumn Papers* 1 (Spring 1989): 81–99.
4. For an overview of outstanding problems and the importance of economic relations, see Zhang Wenjin, "Zhenxi he fazhan ZhongRi liangguode youhao guanxi" (Prize and develop the friendly relations between China and Japan), *Guoji wenti yanjiu* (International problems research) (March 1987): 1–3.
5. Johnson, "The Patterns of Japanese Relations," 415.

History in Chinese-Japanese Relations

From the beginning, the past has entered into the official relationship between the two countries as the basis for "normalization." The Zhou-
Tanaka Communiqué was to serve as a frame of reference for Chinese
discussions in later years:

> China and Japan are neighboring countries separated only by a strip
> of water, and there was a long history of traditional friendship be-
> tween them. The two peoples ardently wish to end the abnormal state
> of affairs that has hitherto existed between the two countries. . . .
>
> The Japanese side is keenly aware of Japan's responsibility for
> causing enormous damage in the past to the Chinese people through
> war and deeply reproaches itself.[6]

A *People's Daily* editorial the day following the declaration of the
communiqué added (after a statement made by Zhou Enlai) that the Chinese made "a strict distinction between the broad masses of the Japanese
people and the very few militarists, and cherish profound sympathy with the
Japanese people who were victimized by war."[7]

The Treaty of Peace and Friendship that China and Japan signed
in 1978 was to reaffirm the principles of the Zhou-Tanaka Communiqué,
and thus it endowed with legal status the recognition of the past incorporated therein. This was to provide the immediate context for the Chinese
response to the issue of textbook revision when it appeared in 1982. The
Chinese viewed the revisions as a betrayal of a common understanding
of the past that had been established during the previous decade. They
also regarded the revisions as an attempt on the part of the Japanese government to subvert an established legal obligation. The phraseology of the
1972 communiqué would provide the Chinese with the basis, as well as the
mode, of their criticism of the revisions.

The first reference in China to the textbook revisions was in a brief
commentary in *People's Daily* on 20 July 1982 entitled "We Must Bear in
Mind This Short Lesson" (*FBIS*, 21 July 1982, sec. D, p. 3). Already on
July 8, the *Dagong bao* in Hong Kong had published a report from Tokyo
that linked "the distortions of history" to the rise of right-wing activity in
Japan (*FBIS*, 23 July 1982, sec. W, pp. 1–2). It is possible that Beijing's

---

6. See the "Quarterly Chronicle and Documentation" section of *The China Quarterly* 52
(October–December 1972): 781–83, for the text and a discussion of the joint statement.
7. *The China Quarterly*, 781.

response was delayed by indecision over how to respond to the revisions. Just the previous month, during his visit to Japan, then Premier Zhao Ziyang had "proposed a set of principles to promote economic ties between the two countries: continued peaceful and friendly relations, equality, and mutual benefit, and a lasting and stable friendship, 'from generation to generation, impervious to international storms.' "[8] It is also possible that protests in Hong Kong, Korea, and elsewhere, especially the protests within Japan against the revisions, forced the Chinese government out of its indecision. From the publication of this first piece, Chinese protests against the revisions gathered speed, until in late August a New China News Agency commentary described the affair as "a great storm . . . in the Asian-Pacific region" (*FBIS*, 13 August 1982, sec. D, p. 2). In early August the protest gathered momentum from the appearance of the film *The Great Japanese Empire* (*Dai Nippon Teikoku*) (*FBIS*, 19 August 1982), Premiere Suzuki's visit on August 15 to the Yasukuni Shrine (*FBIS*, 18 August 1982), and the news in late August that Nobusuke Kishi and his associates were planning to build a "monument to the founding of Manchukuo" (*FBIS*, 1 September 1982). Then, as quickly as they had begun, the protests ceased when, with Premier Suzuki's assurances, the Japanese publishers announced that they would withdraw the revisions (*FBIS*, 7 and 19 September 1982).

The Hong Kong *Dagong bao* report of 8 July, "Japanese Right-Wing Groups and Distortions of History," enumerated revisions in wording in the new textbooks concerning World War II Japanese aggression against China, Korea, and Southeast Asia. The report also pointed out that these revisions were part of a broader ideological shift toward a reassertion of the imperial system of prewar Japan, which was evident from the texts' reaffirmation of the centrality of the emperor in the Japanese political system, the importance of imperial morality in education, and so on. The report, moreover, connected the textbook revisions to increasing right-wing activity since 1981 on various commemorative occasions that celebrated the emperor and the imperial family and called for reuniting "the world under one ruler." These activities culminated in June 1982 with the shooting of a trade union official and the disruption of a teachers' union meeting held to protest the textbook revisions. This right-wing activity, according to the report, was accompanied by the revival of old soldiers' associations who paraded in World War II uniforms, singing old war songs.

When the criticism began to appear in the papers in China, it focused

---

8. James C. Wang, *Contemporary Chinese Politics: An Introduction*, 3d ed. (Englewood Cliffs, N.J.: Prentice-Hall, 1980), 346.

not on this general problem of an ideological shift to the Right, but almost exclusively on the specific textbook revisions concerning the wording of Japanese activities in China during World War II. Three changes received the greatest attention: the change from "all-out aggression against China" to "all-around advance into China," and from "invasion of north China" to "advance into north China"; the description of the September 18 (1931) Manchurian Incident as "blowing up the southern Manchurian railway"; and, perhaps most importantly, the implicit blaming of the victim in the Nanjing Massacre of 1937 by stating that it was caused by "the stubborn resistance of the Chinese troops, which inflicted heavy losses on the Japanese army, who were enraged and, as a result, killed many Chinese soldiers and civilians" (FBIS, 28 July 1982, sec. D, p. 1). In late August, two more criticisms of a somewhat broader nature were added to these basic ones: first, the Japanese Ministry of Education's apparent agreement with the militarists who "called the aggressive war they launched 'the greater east Asia war,' and also described this war, which they launched to seize colonies, as a war 'to achieve national independence in Asia' "; second, the denial of the ministry that Japan had been fascist during World War II. According to the Chinese report, the Japanese Ministry of Education held that while this was the "viewpoint of world history," it was not "Japan's standpoint," and it was necessary to write history "on the basis of Japan's standpoint."[9]

Initially, the Chinese response to these revisions was rather low-keyed. A Foreign Ministry spokesman informed the Japanese minister in Beijing on 27 July that

> the textbook affair runs counter to the spirit of the Sino-Japanese joint statement and the Sino-Japanese peace and friendship treaty, is detrimental to the consolidation and development of the peaceful and friendly relations between the two countries, and will hurt the feelings of the Chinese people; the Chinese government cannot but express the utmost concern. (FBIS, 28 July 1982, sec. D, p. 1)

The criticism, however, intensified almost immediately in response to "excuses" offered by the Japanese government, but especially in response to assertions in Japanese governmental circles that the Chinese attitude constituted interference in Japan's internal affairs. While a Japanese Minis-

9. Chen Bowei, "Newsletter from Japan," Renmin ribao (People's daily), 14 August 1982. In FBIS, 24 August 1982, sec. D, pp. 1–3, especially 2. In my text, I refer to the original publication as People's Daily.

try of Education spokesman told the Chinese minister in Tokyo that Japan would "humbly listen" to Chinese views, three cabinet ministers in Japan expressed resentment of China's "interference" in Japanese affairs, and a Japanese press report divulged that while the Japanese government would offer "explanations" of the revisions, it would not "revise the result of the screening of textbooks" (FBIS, 29 July 1982, sec. D, pp. 1–2). Especially provocative to the Chinese was a statement made toward the end of the month by Yukiyasu Matsuno, director general of the Japanese National Land Development Agency, that

> when Japan "advanced" into another country, the word "aggression" was never used. . . . If someone asks us to change "advance" into "aggression," that means "interfering in internal affairs" and "distorting facts." This will lead Japanese children to say that "our forefathers had done something evil." [10]

The People's Daily commentary of 20 July stated that if the "distortions of history" were not corrected, "people will invariably wonder whether some officials of the Japanese government are still advocating militarism, thus casting a shadow over the friendship between Japan and various Asian countries and seriously impairing the image of today's Japan" (FBIS, 21 July 1982, sec. D, p. 3). In response to the Japanese reaction, the Chinese stopped "wondering." The People's Daily commentary of 30 July, "Honest Advice, Though Unpleasant to the Ear, Induces Good Conduct," stated: "One thing that should be pointed out is that we did not criticize the Japanese Ministry of Education, which tampered with the history of the aggression against China, because we fear the Japanese militarists. To tell the truth, they are no match for the Chinese people." To Matsuno's comments, the commentary responded:

> A handful of Japanese militarists who invaded China did not represent the Japanese people or their forefathers. There is nothing wrong in telling Japanese children that there was a handful of national scum among their forefathers who had once plunged both the Japanese people and the people of neighboring countries into a catastrophe, thus enabling them to learn from this action and be alert against it. (FBIS, 30 July 1982, sec. D, p. 3)

10. "Honest Advice, Though Unpleasant to the Ear, Induces Good Conduct," Renmin ribao, 30 July 1982. In FBIS, 30 July 1982, sec. D, pp. 2–3, especially 3.

Another *People's Daily* commentary published on 1 August, entitled "It Is Better to Be Honest," put the blame even more squarely on the Japanese government. It is worth quoting from at some length both because it is revealing of Chinese objections and because it also gives an indication of the Chinese awareness of the inner workings of the textbook revision process:

> The Japanese Education Ministry's attempt to push the responsibility onto nongovernmental publishing houses does not hold water. . . . Japanese school textbooks are compiled by nongovernmental publishing houses, but they eventually have to be checked and approved by Education Ministry censors and revised according to their views. Moreover, the latter's views are binding. . . . Japanese newspapers have revealed that in the course of screening the textbooks, the censors stressed that "the term 'aggression' implies a concept of value." At that time, the author of the book asked: "Is it not a fact that troops were sent against China? What word other than 'aggression' can be used to describe this?" The censor clearly instructed: "Use the word 'advance'!" On the question of the Nanjing Massacre, the censor's attitude was even more explicit. He instructed: "The word 'after' in the passage 'after the Japanese army occupied Nanjing, it killed large numbers of Chinese troops and people' cannot be used, because it is apt to cause misunderstanding, and people might think that the Japanese army acted like that in an organized way; it must be changed." He also said: "It is hard to confirm that the Japanese army killed large numbers of Chinese troops and civilians, and you should consider amending this." He even took out two books to defend the tampering with history—"The Illusory Nanjing Massacre" and "Shanghai Days—Memoirs of a Journalist," which sang the praises of militarism and had long been spurned by the Japanese people and by historians.[11]

The Chinese response over the ensuing six weeks of controversy took three forms. First, there were diplomatic threats. In early August, the Chinese government publicly hinted that as a result of the textbook dispute, it would not rule out the possibility of canceling Prime Minister Zenko Suzuki's scheduled visit to China later in the year. While this threat was

11. "It Is Better to Be Honest," *Renmin ribao*, 1 August 1982. In *FBIS*, 2 August 1982, sec. D, pp. 1–2, especially 2.

later withdrawn, the government did cancel in early August the scheduled visit of Education Minister Heiji Ogawa "as a sign of its displeasure at the schoolbook accounts that describe Japan's 1937 move into China as an 'advance' rather than an 'invasion' " (*FBIS*, 3 August 1982, sec. D, p. 1).

The second response could be termed a technical-legal-historical response. Chinese publications, with the aid of jurists, argued that while textbook revisions were Japan's internal affair, it became more than an internal affair when such revisions intruded on the history of international relations; these revisions, in the Chinese view, contravened not just the recent agreements and treaties between China and Japan but also postwar court judgments condemning Japanese aggression and atrocities during the war.[12] More importantly, throughout the summer, Chinese publications and historical circles engaged in efforts to demonstrate that during the war, Japanese militarists had done everything that the Chinese claimed they had done. As far as the Chinese were concerned, the substitution of "advance" for "aggression" was nothing less than an effort to "prettify militarism"; one piece, analyzing the Japanese usage of the word "advance," argued that the word actually had a positive connotation in Japanese, which made it doubly offensive.[13] Others argued that "advance" implied that China had no sovereignty and that the "Chinese people were nothing," so that the Japanese could "advance" into China at will. The Japanese perceived in the use of the term perpetuation of the notion that China was merely a "geographic concept."[14] But the greatest effort was devoted to providing, through pictures and survivors' testimonials, evidence of Japanese atrocities in China.

Finally, this historical activity took the form of a mass campaign, as meetings were held all over China to prove that Japanese atrocities had not been restricted to a couple of places like Nanjing and Harbin but rather had been a systematic effort on the part of the invaders that extended throughout the length and breadth of the country. The Chinese press, we may note, also took account, in the course of these activities, of similar

12. For examples of jurists' opinions, see *FBIS*, 5 and 6 August. A very detailed refutation was offered by Chen Tiqiang, vice-president of the China International Law Society, in "The Verdict of History," *Renmin ribao*, 17 August 1982. In *FBIS*, 19 August 1982, sec. D, pp. 1–3.
13. "What Does the Word 'Advance' Mean in Japanese?" *Renmin ribao*, 25 July 1982. In *FBIS*, 28 July 1982, sec. D, p. 2.
14. "History of Japanese Aggression against China Can Never Be Forgotten," *Renmin ribao*, 24 July 1982. In *FBIS*, 26 July 1982, sec. D, p. 4. For "geographic concept," see "Historians Rap Ministry," *FBIS*, 13 August 1982, sec. D, p. 1.

protests against textbook revisions in Taiwan and Korea (North and South), and especially in Japan.[15] The Japanese revelations concerning the details of the revisions provided the Chinese with quite potent information.

As I have already said, the release of the film *The Great Japanese Empire* in early August, Prime Minister Suzuki's visit to the Yasukuni Shrine on August 15, and the news of Nobusuke Kishi's plans to erect a monument to Manchukuo further fueled Chinese indignation. *The Great Japanese Empire*, in its favorable portrayal of Hideki Tojo as a patriot, roused "strong indignation" among Chinese film workers, who supported the calls of progressive filmmakers in Japan to ban "this reactionary film." What further irked the Chinese commentators was that the film, in acknowledging the participation of actors from the "Republic of China," also suggested that its makers promoted a "two-Chinas" cause.[16] Suzuki's visit to the Yasukuni Shrine, where he signed in as "prime minister of the cabinet" provoked a *People's Daily* commentator to ask: "Have some people in the Japanese ruling class really learned a lesson from World War II? If they say they have also drawn a lesson by themselves, then what on earth is this lesson?"[17] Finally, while the Chinese refused to take seriously "first-class war criminal" Kishi's plans to erect a monument to Manchuria, because such plans were very unpopular in Japan, they nevertheless observed that

> Nobusuke Kishi and his ilk want to make clear that the goal of founding Manchukuo was "substantially" "non-aggressive"; and they wish to pass on to the later generations "their ideal and their achievements" in invading the northeast of China. Such wild nonsense has fully exposed this handful of Japanese militarists' ambition to rebuild their "achievement" in aggression.[18]

By late August, a Chinese report from Tokyo entitled "The Whole Story of the Textbook Revision" suggested that the problem might go beyond a few militarists, or even the government. The author, Chen Bowei, wrote:

15. Because there were almost daily reports on protests in Japan, they are too numerous to cite here. For protests in Taiwan and Korea, see *FBIS*, 9 August 1982, sec. D, pp. 3–4.
16. Chen Huangmei (vice-president of the Chinese Film Artists' Association), "What Does the Japanese Film 'The Great Japanese Empire' Show?" *Renmin ribao*, 11 August 1982. In *FBIS*, 19 August 1982, sec. D, pp. 5–7.
17. Wei Zhenzhong, "An Observer's Notes on the Yasukuni Shrine in Tokyo," *Renmin ribao*, 15 August 1982. In *FBIS*, 18 August 1982, sec. D, pp. 2–3, especially 3.
18. "Stop Nobusuke Kishi's Absurdity," *Renmin ribao*, 27 August 1982. In *FBIS*, 1 September 1982, sec. D, pp. 1–2, especially 2.

After the end of World War II, defeated Japan instituted bourgeois democratic reforms to a certain degree. The prewar and wartime autocratic military rule was forcibly ended. However, militarist thinking, deeply rooted in the *social soil,* was by no means eliminated. It has occupied some people's minds like a nightmare. In the view of certain people in the ruling class, textbooks are tools for reviving and cultivating militarist ideology. (*FBIS*, 24 August 1982, sec. D, p. 2; my emphasis)

Another article published in the *Red Flag* about the same time was even stronger in its wording and its predictions concerning the future. The article, entitled "Be Vigilant Against the Danger of a Revival of Japanese Militarism," viewed the textbook revision as the latest manifestation of a century of Japanese militarism and imperialism. The author observed that Japan was presently an "economic big power" because "a considerable part of its capital and wealth [was] in fact plundered from other countries by aggressive war and colonial rule" and stated: "This deliberate distortion of history to defend aggressions in history means that someday Japan will probably retrace the old footpath of militarism. The incident of the distortion of history by the Japanese Education Ministry indicates that this danger is already looming in present-day Japan" (*FBIS*, 3 September 1982, sec. D, pp. 1–5, especially 3).

Just as the rhetoric was escalating, the controversy came to an abrupt end. The New China News Agency reported on 3 September that the textbook publishing house had decided that very day to correct the errors in the textbooks by restoring "aggression" in place of "advance" (*FBIS*, 7 September 1982, sec. D, p. 5). Another report a few days later lauded Prime Minister Suzuki for his efforts "to solve the textbook question" and revealed that the Japanese government had come up with "concrete measures to correct the mistakes committed by the Japanese Education Ministry," concluding that "having been washed by the storm of the textbook issue, the friendship between the Chinese and Japanese peoples will be more genuine and the two peoples will understand each other better. We are looking forward to a successful visit by Prime Minister Zenko Suzuki and the further development of the friendly relations and cooperation between the two countries" (*FBIS*, 10 September, sec. D, p. 4). By September 9 the controversy was over, and the two countries turned to the celebration of the tenth anniversary of "normalization."

In hindsight, the abrupt cessation of the dispute once Japanese leaders had made a commitment to correct the textbook "errors" does not seem very surprising. The Chinese remained vigilant on the issue, however, and there were a couple of references in August and September 1983 to "adverse currents" in Japanese politics (connected, once again, with the Yasukuni Shrine and whitewashing the activities of war criminals). But under the new leadership of Hu Yaobang and Zhao Ziyang in China, following the Twelfth Congress of the Communist Party in the fall of 1982, and of Yasuhiro Nakasone following the elections in Japan soon after, Chinese-Japanese relations reached a new level of amity. The outcry against the textbook revisions in Japan had been of such magnitude that the Chinese had no interest in perpetuating the issue once they had elicited the promise of the Japanese government to resolve it. Most importantly, the Chinese themselves sought throughout the summer of 1982 to contain the issue: Although they were aware of the broader ideological and political issues involved (such as those that had been cited by the *Dagong bao* article on 8 July), they confined their criticisms to specific textual issues of wording; while they were quite aware that the pressure within the Japanese Education Ministry to revise the texts went back to the 1960s,[19] they treated it not as a long-term ideological problem but as a contingent issue; while a number of the critiques of the textbook revisions connected the latter with the history of modern Japanese imperialism, in the end what they chose to stress were the "aberrations" of the World War II period; they insisted repeatedly that while China condemned wartime atrocities, it did not blame the present generation for the past, just as they were ever careful to distinguish extremist militarists from the majority of the Japanese people; finally, even in their diplomatic threats, they were careful not to endanger Prime Minister Suzuki's forthcoming visit, even as they canceled the visit of Education Minister Ogawa. The following statement from a *People's Daily* editorial on 14 August, entitled "Past Experience, If Not Forgotten, Is a Guide for the Future," offers a representative sample of the attitudes that guided Chinese protests even in the midst of escalating rhetoric:

> By recalling the Japanese aggression against China, Korea and Southeast Asia, we do not mean to settle old accounts with Japan. Since the miserable years of the wanton invasion by Japanese aggressor troops and their slaughter of the Chinese people, we have always held that China and Japan, as close neighbors, have a history of friendship lasting more than 2,000 years and that the Japanese

19. Chen Bowei, "The Whole Story of the Japanese Textbook Revision," *FBIS*, 24 August 1982, sec. D, pp. 1–3.

aggression against China only represents a short span in this long history. Moreover, in talking about Japanese aggression, we have always made a strict distinction between the Japanese people and the handful of militarists who were responsible for their war crimes. The Japanese people, who were also victims of Japanese militarism and the war of aggression, are innocent. The militarists drove a large number of Japanese able-bodied men to the battlefield. In the last three years of the war alone, as many as 2.6 million Japanese officers and soldiers were killed in action. (*FBIS*, 17 August 1982, sec. D, pp. 1–5, especially 2)

I will comment on the implications of the 1982 debate and this underlying attitude later. Here I would like to look briefly at the disputes that flared in 1985 and again in 1986 over similar historical issues. These later disputes show, I think, that neither the textbook revisions nor Chinese responses to them were merely passing issues of contingent actions in 1982. The dispute in 1985, in particular, also was expressed in a manner that might shed light on contemporary issues that played a tacit part in shaping attitudes toward the past.

For both the Chinese and the Japanese, 1985 was a significant year in that it was the fortieth anniversary of the conclusion of the war. In this instance, moreover, events shaped up in such a way that the Japanese could claim that the Chinese had played a part in provoking them. Indeed, in September, when the dispute culminated in student demonstrations against Japan in Beijing (followed by several in other parts of China), one spokesman for the Japanese embassy attributed them to the "naïveté" of "people credulous enough to believe the Summer campaign."[20] The reference was to memorials to the sufferings of the Chinese people during World War II that accompanied the celebrations of the fortieth anniversary of Japan's surrender.

The event that triggered Chinese protests this time was the visit of Prime Minister Nakasone to the Yasukuni Shrine on the fortieth anniversary of Japan's surrender on 15 August, which was the first *official* visit to the shrine by a prime minister (accompanied by members of the cabinet) in the postwar period. Considering the symbolic significance of the visit, the official Chinese response (at least publicly) was neither intense nor particularly vehement. A New China News Agency commentary on 21 August stated:

20. "5000 Students at Beida Meet to Commemorate 'September 18 Incident,'" *FBIS*, 19 September 1985, sec. D, pp. 1–2, especially 2.

"In taking this decision [to visit the shrine], the Japanese government has pandered to and actually emboldened those in Japan who have always wanted to deny the aggressive nature of the War and reverse the verdict on Japanese militarism long condemned to the dustbin of history" (*FBIS*, 22 August 1985, sec. D, p. 1). The report, however, concluded with the observation of "unprecedented" good relations between the two countries and a hope that these relations would develop further on the basis of the lessons provided by history. The Chinese press had little to say on the issue over ensuing days, but another report a month later revealed that there was behind-the-scenes activity: "With regard to the official visit by Japanese cabinet members to the Yasukuni Shrine, at which first grade war criminals are worshipped, the Chinese government has made its position clear to the Japanese government, and requested the latter to handle the matter with prudence. Regrettably, however, the Japanese side, ignoring our friendly exhortations, went ahead with the visit . . . hurting seriously the feelings of the Chinese people" (*FBIS*, 20 September 1985, sec. D, p. 1). "We hope," the report continued, referring to the 1972 and 1978 agreements, "that the leaders of the Japanese government will fruitfully honor their promise, that is, Japan will not take the path of militarism again, and they will continue to play their part in consolidating and developing Sino-Japanese friendship and maintaining peace in Asia, and the world."

The most striking response in 1985 came from Chinese students. On 18 September (the anniversary of the Manchurian Incident), students at Beijing University held a commemorative meeting, protesting against the "small group" of militarists in Japan who sought to poison the relationship between the two countries. The next day, joined by students from People's and Qinghua Universities, Beida students marched on Tiananmen Square, shouting slogans such as "Down with Japanese Militarism," "Down with Nakasone," and "Strongly Oppose the Second Invasion" (*FBIS*, 19 September 1985, sec. D, p. 1). The protests in Beijing subsided quickly, although there were student protests elsewhere through early October.[21]

The 1985 dispute is particularly interesting because it reveals a clear connection in Chinese minds between historical and contemporary issues. There is some indication that the campaign during the summer to recall the horrors of World War II provided an occasion to whip up nationalist sentiments that may have been quite independent in its motivations of pro-

21. See the "Quarterly Chronicle and Documentation" sections of *The China Quarterly* 104 (December 1985): 763, and *The China Quarterly* 105 (March 1986): 195.

voking anti-Japanese feelings, although that was one of its by-products. In his 1 August (the anniversary of the founding of the People's Liberation Army, or Army Day) speech, Minister of National Defense Zhang Aiping stated that the "purpose of commemorating the great victory in the war of struggle against Japanese aggression" was to educate the troops and civilians across the country, create a sense of patriotism similar to that which had prevailed during the war, and unite all as one to enhance the struggle for the four modernizations (FBIS, 8 August 1985, sec. K, p. 9). Two issues were conspicuous in these celebrations. The first was the issue of unification with Taiwan. Victory celebrations throughout the summer recalled Chinese unity displayed during the war, including the cooperation between the Communist party and the Guomindang, which had made the victory possible.[22] As late as 1990, one prominent historian gave this as one of the major considerations to keep in mind when writing the history of the war of resistance against Japan.[23]

The second issue was that of economic development. There were already signs in 1985 that the post-Mao reforms had run into some trouble and, as Zhang Aiping's speech suggested, whipping up nationalist sentiments provided one means of reinvigorating the struggle for development. The Chinese government had already come under criticism from some quarters for the concessions it had made to Japan (FBIS, 15 August 1983, sec. D, pp. 1–2), and the progressive widening of the trade deficit with Japan made it into an increasingly significant issue in the reform program. Student activism, which grew with increasing disillusionment with the reforms, found an outlet in 1985 in anti-Japanese agitation. Economic issues were very much in the foreground of the student demonstrations against the "second invasion" during the fall. Both in Beijing and Chengdu, the demonstrations explicitly linked together Nakasone's visit to the Yasukuni Shrine (and hence the revival of Japanese militarism) to the second, economic, "invasion." Ironically, the effort to whip up nationalist sentiment in the struggle for development may have found an easier, and possibly unanticipated, outlet in anti-Japanese feeling. According to one report, a big character poster that appeared at Beijing University during the demonstra-

22. Zhang Aiping was involved in these activities. Xinhua report, 13 August 1985. In FBIS, 13 August 1985. See also FBIS, 14 August 1982, for activities planned for the commemoration.
23. Liu Danian, "Bianxie yibu quanmian xitongde KangRi zhanzheng shi" (Compile a comprehensive history of the war of resistance against Japan), Renmin ribao (5 March 1990).

tions showed a Japanese, saying: "I used to be a Japanese imperialist, decapitating 50 people in Shenyang (during the War), but now I am selling you colour televisions" (*FBIS*, 19 September 1985, sec. D, p. 2).

Both the Chinese and the Japanese governments, however, were more anxious than ever to keep the lid on popular sentiments. Then Vice-Premier Li Peng told the Japanese Foreign Minister Shintaro Abe in October that the Chinese government was "understanding of 'Japan's domestic circumstances surrounding the Yasukuni issue.'" Nakasone reciprocated the same month by informing the Chinese of *his* understanding of the reasons for Chinese resentment.[24] It is also possible that the two governments reached a tacit understanding on the issue, because the following year Nakasone would cancel an officially scheduled visit to the shrine with the "criticisms of neighboring countries in mind."[25]

The textbook issue emerged once again in June 1986, this time over a text produced by a "Forum on the Defence of Japanese Citizens" (*Baowei riben guomin yihui*), which had apparently gotten under way following the furor of 1982. Four things in this text particularly irked Chinese commentators: its description of the "Kingdom of Manchuria" as a "new country that was set up under Japan's leadership . . . encouraging 'cooperation and concord' among the Japanese, Chinese, Manchurian, Mongolian, and Korean nations"; its attribution of the blame for events leading to the war to the Chinese government's mobilization efforts; its statement concerning the Nanjing Massacre that "Japanese people did not know of this incident until after the war and that it is necessary to carry out a clear investigation regarding the 'truth' of the incident"; and, finally, its description of the war as a war for the liberation of Asian peoples: "At that time, Japan called the war the 'great east Asian war' (the so-called Pacific war), and considered the goal of the war to liberate Asia from the rule of the European and American powers and to build an east-Asian co-prosperity sphere under Japanese leadership."[26]

The issues in the dispute that followed were quite similar to those raised in the 1982 dispute. There were, however, two noteworthy points. In 1986, the Chinese were aware of the Ienaga Saburo case, which in their

---

24. *The China Quarterly* 105 (March 1986): 195.
25. Xinhua report, 14 August 1986. In *FBIS*, 15 August 1986, sec. D, p. 1. The following month, Nakasone canceled another visit to the shrine.
26. Rong Sheng, "What is the Japanese 'Textbook Issue' About?" *Renmin ribao*, 22 June 1986. In *FBIS*, 26 June 1986, sec. D, pp. 3–4, especially 4.

eyes rendered even more vacuous than before the disclaimers of the Education Ministry that the writing of textbooks was the responsibility of private
groups, since they could point to the ministry's insistence that Ienaga revise the wording of his textbook in order to purge statements unfavorable
to Japan. More important were statements made by Japanese Education
Minister Masayuki Fujio in late July and early August that the Nanjing Massacre was intended to "break down enemy resistance," that "war means
killing people" and should not be equated with slaughter, and that "world
history is a history of aggression and war. The erroneous view that only
Japan committed aggression must be corrected." Fujio also described as
"incorrect" the verdict on Tojo as an "A-class war criminal."[27]

This dispute lasted longer than the one in 1982, but it was not as
intense. It ended in September following the firing of Fujio, Prime Minister Nakasone's cancellation of his scheduled visits to the Yasukuni Shrine,
and a promise by the Japanese government that in accordance with the
commitment made in 1982, the textbooks would stand as they were. The
Chinese, in return, immediately dropped the issue.

The issue of history has not disappeared, but there have been no disputes over it since 1986. What it has left behind is a Chinese determination
that World War II shall not be forgotten. In addition to existing memorials
to the war, a memorial hall to the three hundred thousand victims of the
Nanjing Massacre was opened in Nanjing in 1985, followed by another in
Beijing in 1987.[28] Plans are also under way to write a Chinese version of the
history of World War II. There the matter stands for the present.

The Past and the Present: Some Implications
of the Dispute over History

In 1965, Sadako Ogata observed that "the Japanese attitude toward
China may be considered a mixture of fear, disdain, and a sense of kinship."[29] We might venture a guess that these attitudes still persist in Japan,

27. Xinhua report, "Japan's Fujio Again 'Whitewashes' War Crimes," 6 September 1986.
In *FBIS*, 8 September 1986, sec. D, pp. 1–2.
28. In addition, a number of books have been published, including translations from
Japanese, that document in words and pictures the Japanese massacres in China. The
evidence that this activity is related to the textbook disputes, needless to say, is circum-
stantial but highly suggestive.
29. Sadako Ogata, "Japanese Attitude Toward China," *Asian Survey* 5, no. 8 (August
1965): 389–98, especially 390.

although the fear may have been alleviated in the intervening years (more on this below). Judging by the disputes I have described above, this "mixture" may characterize Chinese attitudes toward Japan as well. I would like to say a few words here on the reasons for the perpetuation of these attitudes beneath the formal commitment to amity that has governed the relationship between the two countries since 1972.

In a visit to Japan in June 1982, Premier Zhao Ziyang proposed a set of principles to promote economic ties between the two countries: continued peaceful and friendly relations, equality, mutual benefit, and a lasting and stable friendship "from generation to generation, impervious to international storms."[30] These "four principles" would help contain the dispute over history that followed shortly thereafter, and the phrase "from generation to generation" would serve as a staple in the disputes comparable in status to the quotation from Zhou Enlai cited above. In spite of the problem of trade imbalance, both countries have continually stressed the mutual benefits of their flourishing economic relationship, based on the complementarity of the two economies; this has been described on occasion as a "Japanese head on Chinese shoulders."[31] As one Chinese writer put it in 1987:

> Japan is a great country in the world economy. China is a socialist state in the process of development, but it has rich resources and a large population. The two are placed differently in their stages of development, they have different economic structures and different emphasis in development, but each has its superior advantages. . . . As the facts show since the restoration of relations between the two countries, the development of economic exchange has brought benefits to both countries.[32]

The two sides have also stressed continually the close historical relationship between them; "separated by a strip of water" and "2000 years of friendship" appear as clichés in most of the discussions of the past. While Japanese friends of China have constantly reaffirmed Japan's cultural indebtedness to China, at least some Chinese, who have recently turned to an emphasis on the functionality of elements in Chinese culture to mod-

30. Wang, *Contemporary Chinese Politics*, 346.
31. Cited from *Far Eastern Economic Review* in Wang Jianwei, "A Clash of Asymmetric National Powers," 84.
32. Zhang Wenjin, *Guoji wenti yanjiu*, 3. What makes this conciliatory offer all the more interesting is that the essay was written to commemorate the July 7, 1937, Lugouqiao Incident that started the war.

ernization, have found in Japan's success a confirmation of the relevance of China's past culture to the present.[33] Finally, the Chinese at least have perceived, in a close relationship between China and Japan, the key to a place for East Asia in global politics; this was particularly evident in the mid-seventies in the Chinese insistence on the inclusion of a "non-hegemony clause" in the Sino-Japanese Treaty of Peace and Friendship that was directed mainly against the Soviet Union but may be seen from a broader perspective as an attempt to guarantee the autonomy of East Asia.[34]

The dissonant elements in the relationship, however, are equally visible. The emphasis on mutual benefit of economic exchange disguises a painful awareness of economic inequality, as well as an awareness that China may need Japan more than Japan may need China. While the Chinese may offer their resources to Japan in exchange for advanced technology, the exchange (not to speak of the phrase "Japanese head on Chinese shoulders") is reminiscent of the World War II slogan (in which some Chinese shared), "Industrial Japan, Agrarian China." The Chinese are also aware of the political implications of economic inequality: Japan, as a world economic power, is not to be contained within Asia and cannot be trusted indefinitely to promote the economic interests of its Asian neighbors; worse, as a world economic power, Japan views with disdain its Asian neighbors, including China, and may seek to establish a hegemony over them. From this perspective, geographical proximity, the physical basis for "friendship," appears on the contrary as a possible threat, and cultural kinship dissolves before the Japanese urge to escape Asia.

These points are made unambiguously in a book written by a Chinese from Singapore, entitled *The Arrogant Japanese* (*Aomande Ribenren*), that was subsequently translated into Japanese and published in China in 1988. The author, who had spent the previous fourteen years living in Japan, relates the changes in Japanese attitudes in the 1980s (as manifested in the textbook revisions, the visits to the Yasukuni Shrine, and Prime Minister Nakasone's statements on the superiority of Japan as a "single-race nation") to Japan's quest for becoming a world political power to complement its economic power. Japan's professions of "internationalism," as he sees it, disguise this quest for power. The attitude, he argues, goes beyond Nakasone or a few leaders but is common among most Japa-

33. For an example, see Yang Daonan, "World Is Studying the Management Thought in Ancient China," *Economic Daily*, 6 May 1985. These views have become more commonplace since then, with the "Confucian revival" in East Asia.
34. Park, "The 'Anti-hegemony' Controversy."

nese. He finds confirmation for this idea in a book published in Japan in the mid-eighties, entitled *Sayonara, Asia*. His summary of the sense of the book is interesting for what the book might have told its Chinese readers:

> Formerly Japan was part of Asia, and Japanese were Asians, but this is no longer the case. In this great garbage heap that is Asia, there is only one lofty peak that reaches beyond the clouds to the Heavenly Hall of modernization, and that is Japan. In this lofty Hall people live in freedom and comfort; in the garbage heap there is no wealth or freedom. In the forty years since the War, Japan has broken away from Asia; and the gap between Japan and South Korea, and the rest of Asia is bound to widen.[35]

This, the author observes, not only typifies the attitudes of contemporary Japanese but is an attitude that goes back a century to Fukuzawa Yukichi. Asians would be foolish to trust Japan, because Japan's sights are set elsewhere.

While we may not deduce Chinese (or Asian) attitudes toward Japan from such statements, it is fair to say, I think, that a mixture of envy and suspicion characterizes Chinese attitudes toward Japan. At times the attitude has turned into outright hostility, as it did during the student demonstrations in 1985, or the most recent case in 1989 of the "Blood-Bright Dare to Die Corps" (*xieguang gansi tuan*), which threatened to assassinate two Japanese a month unless Japan ceased "its economic activities and sightseeing tours in China."[36]

I am in no position to say whether such attitudes are reciprocated in Japan. The Japanese certainly are aware of China's ambitions to become a world power and possibly of the threat China might present to Japan's economic hegemony as the Chinese economy develops; on at least one occasion, a Chinese trade minister assured a joint Sino-Japanese seminar that Japan need not be concerned on the latter count since it would be some time before China could emerge as an economic competitor to Japan.[37] However ambivalent the Japanese may be in their attitudes toward

---

35. Lu Peichun, *Aomande Ribenren* (The arrogant Japanese) (Tianjin: Xinhua Shudian, 1988), 34. Lu's discussions cover everything from the textbook controversy, to Nakasone's background, to everyday aspects of Japanese society.

36. For this curious group, which threatened to kill Japanese "businessmen, government officials and tourists" in Hong Kong and China, see *FBIS*, 28 July 1989, p. 57. As far as I am aware, nothing has come of these threats, and little is known about the group.

37. Xinhua report, 6 August 1985. In *FBIS*, 7 August 1985. State Councillor Gu Mu:

China, it appears that at the popular level, the Japanese are more sanguine about the relationship between the two countries than are the Chinese.

A survey conducted jointly by Chinese and Japanese researchers among their respective populations in 1988 is quite revealing on some of these perceptions. According to a Chinese report on the results of the survey, both populations gave highly positive responses on the ten-year amicable relationship between the two countries but differed on their evaluations of the current state of affairs as well as on the aspects of the relationship that they stressed the most. Thus, 64.4 percent of the Japanese respondents versus 50.6 percent of the Chinese respondents described the relations in 1988 as "extremely good" or "relatively good." More revealing were the responses to the question of which states were possible threats to peace. Chinese respondents placed Japan third (with 18 percent of respondents) after Vietnam and the Soviet Union and ahead of the United States. Japanese respondents, on the other hand, placed China fifth (with 4.9 percent of respondents) after the Soviet Union, the Democratic Republic of Korea, the United States, and South Korea. Equally interesting were the respondents' evaluations of the aspects of the relationship that they thought were the most important. Chinese respondents placed technical and scientific exchanges first (69.3 percent), with trade and economic cooperation a close second (66.2 percent), and politics and foreign relations a distant third (17.4 percent). To the Japanese respondents, however, cultural exchanges held first place (47.6 percent), with trade and economic cooperation in second place (45.4 percent), and politics and foreign relations in third (23 percent).[38]

No less revealing of such attitudes may be the survey responses of one former Japanese ambassador to China and of Jiang Lifeng, the Chinese author of the report. The ambassador noted that the Japanese suffered from an ambivalence in their attitudes toward Chinese culture: when the present was stressed, they became arrogant; and when the past was stressed, they became servile. Jiang saw things somewhat differently. Commenting on why the Chinese and the Japanese stressed different aspects of the relationship, he observed: "It is natural that the Chinese people,

---

"China, for many years, is most unlikely to pose an economic challenge to Japan, but it can work as Japan's partner."

38. Jiang Lifeng, "ZhongRi lianhe jinxingde shehui yulun diaocha" (Survey of public opinion on the progress of Chinese-Japanese relations), *Riben wenti* (Problems of Japan), 2 (1989): 22–26.

with a long cultural tradition but underdeveloped economy and technology, should hope fervently to absorb Japanese science and technology, and to strengthen economic exchange and cooperation; while the Japanese people, with an advanced science and technology but painfully aware of the need to strengthen cultural spiritual reconstruction, should sincerely hope to understand the Chinese cultural tradition."[39]

These responses, and the contradictions between the two countries of which they are products, suggest why the issue of history (and the issue of culture in general) should be significant both as an articulation of contradictions and as a means of keeping these contradictions in check. For the Japanese, I would like to suggest here, history is a problem to the extent that the legacy of the past serves as an obstacle to the establishment of a new identity consonant with Japan's current status in the world; and the attempts to revise history, viewed not just from an Asian but from a global perspective, represent part of an effort to assert such an identity. For the Chinese, in turn, history (as culture) represents a means of bringing symmetry to what Wang Jianwei has described as an "asymmetric" relationship.

As the Chinese have charged, and many in Japan believe, the textbook revisions and other related historical issues are clearly connected with the reappearance of right-wing and militaristic political attitudes in Japan, no less than with the desires of the survivors of World War II to gain a positive recognition and the efforts of pro-Taiwan groups in Japan to undermine relations with China. But to see only this "militarism," and leave the larger picture out of it, may be misleading. One of the excuses that Japan's Ministry of Education officials gave for the textbook revisions was that because Japan's relationship to Asia had changed since World War II, there was no need to continue to cast a shadow on contemporary relationships by constantly recalling past deeds. This no doubt was disingenuous; on the other hand, it might necessitate a distinction on our part between a militarist glorification of the war and an urge to "forget" the past that might be much broader in its compass than militarists and right-wingers in Japanese politics. Failure to recognize the problems presented by this distinction may in fact end up driving to the Right many who, for lack of a resolution of the dilemma, may find solace in a utopianism of the Right that, however offensive, may nevertheless prove appealing as a solution to the problem of identity. Viewed from a global perspective, the textbook revisions and other historical issues are not merely an expression of Japanese attitudes

39. Jiang Lifeng, *Riben wenti*, 24–25.

toward China or Asia but also part of an effort to "settle the accounts" (as Nakasone put it) left over from World War II. In other words, they are part of an effort to release Japan from the stigma left on it from the postwar settlement, which is an issue not just of Japan's place in Asia but of its place in contemporary global politics as well.

The history of World War II, which to the Chinese *is* the history of the war of resistance against Japan, is important to the Chinese self-image in the contemporary world as well and is also bound up with contemporary issues in China. In his recent discussion of the considerations that should go into the writing of a comprehensive history of the war, Liu Danian singles out four important considerations: that the war represented a turning point between old and new China and ushered in the victory of socialism; that it was a patriotic struggle of the whole of the Chinese people and revealed the importance of unity among all Chinese, including the Communist party, the Guomindang, and the Chinese overseas; that it taught a lesson to both the Chinese and the Japanese people who, in the common suffering they experienced, have realized the necessity of cooperating in the creation of a new future; and that it was of world-historical significance because it was part of a worldwide struggle against fascism.[40]

While all these points may contain kernels of truth, some large, some small, they also suggest rewriting history to achieve contemporary ends, both internally and externally. What I am most interested in here is the concern in the dispute with lessons of the past for both the Chinese and the Japanese people. It is possible to suggest, I think, that in their concern to "consolidate and develop" friendly relations with Japan, Chinese commentators, too, suppressed those aspects of history that they thought might be inimical to relations between China and Japan. It is at least questionable that the Chinese and the Japanese learned the same lessons from the experiences of World War II, that the problems of World War II were a temporary aberration in a two-thousand-year history of friendship, or that the war was the doing of a handful of militarists and had nothing to do with the great majority of the Japanese people, who suffered from it as much as the Chinese did. It may also be suggested, recalling the comments of the Japanese ambassador cited above, that there is a certain advantage to China in stressing two thousand years of friendship against the brief period of "aberration" because the two thousand years are a reminder of Japan's cultural indebtedness to China, just as there are certain advantages for

40. Liu Danian, *Renmin ribao* (5 March 1990).

China to be derived from the distinction between "a handful of militarists" and the majority of the Japanese people. As the discussion above shows, the Chinese have been aware of certain aspects of contemporary Japanese politics that they have nevertheless suppressed in order to contain the discomforting questions raised by historical issues, as with the focus on revisions in wording of historical texts rather than ideological trends in Japanese politics, such as the renewed glorification of the emperor system. Most importantly, the Chinese were aware of the long-term demands in Japan to revise the textbooks but chose to treat the issues in 1982, 1985, and 1986 as contingent and temporary "aberrations."

I do not intend these observations as gratuitous cynicism about Chinese objections to the textbook revisions, nor do I think the two kinds of rewriting of history are identical in their political implications. Rather, a close examination of the disputes reveals that the struggle they produced was not one of remembering versus forgetting but one about two kinds of remembering (or, alternatively, forgetting), each of them bound with contemporary problems, in particular with the pursuit of an identity in the contemporary world. The two pursuits presuppose different visions of history, and this is ultimately what the textbook issue reveals.

I would like to discuss these alternative visions with reference to two films that were released in the midst of the 1982 dispute and were clearly related in both Chinese and Japanese minds to the questions in dispute, although as far as is possible to tell, they were not planned or produced with this particular dispute in mind.

The film to which I have referred above, *The Great Japanese Empire*, was showing in Japanese theaters in July 1982 (I have no information on when it was released). According to a description given by Chen Huang-mei, vice-president of the Chinese Film Artists' Association, who saw the film in Japan in July, the film was intended to clear the name of Hideki Tojo, who was portrayed in the film not as a "war criminal" but as a "loyal official 'dedicated to the emperor and to the country,' who died a martyr's death." The three-hour film covered the war from Pearl Harbor to Japan's surrender, and though it "reveal[ed] certain crimes of Japanese troops in their invasion of Southeast Asia, it la[id] greater emphasis on portraying British and U.S. allied troops massacring the Japanese people at the time of defeat, as though Japanese troops and people were the main massacre targets."[41]

41. For a description of the film, and the reactions of the vice-president of the Chinese Film Artists' Association, see Chen Huangmei, "What Does the Japanese Film 'The Great Japanese Empire' Show?"

Chen did not question the "veracity" of the film, but he did question its re-
versing the verdict on Japanese militarists in its claims to "reassess" the
war and offer a "new understanding" of it.

Against this "militarist" film, which sought to revive the historical
vision of World War II, is another film previewed in late August 1982, *The
Game Yet to Finish*, produced jointly by Chinese and Japanese filmmakers,
on which the immediate verdict of "Chinese historians, film-makers, writers
and friendship association veterans" was: "Truthful to History." The film told
the story of two chess-masters who "had their first friendly encounter in Beijing in the mid-twenties." They started a game, which was broken off by the
turmoil in China at the time. The Japanese chess-master returned home,
where he was joined in 1930 by the Chinese chess-master's son, to whom
he became tutor to improve the young boy's skills at chess. "The Japanese
master, who regarded go-chess as a strong cultural tie transcending war,
so concentrated on teaching the young Chinese that he refused to believe
the news about the Nanjing Massacre." The young Chinese in the mean-
time had married the chess-master's daughter but desired to return home
to participate in the war of resistance. The chess-master decided in the end
to help his Chinese son-in-law return to China but was betrayed by a Japanese right-winger (whose help he had sought), and the young man was
arrested and killed, whereupon his Japanese bride went mad. After the war,
both the Chinese and the Japanese realized that the two peoples had had
no fundamental conflict of interest. "When the two masters realize[d] this,
they finish[ed] their game on the Great Wall." The film, which told the "truth"
about Japanese militarism, among other things, revealed how militarist propaganda had "fooled" the Japanese people and warned the Chinese and
Japanese people, "while engaged in friendly contacts, not to lose vigilance
against the danger of a revived Japanese militarism.[42]

As they are depicted in these descriptions, the two films projected
alternative visions of history on the present and the future. In either case,
present and future young generations were very much on the minds of the
filmmakers. *The Great Japanese Empire* sought not only to clear the image
of Japan's military leaders of the stigma that had been attached to them
since the war but also to recast the war as a utopian project to defend
Japan and to liberate Asia. *The Game Yet to Finish*, portraying the war as

42. See Xinhua report, "Historians Praise Joint PRC-Japan Film," 15 August 1982, for
a description of the film and responses to it. In *FBIS*, 25 August 1982, sec. D, pp. 4–5.
The novel based on the film, published in July, became a bestseller in Japan. In *FBIS*,
9 September 1982, sec. D, p. 5.

an aberration in the lives of friendly peoples, projected on history a more appealing, but equally utopian, vision of everlasting friendship between the two peoples. These two projects, each representing an alternative effort to resolve contemporary contradictions in the countries' relationship and in their self-images, were ultimately what was at issue in the seemingly trivial conflict over wording in the textbook controversy.

• • • •

"A nation's attitude toward its past decides its future," one Chinese commentator wrote in 1982.[43] Attitudes toward the textbook revisions provided the Chinese with a crucial test of "whether Japan can in fact live in mutual understanding with the Asia-Pacific region and establish enduring relations of friendship and cooperation with it" (*FBIS*, 24 August 1982, sec. D, p. 3).

The question, of course, is where such attitudes come from in the first place. The textbook revisions, and the attitude toward the war that they imply, may be viewed as a holdover from, or a revival of, a militaristic past. They may also be viewed as products of a new situation in the relationship of Japan to its Asian neighbors, and the world at large, that articulate through the use of the past novel needs and problems. The question, in other words, is whether attitudes toward the past decide the present and the future, as the Chinese commentator suggested, or whether attitudes toward the present and the future shape attitudes toward the past.

The question may be a moot one if our primary interest lies in condemning a militaristic or right-wing glorification of the war, since it makes little difference in that case whether such attitudes perpetuate a holdover from the past or originate in the present. In either case, the textbook revisions represent an effort to erase memories of Japanese imperialism during World War II, and even to beautify it, as the Chinese charged, possibly as an excuse to legitimize a new type of imperialism (although this aspect of the question was played down by the Chinese). The historicization of the war—that it should not be judged by present-day standards but by the outlook and motivations of its perpetrators—results in the suppression of the other historical question, how "noble" motives led to the consequences they did, which in turn calls into question the motives of those who promote

---

43. "A Danger Signal of a Resurgence of Japan's Militarism," *Hongqi* (Red flag), reported in *China Daily*, 20 August 1982. In *FBIS*, 20 August 1982, sec. D, pp. 1–3, especially 2. In my text, I refer to the original publication as *Red Flag*.

such mystification at present (*FBIS*, 3 September 1982, sec. D, pp. 1–5). Efforts to academicize the questions raised by the Japanese invasion by attempting to determine the number of casualties, or to blame the victims for the brutalities of the war, add injury to insult and raise questions over whether the proponents of the textbook revisions are indeed any different in outlook than their World War II predecessors in the contempt they display toward Asia.

How we pose the question of the relationship between the past and the present is important, nevertheless, in assessing both the contemporary significance of the dispute and the manner in which it was conducted—by the Chinese no less than by the Japanese. I would like to suggest here that the representation of the textbook revisions as a resurgence of past attitudes disguises the origin of these attitudes in a new situation of power and in the problems this situation presents to both China and Japan.

Lu Peichun, the author of *The Arrogant Japanese*, pointed in the right direction, I think, when he observed the connection between the textbook revisions and the increasingly vociferous Japanese claims to world power status in the eighties. Calls to rewrite the history of World War II per se were not novel in the eighties, but this new sense of power may have emboldened its right-wing advocates. It is misleading, however, to attribute the new attitude toward textbook revision merely to the rising influence of a right wing in Japanese politics. It was probably not fortuitous that the calls for textbook revision coincided with assertions of a new sense of Japanese power or the advocacy by activist political leaders such as Prime Minister Nakasone that Japan play a more active role in the world—the so-called internationalization of Japan. It was this new sense of Japanese power, rather than mere right-wing activity or any social animus toward Asia, this coincidence suggests, that was responsible for the intensifying urge to rewrite the history of World War II in keeping with a new conception of Japan's place in the world. In this sense, the textbook revisions may be comparable to moves in Germany to revise the history of the war and reevaluate responsibility for the Holocaust.[44] However distasteful (and disturbing) such revisionism may be, it is nevertheless grounded in the transformation of the power structure established in East Asia (or Europe) in the aftermath of the war.

Japan, however, is a power with a difference. While there is hardly

---

44. For a discussion of the revision of history in Germany, see Charles Maier, *The Unmasterable Past: History, Holocaust and German National Identity* (Cambridge: Harvard University Press, 1988).

any question in anyone's mind presently as to the status of Japan as a foremost economic power in the world, the reluctance among other powers to recognize Japan as an equal has created a rather unique situation. The ambiguous status of Japan as a world power would appear to have a dynamic relationship with the Japanese ambivalence toward Asia, which we noted above. In its striving to be a world power, Japan seeks to overcome the rather deprecatory association with Asia, which has found expression over the years in a Japanese contempt for Asia and an urge to "escape" Asia. At the same time, however, as an object of ethnic prejudice, if not outright disdain, within the global power structure, Japan needs Asia in a real sense as a base of power. It may be this double status within the world system that has led some Japanese, in the midst of calls for a "new global role" for Japan, to also assert that Japan may have a special role to play as a bridge between the First and the Third Worlds, or the north and the south.[45] Specifically where Asia (including China) is concerned, Asia is, economically speaking, Japan's Third World, but a Third World that Japan needs not just as a market or a source of materials but also as a basis of its status as a world power. This, more than any sense of cultural kinship, may explain why, in the aftermath of the Tiananmen Square Incident in 1989, Japan, in the person of Prime Minister Kaifu, has insistently appeared as an advocate of not isolating China.

No less important to understanding the new power situation in East Asia in the eighties are the changes in China's relationship to the world in general and Japan in particular. For all its claims to great power status, based in part on the sheer magnitude of its society and economy and in part on the willingness of other powers therefore to invest those claims with an illusory reality, China is a poor country. So long as China insisted on a socialist identity and a concomitant economic autonomy, it could claim a difference from Third World societies in its relationship to the capitalist world. With the opening to the world in the eighties, this difference vanished rapidly. The leadership's goal to develop the economy rapidly by mobilizing foreign capital, whatever its virtues, has in the short run enhanced China's Third World status by creating a dependency on capitalist economies—in particular, Japan. A close trading partner of China's even before the open-

---

45. For an example, see Masataka Kosaka, ed. *Japan's Choices: New Globalism and Cultural Orientation in an Industrial State* (London: Pinter Publishers, 1989). The intentions underlying the redefinition of Japan's place in the world in this and similar works are entirely peaceful, of course, but the preoccupation with such redefinition that takes Japan's power for granted has created a space for the resurgence (and the legitimation) of other, less worthy alternatives.

ing of the eighties, Japan became in the eighties the foremost foreign power active in the Chinese economy. China's economic dependency on Japan to carry out the reform program is a determining factor of the power structure in East Asia.

Viewed within the global context of East Asia, the relationship between China and Japan appears as one of mutual dependence within an unequal power structure. Japan's status as a global power helps explain why the revision of the legacy of World War II should be important to those who would assert a strong Japanese presence in the contemporary world order; if they did not initiate the revisions, they nevertheless have created a domestic context that legitimizes demands for revision. At the same time, however, given the ambiguity of Japan's status as a world power, which makes for continued reliance on an East Asian identity, Japan's leaders can ill afford to ignore the sensibilities of their East Asian neighbors. This is suggested by the alacrity with which the textbook revisions (and related practices) were retracted when the Chinese made clear the seriousness of their objections.

For the Chinese, in turn, history (and culture) has provided a means, in Wang Jianwei's keen insight, of bringing symmetry to an asymmetrical relationship. It is equally important, however, that in spite of the seriousness of the issues involved, the Chinese made an earnest effort to contain the dispute over textbook revisions. Although Chinese objections to the revisions were measured and specific, they were dropped as soon as the Japanese leadership showed a willingness to retract the changes. Furthermore, the Chinese made a brave effort, contrary to all evidence, to represent the revisions as the doing of a "handful" of militarist remnants from the past. The occasional discussion that sought to pursue the revisions to the structure of Japanese political and economic ambitions over Asia was conspicuous for its rarity. There were obviously internal considerations for staying away from this type of analysis; anxious to invite foreign capital to achieve its developmental goals (and throughout the dispute, the exchange of economic missions continued), the Chinese leadership could not easily condone the kind of analysis that recalled earlier, more radical days of insistence on socialist integrity.

The dispute over textbook revisions had as its subtext another project that in the end provided a common ground that at once divided and unified the Chinese and the Japanese leaderships: how to establish a historical foundation on which to construct a new East Asian order. One of the most conspicuous elements in the efforts to contain the dispute was what I would like to describe here as a myth of East Asia. There was an awareness throughout that neither Japan nor China is any longer a merely East Asian society, satisfied to exist on the margins of a world order centered elsewhere. We may well wonder, indeed, if in terms of their economic relationships and their conceptions of their place in world politics, East Asia represents anything other than a geographical concept to either the Chinese or the Japanese, especially the latter. Separation by a "strip of water" implies proximity but not necessarily a special relationship, not in a positive sense anyway, since proximity may make for ease of aggression and domination as much as for friendship. Indeed, World War II, as an enormous disruptive event in the relationship between the two societies, belies any easy assumption of unity and friendship. For the same reason, overcoming memories of the war has been essential for both sides. Japanese advocates of the revisions sought to achieve this by relegating memories of the war to the past, arguing that those memories should not be allowed to interfere with present and future friendship. In spite of a professed willingness to "let bygones be bygones," the Chinese had little use for this version of the past. They in turn, however, created their own myth by resorting to a long history of unity and friendship, within which the war was represented as an "aberration." A common history provided a point of departure for both arguments. Rather than represent a simple projection of a past reality into the future, the notion of a common history served as a myth with which to reconstruct the past in accordance with present needs and wishes for the future; the copresence of alternative versions of the myth is a reminder of the complexity of present realities.

Efforts to rewrite the history of World War II in East Asia have been bound up with transformations in the world order, and of the place of China and Japan within it, which may well determine the fate of either version of history. There is, however, another possibility. In spite of the repeated references in the course of the dispute to the implication of historical interpretation for the consciousness of the younger generation, there was also an acknowledgment that the younger generation in either country was barely conscious of the war and cared little about keeping its memories alive. The dispute over the past may be resolved in the end not by the ascendancy of one version of history over the other but simply by the fading of memories of the past with the succession of new generations to whom the reality of the world, and of East Asia within it, is vastly different than that of the postwar order. What perils this fading of memory may bring with it is another question.

Archaeology, Descent, Emergence:
Japan in British/American Hegemony, 1900–1950

Bruce Cumings

This is how one pictures the angel of history. His face is turned toward the past. Where we perceive a chain of events, he sees one single catastrophe which keeps piling wreckage upon wreckage and hurls it in front of his feet. The angel would like to stay, awaken the dead, and make whole what has been smashed. But a storm is blowing from Paradise; it has got caught in his wings with such violence that the angel can no longer close them. This storm irresistibly propels him into the future to which his back is turned, while the pile of debris before him grows skyward. This storm is what we call progress.
—Walter Benjamin, "Theses on the Philosophy of History"

In the most general sense of progressive thought, the Enlightenment has always aimed at liberating men from fear and establishing their

Earlier versions of this paper were presented in Paris in January 1991, as part of the Project on the Evolution of Western Societies and the World-System, 19th–21st Centuries, sponsored by the Fernand Braudel Center, the Moscow Institute of World Economy, and the Maison des Sciences de L'Homme in Paris; as the Shelby Cullom Davis Lecture, Princeton University, February 22, 1991; and at Cornell University, in May 1991. I am grateful for their helpful comments to Peter Katzenstein, James Kurth, Immanuel Wallerstein, and the editors of this volume.

sovereignty. Yet the fully enlightened earth radiates disaster trium-
phant.
—Max Horkheimer and Theodor W. Adorno, *Dialectic of Enlightenment*

The breakdown of [the Enlightenment] project provided the historical
background against which the predicaments of our own culture can
become intelligible.
—Alasdaire MacIntyre, *After Virtue*

It is simply not true that capitalism as a historical system has represented progress over the various historical systems that it destroyed
and transformed. Even as I write this, I feel the tremour that accompanies the sense of blasphemy.
—Immanuel Wallerstein, *Historical Capitalism*

How does it happen that serious people continue to believe in
progress, in the face of massive evidence that might have been expected to refute the idea of progress once and for all?
—Christopher Lasch, *The True and Only Heaven: Progress and Its Critics*

Setting aside an apocalyptic awakening of the neighboring San
Andreas Fault, it is all too easy to envision Los Angeles reproducing itself endlessly across the desert with the assistance of pil-
fered water, cheap immigrant labor, Asian capital, and desperate
homebuyers willing to trade lifetimes on the freeway in exchange for
$500,000 "dream homes" in the middle of Death Valley.
   Is this the world-historic victory of Capitalism that everyone is talking about?
—Mike Davis, *City of Quartz: Excavating the Future in Los Angeles*

It is one thing for Walter Benjamin in 1940 to fear a storm blowing
in from Paradise, as the Nazis marched through Europe. It is one thing for
Horkheimer and Adorno, aware by 1944 of the ultimate catastrophe of Nazi
power, to conjure an Enlightenment project gone mad. It is quite another
for American intellectuals across a spectrum of philosophies, from neo-
Marxism through *petit-bourgois* populism to Benedictine Catholicism, to
author influential books arguing (in shorthand), that national development
is destructive whether accomplished by capitalists or socialists and that we
are both relatively and absolutely worse off than before the modern epoch
(Wallerstein); that South Boston offers more hope for our salvation than
Cambridge (Lasch); that the Pacific Rim paradise called Los Angeles, city
of the American future where Horkheimer and Adorno wrote their book in

1944, is a 1990s techno-cultural nightmare (Davis); or that the new dark ages are upon us, and thus we await another St. Benedict (MacIntyre).

All one has to do to dispel this depressing intellectual scene, however, is cross the Pacific—to Tokyo, where the fabric of morality, national development, and urban civility are all intact, and the 1990s bid fair to usher in a century of the rising sun. The trains run on time and kids think drugs are what you buy in a drugstore. And if Marx is dead, no one seems to have noticed.

Had Walter Benjamin not been blocked in his attempt to escape the Nazis through Spain, he might have been carted up and down as "the last European" (his fear of the fate 1940s America held for him) in a country equally certain of its morality, its urban civility, and its belief in eternal progress: it was springtime for the American Century. Not for Americans, an Angel of History that cannot distinguish progress from a heap of debris. Lasch's lower-middle-class populists were safely submerged in a self-confident New Deal liberalism—they were MacIntyre's good Catholics, "left behind" by secular progressivism and "modernization," or condemned to a populist lunatic fringe by social scientists in Cambridge. Instead of Davis's "city of quartz," Los Angeles was the city of dreams, just beginning to sniff a new phenomenon called smog in the mid-1940s.

Our brief tour of quotations—and of Tokyo—has raised a question: is this a paradigm shift, or provincialism? Are we witness to *fin-de-siècle* angst, or declining industrial sectors? Do we herald a new morality, or merely the autumn of the American Century? Methodologically, if the intellectuals no longer believe in progress, how can we think? How do we purge our minds of a "progress" that was the *point d'honneur* of Western civilization and that held much of postwar academe in its thrall (modernization theory, end of ideology, "new" leftism, rational choice theory)?

Let us assume merely for purposes of argument that Wallerstein's blasphemy is correct: the modern system is capitalist, its theory is progress, and that theory is wrong. Without the notion of progress and its corollary "opiates" (Wallerstein's term) of rationality, universalism, and a resulting "truth" known to modern man,[1] how are we to understand our world? If we accept Wallerstein's viewpoint, it turns our understanding of the Enlightenment, the French Revolution, even the Industrial Revolution, into mere moments in the rise and decline of the capitalist world-system, or into mere discourse (not his point), no more and no less compelling than the Confu-

---

1. *Historical Capitalism* (London: Verso, 1983), 80–82.

cian doctrine that the golden age lay in the past, or the Buddhist belief that humans should not disturb the universe, but live ascetically within it. Indeed, Wallerstein's third stanza in the *Modern World-System* quartet is essentially this: a historiographical polemic seeking to deconstruct all the great modern moments save one—the sixteenth-century "big bang" in which the world-system itself was created.[2]

The discourse of progress is inseparable from an industrial mode of production that is its justification, its verification, and, from Wallerstein's point of view, its structural base. If we assume he is also correct here, we must search for a method that does not reflect an epistemology of empiricist rationality, progress, and universalism, yet that is also capable of understanding the mechanisms of industrial capitalism (which the Confucian and Buddhist worldviews cannot).

My position, and the theme of this essay, is that an archaeology of the present and a genealogy of the past can provide us a way of doing so: that is, I follow Nietzshce and Foucault for the purposes of *method,* while taking no position on the implications of their thought for human morality, for how we live.[3] Through an archaeology of the present we can *excavate* the debris gathering at the feet of the angel of history, poke around through the shards of lost worlds and lost worldviews, available to us moderns only as fragments.[4] Through a genealogy of *descent* we can avoid an epistemology of progress that so often defines the discipline of history. Finally, through a conception of *emergence* we can hope to define those turning points when rumblings in the "pre-discursive" (power) detonate changes in the "discursive" (knowledge).[5] In this essay I will first seek to explicate a

2. *The Modern World-System III: The Second Era of Great Expansion of the Capitalist World-Economy, 1730–1840s* (New York: Academic Press, 1989).

3. MacIntyre has effectively done the latter, both in *After Virtue* (South Bend: University of Notre Dame Press, 1981) (which is in many ways a polemic against the modern project via a polemic against Nietzsche, whom MacIntyre rightly takes to be its great interlocuter—see especially the chapter "Nietzsche or Aristotle?"); and in his *Three Rival Versions of Moral Enquiry: Encyclopaedia, Genealogy, and Tradition* (South Bend: University of Notre Dame Press, 1990). The three "versions" are euphemisms for empiricism, Nietzsche and his follower Foucault, and "Thomism" or Catholic thought.

4. This is a central point in the opening argument of MacIntyre's *After Virtue:* "What we possess . . . are the fragments of a conceptual scheme, parts which now lack those contexts from which their significance derived" (1–2).

5. I follow Gary Gutting's discussion in his *Michel Foucault's Archaeology of Scientific Reason* (New York: Cambridge University Press, 1989), 270–72. As he puts it, "The simultaneous application of archaeology to discursive practices . . . and to nondiscur-

method that accounts for the discourse of U.S.-Japan relations, and then examine the relations themselves.

Gary and P'ohang

To make the archaeological metaphor more vivid, we might imagine a Martian reconnoitering our world in the aftermath of a world-historical disaster eliminating humanity but not human chattel. Our Martian would find all the people gone; unable to read the books in the libraries, he would inspect sites of modern civilization in the way archaeologists excavate a site of antiquity. Wandering today as if we were that Martian, we can witness the human wreckage and rustbelt debris of an old steel town like Gary, Indiana existing in global simultaneity with the "vibrant dynamism" (to sample the progressive view), of P'ohang, steel city for the industrialization of the Republic of Korea. Paean to American decline and Korean advance?

On the Monangahela River near Pittsburgh is the great Homestead steel mill, site of a strike central to American labor history. It is now a museum—that institution we designate to be the repository of our archaeological finds.

In the 1940s Pittsburgh was a symbol of American industrial prowess, as well as a headquarters of pollution. In 1990 Pittsburgh has neither steel nor pollution, but has burgeoning service industries and is considered by the cheerleaders of the "boutique bourgeoisie"[6] to be one of the "most liveable cities in America."

In the 1920s Gary had its own measure of tourism, its admirable "life style," its avant-garde architecture, and a considerable measure of culture—"a settled air of community" to cite one source (thirteen movie theaters, 1800 hotel rooms making it the convention capital of Indiana, 1300 retail stores, an opulent bourgeois WASP West Side and a stable working-class East Side, and two identical art deco houses of city and county government, sitting side by side).[7] Today its empty, gutted, or shuttered theaters, hotels, shopfronts, and bourgeois homes, and its shattered human beings, surround the still-functioning art deco buildings of state. In the documentary

---

sive practices . . . enables Foucault to establish an essential symbiotic relation between knowledge and power" (271).

6. James Kurth's term to describe what Americans usually mean by the term "yuppie."

7. Edward Greer, *Big Steel: Black Politics and Corporate Power in Gary, Indiana* (New York: Monthly Review Press, 1979), 78–82.

Roger and Me, the residents of Flint, Michigan resent being placed 300th among 300 American cities: "Haven't they been to Gary?"

Surveying the industrial archipelago of 1993, our archaeology would locate the most efficient integrated steel complex in the world in the bustling city of P'ohang. P'ohang Steel was installed by Japanese technicians, using Japanese technology. It is a paean to Japan's investments in (Belgian-discovered) basic oxygen steel technology in the 1950s, after the United States Air Force had renovated its steel industry by bombing it to bits.

If we observe P'ohang in the 1920s, we find a sleepy port city of a few thousand people and no industry, subsisting in a Japanese colony by exporting some rice. In 1950 P'ohang barely existed, having been blasted to smithereens as it changed hands several times between Korean People's Army forces straining to punch through the "Pusan Perimeter" and American forces using "high-tech" firepower to throw them back. The North Korean siege was broken when General Douglas MacArthur landed at Inch'ôn. Shortly his forces were in Wônsan, where they came upon the up-to-date, technologically sophisticated Wônsan Oil Refinery, a Soviet-Korean joint company. But close inspection revealed this to be a refinery installed in the 1930s by the Japanese. Moreover, the Japanese had used American oil company "blueprints and consultations," a reflection of American dominance in the world oil regime of the 1930s.[8]

The town of Ûnsan was the point at which Sino-Korean forces roared out of the mountains in 1950 and turned MacArthur's Inch'ôn victory into a stark defeat. Moving forward to 1987, we would find the North Koreans inviting Japanese firms to help them upgrade their mining technology at this same Ûnsan, which was the site of Chosen Mining Company operations during World War II and the centerpiece of Korea's most valuable mineral export in the late 1930s—gold, dug from mines that were the technological leader in East Asia.

Descending into the mines, we would uncover not Japanese but American machinery—machinery built by a firm owned by Americans until just before Pearl Harbor (the Oriental Consolidated Mining Company), long after the establishment of Manchukuo and the presumed closing of "the open door." If we were to discover the identities of investors who owned this mining concession, we would find a group of right-wing Republicans associated with Herbert Hoover in the 1920s who also controlled the Home-

8. MacArthur Archives, RG6, Box 78, Allied Translator and Interpreter Service, Issue No. 23, Feb. 15, 1951, quoting original documents captured in Wônsan.

stake Gold Mine in Nevada, the Cerro de Pasco copper mines in Peru, and the Insular Lumber Company in the Philippines: all symbols of American imperialism or untender mercies for labor.[9]

Our archaeology would determine that upwards of 50,000 Koreans were directly dependent on gold-mining companies for their livelihood in the 1930s and that Americans trained "a small army of efficient native miners," Korean mine labor being considered the best in the Orient, and certainly among the cheapest in the world at 60 *sen* per day, about 35 Mexican *centavos*. (The mine used Mexican dollars as currency in this period, as did many foreign enterprises in China, along with horseback guards wearing Pancho Villa bandoliers to guard the loot.)

The Japanese allowed American expansionists to profit from Korean gold mines because they needed American technology. Japan occupied "an intermediate position" in mining, being an imperial power with mines, but requiring advanced technology it did not have to exploit them.[10] In other words, Japan was still "semi-peripheral" in mineral extraction at midcentury.

If we continue backward in time through the Japanese industrial archipelago, we would find that Japanese textile firms, the leading sector in Japan's first phase of industrialization, for decades bought their machines from the renowned Pratt Brothers of England—until about 1930 when they came up with their own "high-tech" equipment and quickly became the most efficient textile producer in the world. They also quickly became England's primary *bête-noir* of industrial dumping, market stealing, and general miscreance. A few years later the obsolescent Pratt machines were stoking Korea's first textile conglomerate, courtesy of "technology transfer" and Korea's labor cost advantage.[11]

Going further back in time, to the 1880s and Japan's first wave of industrialization, we would find fish canneries in Hokkaido, the pioneer Kashima Cotton Mill, the huge Kobe Paper Factory, the first cigarette com-

9. These would be the William Randolph Hearsts, the Mills/Reid family of New York (Ogden Mills was Hoover's Treasury Secretary), the Fassett family of New York Republican fame, and the Adolph Coors family of Denver. See my *Origins of the Korean War,* vol. 2 (Princeton: Princeton University Press, 1990), chap. 5. North Korea requested Japanese technological help for reopening Ùnsan in April 1987, according to Economist Intelligence Unit, *Country Report: China, North Korea,* no. 2 (1987), 46.

10. Foster Bain, "Problems Fundamental to Mining Enterprises in the Far East," *Mining and Metallurgical Society of America* 14, no. 1 (Jan. 1921): 1–34. Also Boris P. Torgasheff, *The Mineral Industry of the Far East* (Shanghai: Chali Co., 1930), 131.

11. Carter Eckert, *Offspring of Empire* (Seattle: University of Washington Press, 1991).

pany, tanning and leather firms, the Osaka Watch Company, the Tokyo Electric Company with its own brand of light bulbs, even tasty Kirin Beer: and every last one based on American technological start-ups, or American expertise. And we would find that Japan's favorite economist in the 1880s was an American, the protectionist Henry Carey.[12]

What is the point of this tour through time and space? Our archaeology would have uncovered in little-known, far-off Korea, and in Japan proper, the modern world-system and the limits of a Japan-centered regional political economy: Japan depended on American and/or British technology, and it was a sub-imperial power, that is, semi-peripheral vis-à-vis the United States, "core" vis-à-vis Korea and China. It was a dependency of both the regime of technology and the system of states. Using the world as our "unit of analysis," our archaeology has also placed us in the anarchic march of "progress," circa 1990, 1950, and 1880, and into an epistemology that makes it impossible to comprehend our world except as a world-system with endlessly shifting points of production.

Sooner or later our archaeologist would conclude that the industrial archipelago he found illustrated little more than the uneven development, the simultaneous creation and destruction, of industrial capitalism. The contemporary discourses of Gary and P'ohang are mutually incommensurable, just as it would be inconceivable to most pundits today that Japan's industrial march was founded in part on the thought of an American protectionist.

Genealogy, Descent, Emergence

Archaeology is useful, but it is not sufficient for our task. We also need genealogy. The former is static: it takes a photograph of Gary and P'ohang at one flash-frozen time. The latter is dynamic, but it does not necessarily imply development. Through a genealogy of the past we can understand not a "progress," but a *descent*, perhaps from that fluorescent point in 1920s Gary, or from the Los Angeles of the 1940s to the Los Ange-

---

12. See Robert S. Schwantes, "America and Japan," in Ernest May and James Thomson, eds., *American–East Asian Relations: A Survey* (Cambridge: Harvard University Press, 1972), 112–16. General Electric, of course, provided everything from electric machinery to equipment to turn out the light bulbs; Kirin was based on the Spring Valley Brewery set up in Yokohama about 1872, by William Copeland. Marx thought Henry Carey was the only original American economist (see his essay "Bastiat and Carey," in *The Grundrisse*); actually Carey was a protectionist who learned much from Friedrich List, whose theories were also favored in Japan.

les of today. But doesn't genealogy also imply *ascent?* From P'ohang in 1920 to P'ohang today? From Japan in 1880 to Japan today?

Genealogy does not imply ascent. It implies *emergence:* P'ohang emergent adds a new word to the industrial vocabulary (and in 1989 a new professorship to MIT: the P'ohang Steel Chair). Japan emergent bids fair to be the hegemon of the next century, but will this mean progress from the American vantage point? Is it in fact Japan that the intellectuals surreptitiously complain about, as "progress" migrates to "the East"?

Archaeology and genealogy give us a method to excavate history and to observe descent and emergence, a way to link discourse with reality, discursive thinking with the world-system or industrial structure. I will use this method to seek an analysis that connects knowledge with power and that is not reductionist—a method that operates at both ends of Althusser's dilemma—what he has called "the necessity—and difficulty—of holding on to 'both ends of the chain' at once: the relative autonomy of a region (e.g., ideology) and its 'determination in the last instance' . . . by the economic." [13] I will attempt a move to what Foucault called "the pre-discursive," the set of relations that unify discursive practice;[14] I will seek the pre-discursive in industrial structure and a specifiable world-system of industrial competition.

The usefulness of this method is that it allows us to see Japan, however close it may be to hegemonic emergence, in "concrete reality", which— in this century—has been a subordinate part of either bilateral American hegemony or trilateral American-British hegemony—save for six months, from Pearl Harbor to the battle of Midway or, if you wish more latitude for Japanese agency, for four years, from the summer of 1941 to the summer of 1945.

To my knowledge no one has ever argued this position before,[15] not

13. Stuart Hall, "The Hinterland of Science: Ideology and the 'Sociology of Knowledge' " in Hall, ed., *On Ideology* (University of Birmingham, 1978), 29–30. I am indebted to H. D. Harootunian for this reference.

14. See Alasdair MacIntyre's commentary on Foucault's *L'Archeologie du Savoir,* in *Three Rival Versions of Moral Enquiry,* 52; also Gutting, *Foucault's Archaeology,* who notes that *L'Archeologie du Savoir* provided "no serious discussion of the nature of the nondiscursive factors and of the influence they exert"; "there is no elucidation of the fundamental nature and ultimate significance of the link between the discursive and the nondiscursive" (259).

15. Of course, the modernization literature created by the Japanophiles of the 1950s– 60s (Robert Ward, James Morley) parenthesized the 1930s–40s as aberrational to the long march of Japanese progress, privileging instead the halcyon years of Meiji and "Taisho democracy." I argue a different point, that Japan in the 1930s–40s was aberrational

because it isn't correct, but for reasons that lie deep within the discourse of industrial competition: steadily thriving within the hegemonic net for ninety years, Japan nonetheless "emerges" in the Western mind at three critical and incommensurable points: at the turn of the century, when it was a British *wunderkind* (but a "yellow peril" to the Germans and the Russians) in the world depression of the 1930s, when it was an industrial monster to the British (but a *wunderkind* to the Germans and the Italians) and in the 1980s, when it was a *wunderkind* to American internationalists and a monster to American protectionists. Here is our metaphor for 1900–92: *Japan as Number Two.* To keep this essay to a tolerable length, I will carry the argument only up to the late 1940s, by which time the essentials of the postwar hegemonic system were in place. I contend, though, that Japan still moves within the system today.[16]

Menu of Quotations

Walter Benjamin said his greatest ambition was to compose a book made up entirely of quotations. Mine is more modest: to compose one section of this paper entirely of quotations.

> Whatsoever of morality and of intelligence; what of patience, perseverance, faithfulness, of method, insight, ingenuity, energy; in a word, whatsoever of Strength the man had in him will lie written in the Work he does. . . . Produce! Were it but the pitifullest infinitesimal fraction of a Product, produce it, in God's name!—Thomas Carlyle[17]

> They are Asiatics, it is true, and therefore deficient in that principle of development which is the leading characteristic of those ingenious and persevering European races . . . but amidst Asiatics the Japanese stand supreme.—*Edinburgh Review,* 1852[18]

> It was part of the Commodore's deliberately formed plan, in all his intercourse with these orientals, to consider carefully before he an-

in its relation to British-American hegemony; I would argue for continuity in Japanese imperialism from 1895 to 1945—as would any of Japan's neighbors.

16. For the postwar period see my "Japan in the Postwar World System," in Andrew Gordon, ed., *Postwar Japan as History* (Berkeley: University of California Press, 1993).

17. This and the next quote are from Daniel T. Rodgers, *The Work Ethic in Industrial America, 1850–1920* (Chicago: University of Chicago Press, 1978), xiv, 230, 241.

18. Quoted in Jean-Pierre Lehmann, *The Image of Japan: From Feudal Isolation to World Power, 1850–1905* (London: George Allen & Unwin, 1978), 46.

nounced his resolution to do any act, but, having announced it, he soon taught them to know that he would do precisely what he said he would.—Commodore Matthew Perry [19]

[Japan] has proved to be the most formidable ground for the development of the *bacillus capitalistic.* It is not yet thirty years since Japan emerged from its "grand revolution" . . . [but] the *bacillus capitalistic* found here the most desirable conditions for its growth . . . especially plenty of extremely cheap labor. [In the not distant future] the *bacillus capitalistic* will be killed by the *phagocitus socialisticus.*—British socialists, 1897 [20]

The Japanese should have no concern with business. The Jap has no business savvy.—Rudyard Kipling (1900)

In one large hall of [Tokyo Commercial] School . . . a number of bays, or recesses, are labelled with the names of the principal mercantile centers of the world, and in each of these a number of students . . . taking the parts, respectively, of bankers, importers, exporters, brokers, insurance agents and shipping agents, carry on active, simulated international trade in strict accordance with the business usages of the places at which they are supposed to be dealing.— missionary observation (circa 1900) [21]

I shall turn Japanese for they at least can think, and be reticent! [Witness] their organization, their strategy, their virile qualities, their devotion and self-control. Above all, their national capacity for self-reliance, self-sacrifice, and their silence!—Phillip Lyttleton Gell (1904) [22]

Witness the magnificent spectacle of Japan today; the State above the individual; common good above personal good; sacrifice of self and devotion to the community.—Sir Oliver Lodge, Fabian (1907) [23]

[The Japanese] shame our administrative capacity . . . shame our in-

19. Perry's *Narrative of the Expedition,* quoted in Peter Booth Wiley, *Yankees in the Land of the Gods: Commodore Perry and the Opening of Japan* (New York: Viking, 1990), 164.
20. Lehmann, *Image of Japan,* 120.
21. Ibid., 132.
22. Quoted in Colin Holmes and A. H. Iron, "Bushido and the Samurai: Images in British Public Opinion, 1894–1914," *Modern Asian Studies* 14, no. 2 (1980): 304–29.
23. Ibid., 321.

ventiveness . . . shame our leadership.—Sidney and Beatrice Webb, 1911

The wily Jap [is] determined to stop at nothing in his efforts to bamboozle shoppers in this country [and is] STEALING OUR MARKETS! [sic]—British businessmen (1936)[24]

To the poltroonery of American liberalism one cannot imagine a better antithesis than the exquisite temperance and the sublime abnegation of the Japanese. Dear, gentle, elegant, heroic Japanese! Be welcomed at our side. We will conquer.—Gazetta del Populo, Turin (1941)[25]

The Japanese are, to the highest degree, both aggressive and unaggressive, both militaristic and aesthetic, both insolent and polite, rigid and adaptable, submissive and resentful of being pushed around, loyal and treacherous, brave and timid, conservative and hospitable to new ways.—Ruth Benedict, 1946[26]

Our economic frontier now embraces the trade potentialities of Asia itself; for with the gradual rotation of the epicenter of world trade back to the Far East whence it started many centuries ago, the next thousand years will find the main problem the raising of the sub-normal standards of life of its more than a billion people.—Gen. Douglas MacArthur, 1951[27]

[The Japanese state elite has] the security, the ability, and an ethos that enable it to concentrate on what is good for the nation as a whole.—Ezra Vogel (1979)[28]

I am really very troubled when I think through the consequences of the rise of Japanese power.—Ezra Vogel (1982)[29]

24. Quoted in Isohi Asahi, The Economic Strength of Japan (Tokyo: Hokuseido Press, 1939), 207–9.
25. Quoted in Time, December 22, 1941.
26. Ruth Benedict, The Chrysanthemum and the Sword: Patterns of Japanese Culture (Boston: Houghton Mifflin, 1946), 2.
27. Speech in Seattle, late 1951, quoted in Michael W. Miles, The Odyssey of the American Right (New York: Oxford University Press, 1980), 170.
28. Ezra F. Vogel, Japan as Number One: Lessons for America (Cambridge: Harvard University Press, 1979), vii.
29. Private seminar on U.S.-Japan relations, Harvard University, 1982; Huntington's statement is from the same source.

[Japan has] these really fundamental weaknesses—energy, food, and military security . . . it is an extraordinarily weak country.— Samuel Huntington (1982)

The most crucial factor determining Japan's sociopolitical reality . . . is the near absence of any idea that there can be truths, rules, principles or morals that always apply, no matter what the circumstances.—Karel van Wolferen (1989)

I believe that the Japanese are individuals. . . . I have met quite a few who want to be taken for distinct persons.—Karel van Wolferen (1989)[30]

[Japan is an example of] state corporate capitalism, as opposed to entrepreneurial capitalism . . . what we used to call fascism.—Jude Wanniskie (1989)[31]

Japan does not aspire to replace America as the world's leader; it will be content to stay number two.—former Minister of Foreign Affairs Okita Saburo, 1989[32]

[The Japanese are] creatures of an ageless, amoral, manipulative and controlling culture . . . suited only to this race, in this place.— CIA-funded conference report, 1991[33]

At a superficial level, my quotations are useful for demonstrating that contemporaneous debate on Japan operates within limits, or within a discourse that has been around since Japan first began industrializing. More than that, this discourse applies equally well to any "late" industrializer, whether Germany of the late nineteenth century or Korea in the late twentieth (increasingly linked with Japan in the American mind as a "threat"). The quotations allow us to place both Ezra Vogel (Japan as model) and Karel van Wolferen (Japan as threat) within a century-long discourse. They allow us to construct an either/or dyad of interpretation, a dualism common to historical interpretation (Gibbon: rise and decline; Toynbee: challenge and response; Fairbank: Western challenge and Eastern response). The

30. The Enigma of Japanese Power (New York: Alfred A. Knopf, 1989), 9, 23.
31. "Some Lines on the Rest of the Millennium," New York Times, 24 December 1989.
32. Quoted in Wiley, Yankees in the Land of the Gods, 483.
33. Andrew J. Doughterty, Japan 2000, 151. This is an unpublished summary account of a 1990 project funded by the Central Intelligence Agency, at the Rochester Institute of Technology.

inscriptions also enable us to recognize a *moral valence* attached to each dyad (model is good, threat is bad; diligence is good, purloining is bad; democracy is good, "state corporate capitalism" is bad; the chrysanthemum definitely beats the sword).

Yet our quotations generate a dyad of incommensurable judgment: are the Japanese a threat or a model? Are they aesthetes or militarists—the chrysanthemum or the sword? Are they innovative, or do they copy? Inventors or purloiners? Is Japan the exception in East Asia, or the rule? (the Webbs and most others thought it the exception at the turn of the century, but would they say so today, with Korean and Chinese industrial prowess?) Is Japan's political economy unique, or does it replicate earlier industrial experience? Is the Japanese state an authoritarian menace or an enlightened pilot (the "benevolent bureaucracy of the future socialist state," according to Beatrice Webb)? Is the Japanese polity *sui generis* (as per the nativist *kokutai* doctrine in 1938 or as Ishihara Shintaro says in *The Japan That Can Say No*), or is it the enlightened if imbedded state of welfare post-industrialism (as Ezra Vogel has it)? Is Japan autonomous or dependent? Do we face today MacArthur's "rotation of the epicenter" of world trade back to East Asia, or have the superpowers merely spent themselves into decline in the four decades of the Cold War, enabling the rise of their former enemies, Japan and Germany? Will Japan be the hegemonic power of the twenty-first century, or was all that talk rendered obsolete when the Berlin Wall fell and a united Germany once again moved front and center in Europe and put all the blather about the Pacific Rim and the "dawning Pacific century" in the shade?

Benjamin liked to quote other people because his thought aimed not at binding general statements but at metaphorical ones, to establish correspondences. Moreover, the quotation—or fragment—offered an alternative to historical narratives that emplotted the tale of progress. His idea was that "the transmissibility of the past had been replaced by its citability"; in place of the authority of tradition, we find a tendency to "settle down in the present," complacently, and to accept its random evidence and its incommensurability.[34] The quotations I have given you may also be taken as metaphors, for Japan observed over more than a century; but the more important point is the *correspondences,* or rather, the incommensurability, the lack of correspondence to any consistent interpretation of Japan other than that it has spent this century becoming an industrial power.

34. Hannah Arendt, "Introduction," in *Illuminations,* ed. Hannah Arendt (New York: Schocken Books, 1969), 38.

Benjamin's metaphor for the historian is thus "the pearl diver," searching for the effluvia of the past to bring up to the surface and to place alongside other effluvia, all in the simultaneity with which we moderns experience the past. And so:

> Quotations in my works are like robbers by the roadside who make an armed attack and relieve an idler of his convictions.[35]

The quotations have much the same meaning for us that antiques have for an antique collector, or that pearls have for a pearl diver—valuable effluvia, but ripped from context—fragments of a lost past but nonetheless precious. The mind reads them and says to itself, you can't have it both ways, or *plus ça change, plus c'est la même chose.* The quotations and dyads are incommensurable, but why? What places the boundary for these antinomies? And the moral valence? What structures the discourse?

Manifest Density: E + D + Em = A

Roland Barthes used Japan not as a mirror to reflect back to the West what is good and true here and sadly lacking there (i.e., the Eastward-gazing function of "Enlightenment" since the eighteenth century), but as a system of difference to develop a radical critique of the West and its assumptions.[36] Barthes developed an optic that offers a parallax view, or a salutary boomerang, to question ourselves. As he said, Japan afforded him

> a situation of writing . . . in which a certain disturbance of the person occurs, a subversion of earlier readings, a shock of meaning.

And later, "Someday we must write the history of our own obscurity—manifest the density of our narcissism."[37]

Our quotations, almost all of them Western, "manifest the density of our narcissism." They do not exist in thin air, however, but have an origin, a cause, and a historical meaning. In *The Genealogy of Morals,*[38] Nietzsche wrote that he ceased looking for the origin of morality behind the world and began looking *in* the world; he found that

---

35. Benjamin, *Schriften* I, in *Illuminations,* ed. Arendt, 571.

36. Barthes, *Empire of Signs* (New York: Hill and Wang, 1982), 3–4.

37. Ibid., 4.

38. Nietzsche, *On the Genealogy of Morals,* ed. and trans. Walter Kaufmann (New York: Vintage Books, 1969), 15–23, 77–78.

the cause of the origin of a thing and its eventual utility, its actual employment and place in a system of purposes, lie worlds apart; whatever exists, having somehow come into being, is again and again
reinterpreted to new ends.

"Japan" is endlessly reinterpreted, but not because of its "progress." The
"evolution" of something, Nietzsche says, is "by no means its *progressus* toward a goal"; words like "progress" and "purpose" are only signs
that some master has imposed upon history a meaning. What we know
as history is always "a fresh interpretation . . . through which any previous
'meaning' and 'purpose' are necessarily obscured and even obliterated."
History is thus "a continuous sign-chain of ever new interpretations."

   Thus, our quotations function as a sign-chain, a genealogy of moral
valence: Japan "stands still," or does what it always has since it joined the
race with the West, but "Japan" metamorphoses with the ups and downs
of Western perception.

   Foucault took up Nietzsche's argument in a famous essay, "Nietzsche, Genealogy, History."[39] Genealogy "opposes itself to the search for
'origins' "; for historians, origins means "that which was already there," as
if it did not require a human being to determine "what was there," but can
simply be "found." The site of historical truth, of true "origin," he says (and
here he draws on Benjamin[40])

   lies at a place of inevitable loss . . . the site of a fleeting articulation
   that discourse has obscured and finally lost.

The genealogical method "excavat[es] the depths," "allow[s] time for these
elements to escape from a labyrinth where no truth had ever detained
them." And so, history

   is the concrete body of a development, with its moments of intensity, its lapses, its extended periods of feverish agitation, its fainting

39. "Nietzsche, Genealogy, History," in Michel Foucault, *Language, Counter-Memory,
Practice,* trans. Donald F. Bouchard and Sherry Simon (Ithaca, N.Y.: Cornell University
Press, 1977).
40. "The true picture of the past flits by," Benjamin wrote. "The past can be seized only
as an image which flashes up at the instant when it can be recognized and is never seen
again. . . . To articulate the past historically does not mean to recognize it 'the way it
really was' (Ranke). It means to seize hold of a memory as it flashes up at a moment of
danger." Walter Benjamin, "Theses on the Philosophy of History," in *Illuminations,* 255.
See also Hayden White's critique of Rankean history in *Tropics of Discourse: Essays in
Cultural Criticism* (Baltimore: Johns Hopkins Unviersity Press, 1978), 51–53.

spells; and only a metaphysician would seek its soul in the distant ideality of the origin.

In other words, my quotations are a discourse with humanly applied limitations and oscillations; their "history" is in the "feverish agitation" and "fainting spells" with which the West greets notable Japanese success, or newfound power.

Foucault goes on to say that *herkunft,* one German word for origin, means something more like "stock" or "descent." An examination of descent "permits the discovery, under the unique aspect of a trait or a concept, of the myriad events through which they were formed." The duty of genealogy is not to demonstrate that the past actively exists in the present, through a predetermined form or through some necessary causality; the past is not an evolution and it does not map the destiny of a people:

> On the contrary, to follow the complex course of descent is *to maintain passing events in their proper dispersion.* [emphasis added]

History is not a determined or meaningful heritage, "a possession that grows and solidifies";

> it is [instead] an unstable assembly of faults, fissures, and heterogeneous layers that threaten the fragile inheritor from within and from underneath.

The "fragile inheritors" of the Enlightenment tradition, as we have seen, now find themselves threatened from within, from underneath . . . and from the East.

Nietzsche also used the term "emergence" (*entstehung*), "the principle and the singular law of an apparition." Descent does not mean uninterrupted continuity, and emergence does not mean "the final term of a historical development," even if both appear as a culmination of trends. "Culminations" are "merely the current episodes in a series of subjugations," and so

> emergence is thus the entry of forces; it is their eruption, *the leap from the wings to the center stage.* . . . Emergence designates a place of confrontation. [emphasis added]

An event (or an emergence) is not a decision, a treaty, or a war, but "the reversal of a relationship of forces, the usurpation of power, the appropriation of a vocabulary turned against those who had once used it." And, thus, his conclusion: "The body [or history, or the descent] is molded by a great many distinct regimes."

In other words "emergence" indicates not just a reversal, but a prior moment of apprehension, when things not heretofore salient suddenly become so and lay the groundwork for a reevaluation. This is a very Nietzschean formulation, but Nietzsche added to this a sense of alarm, a dimension of the unconscious, "an unrecognized motivation serving an unacknowledged purpose," in MacIntyre's apt phrase.[41] Much of the alarmist American discourse on Japan is precisely that.

We may now formulate an equation, to satisfy the positivist penchant for quantitative certainty: let E stand for excavation, D for descent, Em for emergence and A for archaeology, thus: $E + D + Em = A$, our "archaeology of the present," a critical method for doing history that seeks something more than the usual "let the facts speak for themselves" empiricism, something more than mere "pearl diving," and something other than history as "progressus toward a goal."

Japan Emergent

In the 1990s Japan has flashed up at a moment of feverish agitation,[42] but not for the first time. More than 130 years ago Marx noted that Americans, unable to conceive of contradictions in economic relations in the world market as integral to the workings of capitalism, saw such contradictions "as soon as they appear on the world market as *English* relations," that is, as English capital's distortion of the natural order of things.[43] Today the disturber of the natural order of things is Japan. For the past hundred years Western conjurings of "Japan" have expressed the problems of world

41. MacIntyre, *Three Rival Versions of Moral Enquiry*, 35.
42. Good examples may be found on the cover of *Fortune*, "The Big Split" (6 May 1991), or in George Friedman and Meredith Lebard, *The Coming War with Japan* (New York: St. Martin's Press, 1991).
43. Karl Marx, "Bastiat and Carey," in *The Grundrisse* (New York: Vintage Books, 1973), 887. This section is drawn in modified form from my "High Technology and Ideology: How Japan Metamorphoses," originally presented at the American Political Science Association annual meeting in 1983, and published in shortened form in *The Nation* and in *The Insurgent Sociologist* in 1984. It is part of a book-length manuscript that I am working on entitled *Industrial Behemoth: The Northeast Asian Political Economy in the Twentieth Century* (Ithaca, N.Y.: Cornell University Press, forthcoming).

competition for markets and of industrial decline in acute fashion. Historically, when industrial structure is a problem, Japan becomes a problem—although our industrialists would have it the other way around.

I would like to argue that in spite of the sharp reversals in Western discourse about Japan, Japan for most of our century has been caught in the nets of a *regime of technology* and a *system of states*. Japan was not simply in alliance with England from 1902 to 1922, but was content to "prosper in the collective informal empire" of the British and the Americans throughout the first quarter of the century, and to feed off a British-American technological regime without making any significant technological innovations until the late 1920s—and then only in textiles, an industry already in incipient decline in England and America.

Pratt Machines long underpinned the developing Japanese textile industry. General Electric was dominant in the delivery of electricity, and by the 1890s Standard Oil had placed both Japan and China well within the world oil regime, which was increasingly dominated by American firms. Standard Oil's comparative advantage was mostly financial and technical, but it also resided in innovative marketing schemes: a world monopoly, combined with creative ways to sell "oil for the lamps of China."[44] The joint British-American technical condominium was perhaps best symbolized by the British-American Tobacco Company, a subsidiary of the Duke tobacco interests in North Carolina, which got Japan and China hooked on something else, a cigarette habit so deep that "nonsmoking sections" can hardly be found anywhere in either country in 1991.[45]

Even the spearhead for Japan's penetration of Manchuria, the South Manchurian Railway Company, acquired its reputation for advanced and efficient service by importing thousands of the latest American locomotives and railway cars, not to mention tons of American steel railway ties,

44. By 1894, annual American kerosene exports to Japan had reached 887,000 barrels of 42 gallons each. Standard entered the production field in Japan with its International Oil Company, 1900–1906. See Harold F. Williamson and Arnold R. Daum, *The American Petroleum Industry, 1859–1899: The Age of Illumination* (Evanston: Northwestern University Press, 1959), 675; also *Soritsu shichijù-shùnen kinen Nihon sekiyu shi* [70th anniversary history of Japanese petroleum] (Tokyo: Nihon Sekiyu K. K., 1958).

45. James B. Duke formed BAT in 1902, in league with a chief rival, the British Imperial Tobacco Company; Duke held two-thirds of the stock. By 1915, BAT had almost $17 million in investments in China and was one of its two largest employers. (Michael H. Hunt, *The Making of a Special Relationship: The United States and China to 1914* [New York: Columbia University Press, 1983], 282–83.)

all known for decades as the best in the world.[46] Japan has striven and often thrived within this network of dependency, yet almost always has been treated by the West as an independent and often mysterious entity, to be loved or reviled.

Japan's industrialization has proceeded through three phases, the last of which is now flourishing. The first phase began in the 1880s with textiles being the leading sector; the textile phase lasted through Japan's rise to world power, an ascent marked by foreign aggression in every decade after the 1880s (aggression that was errant counterpoint to the roseate imagery of Japanese success, but par for the course among the industrial nations). In the mid-1930s Japan began the second, heavy phase of industrialization, based on steel, chemicals, automobiles, and armaments; this phase was dominant until the mid-1960s. The third phase, of course, emphasized high technology—"knowledge" industries such as electronics, communications, and silicon-chip microprocessors.[47]

Within Japan, each phase, in good product-cycle fashion, has been marked by strong state protection for nascent industries, creative adaptation of foreign technologies, and comparative advantages deriving from cheap labor costs, technological and organizational innovation, or "lateness" in world time. Then there would be a bursting forth into the world market that always struck foreign observers as abrupt and unexpected, thus inspiring fear and loathing as well as awe and admiration. Far from disturbing "the natural order of things," for a century Japan has followed the natural trajectory laid out by leading capitalist ideologues, especially regarding classic notions of the product cycle. In so doing, however, Japan has gotten itself into a lot of trouble.

A Janus-faced, startled surprise greeted Japan's first clear moment of "emergence," its defeat of Russia in 1905. At the turn of the century Japan materialized like a Rorschach ink blot onto which Americans and Europeans projected their own hopes and fears. For Westerners accustomed

46. William Wray, "Japan's Big-Three Service Enterprises in China, 1896–1936," in *The Japanese Informal Empire in China, 1895–1937*, ed. Peter Duus, Ramon H. Myers, and Mark Peattie (Princeton: Princeton University Press, 1989), 35, 57–59; also Ramon Myers, "Japanese Imperialism in Manchuria: The South Manchurian Railway Company, 1906–1933," Ibid., 105–7.

47. Kiyoshi Kojima, *Japan and a New World Economic Order* (Boulder: Westview Press, 1977), 14–15, 120–21; also Hugh Patrick and Henry Rosovsky, eds., *Asia's New Giant: How the Japanese Economy Works* (Washington, D.C.: The Brookings Institution, 1976), 8–9.

to thinking in racial terms, Japanese success was inexplicable because the Japanese were "yellow" and not white (although they soon became honorary whites). Meanwhile, missionaries began referring to "the untiring industry" of the Japanese: "All night long the sleepless sounds of labor are rampant and furious. This habit of ceaseless occupation extends to the very highest classes."[48]

Westerners usually explained all this through a combination of Japanese sweating of labor and shameless copying of foreign models, not knowing that in saying so they simply mimicked British myths of the 1880s about another late developer, Germany. The French were not sanguine about Japan, worrying about "the competition of yellow labor;" even if at present (1905) "Nippon labor does not seem to be the cause of the depreciation of salaries" in the West, it would be so "if Japan, victorious over Russia and master of the Celestial Empire, organized Chinese labor."[49]

British socialists, however, projected their fond hopes and sharp morals onto the Japanese. Beatrice Webb, perhaps with her husband Sidney not the most discerning of Fabians in foreign lands, wrote in 1904 that Japan was a "rising star of human self-control and enlightenment." On her trip to the Orient in 1911, she found the Chinese to be "a horrid race," the Koreans also "a horrid race" (for Sidney these were "lowly vertebrates" who "show us, indeed, what *Homo sapiens* can be if he does not evolve"). Beatrice liked the "innovating collectivism" of Japan and its "enlightened professional elite" with its "uncanny" purposefulness and open-mindedness. Here was the "benevolent bureaucracy of the future socialist state."[50] H.G. Wells, it may be remembered, called his elite "samurai" in *A Modern Utopia* (1905), and in the 1930s the Webbs were to liken Stalin's cadres to "the samurai vocation for leadership."[51]

Why were English of all stripes lauding Japan in the first decade of the twentieth century? The answer is simple: British decline and German and Japanese advance; Germany was a threat, and Japan was the British ally after 1902. After two great waves of industrialization lasting a century and a half, England found itself beset by newly risen industrial powers and by an obsolescent industrial base. A period of fervent soul-searching there-

48. Lehmann, *Image of Japan,* 128.
49. Ibid., 178.
50. Holmes and Ion, "Bushido and Samurai," 320; also J. M. Winter, "The Webbs and the Non-White World: A Case of Socialist Racialism," *Journal of Contemporary History* 9, no. 1 (January 1974): 181–92.
51. Winter, Ibid., 188.

fore marked most debates, with the watchword being efficiency: "Give us efficiency or we die." Alfred Stead entitled his 1906 book *Great Japan: A Study of National Efficiency.* English pundits wished to discover models of efficiency and productivity, and they looked to a "Japan" which, it was thought, "afforded lessons from which the British might learn to solve their internal problems."[52] Here was the reason for all the silly Japanophilia of the period, when the real problems for Britain were declining industries and the threat of Germany.

Germany, for England, was an example of a country pulling itself up from agriculture to industry in the space of a few decades through hard toil, help from the state, protectionism, diligence, "purloined" technology, wicked copying, and "an alert progressiveness, contrasted with the conservative stupor of ourselves (the British)."[53] That is, Germany was for England what Japan is for our industrialists today: a combination of miracle and cheap tricks.

The image of Japan in the West can turn on a dime. During World War I Japan was the scheming jackal, enjoying a war boom and tripled exports but in the 1920s, when it entered a period of economic stagnation and pursued free trade policies, it was lauded for its liberal institutions. The period of *Taisho* democracy was for modernization theorists the progressive culmination of the Meiji success story, marred later by the aberration of the decade of militarism, 1936–45.[54] Whether the 1920s were the exception or the rule of Japanese development, we might at least note that the benign image corresponds to a very benign Japan, undercutting no one's exports and markets and acquiescing in the 1920s international system that defined America, England, and Japan in a perfect trilateral formula: 5:5:3 (the ratio of naval ships in the Pacific, but it can stand for everything else).

By the mid-1930s with the world in depression, protective tariffs everywhere, and Japan embarking on heavy industrialization, "Japan" was again a problem. For liberal internationalists like Henry Stimson, the lament was that Japan, "with a tradition of original friendliness toward the U.S.," should have gone off the free trade regimen and onto such a bender in Manchuria, destroying the "open door."[55] For Guenther Stein, who in 1935

52. Holmes and Ion, "Bushido and Samurai," 314, 328.

53. Ernest Edwin Williams, *Made in Germany* (London: William Heinemann, 1896), 8–9, 162–63.

54. See John W. Dower's introductory essay in *Origins of the Modern Japanese State: Selected Writings of E. H. Norman,* ed. Dower (New York: Pantheon, 1975).

55. Henry Stimson, *The Far Eastern Crisis* (New York: Council on Foreign Relations, 1936), 8–9, passim.

wrote a prescient book with the ironic (for then) title, *Made in Japan,* the country was a model of industrial efficiency that, were it not for tariff walls, "might become the largest exporter in the world—and in a very short time." Stein rightly saw in the heavy industrialization spurt of the mid-1930s "the beginning of a new epoch in the industrialization of the world"; Japan's problem was that it had upset the balance of the world system, "and this is the real reason why other countries complain about her."[56] Within Japan, however, its sharp departures of policy in the mid-1930s were justified, as they had been since 1868, by the requisites of harsh competition in a world that others dominated:

> The chief object of [our] planned economy is successful competition in world markets through a complete industrialization of the country. . . . In the execution of the standardization of national life, which is quite economic in nature, some limitation may be placed upon the laissez-faire policy, but this is a world-wide tendency. . . . [It] is not to be taken as the harbinger of a fascist regime.[57]

Also announced at the time was the first Datsun motorcar, symbol of the "dawning new age," appearing in a Japanese auto market "which has long been dominated by Fords, Chevrolets, and other American cars."[58]

With Japan's attack at Pearl Harbor, of course, its increasingly tough image of the late 1930s turned into one of pure racism. As *Life* said in December 1941, "the whole cartoon aspect of the Jap changed overnight. Before that sudden Sunday the Jap was an oily little man, amiable but untrustworthy, more funny than dangerous." *Time* magazine's issue of the same day (December 22) featured Admiral Isoroku Yamamoto on the cover, garnished with the hue of a moldering lemon, and gave readers instructions on how to tell "Japs" from "Chinamen." By 1943, most of the characteristics that the Fabians had admired were being used to explain why the Japanese were aggressors: the strong group life, the all-powerful state, and "mindless" subordination to authority.[59]

56. Guenther Stein, *Made in Japan* (London: Methuen, 1935), 188, 191, 205.
57. *Asahi Shimbun* (Present-day Nippon) (Tokyo, 1936), 23.
58. Ibid., 119. When I presented an earlier version of this paper in Paris, two French economic historians exclaimed that Japan had made no automobiles until the 1950s. The 1935 Datsun was important, but it was by no means the first Japanese automobile: Isuzu and other firms made autos between 1910 and 1920.
59. Jesse F. Steiner, *Behind the Japanese Mask* (New York: MacMillan, 1943). The commanding interpretation of this dark period in U.S.-Japan relations is John W. Dower, *War without Mercy: Race and Power in the Pacific War* (New York: Pantheon, 1986).

The shifting and incommensurable imagery of Japan in the first half of the century derived from sharp industrial competition in the world-system, a conflict that routinely overlooked Japan's continuing technological inferiority to England and America. But that system is also a system of states, not just markets. How did Japan fit in there?

Japan as Number Two

The conception used in this section assumes the existence of a world market and industrial competition within it, as did the previous section, but I also here assume that the primary and "normal" mechanism that corresponds to the capitalist system of states is *hegemony:* a conception that encompasses empire, colonialism, "neo-colonialism," and what is sometimes called informal empire. Hegemony means the simultaneous *and temporary* "productive, commercial and financial pre-eminence of one core power over other core powers"; the critical element is "productive advantage," which conditions the other two (commerce and finance). Military advantage, conventionally thought to be crucial to hegemony, merely "locks in" hegemony. The hegemonic power favors openness in trade, decolonization or informal empire, and liberalism everywhere—sometimes even in the home market.[60]

Our archaeology has already uncovered in the depths of the "prediscursive" a regime of technology (the productivist aspect of American/ British hegemony) in prewar Japanese industry, moving temporally and geographically according to what is commonly known as a product cycle (American rolling stock in Manchuria, American-blueprinted refineries in Wônsan, basic oxygen furnaces in P'ohang).[61] Now we will excavate "Japan as Number Two" in the discourse of international politics: states arrayed in a hierarchy of power, sometimes known as the balance of power, and states

---

60. Terence K. Hopkins and Immanuel Wallerstein, "Patterns of Development of the Modern World-System," *Review* 1, no. 2 (Fall 1977): 120–21, 130–31. Although I employ this different conception here, I do not have serious disagreement with Peter Duus's use of the well-known Gallagher and Robinson notion of "informal empire," in Duus, Myers, and Peattie, *Japanese Informal Empire,* xiv–xvi.

61. For more elaboration see my "Origins and Development of the Northeast Asian Political Economy," *International Organization* (Winter 1984): 1–40. Theoretically this means that "the continued further mechanization of productive processes is linked to the continual redefinition of 'core'-type productive activities and the continual relocation of core, semiperipheral, and peripheral zones" (Hopkins and Wallerstein, "Patterns of Development", 126).

as both autonomous and penetrated, their structures the outcome of both domestic and international forces.[62] Here, too, the discursive gives way to the pre-discursive, the deep structure of a world-system in which Japan has played an important, but almost always subordinate, part.

An archaeology of Japan in the twentieth century world-system un-earths the following timelines:

a) 1900–22: Japan in British-American hegemony
b) 1922–41: Japan in American-British hegemony
c) 1941–45: Japan as regional hegemon in East Asia
d) 1945–70: Japan in American hegemony
e) 1970–1990s: Japan in American-European hegemony

Here we highlight another aspect of this structure: three of the periods (a, b, and e) are trilateral partnerships, and none is colonial or necessarily imperial. A bilateral regime is predictable in the temporary phase of com-prehensive hegemony (1945–70 for the United States), a trilateral regime in the rising and falling phases of transitional hegemonies. Period c is the exception that proves the rule.

Rather than elaborate this pattern in the pre-discursive of power rela-tions,[63] let us just sample the discursive—found readily in the *oeuvre* of the dean of diplomatic historians of East Asia, Akira Iriye, whose books domi-nate the field. Because Iriye has dwelt at one end of Althusser's "chain," the realm of culture, ideas, and imagery in international relations,[64] and perhaps because of his understated style, few recognize just how deeply revisionist his work is. Iriye has consistently argued through his career

(1) That Japanese imperialism (conventionally dated from the Sino-Japanese War and the seizure of Taiwan in 1895) was subordinate to British imperialism, and coterminous with a similar American thrust

---

62. Wallerstein, *Historical Capitalism,* 56–59.
63. The subject of my current research, and, therefore, both too long and too unformed to present in this paper.
64. Especially in *Across the Pacific: An Inner History of American–East Asian Relations,* his most brilliant and original book; but see also *Pacific Estrangement: Japanese and American Expansion, 1897–1911* (Cambridge: Harvard University Press, 1972), *After Im-perialism* (Cambridge: Harvard University Press, 1965), and the deeply revisionist *Power and Culture: The Japanese-American War, 1941–1945* (Cambridge: Harvard University Press, 1981). All these books operate on the terrain of intercultural imagery and conflict.

toward formal empire in the 1890s, and no different in kind from the British or American variety;[65]

(2) That Japan pursued a "cooperative" policy of integration with the world-system (not his terms) at all times in the twentieth century, except from the critical turning point of July 1941 through the resulting war;[66]

(3) That Japan got the empire the British and Americans wanted it to have and sought to organize an exclusive regional sphere only when the other powers did the same, after the collapse of the world-system in the 1930s (and even then their attempt was half-hearted, and even then the development program was "orthodoxly Western");[67]

(4) That Japan's presumed neo-mercantilist political economy of protection at home and export to the free-trade realm abroad, with corresponding trade surpluses, has been less important over the past ninety years than an open market at home and a cooperative policy abroad.

Japan first "emerged," of course, with its "opening" by Commodore Perry and the subsequent Meiji Restoration, which some Japanese scholars are increasingly coming to interpret as an outcome of world market forces, and when England was the hegemonic power facing growing competition from the United States.[68] Both powers followed a "cooperative" policy toward Japan, however, or what we would call a "trilateral" policy.

65. *Pacific Estrangement,* viii, 18–19, 26–27, 35–36. In fact the United States was for the Japanese both "a model and an object of their expansion." Iriye has a remarkably benign view of both American and Japanese expansion, terming the former "peaceful" and "liberal" because it sought only commercial advantage—that is, what we call hegemony. (See pp. 12–13, 36.)

66. *Power and Culture,* 1–2. From the Meiji Restoration to 1941, he writes, Japan wanted to integrate itself with the regime of the great powers, which he connotes as a policy of "international cooperation" or "interdependence."

67. Ibid., 3–4, 15, 20, 25–27. Iriye dates Japanese plans for an exclusive northeast Asian regional hegemony from 1936, but according to him it still did not have a blueprint in 1939 and was still dependent on the core powers in system until the middle of 1941.

68. Ishii Kanji and Sekiguchi Hisashi, eds., *Sekai shijo to bakamatsu kaiko* (The world market and Japan's opening in the Bakamatsu period) (Tokyo: Tokyo Daigaku Shuppankai, 1982); for an older Marxist interpretation see Ishii Takashi, *Meiji ishin no kokusaiteki kankyo* (*The international environment of the Meiji Restoration*) (Tokyo: Yoshikawa Kobunkan, 1957). The latter views the famous American diplomat Townsend Harris as a representative of American commercial capital, which wanted Japan as a base for trading vessels in the Pacific; the British, however, wanted Japan as a market for British products,

The "hooking" of Japan into the hegemonic system was most obvious diplomatically in the Anglo-Japanese Alliance of 1902,[69] of course, but
this was also connected to the building of railroads in Korea and China,
which Americans (particularly the E. H. Harriman trust) pursued as assidu-
ously as did British interests.[70] But if that episode "locked in" Japan for the
British, it probably was less important historically than the growing American
presence in the technological and energy regime in Japan, and the arrival
of the classic ploy of the rising hegemon: an "open door" policy abroad,
combined with the ongoing development of a protected national market at
home and in America's near reaches (the Monroe Doctrine).

William Appleman Williams was the discerning historian who discovered in John Hay's "open door notes" of 1900 a metaphor for American
expansion, and who grasped that this new form of hegemony had its inception in East Asia.[71] Michael Hunt has detailed an "Open Door constitu-
ency" in American export industries such as cotton and cotton textiles, oil,
tobacco, and railroad equipment; even though residual anti-English sensi-
tivities ruled out a formal alliance with England, American leaders such as
Hay and Roosevelt continued to see an identity of interests with Great Britain (as they had since the War of 1812). Meanwhile Japan was the chosen
junior partner of both: Roosevelt "looked to Japan as an advanced country
and regional power uniquely qualified to instruct backward China" (and thus
steered American policy thereafter toward Japan's colonial and continental
dependencies).[72]

Iriye thinks that the Russo-Japanese War turned Japan into an "imperialist" power, which he seems to define in the narrow terms of forcible
subordination of other nations. Yet he immediately notes, correctly, that as
long as the direction of Japanese imperialism was toward Korea and Manchuria, it had the blessing of Americans (not to mention the British), espe-

---

and since they were the dominant capitalist power, they eventually got what they wanted
in a revision of customs rates that gave England control of Japan as a market (371–72).
See also Wiley, *Yankees in the Land of the Gods,* 482–500.
69. The standard work is Ian Nish, *The Anglo-Japanese Alliance: The Diplomacy of Two
Island Empires, 1894–1907* (London: Athlone, 1966), and his second volume, *Alliance in
Decline: A Study in Anglo-Japanese Relations, 1908–1923* (London: Athlone, 1972).
70. Yasuoka Akio, "The Opening of Japan to the End of the Russo-Japanese War," in
Japan and the World, 1853–1952 ed. Sadao Asada (New York: Columbia University
Press, 1989), 94.
71. *The Tragedy of American Diplomacy,* 2d ed. (New York: Delta, 1972).
72. Hunt, *Special Relationship,* 279.

cially Theodore Roosevelt, and it was accompanied by the usual retinue of cheerleading American scholars.[73]

Roosevelt's successor, Taft, was less enamored of Japan than he was of China (Taft visited Japan in 1905 and decided that "a Jap is first of all a Jap and would be glad to aggrandize himself at the expense of anybody").[74] He was also enamored of "dollar diplomacy" and a sphere of influence in Manchuria. Taft's Secretary of State, Frank Knox, and the classic American expansionist Willard Straight (a longtime advisor to Harriman) developed a "grandiose vision," in Charles Neu's words, for (in Knox's words) an "economic, scientific, and impartial administration of Manchuria," a joint supervision of the great powers, especially England and the United States, and especially over the railways. The goal of the plan was to create "an immense commercial neutral zone"—i.e., an open door—from which all the powers would benefit.[75]

Taft thus inaugurated a pattern that has lasted until the present, in which American diplomacy occasionally flirts with a "China first" policy (Franklin Roosevelt, Richard Nixon, and Jimmy Carter are good examples), only to be called back to the hard reality that Japan, with an advanced industrial base, is the more important power in East Asia. Taft learned that fact by 1910, when his plans to develop Manchurian railways under British-American auspices lay in ruins.[76] Neu notes that Taft's plan did not proceed out of hostility toward Japan—he "admired Japan's achievements and had approved of her absorption of Korea." But just to underline the importance of these events, in 1909 U.S. Navy planners had decided on Pearl Harbor as the chief American base in the Pacific, and in 1910, the Taft administration's General Board "began systematic consideration of war with Japan and by March 1911 had worked out a detailed Orange Plan."[77] (It seemed a bit early to send this chill up the American-Japanese spine.)

73. *Pacific Estrangement,* 47–48. Yale professor Trumbull Ladd, for example, sanctified Japan's reforming (if colonial) role in his *In Korea with Marquis Ito;* the dominant diplomatic historian of the period, Tyler Dennett, and the well-known publicist George Kennan, did the same.

74. Hunt, *Special Relationship,* 151–52, 198, 206–7, 209–10.

75. Charles E. Neu, "1906–1913," in *American–East Asian Relations: A Survey,* ed. Ernest R. May and James C. Thomson, Jr. (Cambridge: Harvard University Press, 1972), 155–72.

76. Hunt, *Special Relationship,* 211–14.

77. Neu, "1906–1913"; the best study of the naval rivalry is William R. Braisted, *The United States Navy in the Pacific, 1909–1922* (Austin: University of Texas Press, 1971).

Shortly after World War I ended, in 1922 to be overly exact, America came to be the major partner in the trilateral hegemony. This was the period when American banks became dominant in the world economy;[78] the Anglo-Japanese alliance had become tattered, and the United States became more important than England in Japanese diplomacy. The Washington Conference was the occasion for this transfer of the baton, a "locking in" with the critical element of global military reach, the American navy.

Bill Williams found an American informal empire beginning in the 1890s and maturing under Wilson and Harding, with both resisting radical change in the East Asian status quo (in spite of the very different rhetoric employed by each). The instrumentality of American-dominated consortia Williams saw as a device for simultaneously constraining Bolsheviks, Asian nationalists, and old imperialists.[79] Iriye really doesn't disagree; he just uses a different discourse to find in the same period the emergence of a new, co-operative, international order.[80] The Washington naval system was explicitly trilateral, in that the United States and England kept their naval superiority, while the United States, England, and Japan all cooperated to keep China a subordinate actor in the East Asian system—amid much American rhetoric about preserving China's (barely observable) national integrity.[81]

Japan adapted to these trends with a low-posture diplomacy throughout the 1920s. Meanwhile it girded its loins at home for trade competition, inaugurating tendencies in its political economy that remain prominent today. Here was an early version of what is now termed "export-led development." Both Johnson and Fletcher date the origins of Japan's national industrial strategy and "administrative guidance" from the mid- to late-1920s; both the Americans and the British were most receptive to Japan's outward-turning political economy.[82] (It has been only in the 1939–45 period and

78. See Harry N. Schreiber, "World War I as Entrepreneurial Opportunity: Willard Straight and the American International Corporation," *Political Science Quarterly* 84 (Sept. 1969): 486–511; more generally see Carl P. Parrini, *Heir to Empire: The United States Economic Diplomacy, 1916–1923* (Pittsburgh: University of Pittsburgh Press, 1969).
79. Williams, *Tragedy*, 78–84.
80. Iriye, *After Imperialism*, 10–22.
81. Hosoya Chihiro and Saito Makoto, eds., *Washinton taisei to Nichi-Bei kankei* [The Washington system and Japanese-American relations] (Tokyo: Tokyo Daigaku Shuppankai, 1978), introductory essay by Hosoya.
82. Chalmers Johnson, *MITI and the Japanese Miracle* (Berkeley: University of California Press, 1982); William Miles Fletcher III, *The Japanese Business Community and National Trade Policy, 1920–1942* (Chapel Hill: University of North Carolina Press, 1989).

the 1980s–90s that this strategy has been perceived as a problem for the United States.)

The Export Association Law of 1925 was an important turning point, stimulating industrial reorganization, cartels, and various state subsidies to exporters; Japan was careful to direct these exports to the noncolonial semi-periphery, not to the colonies, even less to the core markets of America and England.[83] The 1920s also inaugurated a period of import-subsitution industrialization[84] that went hand-in-hand with the exporting program, even if it was more pronounced in the 1930s, when Japan accomplished its heavy-industrial spurt and began its virtuoso mastery of the industrial product cycle.

The result of all this was that in the midst of the world depression and shrunken world trade, 1932–37, Japan's total exports more than doubled and "appeared to flood world markets." Cotton yarn, woven goods, toys, and iron and steel led the advance. Yet Japan registered a trade surplus only in 1935, when its exports were but 3 percent of the world total, compared to 10 percent for the United States. Despite that, Japan's trade partners became obsessed about its exporting. The American economist Miriam Farley explained this by saying Japan had merely "picked the wrong century in which to industrialize"—not a bad observation. By 1936 every major nation had curtailed the influx of Japanese goods, yet Japanese business groups still "tried to induce Americans to invest in Manchuria," even in the late 1930s. Meanwhile, American textile concerns "lobbied for restraints on exports to the United States despite a massive trade surplus with Japan."[85] So it goes.

Concerning the critical 1941–45 period, Iriye notes that until the Japanese military's "turn south" in mid-1941 (a decision deeply conditioned by Soviet power), Japan was still dependent on the United States, which he terms (in a nice summary of the change that came in the early 1920s)

---

83. Go Seinosuke, formerly head of the huge Oji Paper Co. and director of the Tokyo Stock Exchange for twelve years, drafted a report in 1929 recommending, among other things, "a new national committee . . . to rationalize industrial production in order to 'aid industrial development'; "Go endorsed the principle of export planning—selecting products that might sell well abroad and fostering their growth." The plan led to the Export Compensation Act of May 1930, and other measures to aid export industries; the plan was to help exports to Central America, Africa, the Balkans, "central Asia Minor," and the USSR, and it later expanded to include "the whole world except for Europe, the U.S., India, and the Dutch East Indies" (Fletcher, *Japanese Business Community*, 59, 61–62.)
84. Fletcher, *Japanese Business Community*, 28.
85. Ibid., 2, 98–99.

the key to postwar international relations. . . . Its capital, technology, and commodities sustained the world economic system throughout the 1920s . . . as the financial, business, and political center of the world.

The United States invoked the outer limits of its hegemonic power by embargoing oil to Japan, which came as a tremendous psychological shock to Japan and made its leaders assume that the only alternative was war.

Pearl Harbor was an event (a sign) that rendered everything that went before it since 1868 in a different hue—the hue of a moldering lemon, for *Time*'s cover of Yamamoto: behold, the aggressor. It was as if everything presaged it. Today the "reemergence" of Japan and Germany, however much they may have changed in 45 years, again enters a discourse of antinomies: the discourse of eternal mistrust, relating to Pearl Harbor and the crimes of the Nazis. A. M. Rosenthal in late 1990 conjured the "nightmare" that "the Japanese Army will soon again become a political force"; the rightists in Japan "dream, ever, of a new militarism, a new empire. . . . Would you say it could never happen again?"[86]

One would never know that Japan's restoration was America's project for twenty-five years after the war ended. As early as 1942 a small cadre of internationalists in the American State Department and in Japan began moving on remarkably parallel lines to reintegrate Japan into the postwar American hegemonic regime.[87] By 1947 George Kennan had elaborated plans for Japan's industrial revival, and these called for a modified restoration of Japan's former colonial position in northeast Asia.[88]

Stated succinctly, Japan in the postwar period has been an engine of the world economy, an American-defined "economic animal," shorn of its prewar military and political clout. This happened with the emergence of the Cold War, and it deepened as Japan benefited from America's wars to lock in an Asian hinterland, in Korea and Vietnam. In this era, which ran from Truman through Johnson, Japan was a dutiful American partner and the United States was tickled pink at Japan's economic success. As the American capacity unilaterally to manage the global system declined in the 1960s, however, a new duality afflicted the United States-Japan relationship: Japan should do well, yes . . . but not so well that it hurt American interests. (The

86. "MacArthur Was Right," *New York Times,* 19 October, 1990.
87. Iriye, *Power and Culture,* 15, 25–27, 65, 81, 83, 97, 148–49.
88. I have written about this in *Origins of the Korean War, II,* and in "Japan in the Postwar World System," in *Postwar Japan,* ed. Gordon.

symbol of this change is Nixon's New Economic Policy in 1971.) American thinking about Japan remains firmly within that duality today, symbolized by the inability of elites to do more than oscillate between free trade and protectionism, between admiration for Japan's success and alarm at its new prowess.

Conclusion

Behind the bipolar boundaries forged between 1947 and 1950 and the economic pump-priming of two catastrophic wars, the East Asian industrial economies today exercise a powerful gravity on the world system, even if they still remain within the hegemonic boundaries of the postwar settlement. In the 1980s Japan became for the United States what the United States became for England in the 1920s—the center of world financial and technical prowess, yet a power unwilling to "share burdens" in the policing of the world (witness isolationist America in the 1920s and Japan's catatonia over what to do about the Gulf War in 1991).

The capitalist mechanism wedded to resurgent and resourceful East Asian civilizations, however, bids fair to bring things full circle, long before MacArthur's millennium: the "rotation of the epicenter" has put the American economy at risk in a way inconceivable in 1900 or 1950 (we are back to "the pre-discursive," back to Gary and P'ohang). If our analysis is correct, the United States has another decade or two before its premier position in the current trilateral hegemony (United States, Western Europe, Japan) becomes untenable. The twenty-first century may well be one driven by Germany and Japan, or less provocatively, by the European Community and the Pacific Rim—an ironic tribute to their prowess, and to the short-sightedness of American strategy circa 1947 which, predicated on being "Number One" for the ages, may soon make American the junior partner in a new trilateral condominium: America as Number Two.

Yet Germany and Japan are nations with an uncertain relationship to the Enlightenment project: Nazi Germany's barbarous crimes sowed doubts about the very idea of progress in an entire generation of intellectuals, doubt brought to its apotheosis in 1944 with Horkheimer and Adorno's declaration that the Enlightenment "is the line both of destruction and of civilization," an enlightened earth-radiating disaster.[89] By comparison, militaristic Japan was guilty of lesser crimes—garden-variety aggression and slaughter by

---

89. *Dialectic of Enlightenment*, 92.

twentieth-century standards. Yet many observers still assume Japan to be somehow outside the hallowed liberal realm: "Industrialization without Enlightenment" might be the subtitle of Karel van Wolferen's *Enigma of Japanese Power:* Japan is closed and inscrutable, run by a mysterious "system." Its people do not recognize or believe in abstract (Western) universals. They do not privilege individualism.

Here is the problem: if Japan and Germany are the contemporary victors, the Enlightenment project does not explain it. If the rotation of the epicenter places France, England, and America in the shade, what happened to the French Revolution? The British Industrial Revolution? The American *novus ordo seculorum,* now mocked by George Bush's stillborn "New World Order?" What happened to progress?

We are on the verge of a "paradigm shift" because Japan's leap from the wings to center stage induces "a certain disturbance of the person, a subversion of earlier readings, a shock of meaning," and Barthes' truth comes home to us: someday, indeed, we must write the history of our own obscurity.

Society

**Constructing a New Cultural History
of Prewar Japan**

Miriam Silverberg

If the cause of the modern is in America, what is the source of the
modern *in* America?
—Murayama Tomoyoshi, *Shincho* (1928)

The space of modernism, too, is thus differential.
—Perry Anderson, *Marxism and the Interpretation of Culture* (1988)

In January 1925, the *Osaka Asahi* newspaper organized a spectacle.
This gathering of close to one hundred children, whose names contained
the Chinese ideogram "Sho" of the imperial, Taisho reign, is preserved
in a photograph in the pictorial magazine *Asahi Gurafu*. The newspaper
publisher was commemorating the new newspaper comic strip serial *The
Adventures of Shochan*, and children wore knitted "Shochan" hats topped
with pom-poms to that end. But more than the mass-produced apparel was
being advertised. As the cultural historian Tsurumi Shunsuke has pointed
out, the discerning consumer of the photograph was at once made aware
of the comic strip, the hat company that had donated the uniform attire, the
newspaper company, and the imperial reign for which both the children and

the comic book hero were namesakes. The photograph and the brief analysis by the Japanese historian are evocative resources for the construction of a new history of prewar Japanese culture that can illuminate how prewar Japanese mass culture was constructed through the production of cultural institutions, consumers, and cultural practices. They are two of the three forms of resources available to the cultural historian of modern Japan. As this essay will illustrate, the secondary literature produced by Japanese scholars, texts from the era, and the theoretical approaches of Western historians who have addressed the question of the historical significance of modern mass culture in Europe and the United States can all be mobilized to argue that prewar Japanese mass culture was constituted by spectacles, as well as by linkages between such events and the mass media. Moreover, and more importantly, there was a critical tension between the coexistence of an ethnocentric, essentialist, and productivist state ideology and apparatus premised on ultimate allegiance to the emperor, in whom sovereignty resided, and the flourishing of this highly commodified consumer culture selling contradictory images of class, gender, cultural traditions, and leisure. How in fact did the audiences of the *Asahi Gurafu*, the *Shochan* comic strip, the nationally disseminated movies, radio programs, and print media respond to this tension? Did the emperor help to sell hats? Did the comic strip strengthen allegiance to the throne—was it, in other words, a hegemonizing force within a culture industry subsidiary to the state? Did this form of selling a commodified emperor, the hat, the comic strip, the photograph, and the newspaper encourage resistance to state ideology (along with the profit of industry)? Only by coming to terms with the complexities of the experience of prewar Japanese mass culture, an experience mediated by the experience of class, gender, and cultural identity, can we begin to relate the consciousness of the Japanese people to the culture and the politics of the modern Japanese state. The aim of this essay is to set forth some of those complexities and to argue that recent approaches to American and European mass culture suggest to us that neither interpretation (of mass culture as manipulative or of mass culture as resistance) is appropriate but that both must be applied as we begin to investigate how Japanese mass culture of the prewar era participated in, but differed from, cultural currents in the West because of the specific relationship of the state to culture in the Japanese case.[1]

1. Tsurumi Shunsuke identified this photograph as the most telling illustration of the establishment of mass culture by the Taisho era (1912–1926). Rather than reading the photo

It is this different, yet capitalist, cultural history that must be illuminated. At a time when European historians are proclaiming a "new cultural
history," when feminist historians are attempting to negotiate what they see
as the border between literature and history, and when the questions raised
by the poststructuralist enterprise can no longer be ignored as the province
of other disciplines, historians of Japan remain ever the late developers.
We need to write cultural history anew. This should not be seen as a move
away from a social history, for we have barely begun to possess such a
field. Nor should a new cultural history be written or read as a reaction to an
older form of cultural history, for hitherto, with few exceptions, the study of
Japanese culture has been relegated to the limited field of anecdotal, often
antiquarian, literary studies.[2]

---

as representative of the ostentatious consumption and relaxed nature of the era, as Tsurumi does, I would place emphasis on the tension between state ideology and capitalist
culture evoked by Fujita Shozo's reference to the "illicit cohabitation of universalism and
particularity, sensation and empathy, morals and immorality, ideal and reality, aristocratic
spirit and populism, and theory with practice" in his discussion of "the spirit of Taisho
democracy." See Tsurumi Shunsuke, "Taisho ki no bunka," in *Iwanami koza Nihon rekishi*
(Tokyo: Iwanami Koza, 1963), 19:291–93, 315–16.
For the two approaches to mass culture, which the Frankfurt School critics saw as only
oppressive, denying any utopian element or response, see Tania Modleski's introduction
to *Studies in Entertainment: Critical Approaches to Mass Culture* (Bloomington: Indiana
University Press, 1986), ix–xii.
2. On the move from social to a new cultural history, see Lynn Hunt, "Introduction: History,
Culture, and Text," in *The New Cultural History*, ed. Lynn Hunt (Berkeley: University of
California Press, 1989), 1–22; Lynn Hunt, "History Beyond Social Theory," in *The States
of "Theory": History, Art, and Critical Discourse*, ed. David Carroll (New York: Columbia
University Press, 1990), 95–304. For debate over the relationship of language to history,
see Bryan D. Palmer, Christine Stansell, and Anson Rabinbach, "On Language, Gender,
and Working-Class History" and "Responses," *International Labor and Working-Class
History* 31 (Spring 1987): 1–36, and a rebuttal by Joan Scott, "A Reply to Criticism," *International Labor and Working-Class History* 32 (Fall 1987): 39–45. See also the dialogue
between Scott and Linda Gordon in "Book Review," *Signs* 15 (Summer 1990): 848–60.
On the relationship of history to literature, see "Patrolling the Borders: Feminist Histori-
ography and the New Historicism," *Radical History Review* 43 (1989): 23–43; Carolyn
Porter, "History and Literature: After the New Historicism," *New Literary History* 21, no. 2
(Winter 1990): 253–72; Gabrielle M. Spiegel, "History, Historicism, and the Social Logic
of the Text in the Middle Ages," *Speculum* 65, no. 1 (January 1990): 59–86.
Pioneering works in the new Japanese social history in the United States are Andrew
Gordon's work, *The Evolution of Labor Relations in Japan: Heavy Industry, 1853–1955*
(Cambridge: Harvard University Press, 1988) and Anne Walthall's *Social Protest and
Popular Culture in Eighteenth-Century Japan* (Tuscon: University of Arizona Press, 1986).
Tom Keirstead, a historian of medieval Japan, works from the tradition of the European

This essay is a preliminary approach to identifying and positioning the Japanese consumer-subject, who interacted in the urban marketplace of a newly instituted mass culture by challenging the official state ideology of national polity through articulations of class identity, gender identity, and cultural cosmopolitanism.[3] As such, it is one contribution to the construction of a new cultural history of prewar Japan. The first part places this consumer subject within the contexts of class configuration and an integrated mass culture. The second part is a close reading of *Tokyo Learning*, a text produced during the transitional moment of the constitution of a consumer-subject at the turn of the century. In conclusion, I will discuss the relevance of approaches to mass culture in the West to the study of the history of modern Japanese mass culture. The three-part structure does not reflect an attempt to separate text from context but an attempt to work with Gabrielle Spiegel's recognition that the historian of texts is engaged in both a "broadly constructive" act of constituting a historical narrative and in a "broadly deconstructive task" of reading extant texts. Nor should it be read as an example of the colonization of Japanese experience in order to validate Western theory through a non-Western case study. Moreover, I recognize that by referring to the class experience of the consumer-subject in prewar Japan, I am presuming, rather than investigating, the complex history of the formation of class and class consciousness in the Japanese case. I choose to separate secondary from primary sources in order to clarify resources for the construction of a cultural history that can take into account how institutional structures shaped agency, how identity was con-

---

new social history and histories of popular culture and at the same time incorporates the social and cultural theory of Bourdieu, Geertz, Foucault, and Scott in "The Theater of Protest: Petitions, Oaths, and Rebellion in the *Shoen*," *The Journal of Japanese Studies* 16, no. 2 (Summer 1990): 357–88. Takashi Fujitani's theoretically informed work on the cultural history of the emperor in modern Japan is another exception; see his *Power and Pageantry in Modern Japan: A Historical Ethnography* (forthcoming). The "late," and therefore theoretically diverse, nature of Japan's women's history is apparent in the first anthology of historical essays about Japanese women, *Recreating Japanese Women, 1600–1945*, ed. Gail Bernstein (Berkeley: University of California Press, 1991). For a richly descriptive Japanese literary history, see Edward Seidensticker, *Low City, High City: Tokyo from Edo to the Earthquake: How the Shogun's Ancient Capital Became a Great Modern City, 1867–1923* (New York: Knopf, 1983); hereafter cited in my text as *LCHC*; see also *Tokyo Rising: The City Since the Great Earthquake* (New York: Knopf, 1990).
3. The material and conclusions herein result from preliminary research for a book to be entitled *Constructing Japanese Modern Times*.

stituted in relationship to the state, and in what ways the experience of the West was central to the Japanese experience of modernity.[4]

These are not academic questions, enabling us to catch up to Western historians (although we do have some catching up to do inasmuch as we do not already have a vast archive of social, political, and institutional histories to take off from as we begin to interrogate meanings constituted by language in history) in order to claim that we, too, can practice cultural history. The rewriting of modern Japanese political history must take into account Japan's place in the world during the era of colonial expansion beginning at the turn of the century, the extent of public acquiescence to state repression during the 1920s, 1930s, and 1940s, and Japanese conceptualizations of the Japanese place in the postwar capitalist world order. Such history cannot be written without an understanding of the construction of a mass culture that recoded Western institutions and practices for indigenous Japanese consumption beginning in the 1920s. Now, when audiences in the West are captive to commentary that maintains the illusion that either the Japanese have engaged in unreflective cultural "borrowing," or that they continue to reside within an unchanging and unyielding Japanese "culture," the investigation of the construction of the history of Japanese mass culture is all the more imperative.

Placing the Consumer-Subject within Mass Culture

The Japanese New Year's game of *sugoroku,* a Parcheesi-like form of board play, was an appropriate giveaway in the mass-marketing wars of prewar Japan, for the boldly colored mazes well expressed the experience of the urban consumer from the eve of the First World War into the era of Japan's advance into China two decades later. The fortunes of the players lurch forward and pull back as did the Japanese economy after the unprecedented boom years of the First World War. Commentators called the war a "gift from heaven," and indeed the urbanization and industrialization of the economy as Japan moved into the markets vacated by the European

---

4. See Spiegel, "History, Historicism, and the Social Logic of the Text," 75. David Bunn and Jane Taylor warn against a *"new* inequity in international exchange . . . between the production of what is termed 'theory' in the West, and its exchange for raw materials in the form of examples and case studies from the Third World." See David Bunn and Jane Taylor, "Multiculturalism, the International Transfer of Theory, and South African Resistance" (forthcoming).

powers while filling orders for armaments were so intense that more secular analyses must have appeared inappropriate. Between 1914 and 1919, the number of workers in factories employing five or more workers rose from 948,000 to over 1.7 million, and by 1920, 18.1 percent of the populace was living in urban areas. (This was to rise to 24.1 percent by 1930.) As a result of the expansion of heavy industry, especially shipbuilding and steel industries, the expansion of the textile industry (by the end of the war, Japan was second to England in the production of cotton), and the new trade relationships with Europe, the United States, and Asian nations, Japan was also transformed from a debtor to a creditor nation. The first downturn came in 1920 with the collapse of the postwar boom, which resulted from the extension of credit by banking institutions. The economy recovered by 1922 but was again decimated by the earthquake of 1923. A reconstruction boom in 1924 was brought to an end by the financial crisis of 1927, compounded by the worldwide depression two years later. This was attended by the drop in silk and rice prices that devastated the rural sector by 1931, creating conditions of depression that would hold until 1934. The final prewar upswing would not take place until the period between 1934 and 1936, and, as a result of the military spending of these years, accompanied by a reflationary policy, there was virtually full employment by 1937.[5]

The white-collar, nouveau-riche class of salaried workers, bureaucrats, and teachers, which first appeared during the Russo-Japanese War, and which constituted 7–8 percent of the population by 1920, was at first hard hit by the earthquake of 1923. Hardships sustained from the rise in cost of living during the early 1920s were offset by the reconstruction boom of 1924. But the white-collar salaried man had a good life during the 1920s. A college graduate who received the average salary of eighty yen per month supplemented by a bonus worth four months of pay could well afford newly accessible consumer items, such as ready-made clothing, radios, phonographs, cameras, and electric irons, at a time when a made-to-wear suit

5. See G. C. Allen, *A Short Economic History of Modern Japan: 1867–1937* (London: George Allen & Unwin Ltd., 1946), 90–144; Sato Takeshi, "Modanizumu to Amerika ka," in *Nihon modanizumu no kenkyo*, ed. Minami Hiroshi (Tokyo: Bureen Shuppan, 1982), 20–21; hereafter cited in my text as *NM*. See also Minami Hiroshi, ed., *Taisho bunka* (Tokyo: Keiso Shobo, 1965), 66–80; hereafter cited in my text as *TB*. See also Minami Hiroshi and Shakai Shinri Kenkyujo (Social Psychology Research Center), eds., *Showa bunka* (Tokyo: Keiso Shobo, 1987), 19; hereafter cited in my text as *SB*. (Essayists are not listed in either the table of contents or with individual essays published in this volume. For a list of contributors, refer to *Showa bunka*, 545.)

jacket cost ten yen and rent amounted to twenty yen per month (*NM*, 153; *SB*, 68). With one yen he could go to the movies and enjoy a dinner of grilled eel along with a bottle of sake before taking the train home to his suburban "culture house." His fortunes were not totally secure, however, as expressed in the title of a popular novel of 1930, *New Family Sugoroku* (*Shin katei sugoroku*). Salaries and raises were arbitrarily fixed during the 1920s, and, by the end of the decade, many of the new urban consumers were casualties of "enterprise rationalization" and faced unemployment. The popularity of the Ozu movie of 1929, *I Graduated from College But* (*Daigaku wa deta keredo*), and the 1928 *Life of an Office Worker* (*Kaishain seikatsu*), which featured a salaried man who was fired on the day he received his bonus, attest to the precariousness of the new good life.[6]

Small shopkeepers and factory workers also consumed, as Ishikawa Hiroyoshi has shown in his cultural history, which sets forth three socially distinct geographic spheres: the *shitamachi* (usually translated as "downtown") region of self-employed craftsmen and tenement slums; the *yamanote,* middle-class neighborhood of bureaucrats, military employees, teachers, and office workers; and "the other side of the [Sumida] River," where workers in small-scale factories joined ricksha drivers, cart-pullers, rag-pickers, and day laborers at the lower reaches of urban society. There was a major leap in the standard of living between 1919 and 1922, as actual wages rose, and the level of consumption increased 160 percent. (Housing expenditures rose from 10.3 percent to 16.3 percent and clothing expenditures rose from 9.7 percent to 15.5 percent.) After 1922, desires were again refocused, this time from housing and food to what Ishikawa terms "social, cultural desires." Using surveys from the 1920s and 1930s, Ishikawa documents the emergence of "social, cultural desires" for the skilled laborer, who enjoyed such forms of leisure as sports, travel, and reading, from the early 1920s onward.[7]

Prewar Japanese mass culture is often referred to via a series of buzzwords: cafés, one-yen taxis, and *erotic-grotesque-nonsense,* but the extensive research organized by the social psychologist Minami Hiroshi and his associates yields a series of linkages within mass culture and between

6. Imai Seiichi, ed., *Shinsai ni yuragu,* vol. 5 of *Nihon no hyakunen* (Tokyo: Chikuma Shobo, 1962), 155–60. David Bordwell discusses Ozu's representation of the Japanese middle class and provides rich film synopses in *Ozu and the Poetics of Cinema* (Princeton: Princeton University Press, 1988), 33–35, 193–94.

7. Ishikawa Hiroyoshi, ed., *Goraku no senzenshi* (Tokyo: Shoseki Kabushikigaisha, 1981), 50–56, 97–98, 104–9.

mass culture and the state, which creates a dual meaning for the term *mass*. In these writings, *mass* refers to both the techniques of mass production, distribution, and consumption, and the technologies of mass production and distribution. More importantly, these sources reveal to us (unintentionally) how the use of the term *mass* (*taishu*), during the 1920s, served to gloss over the relationship of class to mass culture. Rather, a close reading of that history reveals linkages within culture and between the state (embodied in the emperor) and cultural production. It is clear that the constituent aspects of the material culture of housing and clothing, newspapers, books, magazines, movies, records, and spectacles (including night life), which along with state ideology and policy produced a consumer-subject, were intricately interconnected.

After World War I, consumption, along with production, was rationalized, as department stores offered household goods, clothing, and "mass cafeterias" as the sites of new family leisure activity. By 1919, the major emporiums of Shirokiya, Matsuya, Takashimaya, and Jugo were catering to urban customers and provincial gawkers, and they were followed by Marubutsu and Daimaru in 1920, and Isetan in 1922. By April of 1923, a nationwide consumer organization had been started, and the following year Mitsukoshi customers were asked to vote on whether the pre-earthquake practice of removing shoes at the entranceway should be abandoned (*TB*, 253–54, 361).

Shopping by monthly installment, most mass-produced clothing, and the new forms of housing were undoubtedly accessible only to white-collar consumers, who comprised less than 10 percent of the populace, but the mass media provided consumer items for the urban consumer-subject in all classes. In other words, while the hotel toll roads encouraging tourism, the private railway lines linking passengers to amusement parks, the all-girl Takarazuka theater and music review, and the department stores placed conveniently at railway terminal points provided a nationwide network of consumer activities for the more prosperous on set income, there was the no less obvious network of highly commodified print and broadcasting media, including the movies, that reached beyond the new nuclear family of the new white-collar worker, the *salaryman* (*TB*, 143–44).[8]

---

8. On the entrepreneurial skills of Kobayashi Ichizo, who created two still predominant features of contemporary Japanese mass culture, the terminal department store and the Takarazuka review, see *Taisho bunka*, 143–44. On the emergence of credit, see *Showa bunka*, 68. For the history of Takarazuka, see Jennifer Robertson, "Gender-Bending in Paradise: Doing 'Female' and 'Male' in Japan," *Genders* 5 (July 1989): 50–69.

Print culture cannot be separated from state policy, because the school system had provided a literate readership by the turn of the century, and the fanfare surrounding both the Sino and the Russo-Japanese Wars had primed the population's desire for news. Yet there was a double edge to the power of the press, for just as it advertised for the state, it could also spread news of resistance, as it did during the rice riots of 1918, when news of the "North Coast Woman's Uprising" pushed many into the streets. Newspaper circulation, which had been 1,630,000 in 1905, soared to 6,250,000 (one household out of six) by 1924, and by 1931 the population of 65 million purchased 10 million copies[9] due to the successful marketing ploys of offering new forms of entertainment. Specialized advice columns written by noted women authors, along with religion and agriculture columns, sold newspapers. Comic strip heroes, such as Maggie and Jiggs (in Japanese), sold news magazines. The transformations of *Lazy Daddy*, who catered to working-class readers of the *Hochi shimbun* in November of 1923, testify to the linkages among media. For years, this well-meaning, bespectacled, rotund figure, respectably clad in kimono and kimono jacket, would confront such modern innovations as radio broadcasting and the unemployment line. Lazy Daddy was the subject of thirty-three volumes of cartoons and the hero in a theatrical production.[10]

By the turn of the century, mass magazines had become part of a media network, when the market had been segmented into production of over 180 different magazines for such audiences as elementary school boys and bourgeois housewives. By the late 1920s, in addition to the hundreds of journals aimed at different segments of the populace, the "all-round" magazine (*sogo zasshi*), featuring fiction and roundtable discussions by journalist-critics who made their living by publishing in the popular press, vied for market place. *Kingu* (King), modeled after the *Saturday Evening Post*, sold 740,000 copies at first printing in 1925 after an unprecedented ad campaign that included a *sugoroku* game handout with the purchase of the premier issue, entitled "A *Sugoroku* Race to Tour the Famous Spots in New Tokyo." Within a year, sales reached the 1 million mark. Between

9. Newspaper statistics are from Sharon Nolte, *Liberalism in Modern Japan* (Berkeley: University of California Press, 1987), 19.

10. Regarding *Lazy Daddy* (*Nonki na tosan*), see Maeda Ai, ed., *Taishoki no manga* (Tokyo: Chikuma Shobo, 1986), 70. On the commodification of the newspaper as big business, see Miriam Silverberg, *Changing Song: The Marxist Manifestos of Nakano Shigeharu* (Princeton: Princeton University Press, 1990), 23–24; hereafter cited in my text as *CS*.

1918 and 1932, the number of journals registered with the state more than tripled, increasing from 3,123 to 11,118. During the *enpon,* or one-yen book wars, when publishers, taking their cue from the Harvard Classics, packaged multivolume series of literature and other orders of knowledge, thereby obligating the consumer to buy the entire set, authors amassed overnight fortunes that were consumed by fancy villas or trips abroad.[11]

In the 1920s, print culture was available to all classes of consumers, who were notified of new publications by advertisements in newspapers, magazines, and the one-yen books. Advertising practices were adapted for material culture as early as 1907, when the Mitsukoshi department store invited leading artists and writers to form a "Group on Trends" to advertise variations on clothing fads. By World War I, the advertising industry had become institutionalized through the consolidation of advertising agencies in organizations, through such groups as the Advertising Study Group at Waseda University (organized in 1916), and through such trade publications as *Jitsugyo sekai* (Industrial world), which introduced Scot's *Psychology of Advertising, Kokoku Zasshi* (Advertising magazine), and *Kokoku Kenkyu Zasshi* (Advertising studies magazine) in 1916 and 1917 (*TB,* 132–33).

Movies were a potent medium for multiple marketing strategies. An indigenous film industry, encouraged by the popularity of documentary films of Russo-Japanese War heroism, had been established around 1907. By 1926 there were 1,056 movie theaters showing Japanese and Western films—one theater for every 60,000 viewers, including militant factory workers who on more than one occasion experienced strike lockouts on returning from group outings to the movies. Kikuchi Kan's novel *Tokyo March* first appeared as a serialized novel in *Kingu* from June 1928 through October 1929. The Nikkatsu film studio then produced the film version of the story and advertised the film with photographic ads in major magazines and with the hit song "Tokyo March," composed at the behest of Victor Records, at the suggestion of Nikkatsu. Plays and movies advertised a new genre of popular songs (*ryukoka*), beginning with "The Song of Kachuusha," the theme song sung by Matsui Sumako for the 1914 Imperial Theater produc-

11. On mass magazines, including the impact of a left-wing press, see *Changing Song,* 163. On the statistics of magazines registered under the Newspaper Law, see Gregory J. Kasza, *The State and the Mass Media in Japan, 1918–1945* (Berkeley: University of California Press, 1988), 28. For one history of the origins of the *enpon* crediting the writer and writer/labor organizer Fujimori Seikichi for asking the Kaizosha publisher to offer inexpensive books to workers who were starved for affordable reading material, see *Showa bunka,* 287–303.

tion of Tolstoy's *Resurrection*. These songs challenged the ideology of Confucian family cohesion and Japanese behavior celebrated in official texts, with such lyrics as "My wife has a moustache" or the tirade against "my old lady" who cooks only *korokke* (a newly introduced Japanese variation on the Western croquette).[12]

The new popular songs also advertised the urban cafés, sites of mass cultural consumption mentioned in virtually all accounts of mass culture written since and about the 1920s and early 1930s. By 1933, when 40,000 cafés were operating nationwide, state regulations were instituted to control these special drinking places and eateries. This did not curb café popularity. The following year, these cafés, which catered to the salaried population and to intellectuals, numbered 37,000 (*SB*, 78). The lure of these establishments, which were more bar than coffee house in atmosphere and menu, was as much the liqueurs and whiskey as the sensationalized presence of the "waitress," or *jokyu,* some of whom became regional celebrities. The café waitresses were immortalized in such popular novels as *Jokyu*, serialized in *Fujin koron* (Woman's forum) by Kikuchi Kan, and recognized in the lyrics of movie theme songs. In 1930, Osaka alone boasted 800 cafés and 10,000 waitresses. These bar hostesses numbered 112,000 in 1936 and as many as 90,200 as late as 1939 (*SB*, 78, 169, 477–78). While the "modern girl" has been seen as the embodiment of a new femininity, her significance was as a mythic inspiration or threat. In contrast, the café waitresses were the new women of the era, and their presence as cultural producers reworked everyday relationships between women and men and between Japan and the West. As sex workers selling their companionship, they were the representation of sex, in the sense discussed by T. J. Clarke in *The Painting of Modern Life: Paris in the Art of Manet and His Followers*. The *jokyu* in capitalist Tokyo and Osaka, like the prostitutes in Clarke's bour-

---

12. On the history of the Japanese film industry through the Second World War, see Joseph I. Anderson and Donald Richie, eds. *The Japanese Film: Art and Industry* (New York: Grove Press, 1959), 21–158. See also Peter B. High, "The Dawn of Cinema in Japan," *Journal of Contemporary History* 19, no. 1 (January 1984): 23–57. Regarding *Tokyo March* as an example of the rationalization and repression of the culture of the mid-1920s, see *Changing Song*, 125–26. The theater where *Resurrection* was performed was the *Teigeki* of the most repeated catch-phrase from the earliest days of consumer culture in the 1910s, when Mitsukoshi had organized a campaign around the motto making linkages most apparent, "Today It's Mitsukoshi; Tomorrow, the Imperial Theatre" (*Kyo wa Mitsukoshi; Ashita wa Teigeki*). Regarding *ryukoka*, see Ichikawa Koichi, "Ryukoka ni miru modanizumu to ero guro nansensu," *Nihon modanizumu*, 257–84.

geois Paris, made money visible, especially because their wages usually came only from tips and were not subject to any proletarian contract, but they did organize the *Jokyu Domei* (Federation of café waitresses).[13]

One final link in the network was provided by radio broadcasting, which, more than any other form of media, was oriented to an urban audience. From the outset, in March 1925, it was state controlled through NHK, a national monopoly, but radio participated in the connectedness of mass culture, for newspapers chose to spread the new notions of *rajio kibun* (radio frame of mind) to an audience privy to the broadcast of folk ballads. This was an audio version of the reworked folk traditions found in mass magazines, samurai epics, and in the movies of cult idol Matsunosuke, whose swashbuckling antics glamorized the premodern era. The radio audience, which numbered 3,500 homes in 1922 and 24,500 the following year, also listened to Western music and such programs as "Cartoons Drawn with Sounds" (*Oto de kaita manga*). The "cartoons" went by such titles as "Spring at the Department Store" and featured such representations of cultural shift as the account of the Japanese couple visiting Hollywood who meet Chaplin, suffer at the hands of a pickpocket, and are kept awake by a dance troupe rehearsing in the adjacent hotel room.[14]

State-controlled radio programming was not totally isolated from the less-censored media, as it announced such spectacles as the nationwide high school baseball tournament sponsored by the *Tokyo Asahi Newspaper* from the mid-1910s into the 1930s. The Takarazuka enterprises, encompassing an all-girls review by 1914 after the initial advertisement of a hot springs-amusement park in 1907, provided a spectacle grander than most (*TB*, 144). The Takarazuka women's exposition (*josei hakurankai*), set up on the site of the hot springs in 1913, was but one of many exhibitions,

---

13. T. J. Clarke, *The Painting of Modern Life: Paris in the Art of Manet and His Followers* (New York: Alfred A. Knopf, 1985), 108, 113. See also Miriam Silverberg, "The Modern Girl as Militant," in *Recreating Japanese Women: 1600–1945*, ed. Gail Bernstein (Berkeley: University of California Press, 1991).

14. Takeyama Akiko, "Rajio bangumi ni miru modanizumu," in *Nihon modanizumu*, 253–55. Gregory J. Kasza refers to a "tightly controlled system of mixed civil and bureaucratic management." For a detailed account of the public-interest system, see Kasza, *The State and the Mass Media in Japan 1918–1945* (Berkeley: University of California Press, 1988), 72–101; hereafter cited in my text as *SMM*. It is worth conjecturing how the 25.7 percent rate of radio ownership in urban households as late as 1932, compared to the 4.5 percent rate in rural counties (which would surpass 25 percent in 1940), is related to conscious state policy to limit the diffusion of mass culture and not merely to the poverty in the countryside.

wherein one sector or medium sponsored another. Department stores featured art and photography exhibits, magazines like *Fujin no tomo* sponsored concerts and exhibits, and by the early 1930s, groups of photographers organized into working groups and produced such photo magazines as *Fuoto taimusu* (Photo times) and *Koga* (Bright print). Photographers were also responsible for such events as the 1931 German international moving photo exhibition, which featured 870 prints, including works by Moholy-Nagy. The separation between state and consumer culture was not always delineated in these spectacles. For example, as early as 1907, items in an art exhibit sponsored by the Education Ministry provided the motifs for Mitsukoshi's annual ad campaign (*SB*, 439–40; *TB*, 162–63).

The most spectacular of spectacles, and the most ambiguous regarding the relationship of the subject to consumption and the tension between state and mass-produced consumer culture, were the expositions that were organized in the name of industry and nationhood. The well-advertised and highly organized Tokyo Taisho exposition of 1914 featured booths staffed by geisha (solicited from throughout the city), the nation's first escalator, such new commodities as the gas bathtub, stove, and range (presented by the Tokyo Gas company), and exhibits of the colonized territories of Taiwan and Korea. Eight years later, the Tokyo Peace Exposition introduced an airplane on pontoons and celebrated the empire by adding a Hall of the South Pacific to the reconstruction of the other colonial holdings in the Taiwan and Korea Halls. A third exposition worth investigating was Tokyo's municipal celebration commemorating the end of post-earthquake renovation in 1930.[15]

A peculiarity of the culture presented to the consumer-subject, indeed, one of the reasons I have determined that consumers may not be called merely *consumers* but must be identified as imperial subjects at the same time (although consumers are never really consumers—the term always masks differences), is that all aspects of mass culture set forth above were censored, even as they vied for profit in the marketplace, as documented comprehensively by Gregory Kasza. The press was the most autonomous of the mass media, as revealed both by the ambiguities in

15. For a brief overview of the Taisho exposition, see Takemura Tamio, *Taisho bunka* (Tokyo: Kodansha, 1980), 40–43. The recreation of the colonial holdings, the peace tower, the airplane, and the two-part structure of the spectacle into a bamboo pavilion and a pond's edge linked by a "Peace Bridge" are enumerated in Maeda Ai and Shimizu Isao, eds., *Taisho kooki no manga* (Tokyo: Chikuma Shobo, 1986), 9. See also *Low City, High City*, 257.

the control system and by successful attempts at resistance to censorship. While Home Ministry bureaucrats could suspend publication of journals, ban circulation of specific editions, and mandate the deletion of passages from books and magazines prior to publication, journal editors circumvented such controls through such ploys as distributing a journal before the submission of a copy for censorship, submitting self-censored copies to state officials prior to rewriting the contents before the official printing, using pseudonyms by authors, and using X's and O's or blank type in place of words or passages that would undoubtedly be flagged by the censors. Newspaper management was also subject to an ambiguous, unpredictable system of pre-publication warnings that was ignored by the leading publishers, who either circulated banned editions before receiving official warning or ignored the warnings altogether. Radio censorship was imposed by station officials who telephoned in summaries of programs to state officials prior to broadcast, by instructions regarding taboo content sent to the radio stations, and by NHK inspectors, who activated circuit breakers when commercial advertising was illegally inserted or, less often, when political misstatements were made. The relatively low number of muzzlings for overtly political reasons was undoubtedly due to the fact that all political discussion was banned from the air waves (*SMM*, 29–38; 89–90).

State sensitivity to form, as well as content, is reflected in the regulation of the broadcaster's tone of voice ("coldly neutral") and the supposed prohibition of the terms "extremely" and "absolutely" in regard to any topic whatsoever (*SMM*, 92). Such songs as the notorious "I Don't Want You to Forget Me Now" (Wasurecha iyayo, 1936) were banned because of the erotic style employed by the singer in the refrain consisting of the title words. The fact that the ensuing spawning of a genre of songs with similar plaintive refrains gave rise to the periodization of the time as the "era of 'please, please' (*nehh nehh*) songs" suggests resistance to controls by record producers and consumers (*NM*, 280–83).

Movies were censored earlier and more thoroughly than songs, beginning in May of 1925, through the Home Ministry's motion picture film inspection regulations, which mandated state inspection of all movies before showing. Films undermining public peace, manners and morals, or health could be banned, cut, returned for revision, recommended for withdrawal, or subjected to limited viewing within a highly centralized system of review. Films were not to express any criticism of the political system, including any form of antimilitarist sentiment, and could not refer to class conflict or other group conflict (including gang war), threaten the belief in the Japanese people as a nation, "damage good will in foreign affairs," or show how to commit or conceal a crime. Movies such as Keystone Cops films were banned under the public business ordinance because they damaged respect for the police. Under the mores category, cruelty and ugliness (including bloody battle scenes and physical deformity) were banned, as were sex-related scenes depicting extramarital sex, "kissing, dancing, embracing, nudity, flirting, sexual innuendo, pleasure-seeking," and "others." Also cut were "items related to the ruin of work," items hindering education (by, for example, challenging the authority of teachers), and items challenging most directly the family-state ideology. Anything that ran "counter to the customs of a virtuous home" was forbidden, as were allusions or references to the imperial family. Filmmakers could not show the imperial regalia or any member of the imperial household, including all past emperors, nor could they film any images suggesting the imperial chrysanthemum, including samurai crests—thus, flower crests of twelve to twenty-five petals could be filmed only if clearly distinct from the imperial emblem. Documentary footage of the emperor was also subject to close scrutiny: The imperial household was to be presented accurately, its stylized manner of speech kept intact, but no shots of the exhaust from bodyguards' cars were permitted to be shown (SMM, 55, 57, 61–70; SB, 169, 395–412).

In film, the Showa emperor was highly present through his absence, as has been argued about the Taisho emperor, whose reign ended officially with his death on December 25, 1926. In fact, the Taisho reign, if not its sickly ruler, had been most visibly present in the mass and material culture of the 1910s, when the imperial institution was inserted into the marketplace of mass culture. This was in sharp contrast to the cultural terms of the preceding Meiji era, when, as Carol Gluck has so fully documented, popular culture was mobilized in order to familiarize newly naturalized subjects with the emperor. The enthronement of the second modern emperor, in November of 1915, was commemorated by the highly advertised marketing of items imprinted with chrysanthemum and paulownia patterns by the Mitsukoshi department store, and numerous ads for other commodities had been sold "to commemorate the enthronement." The ceremonies surrounding this ritual were used both to familiarize the male populace with Western clothing and to sell domestic silk products to a populace geared, by Mitsukoshi trendsetters, to the latest colors representing the vivid shades of imperial pageantry. The following year, the discerning consumer was urged to buy earth tones (TB, 162, 164, 166). The media campaign to promote the third, Showa, emperor as "the young prince" was instituted in March 1921, when he was sent on an extensively photographed six-month world tour in preparation for his regency, which was to commence in November of that year, for by October of 1920 the severe illness of the physically and mentally limited Taisho emperor could no longer be hidden from the populace. The photos in newspapers and magazines inserted the new emperor into mass culture as one of the glamorous males to appeal to female readers (*TB*, 225).

In this context, of course, the questions raised earlier in this essay by the photograph of the one hundred namesakes of the Taisho emperor must again be asked: To what extent was the dashing crown prince being used to peddle commodities? Or alternatively, to what extent was the media a medium for the state? Did it serve to illustrate the ideologically freighted "Imperial Rescript on Education," which was recited by every school child? (This was the text that opened with the injunction "Know ye, our subjects" and celebrated the imperial ancestry of the imperial throne as the basis for filial behavior, respect for the constitution, observance of the law, and "courageous" service to the state in order to "guard and maintain the prosperity of our Imperial Throne coeval with heaven and earth."[16]) The histories available offer a rich overview of the cultural resources available to the Japanese consumer but do not give us access to the experience of these subjects. Close reading of texts from the era can. For example, mass magazines from the 1920s and 1930s, such as *Shufu no tomo* (Housewife's friend), beloved by working- and middle-class women, and the more bourgeois *Shukan Asahi* (Weekly Asahi), reveal a shift in valence toward the consumer side of the consumer-subject formulation. A reading of *Tokyo Learning*, published in 1909 by the educator Ishikawa Tengai and accompanied by the endorsements of members of Parliament and the mayor of Tokyo, gives us access to a period of cultural fluidity when experts were trying to hold on to the ideology of an imperial subject, while at the same time recognizing the draw of a consumer culture that challenged both the productivist and statist aspect of Meiji ideology as it encouraged urban Japanese subjects to negotiate unprecedented social relationships.[17]

16. Carol Gluck, *Japan's Modern Myths: Ideology in the Late Meiji Period* (Princeton: Princeton University Press, 1985), 121.
17. A preliminary overview of the complete run of the popular journals of the era, *Shufu no tomo* and the rural-based *Ie no hikari* (Light of the household), reveals that while the imperial presence remains in the form of photographs and introductory articles, the Japanese reader was clearly given access to a much larger proportion of articles and illustrations of new mores and items to be consumed. Here, then, is an example of Carol

Tokyo Learning

Tokyogaku gives us one version of what the Russian cultural historian Boris Gasparov terms the "shape of social behavior" in a rapidly changing urban milieu.[18] This guide to the ambitious young man of the late Meiji era is a key to the cultural codes of that moment, contributing to the history of modern urban Japan as a stratified, fractured place of contention rather than as "congeries" of village communities transplanted into urban space.[19] New identities had to be constructed for and by male and female middle- and working-class consumers, but this was not how the five-hundred-page tract presented the problem. *Tokyogaku* was a guide to success on the battlefield of life; readers were exhorted to adopt the techniques of ingratiation in order to succeed in the business of city life. "Tokyo Learning" (for *Tokyogaku* is short for *Tokyo gakumon,* or "scholarly study of Tokyo"), exhorts the author, is a road map or staircase to success (*TG*, 59, 342). The student of success must gain a new, specialized technique in a city represented as a market-place of business transactions, and this requires mastery of a new lexicon.

Gluck's discussion of the disjunction between *ideology* and *experience,* although I would rephrase this cultural and historical phenomenon as the disjunction between ideology and *practice.* See Gluck, *Japan's Modern Myths,* 267. For Minami Hiroshi's contrasting formulation of a shift from "subject" to "citizen," see *Taisho bunka,* 150–54.

18. Gasparov uses the phrase "the shape of social behavior" and terms "social life as the realization of cultural codes developed by society." See Iurii M. Lotman, Lidiia Ia. Ginsburg, and Boris A. Uspenskii, *The Semiotics of Russian Cultural History*, ed. Alexander D. Nakhimovsky and Alice Stone Nakhimovsky (Ithaca: Cornell University Press, 1985), 16, 21. As Minami Hiroshi has told us, the book was meant for the urban immigrant in response to changing social relationships forged during the urbanization and industrial expansion following the Russo-Japanese War (*Taisho bunka,* 58). American historians have noted how Ishikawa emphasized the power of manipulation as a means of getting ahead in the big city. Henry Smith suggests the evocative translation "Tokyo-ology" for this text; see Henry Smith, "Tokyo as an Idea: An Exploration of Japanese Urban Thought Until 1945," *Journal of Japanese Studies* 4, no. 1 (Winter 1978): 59, and Earl Kinmonth, *The Self-Made Man in Meiji Japanese Thought: From Samurai to Salaryman* (Berkeley: University of California Press, 1981), 274. In Kinmonth's schema, *Tokyogaku* is a textbook for educated youth, written by a textbook publisher.

19. Ishikawa Tengai, *Tokyogaku* (Tokyo: Ikuseikai, 1909); hereafter cited in my text and notes as *TG* or *Tokyo Learning.* For recent revisions of the received wisdom regarding Japanese urban society, see Theodore C. Bestor, *Neighborhood Tokyo* (Stanford: Stanford University Press, 1989), and James A. Fujii's discussion of the writings of Tokuda Shusei in *Complicit Fictions: The Subject in the Modern Japanese Prose Narrative* (Berkeley: University of California Press, forthcoming).

In a glossary contained in the chapter "A Guide to Business," Ishikawa defines the distinctions among businesses, corporations, and companies and the managerial positions within the new corporate hierarchy (*riji, kanji, kaicho*). The author also reproduces such documentation as the articles of incorporation of a joint-stock company (*TG*, 176–86, 271–84). The practice of advertising must also be mastered: *Tokyo Learning* explains that if one wishes to reach a broader audience than those passing by a storefront, pamphlets and marching bands should be employed. The language of advertising is attuned to the psychology of the shopper, as Ishikawa explains in a four-step mini-lesson. An ad should cause the consumer (1) to look, (2) to look closely, (3) to want to buy the item afterward, and finally, (4) to turn that desire into a firm decision. Department store glass counters are one means of creating the desire for constantly shifting fads, which is the agenda of such emporiums as Mitsukoshi. The technique of advertising employs such methods as the repetition of identical images or words and the manipulation of size and titles of famous people or associations. Here the author offers the lesson of the relationship of the Chicago Swift Soap Company to the Women's Temperance Society. Most importantly, the student of *Tokyogaku* must recognize the need to create constant change in order to generate desires (*TG*, 284–91).[20]

Self-advertisement also assures success. The preliminary sections of *Tokyo Learning* on "social interaction" and on "going calling" emphasize that the urban newcomer must take care to go calling at certain times and in specified fashion. One must never visit at mealtime, nor should one expect to be fed. One should select topics for discussion with great care—"one should never discuss sake with a confectionaire"—and one should weigh the value of the gift taken to the target house with great care (*TG*, 31–51). New social gestures are clearly being coded for the student of Tokyo, and the break between rural tradition and urban practice is emphasized by Ishikawa's explanation of the exchange of New Year's cards. A resident of Tokyo who anticipates three days of communal, family-based socializing will quickly be disabused of this idea, for among the successful class in Tokyo, it is considered inappropriate to expect the host of a household to appear. (One's card should be left in the front hallway.) Anyone can make the delivery—even a ricksha driver or an errand boy will suffice (*TG*, 399).

20. For a brief history of the emergence of advertising institutions, confirming Ishikawa's awareness that new practices were being formulated during the closing years of the Meiji era, see Yamamoto Taketoshi, *Nihon no kokoku* (Tokyo: Nihon Keizaishimbunsha, 1986).

Of course the ricksha driver is never an active participant in this practice, for according to the social geography of *Tokyo Learning*, the poor have a different protocol.

The ritualization of the etiquette of social interaction is aimed at attaining and maintaining money. In many ways, *Tokyo Learning* is thus one long illustration of Georg Simmel's theory of the transformation of social relationships and cultural life in a developed money economy. Money not only allows for the anonymity mentioned in *Tokyo Learning*, but it also fosters a new form of relating, based solely on calculation. Of course early modern Japanese consumer culture was not devoid of business transactions to be plotted and executed with exactitude, but Ishikawa's repeated sentiment that in Tokyo "everything is calculated"—for even a glass of water costs— (*TG*, 43) implies a new expression of what Simmel termed the "measuring, weighing and calculating exactness of modern times." The reader of *Tokyo Learning* is urged to "make his own capital." The Tokyoite is on the take and at the same time wary of takers—he can steal the eyes out of a horse (*TG*, 23, 324).[21]

The schema provided in *Tokyo Learning* is one of profound historic discontinuity and social disassociation. The consumer-subjects addressed are interpellated not as imperial subjects with "fixed and unchangeable" roles in a fixed hierarchy prescribed by state ideology but as actively involved in the process of making meaning out of their historical moment through signifying systems, including language, images, gestures, and social behavior.[22] The consumer-subject in *Tokyo Learning* is not a member of a Japanese village transplanted to an urban neighborhood but rather is more akin to Louis Wirth's segmentalized urban personality engaged in superficial, anonymous, and transitory relationships. In a society where kinship and status ties had been replaced by social mobility and a division of labor,

21. On Simmel, see Michael P. Smith, *The City and Social Theory* (New York: St. Martin's Press, 1979), 101–8, and David Harvey, *Consciousness and the Urban Experience: Studies in the History and Theory of Capitalist Urbanization* (Baltimore: Johns Hopkins University Press, 1985), 2–6.

22. I am working from Catherine Belsey's notion of language as one of many signifying systems, specifically, her definition of ideology: "The work of ideology is to present the position of the subject as fixed and unchangeable, an element in a given system of differences which is human nature and the world of human experience, and to show possible action as an endless repetition of 'normal,' familiar action," and her conception of meanings circulating "between text, ideology, and reader." See Catherine Belsey, *Critical Practice* (London and New York: Methuen, 1980), 45, 64, 90, 144.

the only grouping wherein the individual could express his needs was the special interest group. According to Wirth, the anonymity of the urban setting required that the isolated resident use such symbols as uniforms to publicly identify his role in this fragmented society (*TG*, 170, 211).[23] Similarly, in *Tokyo Learning*, presentation of self in public is as crucial as the investigation into an associate's hobbies and financial holdings before an initial encounter—the Tokyo learner, Ishikawa warns, must be neither *haikara* (modishly flashy) nor *bankara* (barbaric) (*TG*, 170). Like Wirth, Ishikawa advocates the importance of interest groups—the geta maker and the book dealer have their organizations, the scholar is urged to attend all professional meetings to ensure his advancement up the ladder, and even the beggars at Ise Shrine have organized (*TG*, 51, 104–5). But unlike Wirth (whose ideas about subjectivity in a fragmented society based on a complex division of labor were influenced by the theory of Durkheim), Ishikawa also acknowledges the importance of class (*TG*, 132, 420).[24]

Class is envisioned as a place on a two-tiered staircase whose steps are occupied by the owners of wealth and the perspiring workers. The industrialists, who are "generals on the battlefield" of Tokyo, are placed within three columns, headed by the "Shibusawa type," whose self-interest is accompanied by an interest in the state. The "Yasuda type" puts self-interest before concerns for the state. The "Okura type," who lacks concern for the welfare of the state, takes third place (*TG*, 118).[25] The concluding section of *Tokyo Learning* is about the "laboring society" in the back tenements, where the head of a household does come out to greet his New Year's callers. The author refers to criminals and pickpocket gangs and hints at a family life differing radically from the idealized family of the successful citizen. The children of the poor have to be taught to wash, and there is

23. Louis Wirth, "Urbanism as a Way of Life," in *Classic Essays on the Culture of Cities*, ed. Richard Sennett (New York: Appleton-Century-Crofts, 1969), 152–53, 156.
24. Ishikawa's discussion of hobbies bears on Minami's view that the manipulation of hobbies was part of a new cultural consciousness differing from the ethos of *bummei kaika* and consisting of the nationwide dissemination of various fads from the Russo-Japanese War onward (*Taisho bunka*, 51–59). For personality types and on creating a personality profile, see *TG*, 61, 215–17. The successful Tokyo immigrant is compared to the effete Edo-ite (*edokko*), whose connoisseurship in the gay quarters, known under the shorthand term *tsu,* is called barbaric. See *TG*, 17, 20, 324, 488.
25. Ishikawa used the term *kaikyu* for class. See *TG*, 352, 374. It should be noted that Ishikawa claimed that classes would disappear in the future, provided that the appropriate social organization could be engineered (*TG*, 375).

constant fighting in the tenements when the head of a household spends income on drink (*TG*, 402, 510–41).[26] The author is aware of class but at the same time is concerned with the consolidation of a "state-society"; he welcomes the central role of the state in furthering a national culture of indigenous morals, customs, and habits. Yet he admits to a tension between conflicting interests: the politician has the state's interest at heart, the wealthy individual may not. Ishikawa tells his readers that just as one category of industrialist may not be interested in paying for the hospitals and schools needed by society that the state cannot afford to finance, so also are there conflicts between less wealthy Tokyo dwellers and the interests of the state. In other words, the self-sacrificing mores exhorted in the morals classes aimed at creating imperial subjects and the battle strategies oriented to the individual's (or the consumer-subject's) struggle for wealth in Tokyo can aim at very different ends.

Tokyo Learning is in part about the Meiji imperial subject, who is the product of the Meiji ideology detailed by Carol Gluck. The unbroken Japanese tradition celebrated in the Imperial Rescript on Education is invoked by Ishikawa in his discussion of the importance of the traditional, gendered division of labor in the Japanese household. But the author of *Tokyo Learning* does protest too much. His discussion of the Japanese woman as national treasure because she is the repository of Oriental beauty, morals, and self-sacrifice (*TG*, 246–47, 251) is too loud, too long, and too much at conflict with the rest of the book's documentation of the fluidity of tradition. Ishikawa's failure to analyze the implications of loaded terms he mentioned, such as "woman-boy" (*onna-boi*) for waitress and "man-boy" (*otoko-boi*) for waiter (*TG*, 445–46, 483), undoubtedly resulted from his refusal to see the fluidity of gender roles that had already begun by late Meiji and would overwhelm the media and mass culture by 1930. Ishikawa knows that by 1909, woman, "Japan's most beautiful artwork," has already moved out of the household and into the factories and that she is not only an imperial subject given the role of good wife and wise mother to a new generation of imperial subjects but also a purveyor and consumer of urban culture at such sites as the department store. (Here Ishikawa illustrates Sharon Sievers's thesis that in Japan, as in other societies experiencing development at a rapid pace, the symbolic function of woman is to provide a psychological an-

26. Ishikawa notes that the Tokyo tenements are in the heart of the city, as opposed to London's poor, who have been placed in the more ideal, marginal site of the East End. For a discussion of the culture (*seikatsu*) of the poor, see *TG*, 538.

chor, representing cultural and social stasis.)[27] When Edward Seidensticker remarked that "the department stores worked the beginnings of a huge cultural shift," he was chronicling the transformation of retail trade,[28] but as *Tokyo Learning* reveals, the department store was also part of a cultural change of consciousness, part of the making of the consciousness of an imperial subject who was also a consumer. The influence of new patterns of viewing, selecting, and purchasing items in a centralized space organized to transform consumption of a limited number of necessities into desire for limitless consumption through new forms of visual and verbal advertisement is hinted at in this document and was elaborated in texts written during the 1920s and 1930s.[29] Richard Sennett has provided a way to connect Seidensticker's institutional history of the department store with a study of the making of the Japanese consumer-subject. In the words of Sennett, "The rise of the department store, mundane a subject as it may seem, is in fact in capsule form the very paradigm of how the public realm as a place of active interchange gave way in people's lives to an experience of publicness more intense and less sociable."[30] Sennett is concerned with the consciousness

27. See Sharon Sievers, *Flowers in Salt: The Beginnings of Feminist Consciousness in Modern Japan* (Stanford: Stanford University Press, 1983), 17. On gender fluidity, see Donald Roden, "Taisho Culture and the Problem of Gender Ambivalence" in *Culture and Identity: Japanese Intellectuals During the Interwar Years*, ed. J. Thomas Rimer (Princeton: Princeton University Press, 1990), 37–55, and Miriam Silverberg, "Advertising Every Body: Images from the Japanese Modern Years," forthcoming.
28. Seidensticker offers a capsule history of how, in 1886, Shirokiya introduced the practice of selling Western clothes and was also responsible for the first shop girls and one of the first telephones. Mitsui, renamed Mitsukoshi in 1904, followed with the sale of hats, leather goods, and sundries. In 1905, Mitsukoshi introduced the glass showcases mentioned in *Tokyo Learning*, along with a second floor. By 1914 Shirokiya was a four-story building with game rooms and exhibition space topped by a tower that competed with Mitsukoshi. By this time, Mitsukoshi also had escalators, elevators, central heating, and a roof garden. See *Low City, High City*, 111–13.
29. See, for example, Kon Wajiro's surveys of department store behavior, discussed in my "Constructing the Japanese Ethnography of Modernity" (forthcoming), and Soeda Azenbo's awe at the power of the department store to encompass all items within its enclosed marketplace, discussed in Miriam Silverberg, "Living on the Urban Edge: Culture and Subculture in Taisho Japan," paper presented at the Association for Asian Studies meeting, Chicago, March 1985.
30. According to Sennett's history of the department store, when Bon Marche opened in 1852 in Paris, it made use of three new approaches to retail trade: (1) there would be a small markup and a large volume of goods; (2) the prices of goods would be fixed and marked; and (3) anyone could enter the shop to browse without feeling obligated to make a purchase. The department store as purveyor of mass-produced goods was "a

accompanying the emergence of capitalist consumption, the same issue raised in *Tokyo Learning*'s discussion of advertising. Crowds of people had to be encouraged not only to look but to buy, and Sennett sees a transformation in marketplace behavior resulting in the emergence of a passive capitalist consumer deprived of personalized contacts with merchants. In order to stimulate this customer to buy, spectacles that made assembly line products appear strange and exotic, and led the consumer to believe in the individualizing effect of the mass-produced and consumed object had to be created. Sennett's brief history of the production of this consumer— an entity who engaged in the gesture of purchasing commodities for public display because of a private fantasy, through a silent and secretive act of selection—suggests one direction for the investigation of the history of the modern Japanese consumer-subject. It provides one documentation of the still unstudied phenomenon in modern Japanese history, whereby in the course of one generation an imperial subject was legislated through state ideology and a consumer-subject was faced with making cultural, and thereby political, choices.

Constructing Histories of Mass Culture

Western theorists and historians have both problematized a depoliticized, dehistoricized study of "popular culture" and questioned outmoded approaches that create false binaries by, for example, opposing high to low and modern to mass culture. For the historian of modern Japan, an additional dichotomy to avoid is the "East meets West" paradigm, which avoids differentiation within both cultures. But to what extent are the European and American histories of the relationship of mass to modern culture and culture to politics relevant in the case of prewar Japan? In other words, how can mass (as class) culture be related to modern Japanese politics and thereby be made meaningful within the context of modern Japanese history?

Only further research can determine to what extent mass culture representations, including those of the emperor, the Japanese family, the Japanese state, and of old traditions and those in the making, celebrated in the Imperial Rescript and reinforced in the *shushin,* or morals, teachings in

---

response to the factory" and also a response to the organizational principles of bureaucracy, because large numbers of employees had to be managed in order to sell the items in uniform fashion. In addition, large numbers of buyers resulting from migration to the city made the high volume, low markup sale strategy and urban renewal possible. See Richard Sennett, *The Fall of Public Man* (New York: Knopf, 1977), 141–43.

the school system, challenged the official ideology presented in the Imperial Rescript and in morals classes. What can be concluded is that the Japanese experience of mass culture was in many ways different from the European and American experiences. A crucial difference exists between Japan and Germany, whose interwar eras have been the source for comparison: While German cultural history was determined by the transition from liberal to monopoly capitalism (as Andreas Huyssen points out in a critique of Adorno), Japan's cultural history was determined by the transition between state and monopoly, or high capitalism, and, moreover, a monopoly capitalism delimited by both an emperor-centered ideology and by constitutional warrants for imperial control. Part of the relevant detail of German history was of course the role of the German Social Democratic party in organizing cultural activity, a development unparalleled in Japanese labor or political history. Frank Trommler has contrasted the formidable size and tradition of workers' culture in Great Britain with a German working-class culture colored by a weak political tradition and the strong position of the SPD. While the links between the working class and cultural activity in Japan have barely begun to be made, neither the British nor the German case is relevant. Not only was the state's control of culture stronger in the case of Japan than in the other two countries during the 1910s and 1920s, the Japanese left-wing was linked neither with a powerful political party nor with cultural institutions, and the Japanese worker was rapidly captive to new institutions and a patriarchal ideology created under capitalism, as Stephen Large and Andrew Gordon have shown. While there is an urgent need for a Japanese labor history integrating the experiences of class, gender, and sexuality, as best illustrated in the work of American labor historians Christine Stansell and Kathy Peiss, the absence of the link between an ethnic and a working-class experience, as explored by such American labor historians as Lizabeth Cohen, is also irrelevant in the Japanese case, nor is the relationship of workers to a "genteel culture," as discussed in Michael Denning's account of dime novels and American working-class culture.[31]

31. See Frank Trommler, "Working-Class Culture and Modern Mass Culture," *New German Critique* 29 (Spring/Summer 1983): 57–70; Christine Stansell, *City of Women: Sex and Class in New York: 1789–1860* (Urbana: University of Illinois Press, 1987); and Kathy Peiss, *Cheap Amusements: Working Women and Leisure in Turn-of-the-Century New York* (Philadelphia: Temple University Press, 1986). Lizabeth Cohen argues that the geographic context of American mass culture—the neighborhoods where movies were seen—promoted ethnic, religious, and working-class affiliations; see Lizabeth Cohen, "Encountering Mass Culture at the Grassroots: The Experience of Chicago Workers in

As Stuart Hall has made clear, the culture of this working class is not easily separated from commercial popular culture or mass culture, but there was a Japanese working-class experience of mass culture, as discussed by the author of *Tokyogaku* and other critics I have called "modern ethnographers."[32] This experience can be compared with the American and European cases. Moreover, there were similarities in the rhetoric of intellectual debate over the nature of the modern phenomenon of mass culture. As Jean Franco, Stuart Hall, and Huyssen have noted, talk about mass culture in the early twentieth century signified an implied "authentic" culture, and this was also the case in Japan. Contrary to the scenario set forth by Hall and adopted by Huyssen, however, the "political and cultural aspirations, struggle, and pacification via cultural institutions" of the masses were not hidden in Japan. It is true that one segment of the intellectual world, spurred

---

the 1920s," *American Quarterly* 41 (March 1989): 6–33. For a sophisticated account of the relationship of ideology to working-class culture, see Michael Denning, *Mechanic Accents: Dime Novels and Working-Class Culture in America* (London: Verso Press, 1987).

I have discussed the absence of Japanese working-class culture in *Changing Song*, 224–25. Minami Hiroshi includes salarymen, bureaucrats, and skilled workers within his category of "post-earthquake middle-class consumers," although scattered references imply a distinct working-class existence, as when Minami notes that the years 1934 through 1936 were the best for the working class because their wages rose, allowing them to come closest to a "modern" American-style lifestyle. See *Showa bunka*, 11, 72, 392. Takahashi Tetsu provides the idiosyncratic concept of a new cultural middle class of suburban proletarians with a provincial, rural consciousness in "Toshika to kikaibummei," in *Jiga to kankyo*, vol. 6 of *Kindai Nihon shisoshi koza* (Tokyo: Chikuma Shobo, 1960), 181, 182, 187. On the transformation from a Japanese craft tradition to a paternalistic ideology, see Andrew Gordon, *The Evolution of Labor Relations in Japan*. Steven Large has compared the "bossification and ossification" of German and Japanese labor elites. In his discussion of "the problem of class consciousness and labor politics in Japan and Germany," he sees Japanese working-class consciousness as weaker than German worker consciousness, while acknowledging the "bourgeoisification" of the German worker. While Large considers such factors as psychological "dependence" (*amae*), the nationalistic dimension to revolution in Japan, social mobility, the power of paternalistic small firms, and Thomas Smith's theory of status over class consciousness as sources for a weak Japanese working-class consciousness, ultimately the following statement by Large is most persuasive for future study of the relationship of Japanese worker to Japanese culture during the imperial era: "We need to know more about the social history of class relations in interwar Japan before we can refer confidently to the 'bourgeoisification' of social movements." See Stephen Large, *Organized Workers and Socialist Politics in Interwar Japan* (Cambridge: Cambridge University Press, 1981), 240–55.

32. Silverberg, "Constructing the Japanese Ethnography," forthcoming.

on by their readings of Nietzsche, Bergson, and Spengler, did echo their European counterparts, in decrying the threats to civilization by mass culture. As Leslie Pincus has pointed out, the aesthetician of "Japaneseness," Kuki Shuzo, managed to displace the manifestation of mass culture in a discourse on tradition, which hid its existence altogether. However, *mass* was associated with class among the Left. In one renowned debate within the literary left-wing in 1928, known as the *Taishuka ronso* (debate on the massification of art), the Marxist critic Nakano Shigeharu asserted that the "masses" were being catered to by the "foot-licking obscenities" of wrong-headed "quack doctors" who fed them comic tales from American magazines in order to teach socialism and decried how the Japanese worker was drawn to historic potboilers about the heroic swordsman Miyamoto Musashi instead of proletarian theater. This was also why the movie theaters were filled with *proletarian* masses of workers and tenant farmers. Rather than covering up class relations, the term *mass* was used as a strategy to discuss class culture.[33]

Andreas Huyssen has called for a reassociation of the avant-garde with mass culture, but in the Japanese case, this is not a necessary move, for in Japan, mass culture was used by the avant-garde, both as a site for production and as a topic for discourse. In addition, the Japanese avant-garde, unlike its European counterpart, was contesting not a bourgeois sensibility or way of life but a state-sponsored culturalism that denied differences within Japan and claimed differences between Japan and the West that did not necessarily hold true at a time when Taylorist principles and Hollywood icons had taken firm hold in Japanese society. The relationship

33. Stuart Hall makes clear that there is no "one-to-one relationship between a class and a particular cultural form or practice; see his "Notes on Deconstructing 'The Popular,'" in *People's History and Socialist Theory*, ed. Raphael Samuel, History Workshop Series (London: Routledge and Kegan Paul, 1981), 231–39.

I refer here to Jean Franco, "Mass Culture. The Ethical Question," Hannah Arendt Memorial Lecture presented at the New School for Social Research, and to Andreas Huyssen's discussion of Hall in *After the Great Divide: Modernism, Mass Culture, Postmodernism* (Bloomington: Indiana University Press, 1986), 47. For an overview of the *minshu geijutsu* (people's art) debate of 1918, which bears on this issue, see *Taisho bunka*, 101–18.

For the most comprehensive discussion of the debate of the *masses,* which raises the issue of the concepts of *minshu* (people) and *gunshu* (grouping), see Takahashi, "Toshika," 189–92. For an overview of the debate, see Miriam Silverberg, "Changing Song: The Marxist Poetry of Nakano Shigeharu," (Ph.D. diss., University of Chicago, 1984), 68–82. On Kuki Shuzo, see Leslie Pincus, "'The Allure of Difference: Iki no kozo' and the Construction of the Japanese Spirit," (Ph.D. diss., University of Chicago, 1989).

of Japanese avant-garde art of the 1920s and 1930s, including surrealism, with a Western, rather than a "bourgeois," experience, bears investigation.

While the influence of Americanization was decried as superficial by critics in Japan on the Left and the Right from the twenties onward, an investigation into the cultural history of the era reveals an alternative, more sophisticated, discourse that takes into account the dynamism in cross-cultural processes. To decry the wages of "Americanism" or merely to list how a new middle class imported ways of life (*seikatsuyoshiki*) is not enough. A new cultural history needs to explore how new attitudes toward food, dress, and sexuality had profound implications regarding Japanese attitudes toward self, others, and the state. In other words, to recount the adoption of Western clothing, bread for breakfast, and new attitudes toward sex, without associating them with new social practices that went far beyond dressing, eating, or kissing, is to avoid problematizing the Japanese experience of modernity. As I have argued elsewhere, a number of Japanese intellectuals who made their living in the mass media during the 1920s and 1930s acknowledged this as they discussed how Japan was capitalist, but not Western; Japanese, but not traditional.[34]

A history of Japanese mass culture must move from the context of the constitution of a consumer-subject with access to a network of cultural institutions to the consciousness of a gendered consumer-subject responding to questions of representations of class and national identity. In contrast to Huyssen's need to see mass culture as the absent other of modernism in his attempt to relink mass with modernist expression, my own agenda is to reconnect the absent other of *modern practice* (as opposed to *Americanism* or *modanizumu*) with the mass culture of prewar Japan. The written and visual texts of the era make clear that the modern sensibility in art and in daily practices (I make no distinction between artistic sensibility and social practice) took on specific form in Japan. Japanese modernity, encompassing the visual aspects of mass culture along with the constitution of new forms of identity and new social practices putting these forms into social relationships, was, to coin a term for the cultural moment in Japan, *constructionist*. In other words, what should be highlighted in a cultural history of the period is the fact that the construction of culture and the conscious-

34. Takahashi sees the production of the "erotically grotesque nonsense" (*ero-guro-nonsense*) dismissed by most as a decadent escape from the trials of the depression as significant. I agree with him, while questioning his characterization of what was being challenged as "feudal notions of sexuality." See Takahashi, "Toshika," 199–206.

ness of this construction (reflected not only in the ethnographies of cultural critics but in the defensive stance of state surveys) are what render the era *modern* and not such changes as the shift from Europe to America, noted by Minami (*SB*, 54), who does not take into full account the cultural continuity of the influence of Europe in the arts and ideology.[35]

The writings of cultural critics and the texts available to us from state commentaries and the mass media of the era (most importantly, the extensive illustrated press with its graphic cartoons, photographs, and menus of daily practices) open up a new vision of how male and female Japanese citizens of different classes integrated the relationship between East and West in different ways, although *not* through borrowing or through a double life enabling them to switch back and forth from white-collar suit to kimono. They constructed an identity informed not by bricolage but by a form of cultural code-switching, whereby aspects of Western material and mass culture were integrated into the experience of everyday practice.[36] Only further research can determine how the consumer-subjects of the era constructed a consciousness and a series of practices as he and she forged

35. According to Perry Anderson, European states on the eve of the First World War (and to a great extent after the war) shared the following coordinates of modernism: (1) a formalized academism supported by regimes still influenced by landowning classes; (2) the emergence of key technologies, such as the telephone, radio, automobile, and aircraft without mass consumption industries; and (3) "the imaginative proximity of social revolution." Within this conjuncture or space of modernism, different forms of modernist artistic expression emerged. See Perry Anderson, "Modernity and Revolution," in *Marxism and the Interpretation of Culture*, ed. Cary Nelson and Lawrence Grossberg (Urbana: University of Illinois, 1988), 323–26. While the relationship between an ancien régime and academism must be reworked to fit the Japanese context, since it may be argued that after the Meiji Restoration or *revolution* of 1868 neither had a hold on sensibilities and, instead, all was up for grabs, the conjuncture was experienced in Japan after the great earthquake of 1923. I argue that the ethnography of modernity was *constructivist* because Japanese cultural critics celebrated technology and aimed to eliminate barriers between work, leisure, production, and culture in order to revitalize everyday life. These thinkers recognized the spectator as participant.

Regarding the European influence on Japanese film during the prewar years, see Yamamoto Kikuo, *Nihon eiga ni okeru gaikoku eiga no eikyo: hikaku eigashi kenkyu* (Tokyo: Waseda Daigaku Shuppanbu, 1983).

36. According to John Gumperz, "conversational code switching can be defined as the juxtaposition within the same speech exchange of passages of speech belonging to different grammatical systems or subsystems." The participants are unaware of which code is in use; they are concerned only with effect. Gumperz also notes how shifts in political ideology result in changes in attitude to code-switching. See John J. Gumperz, *Discourse Strategies* (Cambridge: Cambridge University Press, 1982).

unprecedented relationships within the material world, within and against class, and in the context of a reworking of tradition. To this end, distinctions must be maintained as the tensions between consumer and subject are explored, and as differences are set out—differences premised on the tense relationship of consumer to subject.

The Spirit of Productivity: Workplace Discourse on Culture and Economics in Japan

Christena Turner

Japan's economic success in the contemporary world has elicited considerable respect on the one hand and equally great suspicion and even a certain mystique on the other. Western explanations of this enviable competitiveness inevitably address the potential influence of Japanese culture on Japanese productivity. In particular, there is great interest in the Japanese work ethic, management style, and the elusive motivation of the Japanese worker. Unfortunately, the result of much of the effort to understand Japanese workers and workplaces is a picture with too little breadth or depth. The temptation is to seek a simple answer rather than to understand ongoing Japanese debates and dilemmas. Because "we" want to understand "them," "they" become for us a single, unified group with a single, unified way of thinking. It is not possible to appreciate either Japanese economic success or the role of culture in that success without also appreciating the heterogeneity within Japanese workplaces and the dilemmas of contemporary consciousness for Japanese workers.

Interestingly enough, the meaning of work in Japanese workplaces themselves very often entails some concept of a national or cultural identity. It also involves identifying one or several others against whom the "Japaneseness" of one's own workplace may be balanced. The relationship between culture and economic action is a prevalent concern. There is not, however, one answer or form that this issue inspires. Both the way in which it is discussed and the effect it has on workers differ considerably from workplace to workplace. A number of cultural issues and specific economic goals could be chosen to explore this question. Here, I want to look specifically at the relationship between the "*spirit*" (*seishin*) of workers and the productivity of the firm as it is discussed in three very different workplaces.

The importance of the process through which the meaning of work and the spirit of workers in industrial settings is negotiated lies, for managers, in the commitment and motivation of employees and, for workers, in the meaning of work for life and personal identity. In a country to which much of the world attributes high levels of homogeneity, obedience, and a certain mysterious *cultural* ability to compete economically, the following accounts of specific workplace discourse are meant to give a glimpse of the process through which consensus, agreement, and understanding are contested.[1] They are also meant to indicate the role that notions of Japaneseness (*nihonteki*), the contemporary world (*ima no sekai, ima no yo no naka,* or *kore kara no yo no naka*), newness (*atarashii*), and tradition (*dento*) play in the construction of motivation, commitment, and sensibility for industrial workers in their companies and in their unions.

Ma Joli

Ma Joli is a dressmaking factory in Arakawa-ku, Tokyo. Of its thirty-five employees, all are women, and fewer than ten work part-time. There is no union. There are three men in the company: the owner, the manager, and the cutter. The owner is a former Zen Buddhist priest, and he has a formidable presence: He is tall, about forty-five years of age, and has a strong and decisive voice and manner. The young women think he is handsome, and several have had crushes on him.

I came to this company just as they brought in a new cohort of em-

1. The following accounts are based on fieldwork I did in each of these companies. I studied at Ma Joli from 1979 to 1980 and did follow-up work there from 1980 to 1984. I worked at Universal from 1980 to 1981, did follow-up work from 1981 to 1984, and made two shorter visits in 1988 and 1989. I spent two summers (1987 and 1988) working at the Toshiba factory and made a follow-up visit in 1989.

ployees, and I will focus here on the efforts of these young women to learn to work. The goals of the company were set out rather eloquently in the entrance ceremony for the new workers, by both the manager and the company president. Emphasis was squarely on *"spirit"* (*seishin*). Revolving around spirit were notions of (1) hard work as a way to develop strong spirit, (2) happiness as something that comes with the strong spirit cultivated through achievement at work, and (3) mature social identity as, together with strong spirit, being both a way to achieve and a way to verify the achievement of adulthood (*ichininmae* or *shakaijin*). These young women were just out of high school, so there was also an explicit reference to the transition between the protective (*amai*) environment of home and the harsh (*kibishii*) environment of work. This transition, however, was argued to be good for one, because of its ability to forge strong spirits and thus strong adults. The workplace is, in all these arguments, assumed to be an appropriate site for this self-cultivation.

The president outlined the goals of the company, which the employees were all expected to share now, and explained the harsh nature of their domestic and international economic environments. To compete in such a world, the only real weapon for such a small company is a strong spirit among its workers. In his speech at the entrance ceremony, he said:

> This business is highly competitive and we all have to work together to make it successful. We are under terrific pressure now from Korea and Southeast Asian countries. Korean wages are one-fourth of ours, but their spirit is like that Japan had after the war. They want to work hard and make Korea great. That makes them serious rivals for us. We have to recapture that spirit, the old Japanese spirit. It is our only hope.

He also discussed the laziness of contemporary Japan, praised the postwar frugality, and reminded them that they were too young to realize how luxurious life is in contemporary Japan (*ima no Nihon*). The two things one needed in order to work at Ma Joli were the two most important parts of this Japanese spirit: perseverance (*nintai*) and effort (*doryoku*). These were linked not only to competitiveness and the very survival of the company but to happiness as well: "These two are part of the happy person's character."

The entrance ceremony was a fairly solemn affair: The new recruits sat silently, hands in their laps and heads bowed as he spoke. They livened up a bit later when one of the new young women addressed the whole new cohort with a short presentation. In it she included a story from "old Japan" (*mukashi banashi*) of a prince who loved to eat. The prince sat around eating and eating and not doing much of anything else. One day he was forced to leave this life to do hard work. For the first time, exhausted from hard work, he realized how delicious food really was.

The manager then read from the diaries of the new recruits. They had been asked to write in their diaries each day as they were being trained on the shop floor during their first weeks of work. The young women focused on exhaustion, embarrassment at being troublesome to experienced workers, and insecurity about their ability to be good enough:

> My whole body ached by noon. But there is still something satisfying in this.

> I have to improve quickly so I can stop being so troublesome to the experienced workers.

> The skill it takes cannot be learned in a day, I hope I can be good enough. I will try.

As he read, the manager remarked with satisfaction that they were "learning how hard real work is" and how once they became "spiritually strong" (*seishinteki ni tsuyoi*) many of the difficulties of work and their exhaustion would disappear. The new recruits met these readings and comments with giggles and applause.

The process of learning to work at Ma Joli, of beginning to share the company's goals, of trying to live up to management's expectations, was gradual and anything but smooth. Management demanded a great deal, but the young women had high expectations of themselves, as well. Most were very self-critical during the first few months of work. Their assigned schedule was a rigorous one. They worked most nights until nine or ten o'clock and started each morning at half past seven or eight o'clock. When they had a deadline, at least once or twice a week, they would work overnight. About three months after they all began, there was a particularly trying time when, for more than a month, they worked from seven o'clock in the morning until eleven or twelve o'clock at night. Dinner was usually called in, but when they were very busy, it was skipped. One of the women I came to know quite well lost about thirteen pounds and was diagnosed later with an ulcer. She kept the diagnosis, as well as her appointments with her doctor, a secret. Her doctor was outraged by the schedule she was keeping, and the company was critical when she came back and asked for a more regular dinner schedule. They suggested that she was "weak willed" and that only by becoming "stronger in spirit" would she be able to work just like everyone else. They accused her of asking for special favors.

This was the same woman who recited the old Japanese tale at the entrance ceremony. Her response is an interesting effort to arrive at a coherent sense of meaning in her life and in her work. She accused herself of not being cheerful enough (*akarui*) and of not learning well from her seniors (*senpai*). She resolved not to be defeated by this schedule and to accept the challenge. Her health got worse, and she eventually quit and went home for a break. A month later she came back, having gained back about four-and-a-half pounds and having resolved to manage better this time; she would not become a "whipped puppy" (*make inu*).

The use of the notion of spirit to unite people behind the company's goals casts their acceptance of working conditions in a particular light, one which throws the onus of problems back on their own personal character. For this young woman and others I got to know there, this situation was a very personal struggle, a struggle they shared with their coworkers, but which they shared as separate individuals, each one trying to develop her own personal character, her own personal strength. While they admired signs of success and perseverance in their coworkers, they criticized themselves. Another of these new workers gave me her diary, which she kept for the first month of her time there. In it she criticizes herself and writes:

> After all, I am not yet serious enough; my eyes are always smiling; I will try to be more careful.
> I am not good enough yet. I like people who will scold me harshly. Please scold me more severely.

She also writes of two new recruits who quit and how she tried to talk them out of it. She ends her diary entry that day with, "I will work twice as hard to make up for your quitting. I hope you do well and don't regret leaving."

The two women who quit were both from Tokyo, which raises the issue of the importance of geographical origin in the recruitment of new employees. The manager and the owner emphasized the importance of a rural/urban distinction in the character of high school graduates. Situated as it is in the poorest ward of Tokyo, with a work force of only thirty-five, the company sends its manager to two hundred high schools a year all over Japan—except Tokyo—to recruit about ten new employees. His reason for excluding Tokyo is simple: "Tokyo people are just too spoiled." The manager often invokes the old phrase "*wa kon yo sai,*" (Japanese spirit/Western learning) and complains that, in general, the Japanese spirit is missing in

Tokyo and that it is hard to build a good company with the "Westernized" attitudes of the Tokyo people.

To further stress the importance of this Japanese spirit, fortunately still found in the countryside, the company goes, together, once a year to Southeast Asia for four days. They visit similar factories and talk to people there. The workers are told that they need to know the competition, their strengths and their working conditions, to see what Ma Joli has to compete with and to see how important their own individual efforts and spirits really are. The manager stresses that new machines can increase productivity by 5 percent, but a stronger working spirit of employees can increase productivity by 50 percent.

At Ma Joli, a picture of the "Japanese" (*nihonteki*) is explicitly linked to rural Japan, which is in turn a symbol of the older, as opposed to the newer, way of looking at things. The essence of that older Japan is found in the old tales and expressed in the Japanese spirit—and that is where the uniqueness of Japanese companies can be seen. This is, in turn, argued to be the most important weapon in the fight against foreign competition, the only weapon small and poor companies like Ma Joli have. Japan's Asian competitors—Korea, Taiwan, and some Southeast Asian countries—are thought to have this spirit. In part, this is because they are considered to be historically and developmentally "behind," and thus they have to try harder. Here lies the dilemma in the president's thought: Progress is to Japan's credit, but with this progress has come the loss of a certain strength of spirit and character. What he tries to emphasize is the need to combine the *old spirit* with *new technology* and to create a company—and eventually a Japan—that has both. For the young women working at Ma Joli, their character, their adulthood, and their identity are negotiated in terms of their spiritual strength in the workplace. The spirit of productivity here is a direct link between individual workers, their individual character, and the success of their companies.

Universal Shoes

Universal Shoes, a shoe-making factory of forty-five employees, is located in Kita Senju in Adachi-ku, Tokyo. Half of the workers in this company are male and half are female. They range widely in age from their twenties to seventies. While I was there, this company was being run by its union as part of a post-bankruptcy labor dispute. The union, to which all employees belonged, had taken over operation of the company when the parent company (*oya-gaisha*) bankrupted it following automation of their main factory. The union went to court to fight for back wages, severance pay, and a settlement, and they demanded to be allowed to reopen under their own management. They won their struggle eleven years later and now operate as a workers' cooperative on the original site. The union is formally affiliated with the Socialist party, and Socialist Diet members were present at all major events. While the rank and file do not necessarily share this political affiliation personally, they do share a certain critical stance. In fact, there is much greater agreement about the criticism of capitalism, "Japanese-style management," and conservative politics than there is agreement about the alternatives—like socialism.

The form of this criticism varies from time to time and from person to person. In this union, the rank and file, not to mention leadership, reject openly any efforts by management to motivate workers by referring to "spirit" (*seishin*). Upon beginning self-management, they eliminated slogans, banners, morning recitations, and all other signs of what they refer to as "old" (*furui*), "Japanese-style" (*nihonteki*), and "feudal" (*hokenteki*) management practices. That these elements are essential to productivity is frankly disputed, and the workers and their union claim that productivity has increased since such practices have been eliminated.

To say, however, that such things as reference to "Japanese spirit/ Western learning," which was sometimes quoted at Universal as a joke, were set in the atmosphere of criticism is not to say that Japaneseness was rejected consistently or that the issue of a cultural identity was missing from their workplace. During my months there, leadership tried to formulate a consensus several times, and one of the most complex issues addressed their participation in a large demonstration, their first.

Naturally, protest was not unknown to these workers. They had already been fighting this dispute for three years and had even been leafleting and picketing in front of their own parent-company and at local train stations. Their participation, however, in a large demonstration in the downtown financial district of Tokyo, joined by several hundred other workers from affiliated unions, was a very different sort of activity than anything they had experienced before.

For the rank and file, the problem with this demonstration centered around location, scale, and a sense of powerlessness. The picture painted by the leadership was one of excitement, optimism, and enthusiasm. Leadership asserted the importance of this new tactic for success and lauded the idea as a way to bring their dispute to a quicker conclusion. They spoke of the shock of the banks—of capitalists—when hundreds of people—

workers—would show up on their doorsteps. The rank and file, however, feared embarrassment, humiliation, and ineffectiveness. The clash between values that emphasize strength of character through smooth and harmonious social relations and values that emphasize democratic protest was felt acutely by the rank and file. Union leaders, while sympathetic and understanding about that dilemma, had themselves made an important shift.[2]

The distance between motivation of leaders and the rank and file was evidenced in preparations for the demonstration even on the day before. We all met for a briefing by the general secretary about the next day's schedule. He encouraged people:

> Please try to look determined and enthusiastic! Even if only for fifteen minutes or so at our bank. If everyone could please try and look really involved, we'll appreciate it very much.

This remark brought laughter and released the considerable tension that had been mounting that day and particularly in that meeting. Similarly, he made suggestions about the way they should depart the demonstration. Since it was a cooperative event, they would all go to the sites of each of the other supporting unions' demonstrations as well:

> After our demonstration we are going to continue marching and going to sites of others. About ten of us will be there through the whole day, and we are having the rest of you go home earlier. But please don't look too obvious about leaving. We don't want to give the impression that we are only there for our own interests.
>
> Anyway, please don't make a spectacle of a whole bunch of you leaving all at once. Leave a few at a time. Just sort of sneak behind a tree, remove your headband and chest sign, and walk away looking nonchalant.

Again, people were amused by this picture of themselves, and their laughter brought them to their feet and the meeting dispersed.

The story of this demonstration was itself a fascinating case of a negotiation of meaning through action rather than verbal argument.[3] The result, however, was that through their participation, however reluctant,

2. For a discussion of democratic consciousness in this union, see my "Democratic Consciousness in Japanese Unions," in *Democracy in Japan*, ed. Ellis Krauss and Takeshi Ishida (Pittsburgh: University of Pittsburgh Press, 1989), 299–323.
3. For a full account of this demonstration and an ethnographic account of this company, see my "Breaking the Silence: Consciousness, Commitment, and Action in Japanese Unions," (Ph.D. diss., Stanford University, 1988).

people were brought into contact with hundreds of other workers also fighting in disputes, and, with the exception of a couple of elderly workers, everyone stayed right through to the end—an entire day of walking and demonstrating. Following this event, employees' conversations at work changed in character and topic for several days, and the words "worker" (*rodosha*) and "capitalist" (*shihonka*) were used in conversation much more easily.

My focus here, however, is the nature of this conversation. Socialism poses an interesting problem with regard to the Japaneseness of the workplace in that it is seen as a Western critique of a Western system. While managers at Ma Joli could try to claim a cultural identity in the spiritual dimension of work to offset a sense of "Westernness" about the technology, Universal workers could not claim, in their socialist opposition to capitalism or these particular capitalists, any particularly Japanese character. The dilemma for these Japanese workers was that their unions, their socialist ideology, and even their democratic values were no more "Japanese" than the capitalism they were engaged to struggle against.

The "*nihonteki*" of their lives was as prevalent here as in Ma Joli— more so perhaps, because the factory is located in the old Tokyo (*shitamachi*) area of town, and the workers nearly all came from this area of Tokyo. This geographic identity carries with it a certain cultural meaning, and it is to this that workers turned for their own notions of Japaneseness and culture. The borders of this area itself are disputed. Adachi (where Universal is located) residents claim to be "downtown," but many Arakawa (where Ma Joli is located) residents claim that *they* are "downtown" and that Adachi is not, that it is "across the river." Those who live in the oldest Asakusa area claim that neither Arakawa nor Adachi are "downtown" since Arakawa is across one river and is the site of old crematoriums, and Adachi is across yet another river and is thus simply "countryside" or "rice paddies." Nonetheless, it was an appropriation of the identity of the "downtown" or "*shitamachi*" area and its Japanese value of community and harmony that came, in part, to anchor their sense of themselves in this struggle. They talk about being "very Japanese" in that their human relations are characterized by human-heartedness and reciprocity (*giri-ninjo*), for instance, and in so doing, identify the worst trait of capitalism as the uncaring attitude of the capitalists.

Capitalists are opposed sometimes to labor, but, in conversation, they are more often opposed to "human beings" (*ningen*) and "ordinary people" (*futsuu no hito*). Capitalists are accused of not caring one iota for human beings, not taking account of anything but money. While workers use, and are frequently exposed to, economic and ideological oppositions of capitalists to labor or to analyses of exploitation of labor by capitalists, their own efforts to make sense of their political action more often reference the social quality of their relationship to capitalists. In short, conversations about capitalism reflect a strong emphasis on the social relations of work, particularly the importance of the quality of social interaction and of respect, consideration, and responsibility.

Another way in which people interpret their own political action refers directly to historical continuities of power relationships in Japan. Traditional Japanese power relations are seen to be continuous with contemporary capitalist ones, and the two are posed in just this way. Power relations of the past and those of the present seem to differ only in their labeling. What is *new* as opposed to *traditional* is *protest, democracy,* and even the category *workers* (*rodosha*):

> Our own parents were in most cases not workers. Those with two generations as workers are quite rare, and there are very few with three generations.

Unions stand for some of this newness, and they represent democracy and a certain equality. With a casual reference to postwar American influence, both equality and democracy are often equated with "Americanization." This can be extremely concrete and relevant to daily life, as in the following:

> We poor people have been greatly helped by the democratization and Americanization of Japan. Now we can wear jeans and look casual [he pointed to his own attire] and go anywhere. Before, we needed a new suit, a bath, and hair cream just to go to the Ginza [a chic area of town]! All that cost money, so if you couldn't afford it, it showed. Sometimes you just had to stay home.

There is a desire to reclaim some identity and some sense of validity for their values and actions from Japan and from Japanese culture, and, at the same time, a rush to accept—as a criticism and a dismantling of the oppressive social forms of the "old Japan"—the "new."

The situation is not simple; the word *warikirenai,* signifying an uneasy sense of partial understanding, is common. Popular culture gets drawn into this conversation as well. One Universal worker told me that the problem was that he, like the others at Universal, would really rather just wait for Mitokomon to come in and save them. In a popular TV show set in the Tokugawa period, Mitokomon, a powerful member of the shogun's family, goes incognito around Japan with a team of retainers, all disguised as ordinary travelers. When he stumbles, often by accident, on suffering and injustice, he stops in that area for awhile, bides his time, investigates the situation, and brings it to justice. Only at the end of the whole event do his subordinates reveal his true identity—with a flourish and great awe. This very popular TV show is in its third decade of continuous run. One worker made the link between it and his own company's situation like this:

> In Japan there is no tradition of fighting for yourself, fighting for your rights. You persevere, and, if you are lucky, someone comes and saves you—someone strong and powerful.
>
> Of course, it doesn't usually happen, and that is the real problem. What we are trying to do is new. All of us know it is right and that it makes sense, but it doesn't feel natural.

Toshiba

Toshiba's Yanagicho Works is a high-tech factory, with a union, that employs three thousand workers, 60 percent of whom are what American high-tech factories call "knowledge workers," or engineers and technicians. Both research and development facilities and mass production facilities are located at this site. More than twelve products representing three corporate divisions and five product groups are manufactured there.

The goal of this factory is to maintain an excellent record for innovation and to become even more competitive in the global market than they already are. The motto Speed and Kando (*speed* is in English, *kando* in Japanese) is simple and direct—*speed* refers to innovation and market demands, and *kando* means sensitivity and signifies the need always to be responsive to the slightest indication of a new technology or a new market. The point of their human resource management is similarly to create flexible, highly skilled and highly motivated workers. Naturally, a variety of practices are intended to accomplish this, and they succeed in varying degrees. I will use one, the factory campaign, to illustrate the effort to motivate workers to increase productivity and global competitiveness.

Factory campaigns are a staple of this factory, as they are at Ma Joli. Factory or corporation management starts these campaigns, but in the process of their implementation, they are reviewed and modified by every level of the organization—all the way to the shop floor. The main distinction across levels is that the higher one is in the hierarchy, the more enthused one has to be about the campaign. By the time it reaches the shop floor, individuals have considerable leeway in the degree of their involvement, with many workers nearly oblivious to all but the most specific production targets.

The Creating New Values Campaign was the idea of the general affairs section manager in the General Affairs Department. He was very excited about it when I spoke with him a couple of months after its initial stage had begun:

> This campaign is different, because this time we are trying to create a whole new attitude toward work and a whole new idea about the world.

Why now? Campaign literature itself explains the timing:

> With the appreciation of the yen, the changing structure of international markets, and trade problems, we need to change the very structure of the consciousness of every one of our workers. Only when people can act quickly, sensitively, and vigorously, can business grow and develop.

All previous campaigns in the factory had focused on straightforward goals like raising productivity, safety, or zero-defect. This time, management focused on a much broader range of issues. There were seven themes to the Creating New Values Campaign: increasing consumer orientation, modernizing factories, raising the speed and quality of work, heightening competitiveness, heightening value-added manufacturing, raising self-awareness, and making strong people and a strong culture.

Campaigns last a total of about two years and go through several stages. The first four stages take it from the factory president's office to the departments. The departments send it to their sections, and the sections send it to their shop-floor groups. At each level, ideas for ways to apply and rework the themes both for their own groups and for the factory as a whole are suggested. These are all aggregated again and brought back to the desk of the General Affairs Department chief. At this point, more refined themes are sent back to the departments, sections, and shop-floor groups, who are then asked to set specific goals. After several months, reports are sent back to the department chief. This campaign didn't make it through the final stage; response was so poor from so many areas of the factory, management gave it up.

The problem was vagueness—an inability to figure out what "creating new values" was all about. In particular, "making strong people, strong culture" and "raising self-awareness" didn't inspire much serious thought. Even factory modernization came up with only a couple of useful suggestions—new uniforms and, interestingly enough, a limitation on the number and placement of banners, posters, and slogans.

By the time the first year had passed, the Creating New Values Campaign was virtually stalled. It was evaluated as a partial success. The success was the slogan Creating New Values, which was thought to be effective in keeping people focused on the uncertainty of the future for the contemporary world and on the need to be alert to the possibility of change. The operationalization was too complex and was given up.

The committee in charge of this evaluation had to decide what to do about the faltering campaign. They reviewed each department to determine whether the campaign was having a favorable and significant impact; for example, in the Service Department, one suggestion had led to the production of an eighteen-page booklet about a new on-line information network. This network, called SINFONY, for Service INFOrmation On Line Network for Yanagicho, was indeed a concrete plus, but they decided that it would have been implemented even without the campaign since the Service Department had already been working on it. The ideas about new uniforms and standardization and limitation of signs and banners was good but hardly of major significance in creating new values. In short, it did not seem that the campaign had been a creative interaction between levels of the organization.

The usual path for such a campaign would have taken it through at least another year. The decision was made to subsume this slogan—which everyone agreed kept the feeling of uncertainty and need for readiness to change—under a new slogan, SPIRIT '88. The new campaign combined slogans: SPIRIT '88: Creating New Values! (In this case, *SPIRIT '88* was written in English, in capital letters, and *Creating New Values* was written in Japanese). In addition, management combined six other old campaigns, all successful ones, under it and formed a new promotion campaign committee. By the end of 1989, this slogan had become simply SPIRIT: Creating New Values! and had seemingly settled into a long-range umbrella slogan for more specific campaigns.

Lest you think we have come full circle and are back to Ma Joli's concern with Japanese spirit (*seishin*), let me assure you that this spirit is a more complex and mixed message than that. SPIRIT is an acronym for *Super Productivity by Innovation, Rectification, Integrated Total Operation.* While *'88* focused very clearly on the present, *Creating New Values* pulled toward the future. Of course, *SPIRIT* was also intended to mean *seishin*. Everyone knew that *spirit* was English for *seishin,* and it was part of the campaign to make this association, an association that allows the international language of English to combine with the traditional concept of *seishin* and create a new, updated, more powerful term without the negative associations of the past. The factory president who selected this slogan chose the acronym first, from English, and then chose the English words to give the acronym meaning. The attribution of technological and productivity messages to SPIRIT does, however, round out the circle in another way. If *capitalism* and *Western technology* stand for *Western learning,* as they do in the colloquial usage of the *Japanese spirit/Western learning* at both Ma Joli and Universal, then capitalism and technology have become *Japanese spirit* at Toshiba.

Toshiba's corporate motto is *Gijutsu no Toshiba,* or Technological Toshiba, and a human resources manager at corporate headquarters proudly claimed that "Toshiba is unlike other companies in that it has no corporate culture." The point here, of course, is not that Toshiba has no culture in an analytical sense but rather that part of their corporate image is the irrelevance of "culture" to their corporation and its operation. The appeal is instead to pride in the accomplishment of pragmatic technological innovation and high levels of skill in employees.

In an organization of this size and complexity, there are internal differences in the nature of conversations about culture, Japaneseness, and spirit. There is more being said at the corporate and factory level about competition, newness, and global markets and ventures than about tradition and being Japanese. The link of individual spirit and corporate or factory economic goals like competitiveness and productivity is argued through the mediating concepts of achievement, skill, coordinated teamwork, and precision craftsmanship. However, with a certain denial of nostalgia, of anything particularly Japanese at the level of the factory much less the corporation—with all this comes a shop-floor celebration of their own differences, distinctions, and similarities to "little neighborhood companies."

• • • •

Throughout these cases there is a concern for the nature of the relationship between culture and productivity, spirit and technology, and between Japaneseness and the social dynamics and meaning of work. The importance of this concern is in part the mere fact that these relationships are always in the process of being constructed and defined. This marks the fluidity of contemporary Japanese workplace cultures, points toward the contested nature of shared understanding, and introduces the elements of agency, argument, and process. It also suggests that the important questions are not about the simple, unified nature of "Japanese culture" but rather about the *process* of making work meaningful in Japanese companies. James Clifford has written in his recent *Predicament of Culture* that in cultural analysis we might more profitably look for "connections" than for "unification."[4] These three workplaces are connected in a variety of ways, some direct and some indirect.

On the shop floor at Toshiba, people belonging to a single section talked about being "just like small companies." They demonstrated this in various decorations and unique slogans, and they rehearsed it in section parties and the development of an in-house humor and character often built around their own section chief. In other words, workers and lower-level managers identified their own units within the corporation as sharing some important characteristics—a sense of community and a unique "culture"—with a proud "Japanese" tradition of small companies. The factory itself facilitated this with all-factory events, like the yearly summer festival, where each section builds their own float or display for a parade and a performance.

There are other connections, too. The first time I sat down to talk with the Toshiba union president, he asked me where I had worked before. When I told him I had worked at Universal, he beamed, pointed to his shoes, and said, "They used to come here to sell their shoes. They took a long time to settle that dispute. I admire them. And they make good shoes, too!"

Finally, to finish one of the stories with which I began, the young woman who returned to Ma Joli after taking time off for an ulcer quit again—permanently—a few weeks later. The struggle to learn to work in the way Ma Joli's managers wanted her to work led her outside, to other sources of income, and to other sources of meaning and interpretation. Her father is a worker in a distant city, in a large company with a labor union that belongs to the same federation as Toshiba's and Universal's. For the first time in her life, she began a dialogue about the meaning of work with her father. She heard an alternative view. She made a choice, and eventually found a different job in a small company without a labor union but with much better working conditions.

4. James Clifford, *The Predicament of Culture: Twentieth Century Ethnography, Literature, and Art* (Cambridge: Harvard University Press, 1988).

In reviewing these three cases, a certain trend emerges. It seems harder and harder to make and maintain the kind of link between spirit and productivity that is current at Ma Joli. Outright rejection, like that found at Universal, is no doubt less common than a tolerant apathy, like that at Toshiba, but the tendency for the link to be less convincing over time seems clear. It is, for one thing, the express purpose of the Toshiba union to keep watch on company campaigns and to make sure they don't worsen working conditions. So, while there is a trend away from the credibility of individual spirit and productivity being linked in the direct way they were at Ma Joli, there continues to be an important issue of identity, culture, and economic organization and competitiveness that is negotiated in a variety of ways. At Universal, the location of the factory was pertinent; at Toshiba, the character of the section was pertinent.

How the issues of spirit and productivity or culture and economic action are discussed and what conclusions and meanings are shared by workers vary greatly across workplaces. For Japan today, it is true that these issues are the focus of some serious contention, and thus it is around their discussion that important social and cultural issues are negotiated. I would suggest, however, that this focus itself is historically specific, stemming from the particular circumstances of recent and rapid industrialization and ascendence to global economic power, and from a need to assess national and cultural identity in the context of that process.

Culture

The Novelist in Today's World: A Conversation

Kazuo Ishiguro
Oe Kenzaburo

Oe: We know that your father is a marine scientist, but exactly what branch of marine science does he specialize in?

Kazuo Ishiguro was born in 1954 in Japan. He went to England at the age of five when his oceanographer father was invited to participate in a British government research project. He attended British schools and graduated from the University of Kent, where he majored in English literature. He later studied creative writing at the University of East Anglia graduate school. His first novel, *A Pale View of Hills* (London: Faber & Faber, 1982) was awarded the Royal Society of Literature Prize, and his second, *An Artist of the Floating World* (1986), received the Whitbread Book of the Year Award. His latest book, *The Remains of the Day*, won the 1989 Booker Prize, Britain's most prestigious literary award. Oe Kenzaburo, born in 1935 in Shikoku, is a leading contemporary novelist in Japan. Among his best known works are *Man'ei gannen no futtoboru* [A Football Game in the First Year of Man'ei] (Tokyo: Shinchosha, 1973; translated as *The Silent Cry* by John Bester, Kodansha International, 1974), *Do jidai gemu* [Contemporary Games] (Tokyo: Shinchosha, 1979) and *Atarashii hito yo mezameyo* [Wake Up to a New Life] (Tokyo: Kodansha, 1983).
This conversation was held in November 1989 during Mr. Ishiguro's first return visit to Japan in thirty years on the Japan Foundation Short-Term Visitors Program and was originally published in the *Japan Foundation Newsletter*, vol. 17, no. 4.

Ishiguro: He's an oceanographer, so it's not so much marine science. He's studied wave patterns. It has to do with the tides and waves. His speciality in the 1960s was relevant to the British government's research on the North Sea, an area they were very interested in at that time because of the oil.

Oe: But reading your novel *An Artist of the Floating World*, I was struck by the excellent descriptions of life in Japan, of Japanese buildings and landscapes. I would like to ask where you acquired this basic knowledge about your Japanese landscapes and characters, and to what extent they were a product of your imagination.

Ishiguro: Well, I think the Japan that exists in that book is very much my own personal, imaginary Japan. This may have a lot to do with my personal history. When my family moved from Nagasaki to England, it was originally intended to be only a temporary stay, perhaps one year or maybe two years. And so as a small child, I was taken away from people I knew, like my grandparents and my friends. And I was led to expect that I would return to Japan. But the family kept extending the stay. All the way through my childhood, I couldn't forget Japan, because I had to prepare myself for returning to it.

So I grew up with a very strong image in my head of this other country, a very important other country to which I had a strong emotional tie. My parents tried to continue some sort of education for me that would prepare me for returning to Japan. So I received various books and magazines, these sort of things. Of course, I didn't know Japan, because I didn't come here. But in England I was all the time building up this picture in my head, an imaginary Japan, if you like.

And I think when I reached the age of perhaps twenty-three or twenty-four I realized that this Japan, which was very precious to me, actually existed only in my own imagination, partly because the real Japan had changed greatly between 1960 and later on. I realized that it was a place of my own childhood, and I could never return to this particular Japan. And so I think one of the real reasons why I turned to writing novels was because I wished to recreate this Japan—put together all these memories, and all these imaginary ideas I had about this landscape which I called Japan. I wanted to make it safe, preserve it in a book, before it faded away from my memory altogether. So when I wrote, say, *The Artist of the Floating World*, I wasn't terribly interested in researching history books. I very much wanted to put down onto paper this particular idea of Japan that I had in my own mind, and in a way I didn't really care if my fictional world didn't correspond to a historical reality. I very much feel that as a writer of fiction that is what I'm supposed to do—I'm supposed to invent my own world, rather than copying things down from the surface of reality.

Oe: That seems to be a very concrete illustration of the way a writer's imagination takes shape. In my book *The Silent Cry*, I wrote about Shikoku. I was born and grew up in a mountain village on that island. When I was eighteen, I went to the University of Tokyo to study French literature. As a result, I found myself completely cut off from my village, both culturally and geographically. Around that time my grandmother died, and my mother was getting older. The legends and traditions and folklore of my village were being lost. Meanwhile, here I was in Tokyo, imagining and trying to remember those things. The act of trying to remember and the act of creating began to overlap. And that is the reason why I began to write novels. I tried to write them using the methods of French literature that I had studied. Reading your novels, and thinking about the history of English literature, I get the strong impression that, in terms of method, you are a novelist at the very forefront of English literary history.

I was interested in the way that *An Artist of the Floating World* begins with a description of a large building, and how we enter the world of the novel through that building. In the same way, *The Remains of the Day* begins with a description of a large mansion. As a way to enter the novel, it overlaps to a great extent with the earlier book. It was easy for me to see how the two books—*An Artist of the Floating World* and *The Remains of the Day*—are connected, and how one develops the other. Reading the two books together and observing this overlapping, I thought to myself that here was certainly a great novelist.

Ishiguro: That's very flattering. I'm very interested to hear some of the background about your being cut off from your past in Shikoku. Are you saying that the urge to remember or stay in touch with your past was actually crucial in making you become a writer?

Oe: I have a book that is just coming out in French translation from Gallimard: *M/T et l'histoire des merveilles de la forêt*. The "M" is for matriarch and the "T" is for trickster. A while ago I wrote a book called *Contemporary Games*, about the myths of the village and the universe of the village. As I wrote *M/T et l'histoire,* I listened once more to my grandmother talking about cosmology, and wrote it down just as it was, in her own words. In fact, the history of my village is already lost. Almost everyone has forgotten it. For example, there is a place where dozens of people were killed in a riot, but no one remembers that. My family, and especially my grandmother, remembered those things very well, and told me about them. Until I was fourteen, I grew up in the village, listening to these stories. Then I moved to the city and was completely cut off, while they were all dying. So now the only person who remembers the central part of the myths of that village is me. This is what I want to write about now. I want to write a book that will sum up, or finish, all of my work up to now. These things will be the main theme of the book, and right now they are what is most important to me.

Ishiguro: I hope the English translation will be appearing very shortly. I look forward very much to reading that. Reading *The Silent Cry*, and I think it is an extraordinary work, one of the reasons why I think it's such a special work is that it's often difficult for a writer to get a certain distance from very personal events in his life that have touched and disturbed him. This book seems to be that kind of book, but at the same time you somehow seem to have kept control, to have maintained an artistic discipline, so that it actually becomes a work of art that has meaning for everybody. It's not simply about Mr. Oe. It strikes me that one of the ways in which you managed that is a certain kind of humor, a unique tone. It's very different from the kind of humor found in most of Western literature, which is mainly based on jokes. Everything has this peculiar sense of humor, which is always on the verge of tragedy—a very dark humor. This is one of the ways in which you seem to have been able to keep under control events that must be very close to you. Mr. Oe the artist has always managed to keep in control of the work. But do you think this sort of humor is something unique to your own writing or have you got it from a larger Japanese tradition?

Mishima's Image of the Japanese

Oe: It's interesting that you should ask that, because one of the things I feel is unique about your work is your control over the distance from the periods and characters in your work. All of your books have a distinct tone, even though they are connected on a deeper level. So I appreciate your comments about the tone and distance in my works.

I think that the problem of humor, which you just brought up, is a very important one. This is one of the points in which I differ from Mishima Yukio. Mishima is very strongly rooted in the traditions of Japanese literature. Moreover, they are the traditions of the center—Tokyo or Kyoto—

urban traditions. I come from a more peripheral tradition, that of a very provincial corner of the island of Shikoku. It's an extremely strange place, with a long history of maltreatment—out there beyond the reach of culture. I think my humor is the humor of the people who live in that place. Mishima had a great deal of confidence in his humor, so perhaps it's accurate to say that his humor was the humor of the center, whereas my humor is the humor of the periphery.

Ishiguro: I would be quite interested to hear what you feel about Mishima. I'm often asked about Mishima in England—all the time, by journalists. They expect me to be an authority on Mishima because of my Japanese background. Mishima is very well known in England, or generally in the West, largely because of the way he died. But also my suspicion is that the image of Mishima in the West confirms certain stereotypical images of Japanese people for the West. And this is partly why I think he is much easier for Western audiences. He fits certain characteristics. Of course, committing *seppuku* is one of the cliches. He was politically very extreme. The problem is the whole image of Mishima in the West hasn't helped people there form an intelligent approach to Japanese culture and Japanese people. It has helped people perhaps to remain locked in certain prejudices and very superficial, stereotypical images of what Japanese people are like. Most people seem to regard Mishima as a typical Japanese, in some sort of way. Of course, I never quite know what to say in response to this, because I know very little about Mishima, and very little about modern Japan. But that is certainly the impression that I get—in the West he is being used to confirm some rather negative stereotypes. I wonder what you think about Mishima and the way he died, what that means for Japanese people, and what that means for a distinguished author such as yourself.

Oe: The observations you just made about the reception of Mishima in Europe are accurate. Mishima's entire life, certainly including his death by *seppuku,* was a kind of performance designed to present the image of an archetypal Japanese. Moreover, this image was not the kind that arises spontaneously from a Japanese mentality. It was the superficial image of a Japanese as seen from a European point of view, a fantasy. Mishima acted out that image just as it was. He created himself exactly in accordance with it. That was the way he lived, and that was the way he died. Professor Edward Said uses the word *orientalism* to refer to the impression held by Europeans of the Orient. He insists that orientalism is a view held by Europeans, and has nothing to do with the people who actually live in the

Orient. But Mishima thought the opposite. He said that your image of the Japanese is me. I think he wanted to show something by living and dying in exact accordance with the image. That was the kind of man he was and why he gained literary glory in Europe and the world.

But what in fact happened is that Mishima presented a false image. As a result, the conception of Japanese people held by most Europeans has Mishima at the one pole and people like Akio Morita, chairman of Sony, at the other pole. In my opinion, both poles are mistaken. But if this is the case, where can we look for a more accurate image of the Japanese people? Going back to your book *An Artist of the Floating World*, at the very end there is a scene with a number of young Japanese, and the artist, who is looking at them in a warmhearted way. I think that people like those young Japanese really do live in Japan, and that they are the ones who have brought prosperity to the Japanese economy. Of course, Mishima had nothing to say about them. And writers like me, who take a negative view of Japan, have not captured them either. So I think that your novel exerted a good influence on perceptions of Japan in Europe, a kind of antidote to the image of Mishima.

Method of the "Homeless Writer"

Oe: I have a question I wanted to ask. Reading your work and talking to you, one does not at all get the impression of someone born in Japan. In the case of Conrad, one of my favorite authors—to me, he is a kind of ideal novelist—one gets the strong impression that he is a genuinely English author, as well as a true European. On the day when you received the Booker Prize, there were reports in the Japanese mass media of your remarks on Salman Rushdie.[1] There were many people who were moved by those remarks, including myself. We felt that this person was a genuinely European novelist, a genuinely European personality, that this was real European intelligence.

The Japanese themselves want to be perceived as peaceful and gentle, like Japanese art—landscape paintings and so on. They don't want to be seen as economic imperialists or military invaders. They would like others to think of flower paintings, something quiet and beautiful, when they think of Japan. When your books first began to appear in Japan, that was

---

1. In his acceptance speech of the Booker Prize, Ishiguro said: "It would be improper for us not to remember Salman Rushdie this evening and think about the alarming situation and plight in which he finds himself."

how they were introduced. You were described as a very quiet and peaceful author, and, therefore, a very Japanese author. But from the first, I doubted that. I felt that this was an author with a tough intelligence. Your style always involves a double structure, with two or more intertwined elements. And in fact, that has been demonstrated again with each of your books. I also felt that this kind of strength was not very Japanese, that this person was, rather, from England.

Ishiguro: Well, I don't try to be a quiet writer. That's really a question of technique more than anything else. There's a surface quietness to my books— there aren't a lot of people getting murdered or anything like that. But for me, they're not quiet books, because they're books that deal with things that disturb me the most and questions that worry me the most. They're anything but quiet to me.

On the question of being a European writer, I think that partly this has been the effect of my not knowing Japan very well. I was forced to write in a more international way. If I had continuously returned to this country after I left it in 1960 and was more familiar with Japan all the way through my growing up, I think perhaps I would have felt a greater responsibility to represent Japanese people in this way or that way, to be a kind of spokesman, if you like, of Japan in England. But as things worked out, I didn't return. This is my first return to this country in thirty years. I was very aware that I had very little knowledge of modern Japan. But still I was writing books set in Japan, or supposedly set in Japan. My very lack of authority and lack of knowledge about Japan, I think, forced me into a position of using my imagination, and also of thinking of myself as a kind of homeless writer. I had no obvious social role, because I wasn't a very English Englishman, and I wasn't a very Japanese Japanese either.

And so I had no clear role, no society or country to speak for or write about. Nobody's history seemed to be my history. And I think this did push me necessarily into trying to write in an international way. What I started to do was to use history. I would search through history books in the way that a film director might search for locations for a script he has already written. I would look for moments in history that would best serve my purposes, or what I wanted to write about. I was conscious that I wasn't so interested in the history per se, that I was using British history or Japanese history to illustrate something that was preoccupying me. I think this made me a kind of writer that didn't actually belong. I didn't have a strong emotional tie with either Japanese history or British history, so I could just use it to serve my own personal purposes.

The Problem of Audience

Ishiguro: I wonder, Mr. Oe, do you feel responsible for how Japanese people are perceived abroad? When you are writing your books, are you conscious of an international audience, and what this will do to Western peoples' perceptions of Japan? Or do you not think about things like that?

Oe: I was interviewed once by a German television station. The interviewer had translated one of my books into German. He asked me whether it was very important to me to be translated into German. I said no, and a deathly silence fell over the studio. The reason why I said no is simply that I write my books for Japanese readers, rather than for foreign. Moreover, the Japanese readers I have in mind are a limited group. The people I wrote for are people of my own generation, people who have had the same experiences as myself. So when I go abroad, or am translated abroad or criticized abroad, I feel rather indifferent about it. The responsibilities I feel are to Japanese readers, people who are living together with me in the midst of this environment.

Speaking as a reader, foreign literature is very important to me. William Blake is important to me. I've written one book based on Blake, and one based on Malcolm Lowry. Another book was about a Dante specialist who lives out in the country. With respect to Dante, I have been influenced in various ways by scholars from your country. So in that sense I have been much influenced by foreign literature. I read your books in English, for example. Still, I think that when I write my books, I write them for Japanese readers. I feel a certain sense of responsibility that I just can't break out of, even though I feel that there is probably something mistaken about that attitude. Naturally, I believe that a real novelist is international, like yourself. In your case, of course, I think that in addition to being international you are also very English. In *The Remains of the Day* you discovered viewpoints from which it is possible to describe both English people and Americans well. The viewpoint is completely different from that of a Japanese person or a Chinese person. From a certain viewpoint, it is possible to see an English person well, and also an American person. And that viewpoint has produced your style. I think that this sort of author is genuinely European, international in an essential way. So it might be that I am a more Japanese author than Mishima. I hope, myself, that younger Japanese authors will be able to discover a more international standpoint or outlook.

Ishiguro: There never seems to be a clear relationship between the audience an author thinks he is addressing and the audience that, in fact, the author does come to address. Many of the great classical writers, whether the ancient Greeks or whoever, had no idea they would eventually address people from cultures very, very different to themselves. Possibly Plato was writing simply for the people who were living in Athens at the time, but of course we read him many, many years later, in very different cultures. I sometimes worry that writers, being conscious of addressing an international audience, could actually have quite a reverse effect, that something very important in literature might actually die because people water down their artistic instincts. It's almost like a mass-marketing exercise.

Particularly because this is a time when American culture, or what you might call Anglo-American culture, is pervasive all around the world—in Asia, Latin America, and so forth—it seems to be growing and growing. Perhaps it is very important that writers don't worry at all about this question of audience. You, yourself, Mr. Oe, may think you are only writing for your own generation, for Japanese. But your books are read by lots of people outside that group. People want to translate your work. It seems that as the years go by, your reputation grows, and in different parts of the world. This shows that someone can be addressing a small group of people, but if that work is powerful and sincere, it has a universal, international audience.

On the other hand, I know that there are many writers who are consciously trying to write the novel that is all ready for translation. And of course nobody particularly wants to read these things, because they have lost some sort of initial strength that comes from the intensity of addressing a small group. Perhaps whether a writer is international or not is something that the writer cannot control. It's almost accidental. But often, I think, the deeper the work, and the deeper the truth of the work, the more likely it is to be international, whether the author is consciously addressing a small group of people or a large number of people. Do you think younger writers in Japan are worried about this question of how international they are?

The Meaning of "International Author"

Oe: In last evening's edition of the *Asahi Shimbun*, there was an article about how a translation of a work by the novelist Murakami Haruki is being read widely in New York. The article quoted a review in the *New York Times* to the effect that it was now possible to imagine a literature of the Pacific Rim.

For the past week I have been thinking about just what sort of novelist you are. My conclusion is that, rather than being an English author or a European author, you are an author who writes in English. In terms of furnishing the materials for literature, there is a tremendous power in the English language. Somehow it seems that the initiative in world literature has been with English, especially in the field of the novel. As long as he has the English language, an author can leave England and still remain a great writer. Lawrence was that way, and Laurence Durrell, also E. M. Forster. I felt that by thinking of you in this way, as a writer of English, I had got hold of something essential. By way of comparison, Murakami Haruki writes in Japanese, but his writing is not really Japanese. If you translate it into American English, it can be read very naturally in New York. I suspect that this sort of style is not really Japanese literature, nor is it really English literature. But as a matter of fact, a young Japanese author is being read widely in the United States, and I think that this is a good sign for the future of Japanese culture. A young Japanese writer has achieved something that I was never able to achieve, nor Mishima, nor Abe Kobo.

Ishiguro: I think I, too, share these same worries. I attended a lecture by the European intellectual George Steiner, who is at Cambridge and very well known in Britain. I think you are familiar with many of his ideas. One of his constant worries is about all the cultures of the world disappearing because they are swallowed up by this ever-growing, large blanket called Anglo-American culture. He is very disturbed by the fact that scientific papers in China, and certainly here in Japan, are often written originally in English, because they have to be presented at conferences where only English is understood—that in the communist countries the young people listen to the latest Western rock music. He is very afraid of a certain kind of death of culture, because this bland, colorless, huge blanket called Anglo-Americanism is spreading around the world. In order to survive, people have to sacrifice many things that make their culture unique and, in fact, make their art and culture mean something, and, instead, contribute to this meaningless blanket, this strange thing that is conquering the world.

   I think that is quite an important thing to be concerned about. Certainly my generation of writers in Britain have perhaps not worried about that kind of thing enough. We have perhaps been concerned about the opposite problem, of not being international enough. I think this is certainly a problem that we have to think about. I think it will be very strange if we all contribute to the same sort of culture, if we're all addressing the same sort of audience. We could all end up like international television. A lot of television programs are now rather superficial, but they're international. It would be sad if literature and serious art were to go the same way—to the lowest common denominator, in order to appear international.

There is a sense among younger writers in England that England is not an important enough country anymore. The older generation of writers assumed that Britain was a very important country, and so if you wrote about Britain and British problems, it would automatically be of global significance. The younger generation of writers in England are very aware of the fact that this is no longer true, that England is now rather like a little, provincial town in the world. Some younger British writers have a kind of inferiority complex, that is, they have to consciously make an effort to address international themes, because if they simply write about life in Britain, nobody is going to be interested. Perhaps that feeling doesn't exist in the United States or Japan, in that there is a strong sense that these two societies are now somehow at the center of the world, and the twenty-first century is going to be somehow dominated by these two powers. But certainly, living in England, I feel that same pressure, that I have to be international. Otherwise, I'm going to end up in the same position as Danish or Swedish writers, of being very peripheral, because a lot of the great questions of today are passing Britain by. In a way, I think young Japanese authors don't need to feel that sort of inferiority, just because of the way history is moving.

The Role of Peripheral Literature

Oe: Of course, I have nothing against the fact that Japan is becoming rich because of radios and automobiles. I don't own an automobile, but I do have a radio. But I do think that the state of the economy and the state of literature are unrelated. Instead, I think Japanese authors should clearly realize that Japanese literature is very peripheral. When a peripheral literature attempts to become a central literature, one of the things that happen is that it tries to become exotic. I think Mishima tried to create a literature of the exotic. But I believe that attempt was mistaken. Paradoxically, it may be possible for Japanese writers to play a certain role in world literature if they express Japanese concerns in a literature of the periphery.

   I am familiar with George Steiner. He seems to be very fond of the idea that things are dying—first it was tragedy, and now it is culture. I think that the image of Anglo-American culture as a huge blanket spreading across the world is one of his best. I can't really agree with what you said about England being a peripheral nation in terms of the world economy and international relations. I believe that in terms of culture, England still occupies a very important place in the world, and will continue to do so in the future. Looking forward to the twenty-first century, it doesn't seem to me that

Japan will become a cultural center just because of its economic strength. I don't believe that American cultural spokesmen will have a very great deal of power, or that Soviet cultural spokesmen will be very powerful. I think that in the twenty-first century, statements by isolated writers and scholars from small countries that appear to be in the periphery will play a very important role in world culture. One example is the novelist Italo Calvino, who recently died a tragic death. He was scheduled to deliver the Mellon Lectures at Harvard University and was working on the manuscript for those lectures until he died on the day before he was to leave for the United States. The manuscript has been translated into English as *Six Memoirs for the Next Millennium*. Reading it, I think that this work by a novelist from Italy, a country that is economically and politically on the periphery, contains things that will be of central importance in the next century. Another example is the Czech novelist Milan Kundera, now living in exile in France. But reading, for example, the Israel Address, which is found at the end of his book, *The Art of the Novel*, I think we will find the most central expression of how a writer will have to live and act today. So I think what writers from Japan must learn is that they need to think about how they can contribute to world culture as representatives of a small, but cultured, nation in Asia. Moreover, they should do so without the help of businessmen or politicians. Simply as writers, they will have to open up, on their own, a road to England, or a road to France.

Front Lines of Today's Intellectual Battles

Ishiguro: I would like to add to my earlier remarks. It wasn't simply because Britain was declining as an economic power that I was suggesting writers in Britain had a sense they were peripheral. I don't think it is really so much in connection with economic power. In fact, I think, it is in some ways quite the reverse.

Writers from Britain and, to a certain extent, writers from Germany and France—and I myself have had this experience—go to an international writers' conference and somehow feel inferior, compared to writers who come from places like Africa, or Eastern Europe, or Latin America, in the sense that in many of the great intellectual battles between liberty and authoritarian regimes, or between communism and capitalism, or between the Third World and the Industrialized World, the front line somehow seems to be in these countries, and there seems to be a more clearly defined role for writers like Kundera or some of the African writers. Writers from all the Eastern European countries always seem to have some sort of clear political role to play. This may well be a mistaken assumption, but it's an easy assumption that comes over a lot of us who come from the more safe countries, if you like, the safe, prosperous countries like Britain, or West Germany, or France, although the situation has suddenly changed for the West Germans.

Somehow, in terms of the really important things happening in the century, in historical terms, if we are writing from a position like Britain, or Sweden, or France in the latter part of the twentieth century, we are writing from somewhere very far away from where the main events are taking place, and we somehow lack the natural authority of writers who are living in Czechoslovakia, or East Germany, or Africa, or India, or Israel, or the Arab countries. And I think this is the reason for this inferiority complex, rather than simply that Britain is not quite as important an economic power as it used to be. Of course, it is still a very powerful economic force. But just in terms of the great intellectual debates that seem to be central to the latter part of the twentieth century, there is the feeling that perhaps we in England are in the wrong place to view the big battles.

Perhaps it's a good thing that British writers feel they have to travel, or that at least in their imaginations they would have to travel. So I think the younger generation of British writers, much more than the older generation, tends to write novels that are not set in Britain, or at least not set in their time. They will look back through history for a time when Britain itself was in crisis, and so the war figures quite large. Or they have to use their imaginations to create completely imaginary landscapes. This kind of thing is happening more and more, and I think it comes out of this idea that somehow England is far away from something important happening politically and socially in the world. Perhaps writers in Japan and the United States do not feel it quite so much, because there is a sense that somehow, quite aside from the economic question, Japan and America are at the forefront of something crucial that is about to happen in the world. I think that has a certain effect on how writers view their work, where they go for material to feed their imaginations.

Oe: When I myself go abroad to participate in various conferences, it is always simply as an individual writer. I think that the things I have talked about have been more or less unrelated to Japan's economic growth. My sense of Japan is that it is still a peripheral country, and that in spite of its economic power, it is still not living up to its international role, particularly in Asia. Thinking back, I think I may share some of the responsibility for this state of affairs, so I talk about that and the sort of things that a writer, as a writer, might be able to do to compensate.

For some reason, Japanese writers tend to stay away from international writers' conferences. Up to now, at least, there have not been many authors who have gone to speak out about Japan's place in the world, about the contradictions felt by Japanese writers in the midst of economic prosperity, about the things which trouble them deeply. So, for my part, I am trying to do that, little by little. Japan has many very capable businessmen and politicians, but as a novelist, I want to speak out internationally about things that they never mention. And I think it is meaningful for writers from abroad, especially young writers like yourself, to come to Japan to look closely at this country and to meet Japanese intellectuals. I hope this will lead to a deeper understanding of things such as the difficult role played by Japanese intellectuals amid material prosperity, and to cultural encounters at a genuinely substantial level. So in that sense, welcome to Japan!

Ishiguro: Thank you very much. It was an interesting conversation.

Soseki and Western Modernism

Fredric R. Jameson

Analyzing translations—even in the era of the misreading (strong or otherwise)—can lead one into the comical situation in which it is the translator (in this case, V. H. Viglielmo) whom one is, in reality, comparing to Henry James, all the while imagining oneself to be thinking about Soseki. What has disappeared is not merely the resistance of the original language (its untranslatable sentence structure, or, the other way around, what it cannot, as one individual language among others, structurally do) but, above all, its historicity. Adorno is not the only one to have thought that the most immediate experience of history afforded by a literary work lies in the very texture of its language. But translations do not yield that sense of the passage of time any Japanese reader must feel on confronting a text written in 1916. Yet, whatever has become outmoded in Soseki's last, unfinished novel, *Meian*,[1] is an index of its historical situation fully as much as those

1. Natsume Soseki, *Meian* (Light and darkness), trans. V. H. Viglielmo (London: Peter Owen, 1971); hereafter cited in my text by page number only. Besides the extensive and valuable translator's introduction to this volume, I have consulted Kathryn Sparling, "*Meian*: Another Reading," *Harvard Journal of Asiatic Studies* 42 (June 1982): 139–

stylistic and linguistic things it was able to do that, for whatever reason, later users of the language could no longer achieve. Finally, however, the ridicule to which a critic of translations exposes himself is the milder one—more humdrum, and the least interesting of all—of simple gestural and contextual miscomprehension, about which native speakers shrug their shoulders, not even offended: that stars mean it's time for Christmas shopping (seasonal marker), that raising your hand in the classroom means you need to go to the bathroom (cultural code). Instead, the alien critic invents a whole cosmology for the former and reads a fundamental gesture of resistance and subversion into the classroom interruption. These often uninteresting discrepancies, however, are the obverse of a phenomenon in which literary critics have long been passionately interested, namely irony: the non-native speaker in the situation of translation seems the outside—unfamiliar—which inside familiarity utterly domesticates; modern irony, however, seems to involve the inverse situation: one of inner comfort and familiarity with which, on the inside, each is deeply comfortable; the self as the old clothes we wear around the home—which, however, looks different and unfamiliar, somehow shocking, from the outside. Soseki's novel is about the structure of the ironic situation, and about it in its very novelistic form. Meanwhile, the whole cultural period to which this novel somehow corresponds—that of high modernism, which in the Far East seems peculiarly to coincide with the period of realism (and this belatedly, according to Western chronology), rather than to follow and to replace and discredit it—is itself equally deeply obsessed with irony as such, in which modernism thinks it glimpses a metaphysic and a philosophical and moral value, fully as much as this or that mere technique. Perhaps, therefore, mistakes that call for irony are less misplaced in a study of this particular novel than in texts from other corners of time and space.

Meanwhile, the very hermeneutic of this particular narrative—the concealment of Tsuda's complaint—evidently a venereal disease of some sort, if not hemorrhoids, and the euphemistic evocation of Kobayashi's adherence to the socialist movement—these reticences, and the complicity they demand from the reader, are something like the inscription, in reverse, of the kind of contextual blindness here anticipated.

76; and Masao Miyoshi's chapter on Soseki in his *Accomplices of Silence: The Modern Japanese Novel* (Berkeley: University of California Press, 1974). In addition, I have been privileged to hear Oe Kenzaburo's interpretation of this unfinished text and have profited from the perceptive reactions and helpful advice of Ted Fowler.

The idea of familiarity, however—from Baudelaire on, one of the great obsessive themes of the modern, generally—reminds us that translation tends to block out what makes up the most confusing and vivid feature of our experience of Otherness, namely, the unfamiliar itself—what is seemingly uninterpretable and doesn't compute, what seems to mark deep characterological and cultural difference. Most often, a little "familiarity" dissipates the illusion of difference and shows that the strangest locutions (or the simple-minded designations of the various pidgins) are perfectly ordinary thoughts and expressions that are familiar on the inside to any native speaker and need to be replaced by something equally familiar for the foreigner, as well. Not people but situations are radically different; on the other hand, nothing mars a translation more than the attempt to render an idiom idiomatically. But even that is an impossible situation, since the avoidance of the idiomatic causes an impassivity to rise upon the textual surface that is deeply neoclassical and becomes a textual connotation and a stylistic ideology (the absence of style is a style in its own right) that may be culturally and historically utterly inappropriate.

But the absence of difference then generates yet another kind of comedy, as the reader tries desperately to decide what this unknown but non-alien (qua translated) object is basically like: It is a psychological comedy, and you tend to laugh at the people who are unprepared for new experiences but must first assimilate them somehow to what is already known and long since inventoried and cataloged. Still, Proust himself described at great length this anxiety of the New, which we seek to assuage with comparisons until enough time has passed for a certain new familiarity to take its place among our habits, at which point Soseki's once unfamiliar name becomes a word for an independent object, a thing in its own right, a style or work that no longer has to be like anything.

It may still, of course, be "related," but I must confess that I have always found Wittgenstein's overused concept of the family likeness oddly feeble and lacking in explanatory power, although it is refreshing to be able, henceforth, to forget about that even older chestnut, "influence." Is Soseki's resemblance to the generation of Henry James and the ironists who followed him a genuine historical problem, and one that ought to summon forth a whole multidisciplinary research effort in order to avoid trivializing notions of influence, on the one hand, and metaphysical or cosmological notions of translational generational rhythms, on the other? Is modernization a useful clue, insofar as it designates a feature, a very dramatic feature indeed, that is common to the social situations of the writers on both sides of that particular globe-in-history? What seems certain to me is that the traits of similarity, the shared components, of these distant works are put together differently in each case, thereby facilitating identification, since we are no longer tempted to confuse the parts of the structure with the empirical qualities of the individual work.

Meanwhile, the nascent abstraction of both movements, of *Meian* fully as much as the works of the European ironists, seems to have left its trace in the critical methods that themselves emerged in the moment of nascent modernism and, in particular, in a focus on the form-problem, which can also be compared to the phenomenological bracketing or suspension of content. In a situation, in other words, in which the achievement or construction of form is the paramount interest of the critic and can eventually be marshaled in support of primary historical theses (as in the work of Lukács, most dramatically, but not exclusively, in *Theory of the Novel*)— in such a situation, content tends to be degraded to the status of a mere pretext for the achievement of the form; and I will not proceed otherwise here. I say so because the echoes I have retained from the Japanese critical debates on *Meian* turn essentially on what I consider to be matters of content, namely Tsuda's spiritual state, his putative regeneration, and the like, the whole (unfinished) novel coming to seem a psychodrama of archetypal proportions, about which it might be more accurate to say that it is the illusion or appearance of interpretable meaning thrown off by some initial psychological content.

Perhaps, indeed, the temptations of such moralizing and archetypal readings are generated by the very simplicity of the plot itself, which relates a series of interviews and conversations from the life of a man who has just undergone a minor surgical intervention and goes to recuperate in the countryside. His problems with his wife O-Nobu, with his sister, and with other more wealthy or distinctly less well-to-do acquaintances are conveyed in some detail by way of this occasion or narrative pretext: Its slightness causes the more detached observer to return to the character of Tsuda himself, with a view toward determining whether it holds some clue to the reason for showing us these interactions in the first place. Yet in the process of reading the novel line by line, larger questions of that kind tend to be eclipsed by a fascination with the sheer narrative present.

At any rate, my own experience of the novel had little in common with the kinds of interpretations just mentioned, as though the absence of significance, or the need to discover it or reinvent it, did not have much urgency. My reading is probably also an interpretation, essentially a utopian one, but one that can be characterized as having to do with a formal experience of great purity (in the sense of specialization rather than moral qualities), of a registration of interpersonal relations of extraordinary exactitude, implying a narrative machinery of a unique kind, theorized long after the fact in discussions such as Nathalie Sarraute's about the *subconversation,* [2] and suggesting literary parallels that are at best anachronistic and at worst culturally and generically inappropriate. I think, for instance, of the plays of Racine, but only in the sense in which it can be affirmed, say, that of the fifteen hundred alexandrines of *Andromaque,* his first major tragedy, no more than a handful serve uniquely to convey information; every one of the rest can be shown to be overdetermined in such a way that whatever else the verse is meant to say, it also functions as an instrument in the mouth of the speaker designed to work the conversation partner over (most scenes involve no more than two actors, in an intense exchange whose deeper truth, if not its outer form, is stichomythic), whether to touch, to humiliate, to manipulate, to revile, or to fawn or grovel. The theatrical medium and the aesthetic of the unities become the vehicles as well as the cause, along with the condition of possibility, for a bravura organization in which the right speaker erupts on the stage at the right time, so that a plausible accident (which advances the plot) always motivates the copresence of the next and most appropriate partners. (The stage directions of another play, which house all these meetings in an anteroom, beyond the living space and the chambers of state alike, seem in a deeper sense to mark them all, lifting up the stage into a place beyond the world, in which purely interpersonal interaction at its most intense can alone happen.) The comings and goings of Soseki's characters sometimes strike one like that (most take place in that space beyond the world that is Tsuda's peculiar upper-story "hospital room"); and their specific motivations (to tell so-and-so not to come today, the dispatching of endless messengers and telephone calls, the nonetheless unlikely and undesirable coincidence of two visits, etc.) are all as elegantly drawn back into the movement of the interpersonal dialogue as the analogous plot machinery in Racine. What is different, above and beyond the secular impurity of the bourgeois urban drama, is the obligatory presence of the object world in the novel; it can be removed from drama, as triumphantly in Racine himself, while elsewhere in the history of theater a too-insistent object turns back heavily into a symbol, as in Ibsen's duck or gun. In the

---

2. See my *Fables of Aggression: Wyndham Lewis, the Modernist as Fascist* (Berkeley: University of California Press, 1979), 50–61.

novel, however, it is the absence of the object-world that attracts attention (as in the aesthetics of Woolf or Gide, which aimed at reducing external description to a minimum and, thereby, at once seemed mannered): The form itself leaves residual traces:

> He went out into the road, and slowly walked away from the Yoshi-kawa home. But this did not mean that his mind could withdraw as rapidly as his body from the parlour where he had just been. As he made his way through the relatively deserted evening streets, he could still clearly see the bright interior of the room.
>
> The coldly gleaming texture of the cloisonné vase, the colours of the brilliant pattern flowing on its smooth surface, the round, silver-plated tray which had been brought to the table, the cube sugar and cream containers of the same colour, the heavy curtains of bluish-black fabric with a brown arabesque design, the ornamental album with three of its corners set in gold leaf—these vivid images passed in a disorderly manner before his mind's eye even after he had gone out from under the bright light and was walking in the dark out-side. (20)

Perhaps this cushioning layer of objects and residual furnishings explains the incomparable distance between the violence of Racine (aris-tocratic elegance is at one with such violence in its very origins, whereas bourgeois elegance has virtually the inverse function of repressing it) and the chamber music of Soseki, which can, to be sure, reach moments of great intensity but which seems to offer the utopian de-materialization and stylization of the outside world and whatever in it is sordid and marked by sheer need. But it does this by including passion, need, social class, and money rather than by leaving them out; by translating all those things into its own idiom—the interpersonal language exchange—just as there is some distance between a brute fact or event and the *récit* in which its occurrence is put into words. Kobayashi's lower-class shabbiness and willful psychic ugliness ("Mrs. Tsuda, I live to be disliked. I purposely say and do things people don't like" [154]) enter the round of instruments in a way in which, for example, a Dostoyevskian character of his type could not be imagined within the country houses of a Henry James novel. As for money, it is a fundamental, although curiously eccentric, datum of the plot: Tsuda's father has suspended his monthly allowance, while on top of that he needs a medi-cal absence from his job and a period of recuperation in the countryside (from whom is he to borrow money? or who can influence his father?). But in fact, money—so often, in any case, as canonically in Simmel, associated with abstraction as such—provides the pretext for the very rarefaction of narrative we have been discussing; giving the characters something to talk about, it opens the space for their interaction. Money is here in a league with interpersonality rather than with what distracts from it or tears through its delicate web of relationships. Quite unexpectedly in a sense unmentioned by Simmel in his famous essay,[3] it provides the formal ground for abstraction in the ceaseless weaving of well-nigh decorative arabesques that are composed of dialogue sentences and replies: "a lace made of rope," Cocteau described his plays (which he rather preciously termed "theatrical poetry"); perhaps something similar might be observed about these scenes of Soseki, than which nothing could be further from actual theater or from the dramatic in any conceivable generic sense. Still, as Gore Vidal once observed, dialogue is not prose, so that this novel offers us sheet upon sheet of an arrangement of writing that is not poetic at all but not subject, either, to the normal kind of story reading.

Still, a dialectic is generated by the extreme compression of this particular pole of the novel's language, so that one has the sense of endless murmured conversations, in quiet tones, linked or interrupted by the movement of the characters on peaceful trolley cars in that small town that is the Tokyo of the pre-earthquake period. The point, however, is that the urban transitions stand out and that, however muted, they designate the presence—not always perceptible as such—of a spatial dimension underpinning this extraordinarily de-materialized narrative seemingly tressed from interweaving human voices. The overemphasis on rarefied spoken language, however, calls up its dialectical opposite in the emergence of a spatial grid that links the various scenes of dialogue—houses and rooms—in a network presumably characteristic of some uniquely Japanese construction of urban space and landscape that erupts in the great concluding sequence in which we leave built space for the countryside and the inn and hot spring in which the novel presumably concludes. I will return to this remarkable and unexpected spatial experience in a moment.

But the construction of some absolute conversational element in the

---

3. The reference is to his classic "Metropolis and Mental Life," in which the nervous specificity of big city life and the urban mentality is linked to money and its abstractions. In his rather different, and more socially critical, reading of the novel, Miyoshi underscores the theme of money, particularly in relationship to Mrs. Yoshikawa (see Miyoshi, *Accomplices of Silence*, 90).

novel demands not only that it be limited by an external space of a different kind but also that it be enabled by an inner form, which would not merely "motivate the device," by providing an implicit philosophy of the subconversation, but which would also, by incorporating narrative expectations, allow these moments to function like stories.

In Soseki, indeed, we seem to surprise the simultaneous existence of the two distinct and seemingly antithetical distortions of narrative raw material observable in the West: These were, on the one hand, a postulation of enormous length and distention, and, on the other hand, a minimalism tending toward a veritable instant without duration, continuity and discontinuity, respectively, of so peremptory a type that either extreme offers the radical stylization that modernism strove for in its flight from commonsense realism and the ratification of the status quo implicit in the various literary verisimilitudes. Thus, in music, we find the enormous movements of Mahler's symphonies, which play havoc with the memory and attention span of its listeners in order to incorporate an extraordinary range of intense styles or experiences of all sorts, from vulgarity to mystical ecstasy, from heroics to pastoral experiences of nature, from Italianate emotion and recitative to the Viennese bittersweet. But here the dialectic of length and instantaneity becomes clarified, since immoderate duration tends to impede the establishment of perspectival order, the positioning of any individual part or detail within a larger whole. In other words, beyond a certain point, length ceases to be monumental and returns the listener's punctual experience to a new kind of absolute present. The aesthetics of that absolute present, then— Schoenberg's expressionism, say, where the musical work is reduced to units of one to three minutes in length—perhaps only overtly disengages the inner truth of the aesthetics of infinite duration.

Still, in the West, these two ways (which thus, like Proust's, ultimately and dialectically rejoin each other) have been felt to be aesthetically and philosophically distinct, Beckett's breaks and silences seeming to share with the eternity of Proust's three-hundred-page-long receptions and dinners only a will to do violence to normal middle-class perception (and to the reading that accompanies that). This is why any speculation about Soseki ought to include a discussion of whether in Japanese social life in this period there existed the same kinds of bourgeois stereotypes about everyday life that were constructed in the West during the realist period and which had in the modern already entered into crisis and become the object of satirical or utopian contestation. I've suggested above that the sequence of stages implied here is purely ideal (and also local) and that one could imagine a situation, in the modernizing East, in which the construction of bourgeois everyday life (the realist moment) took place simultaneously with its modern moment. Indeed, the wondrous rhythms of the daily life of Soseki's characters—what Genette called the iterative; what, in Proust, constructs the very idea of a routine and a daily life in the first place—are here seemingly at one with a virtually modernist distension of temporality, such that enormous conversations or interviews between the main characters swell to fill the entire novel. Read thus microscopically, held up close to the eyes, Soseki does not seem much shorter or swifter than Proust himself, despite the fact that *Meian* is virtually all dialogue, in contrast to that single enormous explanatory Proustian paragraph into which bits of dialogue are inserted.

But in Soseki, stylized length (the climactic central conversation lasts some fifty pages) is accompanied by a systematic fragmentation and autonomization more characteristic of the minimalists, if not of Brecht himself, who systematically broke his scenes up into complete miniature gestures, each one (a *gestus*) labeled with a title and a potential moral. The analysis of Soseki's narrative flow into small numbered sections has a similar effect on perception, combining the minute with the infinite; that such an arrangement owed something to journalism and serialization is scarcely an alternative causal explanation, since the form of the newspaper ultimately loops back into the general determinations of bourgeois culture in its own right, while such seemingly external economic necessities are always overdetermined by being drawn within the work of art and transformed into the pretexts for its new formal innovations.

But where everything is dialogue, the traditional, non-dialogical components of narrative now tend to implode and to find their equivalents within the unidimensionality of the spoken exchange itself. Whence the extraordinary drama of these seemingly placid and desultory conversations that must now stand in for the larger struggles and adventures that once seemed to characterize life itself and its epic narratives. All of the excitement and the tension of these last will now be miniaturized and retranslated into the conversational exchange itself, whose predominant inner form now comes to be the *agon*, or the life-and-death struggle or duel, between two protagonists (these change and shift throughout the novel, but the deeper sense of all conversations being one ultimate agon persists throughout the scenes). Actually, in this novel, a more familiar local reference prevails: "In a certain sense, when [O-Nobu] and Tsuda privately viewed their relationship, very similar to that between *sumo* wrestlers facing each other in the ring every day, they felt that it was of a kind where she was always his opponent and occasionally even his enemy" (80–81). It is important not to overshoot the mark here and to conclude that this antagonistic relationship characterizes only the married couple itself; in fact, it organizes all the encounters in the novel in one way or another.

Inevitably, then, the account of such conversations will come to be framed in military terms, particularly since tactical or strategic winning or losing, advancing or falling back, need not be completed by the larger picture but can be read off the present like the score in a basketball game. The military agon is thus perfectly consistent with the perpetual present of the narrative, since finally in warfare only the present counts, while a variety of moves can be subsumed under it: "O-Nobu wondered how she should behave, now that she was being treated as a child by her uncle in this way, so as to provide an easy transition from the awkward situation" (123). What counts in a moment like this is not particularly any longer-term relationship with her uncle, nor any decisive revelation of O-Nobu's own character, nothing that would cause her to make a fundamental decision or a basic characterological change or life decision; rather, it is simply whether she wins or loses, whether she cuts her losses and decently escapes, or remains subjected to overwhelming superiority on the other side.

The formal simplification of complex and often traditional situations into simple winning or losing is a narratological variant of Weber's rationalization and is surely characteristic of a capitalist or money economy as such (it is first dramatically rehearsed in Balzac). It should be clear how such a zero-sum logic can coexist for a time with the demands of more traditional social interaction (as in the familial and hierarchical situation from which the previous notation was drawn) but will end up emptying this last of any meaningful content or value.

This is not, however, a matter of personal or collective psychology: The following strategic appreciation has, for example, nothing to do with either national aggressivity or some "argumentative character" that might be attributed to O-Nobu personally: "She boldly jumped ahead. She decided to break through all the round-about talk entwined with personal considerations and to meet O-Hide directly" (241). By the same token, a rather different dramatistic assessment at a different moment in the agon does not necessarily signify passivity:

> O-Nobu shortly came to a decision. It was quite simply that to make the problem meaningful she would have to sacrifice either O-Hide or herself, for if she did neither, the discussion would never amount

to anything. It would not be difficult to sacrifice her opponent. If she only broke through somewhere at one of O-Hide's weak points, that would suffice. Whether that weak point was actual or hypothetical was not then O-Nobu's concern. By comparison with the effect she was attempting to obtain merely from O-Hide's natural reaction, the investigation of the truth or falsehood of O-Hide's weakness was an unnecessary consideration. But she still sensed a certain danger in her action. O-Hide would undoubtedly become angry. And to make her angry both was and was not O-Nobu's objective. Therefore O-Nobu was necessarily perplexed as to how to move.

Finally she roused herself to seize a certain opportunity. And as she did so she had already decided on sacrificing herself. (238–39)

What this kind of structure does tend to produce, as a new kind of form-problem for the novelist, is some sense—hitherto absent from either reality or from the reader's narrative habits—of what it would mean to "win" or to "lose" these struggles: "It was as if Mrs. Yoshikawa had already defeated Tsuda by showing him clear-cut evidence that he still was attached to Kiyoko. His attitude, equivalent to one a person might have after a confession, strengthened Mrs. Yoshikawa, as she put an end to one phase of the contest between them" (264). Despite the thematization of "egotism" here and there in the novel and among its critics, events of this type do not signal a world of characters committed to the will to power, not even, as in Proust, the ineradicable force of some deeper ultimate selfishness of the individual subject. The satisfactions of amour propre are less significant here than the opening up of some well-nigh infinite chain of future manipulations, which only intensify our ultimate question as to where they lead and what they can possibly construct or produce as the ultimate "end" of this linked series of "means." Fortunately, the absent conclusion leaves this question permanently open; surely Soseki could never himself have answered it in any satisfying way (and the plausibility of the surmises of his commentators, that the final meeting with Kiyoko would have marked some deeper regeneration in his character, strikes me as being aesthetically unsatisfactory—a sentimental way of finishing the novel off that would surely have diminished the power of the remarkable effects we are here describing).

On the other hand, the language of battle permits a larger absent form to arise from these present instants of confrontation in a way that no more realistic account of the interchange—where form and pretext would remain indistinguishable—could have conveyed. So it is that we feel the great impending curve of the agon on its downward slope: "O-Nobu realized that she was more flurried than her husband. When she forsook the argument upon realizing that if it went on in this vein he could no longer be defeated, she turned aside adroitly before betraying her own weakness" (281). Still, a glimpse like this of the movement of the agon as a whole then raises the equally embarrassing question of what it would mean to be defeated in it, where answers having to do with vanity or subordination equally risk trivializing the event itself. Formal abstraction of this kind is possible only where the content of the drama, of these human relations themselves, can be suspended and questions of ultimate ends bracketed.

Meanwhile, the form—about which we remember that it no longer exactly involves prose as such—presses language itself up against its most extreme expressive limits, as though to invent, from out of itself and from the very material of a language that can no longer say anything, new and linguistic, yet material, modes of expression. This is most notably the case with the look or glance, which here acquires a heightened power, as though indeed the eye were able by some inner intensification literally to gleam more sharply and brightly: not only O-Nobu's looks, which continue to startle her husband as though she were always up very close to him, but in the various duels and encounters of social life, looking is like saying something. Indeed, in the following episode the look is uncharacteristically felt from the inside rather than seen by its destinatee or victim: "At the moment O-Nobu gave O-Hide this one glance she sensed that O-Hide already understood her present mood. But this was after the single glance had suddenly flashed from the deep spring of her artifice, which she could in no way control. Since she did not have the power to check this small act, which by chance had sprung from some unfathomable area of her being, she could do nothing but tamely await its effect" (233). We cannot accept the idea that looks are physiological events (if only because that would commit us to participate in a certain kind of scientistic-materialist ideology); rather, they must be seen as narrative constructs, the empty place of an exchange, from which words, sentences, and the very acts of language are constitutively lacking. The look then becomes a kind of narrative space that the novelist can cover with sheets of decoration of a functional kind, the most extreme example of which must surely remain this classical passage from Proust, which, preposterous on any literal reading, can stand as a microcosm and an emblem of at least one remarkable modernist linguistic strategy (it is a question of an acquaintance who, in Horatian fashion, denounces over and over again the city, high society, and social snobbery, but who is, in this episode, suddenly revealed to be a snob himself, since he is unwilling to introduce Marcel's bourgeois family to the aristocratic lady he happens to be accompanying):

> Near the church we met Legrandin coming towards us with the same lady, whom he was escorting to her carriage. He brushed past us, and did not interrupt what he was saying to her, but gave us, out of the corner of his blue eye, a little sign which began and ended, so to speak, inside his eyelids and which, as it did not involve the least movement of his facial muscles, managed to pass quite unperceived by the lady; but, striving to compensate by the intensity of his feelings for the somewhat restricted field in which they had to find expression, he made that blue chink which was set apart for us sparkle with all the zest of an affability that went far beyond mere playfulness, almost touched the border-line of roguery; he subtilised the refinements of good-fellowship into a wink of connivance, a hint, hidden meaning, a secret understanding, all the mysteries of complicity, and finally elevated his assurances of friendship to the level of protestations of affection, even of a declaration of love, lighting up for us alone, with a secret and languid flame invisible to the chatelaine, an enamoured pupil in a countenance of ice.[4]

Whatever the inner elasticity and limits of what we have been calling the agon-model, however, it is important to note that Soseki disposes of other, more melodramatic inner forms with which to preserve the tension of his dialogues: The most obvious is that of the mystery, the withholding, the expectation of the secret or the revelation (which Barthes called the "hermeneutic code" in *S/Z*). To begin with, he has himself withheld the matter of Tsuda's earlier lover, Kiyoko, so that allusions to this earlier secret (by Kobayashi and Mrs. Yoshikawa) remain suitably dark and mysterious. This also means that the agon between interlocutors can take the additional form of a struggle for the secret, the avowal, the mystery, the denunciation, or the confession, as though the plot of the mystery story had been interiorized, and attention to its larger movements now adapted to the parrying of observation and response in a miniature reproduction of its form within the limits of the verbal interchange.

Finally, one must note the emergence of a kind of rationalization

---

4. Marcel Proust, *The Guermantes Way*, trans. C. K. Scott-Moncrieff, in *Remembrance of Things Past*, vol. II (New York: Vintage, 1983), 136–37.

of the form, which comes closer to something like a philosophy of human relations (or of language itself). At these moments, conversation—while remaining agonistic—no longer seems driven by the will to win a struggle, but rather by the need to express and to verbalize: "Both O-Hide and Tsuda were primarily bothered by how best to solve the practical problem, and yet neither had the courage to probe verbally to the depth of the matter" (176). Something even more fundamental than the intimacy and hostility between brother and sister seems at stake in a verbal grappling of this kind: "And yet they were both already inextricably involved with each other. They could not really be satisfied unless they extracted, by means of conversation, a certain something from the other's heart" (183). This is not, I think, the Hegelian struggle for recognition, which on the German philosopher's view marks the very nature of interpersonality ("each consciousness desires the death of the other one"). Rather, in Soseki's world, some larger network of forces[5] seems to hold these individual subjects in its grasp and to determine convulsive efforts by each of them that are not individually desired:

> The three had fallen into a strange predicament. Since by force of circumstances they were linked together in a special relationship, it had become increasingly difficult for them to change the subject of the conversation; and of course they could not leave. Thus, while remaining where they were, they had to resolve their problem one way or another.
>
> And yet, seen objectively, it certainly was not an important one. In the eyes of anyone able to view their situation from a distance dispassionately, it could not but appear insignificant. They knew this very well without needing to have it brought to their attention. They were, however, forced to quarrel. Some controlling power extended its hand from an unfathomable, remote past, and manipulated them at will. (197)

Indeed, a final remark of the novelist would seem to project all this out into the metaphysical itself:

5. In a different kind of overtone or afterimage, this sense of a larger determination can also take a more personal form: "But O-Nobu was even more greatly concerned with another problem. She even went so far as to think that a plot had been hatched against her and was secretly progressing somewhere" (273). Even the mildest forms of paranoia are, however, also distorted projections of cognitive mapping and secular degradations of a religious conception of Providence.

> From the context of the situation she was forced to adhere to that one point with the force of her entire being and to the limit of her powers of thought and judgment. It was her nature to do so. Unfortunately, however, the entirety of nature, which included her own, was greater than she. Extending far above and beyond her, it did not hesitate to cast an impartial light on the young couple and even to attempt to destroy her in her pitiable state. (283)

But from the formal standpoint that is ours here, the philosophical implications of such a passage, which suggest a worldview of Soseki's own and a kind of vision of life to be rhetorically conveyed by the construction of the novel, are beyond our reach. We must say, on the one hand, that such philosophical views are of significance here only insofar as they ultimately enable the formal development we have been examining and, on the other hand, that a philosophical consideration of them in their own right would have to give place to a consideration of the period ideologies and the social context in which such a metaphysic could be entertained in the first place and which could alone suggest its ultimate personal and social functionality. In the dialectical analysis of literary form, then, such questions of philosophical content or message are either too much or too little; either they overshoot the formal mark by raising illicit questions about the meaning of life, or else they have not been sufficiently pursued to the point at which they become part of a more general social and historical inquiry into the period.

Surely this rather austere view of metaphysics is consistent with Soseki's own narrative procedures: They are, for example, utterly resistant to questions of psychology, something worth stressing in a residual situation in which conventional views of modernism still see this last as an essentially subjectivistic movement, whose innovations lay in introspection and in the discovery of deeper psychological quirks or pathologies. In fact, however, what can be witnessed in all the moderns is rather a distancing from psychology in this sense and a reification of the feelings or emotions that names them in new ways and allows us to walk around them and to contemplate them like so many objects. Surely Lawrence's canonical attack on traditional characters and on the ego itself ("it is the inhuman will . . . that fascinates me" [letter to Edward Garnett, June 5, 1914]) is also an attack on psychology and subjectivity in the name of objectifying modes of figuration. In Soseki, also, feelings stand out sharply and vividly, but only because they are so rare as to constitute virtually meteorological events:

The spectators were indeed strange, for they did not in the least complain about the long intermission during which there was nothing at all to do. Without showing a trace of their previous boredom, they were tranquilly absorbing desultory sensations in their vacant minds, and were being swept along frivolously with the passing moment. They appeared drunk from the very breath which they breathed on one another, and when they had recovered a bit from it, they would immediately turn their eyes and observe someone's face; they then would just as quickly discover therein a certain intoxicating substance. They appeared to be able to acclimatize themselves instantly to their companion's feelings. (84)

The fact that this peculiar intensity of feeling is associated with the theater and its spaces distances it still further and frames the affect, estranging it and suggesting that the very feelings that materialize so vividly against the blankness and impersonality of the narrative have some deeper constitutive relationship to the aesthetic and to representation itself.

Even irony itself can be seen as the intrusion of an outside into this seemingly sealed inside that is conversational impersonality, for irony can essentially be described as a brusque movement in which the inside becomes aware (in pride or shame, as Sartre might have said) that it has an outside in the first place. In this sense, O-Nobu's thoughts about Tsuda ("It suddenly occurred to O-Nobu that Tsuda was extremely egotistical") are as ironic as anything he might suddenly think about himself, since by way of their conversational intimacy his own "character" belongs to her as well. It is indeed as the discovery of something like a "character," an external being that other people see and that is radically distinct from that intimate consciousness that cannot be characterized in such characterological language, that irony is to be understood, as both a psychological and a social, or aesthetic, matter. The unfurling of a wave of modern irony over late nineteenth-century European culture—beginning with Flaubert and Baudelaire, and then becoming the explicit program of a host of novelists from Henry James to Gide, not to speak of the relativism of newer playwrights like Pirandello or of the point-of-view poets like Fernando Pessoa, with their multitudinous personae—is a sociological event, as well, and signals the porosity of the middle classes to their Others, whether within the nation-state, in the form of hostile subaltern classes, or outside it, in the form of the colonized. That this drama should play itself out in the limited symbolic forms of the moral or ethical, where a single sovereign consciousness is suddenly made to feel its degradation, as archetypally in Kafka's "The Judgment," is an index of the complexity of the differentiations of modern culture and society and also a warning against the literal reading of aesthetic appearance: Nowhere are hermeneutic and interpretive operations, or, indeed, dialectical modes of comprehension, more urgently demanded by the content of the cultural text itself than in these symptomatic structures (which have been deformed and canonized in the academic versions of the modernist "classics"). Here, too, then, Soseki displays a significant variant form of this trans-modern phenomenon, which we have learned mainly from Europe, but about which this remarkable non-European text can be expected to have new lessons.

I would be tempted to argue that the themes of "egotism" (sounded in the previous quote), along with those—dear to the critics—of moral degeneracy and regeneration are something like "motivations of the device": Paul de Man was using an essentially Russian-formalist logic when he argued that guilt and the content of the moral fall derive from the form of the confession, rather than the other way around (the peculiarities of the James-Lange theory of emotion also come to mind, in which the "feeling" follows on the physiological symptoms, anger deriving from bodily heat and tension, etc.). In this particular instance, however, since we do not possess the essentials of Tsuda's ironic unmasking and indictment (which the ending alone would have disclosed, although dark mutterings from Kobayashi and Mrs. Yoshikawa enforce the sense that there will eventually be such a revelation), the form is, as in a laboratory experiment, disclosed to us in a virtually pure, self-bracketed way, mapping out an immense interior space about which we can only say, from within, that it has an outside, without knowing what that outside might be. This space is intolerable, but it is also what I am here characterizing as utopian.

Before we reach that point, however, we must lay in place the final and most momentous effect of this conversational interiorization, which is the convulsive emergence, in the final section, of what I hesitate to call "nature," for fear that concept plays a different role in the equivalent Japanese ideological construction. Yet when Tsuda leaves the city, a radical shift in narrative can be observed, as well as existential experience, in which the provincial inn plays a fundamental role, not so much because of its relationship to the countryside and the peasantry, as within itself, where a virtual labyrinth is opened up. I have already commented on the distinctiveness of the urban map offered by *Meian*: a network of nodal points and characteristic inner spaces, rather than a set of relationships, or the geometry of avenues, or the profile of a city, with its staggered monuments and facades. When the content of the conversations has faded from the memory, the reader retains these spaces—the peculiar upper room in the clinic, the shabby wine shop in which Tsuda and Kobayashi discuss the lower classes, the bourgeois living quarters of more or less affluence and of the more prosperous protagonists, as well as the petty-bourgeois households of the less so: These are valuable experiences indeed, which it is not the least triumph of the novel to have conveyed, so economically, and as it were laterally and in passing, without any commitment to a heavy-handed aesthetic of description or of place.

But now, in the inn, interior space as such becomes immensely involuted, its multitudinous articulations turned within, so that Tsuda wanders up and down its split levels and uneven staircases as in a maze, not omitting at a climactic moment to see someone unfamiliar coming toward him who is, in reality, his own self in the mirror (345). But this peculiar experience, which now makes up the adventures of the narrative at some length and provides a very different kind of reading experience than the preceding dialogues (which virtually make up the rest of the novel), is perhaps itself only the exfoliation and outer skeleton, made thing-like and built into compartments and rooms and corridors, of the truth of the earlier narrative itself. Here, too, the sense of an outside, beyond which other people mysteriously and unfathomably exist, is the dominant: Voices from beyond walls or outside windows, and anxieties felt on rounding a corner or hearing a footstep, all make the experience of a labyrinthine inner house into the perpetual surmise of the existence of the Other, just beyond the partition. Yet, this is now intensified dialectically to the point of taking on a new linguistic mode from the preceding form in which the intimation of the Other was conveyed: from intersubjectivity to place, from language to things and the visual, from speech to ambulation. It is an extraordinary shift, which then breaks off before any official meaning (presumably derivable from the now vanished and eternally silenced "authorial intention") becomes clear or gives a clue.

I call what happens in this work utopian not because it is pleasant or gratifying: Indeed, the conversational element *Meian* gradually constructs—like so many of the ironies of the European modernist "point of view"—is likely to grow constricting for the reader, and even stifling, if only because an existence of unbroken subjectivities is established from which we never have any relief. To be sure, we never think much of Tsuda himself (although we may never be quite sure why not), but even the noblest subjectivity or conscious point of view would surely here at length become intolerable. Yet pure intersubjectivity—which is wrong and ideological as a philosophical "system," since it suppresses the facts of life of omnipresent alienation and reification—becomes utopian again precisely to the degree to which it does more than imagine, it symbolically constructs and projects, a world from which alienation and reification have been, however violently or by fiat, excluded. This is the approach to the human age, to a condition in which matter is transformed by human praxis, such that it can never be encountered directly, in its contingent and antihuman state: something here, to be sure, realized only ironically, as when money becomes "humanized" and "spiritualized" by passing into the conversations of people still bedeviled by it. Yet it is enough: The utopian dimension of the literary or cultural work can never be separated from its ideological existence and its complicity within a production system necessarily based on misery and blood guilt: Yet something has been gained when, for an instant, like a mirage, it can be glimpsed projected beyond that. The dimensions of the utopian achievement, however, must then be measured by replacing the text in everything it thereby had to overcome and returning this remarkable narrative music to the social material that had to be refined and transformed into sound in order to compose it.

America's Japan / Japan's Japan

H. D. Harootunian

1

Ever since the first moment Japanese and Americans encountered each other in the nineteenth century, to embark upon an often fateful course of interaction, the promise of a dialogic conversation has usually slipped out of reach. From the very beginning, the interactions, these days called a partnership, seem to have followed a course in which verbal misunderstandings merely compounded more basic misrecognitions prompted by vastly differing historical experiences and the consequent formulation of interests that invariably produced mismatched expectations. At the risk of summarizing the whole of this interactive history by appealing to a paradigmatic event that promises to play the role of a muscular metonymy, it is fair to say—in retrospect—that misunderstanding attended the first negotiations between Japan and the United States and now seems to have prefigured the subsequent history of relations. When the first American consul, Townsend Harris, arrived in Japan in August of 1858, not long after Commodore Perry had hurriedly come and left (much to the consolation of Tokugawa officials), to complete the work begun with the earlier move to open up Japan for trade and diplomacy (1854), his presence was neither expected by Japanese authorities nor, as it has become apparent, desired. Not even John Wayne, in that now long-forgotten classic movie *The Barbarian and the Geisha,* was able to convey the sense of perplexity Harris must have experienced when greeted by the puzzled Shimoda officials who had not expected the American's arrival. The confusion may have been compounded by the problem of translation, if Sam Jaffe's portrayal of Harris translator Henry Heuskins is accurate, since both his Dutch-accented English and English-accented Japanese sounded like the same unintelligible language. Be that as it may, the movie might still be viewed as a gloss on this history of misrecognition.

The reason for Harris's cool reception among shogunal officials stemmed not simply from internal political struggles plaguing the bakufu leadership but, just as importantly, from the wide margin of interpretability allowed by the language of the Treaty of Kanagawa of 1854 between the United States and Japan. Perry left Japan, after the signing of this convention, believing that one of its provisions (Article XI) gave the United States the right to send a diplomatic representative to Japan within a year and half of the signing. The Tokugawa authorities who negotiated the treaty had reassured themselves, owing to intense antiforeign opposition defending the "ancient law" of seclusion, that diplomatic representation would be made only if both governments agreed to do so. While the language of the English original called for the appointment of "consuls . . . or agents to reside in Shimoda at any time after the expiration of 18 months, provided that either of the two governments deem such arrangements necessary," the Japanese version eliminated the subject of the clause and thereby permitted a reading that assumed either one or the other or both. The following clause, "If conditions are such that it becomes an unavoidable matter," was read differently by each participant, and usually in terms of its own immediate interest. The United States seized upon it as an occasion for opening up Japan to American trade, whereas the Japanese saw in it a solution to maintaining seclusion and keeping foreigners out.[1]

It might be argued, on the basis of this inaugural misrecognition, that Japanese/American relations derived from and were set upon their course by an act of interpretation, whereby the United States jumped to occupy the "enunciative voice" to determine the meaning of a statement before the Japanese were able to press their own claim. On their part, the Japanese appeared to have been assigned to the status of second-term,

1. This episode is reported in Hugh Borton, *Japan's Modern Century,* 2d ed. (New York: The Ronald Press, 1970), 38–49.

or silent, interlocutors whose interests, hereafter, were to be represented to themselves by another. Sometimes the interaction has resembled the relationship between ventriloquist and dummy.

Despite the problems involved in loading this episode with paradigmatic force, it's hard not to see traces of it reappear in the history of relations between the two countries since the 1850s and to recognize the guiding role it has played in structuring what might be called America's Japan during the period of postwar occupation. This is not to say that contact between the two countries was marked only by traumatic episodic encounters precipitated by crises in the world system. During the 1920s and early 1930s, Japanese actually experienced what might be described, momentarily, as the time of Japan's America, when material culture, the culture of modernism, rather than diplomatic engagement or war, defined the mode of interaction. It should be noted that this Americanizing interlude was voluntarily welcomed by Japan and involved no crisis over the claims of interpretation and the establishment of meaning. While this phase of Americanization was occasioned by World War I, especially the ascendancy of the United States and American capitalism immediately after the war, and the spiritual depletion, if not physical exhaustion, of the "European Civilization", Japanese had so enthusiastically embraced in the Meiji period, it differed from the later post–World War II effort to democratize Japan under the auspices of an army of occupation. If war provided the opportunity for two distinct moments of the Americanization of Japanese society, the earlier process marked a transformation of Japanese society into a culture of capitalism, commodification, and consumption, driven by greater integration into the world system, which effectively managed to displace the politics of social democracy, while the latter was a forced march, which tried to implement the conditions for the realization of a lasting democratic order. The earlier appeal of Wilsonian democracy in Japan immediately after World War I and the promise it held for social transformation in the 1920s gave way to an enthusiasm for American material culture as a substitution, marking a consequential shift from active political participation to consumption, from the domain of politics to the space of culture. For Japanese, modernity meant speed and the spectacle of shock and sensation, and was often symbolized by film and radio, Americanization, and new subjectivities such as the ubiquitous *moga*—modern girl—and *mobo*—modern boy—found in the great metropolitan centers of Tokyo-Yokohama and Osaka-Kobe. In Japan, no less than in any other industrializing society, the heroism of production was being replaced by heroic consumption, which resulted not so much in a clash between new and established values as in a struggle of desire against values in general. More importantly, commodity culture meant consumption and the gendering of objects for consumption, even though social discourse frequently sought to efface the role of both class and gender in the general interest of trying to identify the grounds of an authentic culture as the source of national subjectivity. Ironically, the later phase of Americanization, which aimed at implanting democratic values and institutions through the policies of Occupation fiat, invariably recuperated the earlier regime of commodi- fiction and consumption as a displacement for political action. In time, war defeated Japan's America and opened the way for the Occupation's version of an America's Japan.

We are all, by now, familiar with the effort of the American Occu- pation after 1945 to install a narrative to represent Japanese aspirations that derived from an idealization of the American experience, as if it was their own. In this regard, the literary critic Kato Norihiro has reported the observation, in his *Amerika no kage*—America's shadow—(taken from an article by Douglas Ramsey), that the photograph of General Douglas Mac- Arthur standing with Emperor Hirohito, taken at their first meeting in 1945, can be read as a momento of a marriage with all of its attending associa- tions of a sexual relationship and conjugal bliss between Japan and the United States at the beginning of the Occupation. In this reading, America is seen as male, represented by big Mac, dressed casually, in an open-collar shirt, dominant, stern but benevolent; Japan, the bride, played by Hirohito (not so far off the mark since emperorship in Japan has profound historical roots in matriarchy, allegorized in the myth of the sun goddess) appears as female, small, nervous, almost shrinking before MacArthur's towering height, dressed formally in cutaway jacket, striped trousers, tipped collar; fragile, certainly compliant, yielding, and totally subservient. Moreover, this picture conforms to the description offered years later by E. O. Reischauer in his book *The Japanese,* in which he referred to the relationship between the two countries as a "skillful blending," the model of an ideal and suc- cessful bourgeois marriage.[2] For a less allegorical model, there is the movie *Sayonara,* in which Marlon Brando played male America to Yoko Tani's female Japan.

If the Occupation is seen as a bourgeois wedding between the United States and Japan, the actual intent of the coupling was to transform the bride by bringing her into the groom's household; through marriage the

2. Kato Norihiro, *Amerika no kage* (Tokyo: Kawade shobo shinsha, 1985), 24–25.

bride would be resocialized into the groom's world of middle-class values and the standards of civilized life, now read as the "free world." This narrativizing of Japan by the American Occupation became the central plot of social sciences in the 1950s and 1960s and what then came to be known as modernization theory. The struggle to preserve the values of the free world and to prevent the spread of communist revolution was inscribed in a theory of development that sought to promote a universal/rational ethos against the forces of politically deformed particularisms, peaceful transformation over revolutionary upheaval. Modernization was simply a transformation of imperialism and colonialism, which by the end of World War II were held in disrepute, not because of a general acknowledgment that they signified domination, exploitation, and oppression but because of the alibi that they were no longer, if ever, profitable. The most spectacular application of this theory of modernization, and perhaps its most enduring achievement, was the example of postwar Japan, already made to enact a narrative devoted to the story line of reform, reconstruction, and democratic renovation. By 1948, moreover, American policy was already anticipating the struggle between differing developmental strategies and began to move actively to transform the former foe, Japan, into friend and partner.

I would like to propose that this Occupation narrative and its subsequent articulation in countless studies devoted to demonstrating the modernization of Japan combined to establish the terms for constituting America's Japan and to mark the place of a new stage of imperialism and colonialism without territorialization. (I realize that an American military presence has been evident in Japan since the end of the Occupation in the early 1950s, but the governance and administration of the country have been in Japanese hands.) By the same measure, this modernization narrative provided the means for not imagining a Japan's America, as if both speakers were equal, but rather a Japan's Japan which simply managed to supplement (not in a Derridian way) the image already authorized by the representation constructed by both the Occupation and its later theoretical projection and empirical verification. Modernization theory, as it was increasingly "applied" to explain the case of Japan, prompted Japanese to incorporate American expectations to fulfill a narrative about themselves, produced by others, elsewhere, that had already demanded the appeal to fixed cultural values—consensuality—uninterrupted continuity, and an endless present derived from an exceptionalist experience. In this way, modernization theory, which betrayed the conceit of an earlier social science that had bracketed history altogether, was used to encode Japan and invite the Japanese to locate themselves in the account by summoning values and experience attesting to a cultural endowment that had survived since time immemorial (a social Darwinist inflection that privileged enduring values supposedly because they had survived) as an explanation for both economic and technological success and the absence of conflict in the nation's history. In this narrative both the Meiji Restoration of 1868, which represented a genuinely transforming moment, and the Pacific War were either marginalized or explained as aberrations.

The Occupation narrative sought to "re-make" Japan as a "free" and "democratic society," and, thereby to reinstate an earlier course which, according to a number of interpreters, had been derailed in the 1930s. In this regard, Mary Layoun, in an unpublished manuscript, has correctly argued that the Occupation plot line, resituating a capitalist organization of production, displaced certain "narratological roles, such as the strike, to satisfy or accommodate shifts within . . . American policy toward Japan." American authorities believed, out of some combination of missionary optimism and New Deal reformist zeal, that Japan could be reconstructed and set upon its democratic course, if some tinkering was done. Embedded in this plot was the imperial figure of a theory of development which, once articulated as normative science, authorized the exportation of its program everywhere to secure nonaligned societies in the struggle between the "free world" and the communist bloc. The apparent advantage of this theory of development, as it was put into practice, was that it seemed to offer a viable alternative model of change to the Marxian insistence on the role of contradictions, class conflict, and revolutionary violence. In time, this Occupation narrative for Japan was reconstituted into a larger narrative of modernizing progress that would seek to uphold Japan as a showcase or, better yet, storybook example of its promise.

Whereas the Occupation effort had no need to account for the reasons that prompted Japan to embark upon a ruinous war, the modernization story line was obliged to construct an explanatory strategy that might be able to represent the recent historical experience as the expression of an evolutionary and progressive transformation, yet still account for the reasons why Japan went to war. Such an explanation would have to show that Japan was temporarily "derailed" in the 1930s from its true democratic vocation by appealing to structural dysfunctions caused by an immature social system incapable of accommodating stresses and strains, certifying a functionalist conception of the social order that seemed to have more in common with a plumbing system and clogged pipes than a human society.

In this scenario, the values of instrumental rationality, derived from the fantasy image of the market, and the progressive modernization of means were reread politically as "democratic," even though this move was avoided in the first discussions devoted to planning a study program on Japan's modernization. Much of the impulse for this approach in the study of Japan was provided by the "experience" of the American Occupation and its decision to reconstruct Japanese society for production and its fear, after 1947, of an imminent communist revolution. But it was systematized, and given empirical force, through the appropriation of a model of development by historians and social scientists of Japan who quickly "renarrativized" the nation's history into a metonymic substitution for an imagined whole that signified transformation through adaptation and value integration. According to this program, as envisaged by proponents of Japan's modernization—principally the Conference on Modern Japan—Japanese history showed how the nation had successfully evolved peacefully from a feudal order, whose values had survived intact to mediate this development and whose more baneful remnants would eventually be eliminated by the force of rationality. In other words, Japan's successful modernization constituted no abrupt break with a feudal past, as had, say, the French or even Russian Revolution, which, in any case, was appropriated by modernizers to navigate the uncertain transition to modernity. This view was best expressed in all those accounts that sought to show how traditional values were pressed into the service of mediating vast and even traumatic changes that otherwise would have torn society apart. Later, this particular privileging of sturdy traditional values, the force of a feudal unconscious capable of surviving history, authorized Japanese to appeal to an exceptionalist culture to explain their unique economic and technological achievements in the postwar period. Paradoxically, the very feudal unconscious Marxists had once identified as the cause of Japan's uneven development and social contradictions now became the principal explanation of Japan's successful modernization. In the hands of modernizers, Japan's cultural endowment either prefigured or provided analogues to the rationality that had made the West modern and powerful. Modernizers looked to the enthronement of reason and its political management in the present as the quintessential representation of Japan's development and the meaning inscribed in its history. Yet the easy equation between rationalization and political modernization made the move to a democratic society appear to be a natural result, even though the relationship was never adequately theorized and the genuine distrust for mass democracy was never exorcised in either American or Japanese considerations. As a result, Japanese society was made to appear conflict-free and consensual, and, in time, came to be reread as a superior and even more efficient expression of liberal democracy.

This version of America's Japan was produced in the 1960s and early 1970s by a self-anointed group called the Conference on Modern Japan. Many of its principal participants were former occupationaires or sons of missionaries or both. During its time, the conference produced six large volumes of papers loosely organized around the theme of Japan's modernization, and it generated countless studies in dissertations, articles, monographs, and books, which still seek regularly to demonstrate the singularity of meaning illuminated by the narrative of modern Japan. The purpose of these studies has been to show the persistence of common sense in understanding Japan, almost as if students outside Japan were compelled to reproduce the very consensus attributed to Japan's success as a rational order. This nostalgia for consensus and the effectivity of such an order have often appeared in those studies that recently have sought to hold Japan up as a mirror for the United States.

The Conference on Modern Japan met formally in the resort town of Hakone in August 1960 for three days in the spiritually invigorating if not oxygen-thin air of Mt. Fuji. The transcript of the proceedings announced that the purpose of the meeting "was not [to allow] individual presentations related to the modernization of Japan but to conduct a debate concerning the problem of Japan and the idea of modernization." Another goal was to plan a series of seminars to begin the following year. Hence, the discussions in Hakone sought to "move from the general to the specific,"[3] unintentionally following Marx's advice in the *Grundrisse* that science proceed from the abstract to the concrete. What this move from the general idea to its constituent parts meant was a rejection of a view steeped in values (echoing the then current absorption of social science in the pursuit of an objectivity paralleling the physical sciences) in favor of one purporting to recover the concept of modernization by establishing plural, objective standards. In the Japanese version of the transcript, these standards came to constitute an economy of inclusion that involved "self-evident" categories such as high levels of urbanization, broad levels of literacy, relatively high levels of manu-

3. I have relied extensively on the informative book by Kinbara Samon, '*Nihon kindaika'ron no rekishizo* (Tokyo: Chuo Daigaku shuppanbu, 1968), 26–38. I have also consulted the mimeographed version of the meetings transcript, in both Japanese and English.

facturing, and the production of commodities, all taken from the work of Almond and Colemen (*The Politics of Developing Areas*). In those years this text was regarded by social scientists as a near-perfect and objective taxonomy of modernization and a guide-book for the installation of a rational, read consensual, "political culture," because it was steeped in shared core values. According to one of the principal participants, the conference's chair, J. W. Hall, the conference hoped that this taxonomy would show that modernization was something more "comprehensive than such processes as westernization or industrialization, or such systems of social organization as absolutism, capitalism, and socialism." Despite the obvious gesture to make such categories appear neutral, to dehistoricize them by appealing to a Parsonian misreading of Max Weber's conception of *zweckrationalität* and, thereby, to avoid the excesses of a value-centered view, the historian Inoue Kiyoshi was correct when he later observed that the classification system betrayed a kinship with capitalism, which was presented as a natural development of the human species.[4]

If Talcott Parsons was visible everywhere, the invited surprise mystery guest was the ghost of Herbert Spencer, an old friend of Meiji Japanese, who worried about getting out of feudal standstill and onto the track leading to rational progress. While the Americans were convinced that instrumental rationality, a dehistoricized means/end relationship, constituted the objective standard for measuring modernization in a number of spheres such as politics, economics, social organization, and even culture, the Japanese participants saw in the claim of neutrality the absence of history and the various ways capitalism was bonded to local experiences. Clearly, different histories were being summoned. Yet, none of the participants on either side ever questioned the problematic status of privileging as a standard criterion of the relationship between means and ends and its authorization of a protean binarism that generated a whole catalogue of distinctions that automatically aligned societies according to their proximity to the universal or particular and the instrumentality of a culturally specific conception of rationality masquerading as a universal value.

Here, it seems, was the real nub of the issue and the point of difference between the two discourses. The American position was linked to a methodological conviction to "construct theory from facticity" as the only scholarly ideal both parties should pursue. The first volume of essays announced the aim of "retelling" Japan's modern history based on greater

4. Kinbara, *'Nihon kindaika'ron no rekishizo*, 240.

and more precise attention to "empirical data" and a "less confining" reli- ance on general theory.[5] This presumption authorized a program leading to an understanding of "Japan within the concept of modernization," which was presented not as a theoretical construct but merely as a description of the way things are. But the Japanese view projected a different "inter- est" or "problem consciousness," as it was often called, which sought to explain "why modernization was a problem." The political theorist Maru- yama Masao, responding to the claims of normativity ascribed to the sev- eral categories of modernization, called into question the absence of any concern for the status of individual value systems.[6] Toyama Shigeki, a his- torian, condemned the conference for emphasizing the leading role played by capitalism and industrialization in the process to the exclusion of pre- modern elements derived from peasant life, and for its "indifference toward the continuation of militarism and despotic leadership . . . and its appar- ent neglect of the role of patriarchy and social hierarchy in dominating the everyday life, despite the universalization of education and the spread of modern thought."[7] This observation corresponded much more closely to Max Weber's original formulations concerning the bureaucratic domination of everyday life than the optimistic misrecognition made by Talcott Par- sons that had become regarded as common sense among American social scientists. Yet, the really important difference came with the articulation of an American faith in the possibility and necessity of linking "tool concepts" to a "universal" principle of analysis and the opposing Japanese contention that believed in the importance of historically mediated concepts, differ- ing temporalities, and local experience.[8] While this difference constituted a kind of blindness around which the debate over modernization was orga- nized, and which subsequent studies tried to suppress, it is clear that what the Japanese were seeking to re-present was, in fact, the very purpose of such a project. They were intent to lay claim to the right to represent their own historical experience to themselves, if not to an other, and to renew a struggle that had marked the production of cultural theory in Japan from the time of the Meiji Restoration of 1868. Plainly, the Japanese were appealing to narremes derived from the prewar debate over the nature of Japanese

5. John W. Hall, "Changing Conceptions of the Modernization of Japan," in Marius B. Jansen, ed., *Changing Japanese Attitudes toward Modernization* (Princeton: Princeton University Press, 1965), 40.
6. Kinbara, *'Nihon kindaika'ron no rekishizo,* 28.
7. Ibid., 29.
8. Ibid., 30.

capitalism that had attempted to account for the debilitating contradictions of the modern historical experience and to find in the 1930s the reasons for Japan's drift toward fascism and absolutism. Few, on either the Japanese or American side, were willing to entertain the philosopher Tosaka Jun's prewar analysis that liberalism itself was the cause of the development of fascism. When contrasted to the rather narrow research agenda implemented to grasp a modernization process, whose sole aim was to demonstrate the "differences . . . in proximate methods," we can see that the Conference on Modern Japan would settle for nothing less than the construction of a new narrative capable of signifying the "rational control of its (human society) physical and social environment."

To be sure, the move toward modernization must be related to a Cold War context that had already encouraged the mobilization of resources at major American universities devoted to the study of the Soviet Union. In fact, it seems entirely likely that the earlier examination of Russia's modernizing process became both the inspiration and the model for the decision to study Japan, inasmuch as the strategy invariably invited comparisons. Just as the study of the Soviet Union was linked to policy-making and intelligence-gathering, so the subsequent study of Japan's modernization would affirm a nonrevolutionary model of development in the Cold War struggle between the "free world" and the communist bloc for the hearts and minds of the peoples of the unaligned nations. This linking of Japan's modernization to American development policy has come back decades later in the form of both all of the pleas advising the United States to model itself after Japan and the whining of "bashers" who blame Japan for America's decline. Yet, its principal purpose initially was to resituate the former imperialist Japan within the new framework of American imperialism and call it by another name.

By 1958, W. W. Rostow had published his famous noncommunist manifesto, *The Stages of Economic Growth,* which envisioned the "industrializing process" in a comparative context of global development and took the study of modernization beyond the Soviet case. This text became the basis of E. O. Reischauer's influential *Nihon kindai no atarashii mikata* (New view of Japan's modernity); which was read widely in Japan but never appeared in English. Reischauer wanted to show how Japan had successfully avoided both the excesses of conflict and political totalism in the passage to a modern order. But it is important to recognize the difference between Rostow, who emphasized the primacy of economic development, which would lead to political democracy, and Reischauer, who emphasized politics and, thereby, opened the way for a reassertion of the state and state capitalism masquerading as social democracy.[9]

It is precisely this conviction that helps explain the appropriation of Rostow's stage scheme of development by Reischauer, who became Ambassador to Japan after Kennedy was elected to the presidency, and it accounts for the turn toward a consideration of indigenous value as the "vanishing mediator" in the modernizing process in the action theory of R. N. Bellah. Where Reischauer departed from Rostow was in his decision to emphasize the political dimension of modernization, which he believed constituted a crucial supplement to economic growth. For societies that had lagged in the modernization process (Nazi Germany, Fascist Italy, the Soviet Union, and prewar militaristic Japan), which had equated economic underdevelopment with political authoritarianism without necessarily favoring the former over the latter, disruption reflected "political polarization" which, he argued, stemmed from a commitment to rapid development, rather than an evolutionary growth which characterized the "democratic states" of Western Europe, North America, Australia, and New Zealand.[10] Already committed to the role played by traditional, principally political values as the mediator that nurtured evolutionary transformation, Reischauer was convinced that even latecomers like Japan, despite the aberration of war, had avoided revolutionary upheaval in modern history because of such mediation. The argument suggested that Japan was really not other to the West (later verified by Robert Bellah's search for an analogue to the Protestant ethic in Tokugawa religions) and, therefore, already enjoyed the identity of selfsameness rather than difference and lack that marked the place of otherness reserved for Third World societies in Africa, South and Southeast Asia, and China. Japan became Echo to America's Narcissus.

In authenticating this vision, Reischauer presented his credentials as a longtime fighter against Marxism. In tones recalling more recent replays of Rambo-like machismo, he announced in a speech shortly after becoming ambassador that "this classical Marxism is our true foe in Japan. I have never shirked from an opportunity to inflict a blow against it. Of course, one does not use such words. The words I do use are: 'Taking on a new view of history.' They are the party of a period now past. We are the wave of the future."[11] "In this way," Reischauer continued, "I have always continued the

9. See ibid., 85, for Reischauer's explanation.
10. Ibid., 88–89.
11. Kawamura Nozomu, *Nihon bunkaron no shuhen* (Tokyo: Ningen no shakaisha, 1982), 80.

struggle and they (Marxists) have acknowledged this to be so. They have referred to it as the Kennedy-Reischauer assault." [12] The political program lodged in this new view of history, unintentionally echoing Takata Yasuma's prewar declaration of a "third view of history" in his own struggle against Marxism and idealism, was the attack on Marxism that he, as ambassador to Japan, would make as his personal mission. His strident language already disclosed a willingness to enter into combat. To this end, Reischauer separated Japan from the "poorly developed countries," reinforcing Japan's withdrawal from the Asia it had so recently colonized and plundered during the Pacific War, and affirmed Japan's own decision to identify with the First World rather than the Third World. These countries, he argued, "cannot be considered to be like Japan, which was able to accelerate the modernizing process while being conscious of the modernization of the West in the world." "From the standpoint of world history," he told his audience, "the most important thing has been the history of Japan in the last 90 years. The reason for this is because it accelerated the modernizing process and used the . . . pattern of the West. But it is because it realized great success that it is a unique case within this [pattern]. There are a number of troublesome problems, such as militarism, but if seen from a broader perspective, Japan is a success. The case of Japan should become a textbook for the developing nations." [13]

In this program, Reischauer saw the United States as the most successful example of the historical development of modernization. He complained that some people have mistakenly seen the term modernization as a prescription, as "something that ought to happen," but he was convinced that it was something that simply happened under certain conditions, as if a dictation from nature itself.[14] Because of the natural occurrence of modernization, the process was exempt from value judgments of whether it was good or bad. The real was simply the rational. The "presentism" Reischauer celebrated, his exuberance for the way things are, was matched by an enthusiastic appeal to the methodological neutrality that had been expressed in the American view at the Hakone Conference, "the open approach," as it was called, with its valorization of technological progress, rationality of means, and the desirability of industrialization devoted to the production of consumer goods. This sentiment was made into a catechism of faith by one of Reischauer's most devoted students in a speech delivered at the Inter-

12. Ibid.
13. Ibid., 80–81.
14. Kinbara, 'Nihon kindaika'ron no rekishizo, 94.

national Christian University of Japan in 1961 when he announced that the important thing was not what people read but that they were able to read, not what they do as free individuals but that they participate functionally in a mass society, not what they produce but that they produce things. "At the same time one makes arms, one also makes automobiles; at the same time one organizes concentration camps, one organizes schools to teach freedom. This is all modernity."[15] But this description could just as easily be applied to fascism.

Finally, modernization theory acquired a complex theory of action, as articulated by Talcott Parsons, which offered the prospect of a stable social imaginary rooted in the claims of normativity, central or core values capable of securing integration, and the primacy of the present and the way things are. This vision of normalcy undoubtedly derived from Parsons's romanticization of small-town America, probably rural Ohio, and what for him, growing up in this safe, stable, and comfortable environment, appeared to be an endless summer, a present that had no need for either past or future since society had achieved optimal perfection. The appropriation of Parsonian theory was made by R. N. Bellah in a work called *Tokugawa Religion,* which made available a powerful and influential formulation that sanctioned the role of traditional or core values, derived from the cultural endowment, as the privileged mediator for modernizing changes, the rational means employed to secure the ends of social change, that is, the establishment of capitalist society. The work provided a strong argument for empowering what were identified as traditional values, which, despite the risk of reification, were mobilized because they had been able to survive by making necessary adjustments. Such values also attested to the bonding between norms capable of securing integration and a society's competence to absorb the shock wave of modernizing changes without resorting to disruption and violence. The irony of this argument has been that it produced a pre-emptive closure by making the Japanese "textbook" inaccessible to precisely those Third World societies it was supposed to inspire to follow the Western pattern. Only advanced societies like the United States are able to learn from Japan, not Third World societies, since Japan now does better what Americans used to do. In all fairness to Bellah, he has not resorted to this kind of hysteria prompting Americans to seek enlightenment in the Japanese model, driven by concerns to be number one, but, rather,

---

15. Marius B. Jansen, "On Studying the Modernization of Japan," *Asian Cultural Studies* 3, (Tokyo: International Christian University, 1962), 1–11. Quoted in Kawamura, *Nihon bunkaron no shuhen,* 82.

has rewritten *Tokugawa Religion* and called it *Habits of the Heart,* to remind middle-class white Americans, somewhat nostalgically and melancholically, of those sturdy religious (core) values of small-town America that once made society whole and integrated. Yet, Bellah's conception of how cultural values mediate change risked producing precisely the kind of exceptionalism that informs current Japanese cultural theory on what it means to be Japanese, just as Parsons's appeal to universalism betrayed the powerful exceptionalism that had always marked the place of small-town America and its values. As a testament to the truth that some things never die, we can still hear exhausted echoes of this conceit in the works of all those writers, like the historian of Chinese philosophy Wei-ming Tu and others, who have tried to argue that Confucian values undergird the industrial and commercial transformation of the "four little dragons," long after Bellah himself has abandoned the theory. It is important to note that the articulation of this theory, which assigns to core values—tradition—the job of guiding the ship of society through the perilous shoals leading to modernization, was never far from promoting authoritarian modes of social control for the realization of a stable political order conducive to the changes demanded by capitalist transformation.

In the preface of the Japanese edition of the earlier book, Bellah explained the plan of applying Parsons's theory of social action.

> As for the theory of social action, the value and social systems are important factors in the historical process. I am convinced that these cannot be explained by class interest. . . . Insofar as the theory of social action clearly functions in the present social process, it is completely different from the idealist approach in respect to its basic supposition because it considers the importance of values. For action theory, the political system operates as the axis of the social process and the institution of society. It receives influence from economic or class energies but it is never determined by them.[16]

Action derives from the force of values that have already proved their adaptability for survival. In this view, Japan had embarked upon modernizing reforms before the achievement of modernity, by relying on traditional relationships and values. Yet this premodern experience plainly prefigured the later realization of a rational, modern order. Tokugawa Japan amply demonstrated the primacy of what Bellah called political and adaptive values, which were particular rather than universal, usually assigned to economic

16. Quoted in Kinbara, *'Nihon kindaika'ron no rekishizo,* 96–97.

values, and showed already their elastic capacity to accommodate change. In the sphere of religio-cultural values, Bellah believed he had found the form of this premodern rationality, the "functional analogue to the Protestant ethic."[17] In the Japanese religious experience of Tokugawa Japan, Bellah proposed it was possible to identify those rationalizing tendencies in religion that would supply the necessary motivation for inducing Japanese to accept vital social changes in the interest of collective survival. Later, in 1965, Bellah affirmed the importance of this hermeneutic in an article in which he asserted that the problem of modernity was manifested not in the circumstances of political and economic systems but only as "spiritual phenomena" and "varieties of mentalities." The change toward the modern required a "social psychological revolution."[18] Such spiritual revolutions, he added, have usually succeeded only in circumstances in which it has been possible to preserve social identity yet encourage change. It is evident from this observation that he was convinced that the continuity of social identity would be the greatest guarantee against the necessity of reorganizing the structure of society at its deepest levels. Observable cultural specificity— social identity—would always secure a social order in the assurance of stability and serve as a hedge against the specter of revolutionary upheaval. It was precisely in this narrative mode that Japan's history was emplotted and why proponents of modernization theory (invariably students of Reischauer and their camp followers) sought to dismiss, discredit, and even efface the work of E. H. Norman and others who had encoded the Meiji Restoration as an instance of revolutionary change and transformation.

While Bellah's intervention offered a persuasive explanation for yoking rationalization to religio-cultural values that were capable of supplying the mediation for social change, it also provided powerful and lasting reinforcement to a theory of modernization that already favored continuity and consensus over conflict and rupture, the identity of the past in the present over historical difference, and the stability of fixed values driving change over discontinuous perspectives demanding new starts. Moreover, it was precisely this "instrumentalizing" of culture that was increasingly used by Japanese to explain both the withdrawal of democratic promise in the 1960s and the identification of global economic success with an exceptional cultural endowment. And it was this linkage of "modernism" and "Japanism" that the critic Takeuchi Yoshimi believed would doom postwar Japan to repeat in a new and more powerful register the very history the war

---

17. Robert N. Bellah, *Tokugawa Religion* (New York: The Free Press, 1985), 2.
18. Kinbara, *'Nihon kindaika'ron no rekishizo,* 97–98.

was supposed to have overcome. Without saying so directly, Takeuchi already saw the terms by which America's Japan could become the model for Japan's Japan when he declared that no difference separated "Japanists" (*Nihonshugisha*) from "modernists" (*kindaishugisha*).[19]

2

Between the 1950s and the 1960s, the promise of postwar social democracy began to fade as the result of a combination of external and domestic forces that ultimately constituted a historical conjuncture that promoted revitalization of the state and the economy. These changes were signified by a shift among modernists such as Maruyama Masao and Shimizu Ikutaro toward the American theory of modernization and the production of a state ideology centered on attempts to substantiate the "symbolic" character of the imperial institution. The Marxist critic Ueda Koichiro saw in these years of "intellectual outburst" a turning point in the postwar discussions on politics and society; outside Japan they were marked by the Hungarian uprising and the beginnings of a critique of Stalinism, while at home he noted a turn toward state-sponsored capitalism.[20] The question that agitated thoughtful people was how best to take hold of this conjuncture and make theoretical sense of what was happening in Japan. Modernists, who earlier had been committed to finding the grounds for a responsible subject and establishing an ethos capable of generating a politics of accountability, now appeared to abandon these goals for theories that promised the realization of a "production society" by the end of the 1960s. This change corresponded to a shift in how the war and responsibility for it had been understood. Whereas in the earlier years of the postwar period, there was a willingness to see Japan as victimizer in Asia (a memory recently revivified by the resurfaced image of the state's wartime monopolization of a network of whorehouses, euphemistically called "comfort stations," for Japanese troops, forcibly stocked by primarily unwilling Korean women, who have lived decades with the sure knowledge that the Japanese government claimed no direct knowledge of or responsibility for this most brutal of exploitative oppressions), this view was gradually replaced by one that portrayed Japan as victim. The shift and the subsequent loss of memory was related to the Occupation's decision to turn former foe into friend after the collapse of Nationalist China.

19. Takeuchu Yoshimi, *Shinpen Nihon ideorogi,* vol. 2, *Takeuchi Yoshimi hyoronshu* (Tokyo: Chikuma shobo, 1967), 273–82.
20. Yoshida Masatoshi, *Sengo shisoron* (Tokyo: Aoki Shoten, 1984), 96.

In these circumstances, theory turned first toward envisaging Japanese society and social structure along the lines of the business firm, which, in turn, derived its representational form from the "household" system. The irony of employing the metaphor of the household as the basis of the state before the war and its reincarnation in the firm after the war apparently failed to catch the attention of those sober social scientists who were busily at work imagining a fit between the public realm and daily life. Once Japanese society was envisaged as a large firm that resembled the household, this image was normatized and theory, as such, was effaced and ultimately eliminated as a space for construction, imagining differing alternatives and criticism. What was produced in discourse as an image, merely a representation, was presented as social reality and the way things are in Japan. The catalyst and marker of this change were the mass demonstrations that began in the late 1950s and culminated in the protest of 1960, provoked by the willingness of the government to revise the joint U.S./Japan Security Pact and the success of the leading political party, the Liberal Democratic Party, to prioritize "income doubling," industrial expansion, and increased GNP in the coming years. In the Japanese intellectual world, the resistance against revising the security pact came to symbolize the subsequent contest between the ruling party, trying to consolidate its control, and an amalgam of opposition parties, the left and student groups, attempting to seize the opportunity to realize the promise of a social democracy accountable to plural interests. Takeuchi Yoshimi saw in this political contest the promise of a genuine "Japanese Revolution." The issue was seen as a struggle over the choice between democratic politics or economic growth. In this breech, modernists retreated from positions they previously shared with Marxists devoted to barring the return of militarism and a powerful state. By the same token, they embarked upon a critique of the methodological claims of Marxism. In this way, the earlier modernist sentiment to resituate the promise of an "enlightened" political ethos, supported by the concept of a responsibly informed subject capable of acting, decomposed into pallid affirmations of high growth and the expansion of Japanese capitalism as merely the *sign* of democracy. Whereas earlier modernists aligned their interests with Marxists in a general assault against the re-emergence of a statist hegemony, now, in the decade of the sixties, they were defending American military and economic assistance and risking complicity in an imperialist expansion that they believed had condemned Japan to war and defeat twenty years earlier.

According to a number of observers of this scene, the modernist move coincided with the articulation of what came to be called the

"Kennedy-Reischauer Line."[21] In the eyes of many, the reaffirmation of a state even more powerful than its prewar predecessor benefited immensely from its close association with the American conception of modernization and its privileging of a rational polity devoted to economic growth and the articulation of cultural values capable of securing integration and preventing wrenching discontinuities. It should be pointed out that the so-called symbolic emperor, dreamed up by Occupation planners persuaded that Hirohito should not be tried as a war criminal, constituted an ever-present reminder of precisely those cultural values modernizers had fixed as the guarantee of continuity.[22] In fact, this new "symbolic emperor" seemed to acquire even more materiality and greater identification with core cultural values in the several moments constituting the process of refiguring the imperial institution.

In the context of the 1960s, "high economic growth" led to the staging of a number of dramatic economic booms, and the LDP enhanced its own hegemony by effectively displacing the political and social goals of an earlier period to the prospect of economic well-being. Once the effort to renarrativize society as a successful example of modernization was on its way, portraying an unfolding plot that would culminate in the realization of a "manufacturing society" or an "information society," the ground was prepared for the rearticulation of an image of Japanese exceptionalism and "realist political theory," and the final conflation of an ideology comprised of fixed cultural values and Japanese capitalism. Under the sway of this story line, the fixed cultural values modernization theory sought to uphold as the agents mediating evolutionary change were now employed by Japanese to explain why their achievements were so unique. The textbook case that was supposed to provide guidance to less developed nations could no longer offer useful knowledge, because the cultural values that mediated Japan's successful progress were irreducibly Japanese. The very rationality that religious and cultural values seemed to offer was embedded in an exceptionalist experience that was more racial than rational. Yet, I have already suggested that this exceptionalism was very much a part of the modernizing program, even as it was imagined by American social scientists. Only the epigone Ezra Vogel, whose nostalgia for an imaginary America, tidy and orderly and led by people like himself from the Kennedy School of Public

21. See Yoshida, *Sengo shisoron,* 97.
22. On the question of the so-called symbolic emperor and his relationship to culture, see my " 'Ichiboku ichigusa ni yadoru ni tennosei,' " *Shiso* 11 (1990): 85–101.

Affairs, called attention to Japan as a model for the United States, not the Third World, to follow.

Contemporary Japanese cultural explanations have, in following the discursive conventions of modernization theory, sought to elide daily life with the way things are—*genjitsu,* or present-mindedness—to show the very identity of past and present in the transmission of certain cultural values, as if no real difference separated Japanese today from their remote past. In fact, in the long and exceedingly detailed social scientific analysis by Murakami, Sato, and Kumon, *Japanese Civilization as Household Society* (1970), there appears to be no substantial difference between contemporary society and the Stone Age. This move to celebrate an endless present is so important because discussions centering on daily life before the war, as such, were frequently employed to contest the present as a massive simulacrum of Western society and to master the excess of history that resulted in ceaseless succession. In the context of these earlier discussions, the figure of daily life, in one form or another, was situated as the scene of radical difference and the site of innumerable unresolved contradictions. Yet, it was summoned to manage what appeared to contemporaries in the 1920s and 1930s as wrenching, epochal changes; that is to say, daily life was employed as a figure outside time to mediate an unmasterable modern history. In the hands of postwar thinkers, this "presentism" reflected simply an affirmation of the way things are and the recognition that history had come to an end in a perfected present. The emphasis on presentism, as formulated by thinkers like Shimizu Ikutaro, what he called affirming "actuality," represented an abandonment of all ideals and a Japanese call for the end of ideology, mimicking a move that modernization theory had already made when it discounted the role of ideology altogether in understanding society. Such a view implied strongly that the goal of modernization had been realized, the project of modernity completed, and it was now important to retain the image of a stable social order against the threat of future change by appealing to enduring cultural values and form. In this scheme, there is no place for history to occupy.

What I would like to suggest is that America's Japan became Japan's Japan once it was recognized in the 1970s that the goals of modernization had been reached, income-doubling secured, and high economic growth realized. What had originally been conceived as a means to explain how societies, in this instance Japan, could become modernized without relying on the agency of conflict and struggle, became an ideological device employed by the state to justify the status quo and to eliminate the realm of criticism that once belonged to the space of culture. A developmental theory that stressed the evolutionary conception of history became the ideology of a developed sociopolitical order that was determined to eliminate the prospect of any serious threat to the way things are. Yet even in this "history," there was a clear emphasis upon the persistence of cultural values, capable of aestheticizing daily life, which had passed the test of survival by both resisting change and demonstrating their continuing usefulness in the task of guiding society over the long duration in an evolutionary development. But such a view of values plainly worked against history and pointed to a time when it, too, would end or be overcome.

Accordingly, the rise of a conception of a mass society and its corollary—that all Japanese belonged to a vast middle stratum because they were Japanese—has necessitated that discussions on the nature of social theory and cultural profile be grasped from a "new perspective." What this entailed was a turn to culture to explain the status of contemporary mass society, to affirm it rather than to offer the space of critique, and the subsequent appeal to a premodern endowment as an irreducible essence to sanction, not to resist, the modernizing changes Japan has realized. But to summon culture, as such, and to mandate the coexistence of what was being called the "Japanese thing" as the sign of an insurmountable presentism required separating cultural forms and values from their historical conditions of production; it also ran the risk of providing support to an atemporal order in the present, which seems very close to the America's Japan of modernization theory. This practice has invariably resulted both in projecting the picture of a timeless culture that might function as an adequate displacement for history and in recruiting elements of a past or daily life from their embeddedness to show that Japanese have not really changed since the sun goddess was persuaded to leave the "heavenly rock cave." The constant reminders of enduring cultural values and the repetitious reification of the timeless folk, village, and household—what Yoshimoto Takaaki has called the "imaginary community" (genso kyodotai) and what I see as a national poetics, which are ceaselessly promoted as enduring presences in contemporary Japan—attest to the ideological force of continuity and value integration and supply the "common-sensical" means for differentiating Japanese from others.

This discourse on Japanese culture and its enduring presence was effectively articulated by a large number of writers and thinkers of the late 1960s, and it continues to capture the popular imagination in countless books, articles, and media events calculated to remind Japanese that this cultural uniqueness and difference account for the nation's vast economic and technological successes. One of the most vocal defenders of this cultural ideology has been the critic Eto Jun, who has waged a tireless campaign, virtually a war, against what he has called the illegality of the American Occupation and Japan's unconditional surrender. In a discussion with E. O. Reischauer, Eto proposed that even though modernization has become a problem everywhere, the Japanese experience shows that the "destruction of the self" is different from what occurred in Europe and the United States.[23] Whereas the self has decomposed into atomized fragments in these places, in Japan it has retained a firm identity because of its integration into the larger social group. This argument was effectively made before Eto's revelations by the sociologist Nakane Chie in an influential book describing Japanese society as vertically organized and arguing for the impossibility of individual identity outside the group. In Eto's case, the argument easily reduced history to culture. Eto's critique was aimed at the Occupation, which, he proposed, wrenched the Japanese from their own history in the interest of democratizing and Americanizing Japan. The history he wished to recall was an imaginary that had been rooted in the values employed to justify and carry out the war. For him, the consequence of this rehistoricization of Japan was mirrored in the production of a mediocre literature in the postwar period. This literature, he wrote, rejected the past altogether for an advocacy of "distinctiveness" and novelty. But, he continued, "must literature be only this kind of activity? Should not the creation of literature be a continuous endeavor that seeks ceaselessly to reunite the self with the past? Won't it encounter those things that should be called the true self, according to those facts that have been confirmed and point increasingly to an organic whole of culture that it will one day restore?"[24] The "organic whole" he wished to restore referred to an integrated totality secured by imperial sovereignty and closely resembling the ideological representations of emperor and community that were being made during the 1930s.

By the same measure, the attempt to resituate timeless cultural forms in the postwar period in order to overcome contemporary history preoccupied the writer Mishima Yukio, who, with contemporary critics such as Kobayashi Hideo and Fukuda Tsuneari, produced an ideology of cultural totalism to serve the political and economic systems at that time. Mishima's rejection of postwar history stemmed from a conviction that the times demanded a rearticulation of a theory of cultural holism that would

23. Yoshida, *Sengo shisoron*, 90.
24. Ibid., 141.

center pure form, once more, unmediated by the necessities of history. The model he offered of a culturally whole Japanese order free from the history of the "post-war" demanded a break with the West, even though he was Japan's most "Western" writer. The backdrop for his own anticommunist manifesto, "Essays on the Defense of Japanese Culture," (*Nihon boeiron*) was the emerging Japanese superstate of the late 1960s, which, according to his text, was now compelled to defend culture against its destruction by socialism. Mishima was already complaining about his present, and the showy "culturalism," as he called it, that incessantly transformed culture into "things." Often, he echoed the complaints by cultural critics in the 1930s who worried that spirit was losing out to the machine and consumption. Everywhere, he saw only "ornamentation," "exhausted emotionality," and the "elimination of the real." Contemporary cultural life was counterfeit, "diluted for mass consumption," revered as a thing, and removed from the source of all things—the emperor—that had given it enduring expression.

Like many of his contemporaries, Mishima was convinced that cultural and aesthetic form constituted the trace of national spirit and was the surest defense against the erosions inflicted by time and history. He was persuaded that timeless form was manifested in continuities or repetitions which, like the punctual rebuilding of the Grand Shrine at Ise every twenty years, have always defied mere history. But the greatest sign of repetition, continuity, and the autonomy of form was the emperor, who was always "present," even when absent in certain periods of Japan's history. The emperor represented a "free creative subjectivity," who acted as a signifier (or perhaps a transcendental subject) that authorized cultural signification but who was not bound to a signification, and was always capable of transmitting form itself on its endless itinerary through time. To defend "culture" meant ridding society of egoism and encouraging self-sacrifice in order to conserve the "continuity of destiny."[25] Accordingly, the "mother's womb" of this vast cultural idea, whose surplus always escaped being assimilated to the logic of history, representing a general economy of excess and expenditure, was an imaginary community, itself a form that remained immune from history. The lynchpin in this vision of cultural wholeness was the emperor, the *tenno,* as he preferred to call it, who represented fully the "ideal of cultural continuity." In Mishima's scheme, the tenno would join "absolutistic ethical values" to an "undifferentiated inclusive culture."[26] It should be

25. Ibid., 104.
26. Ibid.

pointed out that Mishima's conception of kingship was closest to the post-war construction of a symbolic emperor and its identification with the realm of culture, and it disclosed a perceptive grasp on his part of the vast powers associated with this new and revitalized image of imperial authority. While Japan was still a ways from realizing this goal, he was confident that through the implementation of a law calling for "public safety," it would be possible to establish an arrangement that could combine the "*kokutai* (national polity) of the Tenno's state" and "capitalism together with a system of private property,"[27] a classic reformulation of fascism. It was for the realization of this ideal that he staged his last, great spectacle—suicide by ritual decapitation, which, far from moving his countrymen and women to follow his call for action, was simply a commodity that was rapidly consumed and forgotten.

If Kobayashi Hideo offered up a similar defense of culture by poeticizing daily life, as has been argued, he refrained, to the last, from projecting a specific political program devoted to organizing a vast spectacle deployed, as had Mishima, to jar the Japanese into recognizing their "Japaneseness." Yet, his decision to root daily life in a traditional mode of cognition, which itself was embedded in language and life, brought him very close to Mishima's project of an aesthetic ideology that the timeless form of emperor both represented and authorized. Kobayashi had already distinguished himself before the war as a theorist of a genre of writing called "pure literature," which, in the 1930s, represented an effort to rescue literary production from Marxism. In an early work on Dostoevski, he disclosed what became, for him, an insurmountable allergy to history and the historical because it appeared to have no purity as a mode of understanding, mired in the mundane and the mediocre. History was nothing more than low-grade fiction, at best accident and contingency, since "men do not see historical reality" but only "create" it by seizing hold of "historical materials that have been given to them."[28] To see history and to grasp the true and enduring forms of life, he wrote, it was necessary to possess the "genius of the poet" or to be one who is in a position to "polish mightily the mirror of the self," an obvious reference to the Buddhist gesture of "polishing the dust from the mirror" in order to see the genuine reality rather than mere desire. Only in this sense is history a worthy pursuit since it "is a classic, it is the mirror" that reflects enduring cultural forms.[29] The presence of timeless

27. Ibid., 105.
28. Ibid., 111.
29. Ibid., 113.

forms constituted for Kobayashi a kind of eternal "now-time," a view that closely resembled conceptions of native ethnology developed by Yanagita Kunio and Orikuchi Shinobu, the deployment of a figure outside of time to mediate contemporary historical change.

During the war, Kobayashi carried on this project to naturalize history into the site of timeless cultural form and the repository of enduring forms that had escaped mere history. In making this move, he rejected any effort to identify those factors and events that might have been involved in producing a specific historical moment. This elision of history and culture was realized in his major text on Motoori Norinaga, which he completed well after the war had ended. In this text, he returned to the exploration of "seeing" and "vision," and he appealed to Buddhist modes of "knowing," which he contrasted with Western "realism" based upon "observation." Yet, it was the great eighteenth-century nativist Norinaga, the subject of Kobayashi's book, who provided him the methodological and philosophical means with which to identify spirit and "thingness" in "direct experience," even though he had studied Bergson as late as the 1950s. It was Norinaga's conception of empathic understanding of things, *mono no aware,* embedded in native daily life, language, and culture, that supplied the model for "seeing" and "knowing" what could not be grasped by other theories of cognition. Norinaga had been convinced that true Japanese emotionality had been lost because of the dependence on imported and alien principles of knowledge, such as Buddhism and Confucianism, and language, such as Chinese and its ideographic system of notations. According to Kobayashi, the revival of a natural emotionality as imagined by Norinaga invited a determinate stand against "rational norms" that had governed Japanese conduct and demanded a rejection of fixed principles altogether as inimical to native Japanese sensibilities. But the great appeal of this theory of cognition lay in its capacity to induce acceptance of the way things are, to affirm any historical givenness, and any present as it has been received.[30] What attracted Kobayashi to Norinaga's hermeneutic was the prospect of realizing a natural emotionalism freed from artificial, normative constraints of society, politics, and history—one that was more passive than active, and always prepared to receive. In a certain sense, he saw his time as an allegory for Norinaga's past, in which the great nativist struggled to free Japanese sensibilities from alien and alienating constraints in a time of great urban affluence and cultural transformation; yet, by the same measure, it is possible to

30. Ibid., 123–30.

read Norinaga and his time as an allegory for Kobayashi's present, in which the promise of *mono no aware* would liberate Japanese once more to see those true and enduring cultural forms that affirmed them in an unchanging and unchangeable Japaneseness.

Despite the prevailing nostalgia among cultural theorists (in a country where it now seems everything ends up as cultural theory) to resituate enduring cultural values within the confines of a modern industrial and technological society, these interventions have functioned more to reify the life forms of daily existence and to reaffirm the present as it is. Cultural theory has often failed to masquerade its complicity with social theory and its own effort to secure a ground of consensus as the principal condition for Japan's contemporary economic success. While such gestures invariably seek their genealogy in the prewar discourses on culture and society, the differences are substantial, and they disclose how the world has changed. Whereas prewar writers and thinkers summoned culture—spirit—as the best and last defense against the excesses of technology and commodification, the defense of spirit against the machine and commodity form, postwar writers have transmuted forms of daily life—the village collectivity, the household, the smaller units of rural life—into principles of organization, Kobayashi's "enduring thing," capable of serving and advancing new modes of commodity production. But we have come to know that these forms are situated at the end of a signifying chain, not at its beginning, even though cultural theory has sought relentlessly to produce this effect. Moreover, we have also come to recognize in this present historical conjuncture that they are not simply resuscitated remnants made to signify the wholeness and continuity of culture. The repetitious display of cultural ideologemes signifying uniqueness in daily life calls attention to the ceaseless effort to persuade Japanese that they have not yet become anything other than what they have been since the beginning of time in a world where everything else is changing, despite the spell of a history that constantly tries to hold them in its grip. Yet, this persisting reliance on cultural strategy and the tireless and often tiring appeal to timeless forms as a defense of the present against the assault of both a history that has passed and a history not yet imagined— what Marx once referred to as the "poetry of the future"—merely attest to how Japan's Japan still manages to echo the plaints of America's Japan.

In a Labyrinth of Western Desire:
Kuki Shuzo and the Discovery of Japanese Being

Leslie Pincus

> Contemporary Japan has come face to face with a crisis. Every aspect of our life is tainted by the West, a condition commonly believed to be "modern." But this is a dangerous delusion, one which must be dispelled.
> —Kuki Shuzo, "Japanese Culture"

After nearly a decade in Europe, Kuki Shuzo, scholar of Western philosophy, returned to Japan in 1929, soon to publish the work for which he became best known, *"Iki" no kozo* (The structure of Edo aesthetic style).[1] An elusive sense of style and deportment, *iki* circulated in the erotically charged atmosphere of the Edo pleasure quarters, the Kabuki theaters, and the popular arts of the late Tokugawa period (1600–1867).[2] The adepts of

---

1. Kuki Shuzo, *"Iki" no kozo*, in *Kuki Shuzo zenshu*, ed. Amano Teiyu, 12 vols. (Tokyo: Iwanami Shoten, 1981), 1:1–85. Subsequent references to this work and others included in *Kuki Shuzo zenshu* will hereafter be cited as *KSZ* with volume and page numbers.
2. Although the term *iki* is translated in Japanese-English dictionaries as "chic" or "stylishness," I use the Japanese in provisional deference to Kuki's central claim that the phenomenon of *iki* is culturally incommensurable and consequently untranslatable.

this style included the geisha and *tsu,* or connoisseur/dandies, who patronized the popular arts and frequented the (increasingly unlicensed) quarters where an official Confucian version of order and propriety no longer held sway. The qualities celebrated in the aesthetic style of *iki*—a restrained wantonness, a playful bravado, expertise in the practices of the quarters—expressed the cultural autonomy of a rising mercantile and artisanal class and its resistance to a near bankrupt *samurai* bureaucracy.

Since its publication in 1930, *"Iki" no kozo* has been neglected, admired, and reviled in turn. Some hail it as a text that successfully captures the essence of Japanese culture. Others condemn it as a pernicious example of *Nihonjinron*, that ubiquitous discourse on Japanese uniqueness. Most recently, *"Iki" no kozo* has come up in the context of "Postmodernism and Japan."

Why has a study of an early nineteenth-century aesthetic style become the occasion for such disparity of opinion, and why does it figure in modern (and postmodern) debates on culture, whether in the 1930s or the 1980s? In an attempt to address these questions, we might do well to turn first to the postmodern context. I would suggest that in *"Iki" no kozo*, postmodernism recognized a voice that anticipated the ambiguities and mixed messages of its own critique of modernity. According to prevailing definitions, the identifying mark of the postmodern is an incredulity toward the grand narratives that have ruled over modernity, whether a dialectics of spirit, a hermeneutics of meaning, the emancipation of a rational subject, or the creation of wealth.[3] Generated by a desire to suspend the hierarchical distinctions put in force by the Enlightenment, postmodernism has devoted itself to the articulation of difference, to identifying those marginal sites that escape the control of a ruling center. Yet, by its own admission, the postmodern is regularly revisited by the very unities it hopes to exile. Roland Barthes once commented that the attempt to imagine a symbolic system outside the limits of Western metaphysics is "like trying to destroy the wolf by lodging comfortably in his gullet": The values we drive out, he explained, return in the language we speak.[4] Some have cautioned that the postmodern project, in its playful zeal to escape the language of its modern

3. Jean-François Lyotard, *The Postmodern Condition: A Report on Knowledge*, trans. Geoff Bennington and Brian Massumi (Minneapolis: University of Minnesota Press, 1984), xxiii–xxiv.
4. Roland Barthes, *Empire of Signs*, trans. Richard Howard (New York: Hill and Wang, 1982), 8.

predecessors, has simultaneously diminished possibilities for critical theory. More urgent is the question of whether *difference* itself risks becoming a hegemonic concept, whether its celebration once again serves to suppress the voices of those others for whom the postmodern supposedly speaks.

A good half-century before the advent of postmodernism, a similar set of contradictions beset the critical reflection on modernity that took place in Japan, with this exceptional circumstance: The Japanese reflection of the interwar years was colored by more passion and more pathos than its European postmodernist successor, because the grand narratives opposed by the Japanese had so recently been imposed, or self-imposed, under the impending threat of colonization. The most dominant of those narratives that came into force along with Japan's forced entry into the world market was summed up in the slogan "Civilization and Enlightenment." This ideological notion subjected Japan to a universalizing schema of linear historical development, a schema in which a modernized West inevitably prevailed. As something of an afterthought to Japan's successful modernization, more than a few writers and theorists during the 1920s and 1930s attempted to restore to Japan its difference from reigning Western values, values that were, however, already deeply entrenched in the specialized languages and everyday life of Japanese intellectuals. After several generations of successful assimilation to the West, Japan had little choice but to delineate Japaneseness against, and within, dominant Western discursive modes. And, like postmodernism, this renewed recollection of Japan wavered precariously and ambiguously between critical protest and reaction.

Kuki Shuzo, a significant contributor to this beleaguered project, identified *iki,* an aesthetic style from an era that closely preceded Japan's dramatic encounter with Perry's "black ships," as a privileged signifier of the distinctiveness of Japanese culture. The foe from whom he had to wrest *iki* was, however, not the West so much as it was Japan's own Enlightenment, under whose reign the culture of the Tokugawa era had become the object of disrepute and neglect. With the publication of *"Iki" no kozo,* Kuki aspired to resituate a marginalized historical moment in the center of Japan's self-understanding. Yet, ironically, the terms in which he articulated Japan's difference from the West were clearly marked by a long and productive apprenticeship to European letters. It should not be surprising, then, if *"Iki" no kozo* is haunted by the specter of Occidentalism it sought to banish. The question that Fredric Jameson first addressed to postmodernism—does it transcend, or does it reproduce, the logic of what it opposes?—has disturbing (if retrospective) relevance for the endeavor to recover Japan's cultural authenticity during the interwar years.

European Universalism, Race, and the Recollection of "Japan"

In his exploration of the ambiguities posed by *"Iki" no kozo*, Karatani Kojin observes that Kuki's attempt to define a sensibility exterior to Europe's modernity took the form of "a citation of the anti-Western elements in Western thought."[5] Kuki endorsed the German neo-idealist defense of culture, applauded Bergson's sanctification of subjective experience, and followed Heidegger in pursuit of authentic (and de-centered) being. He embraced the European cultural hermeneutic for its methodological capacity to reclaim a selectively cherished past. In the most general terms, this extended episode in the history of European philosophy represented an attempt to stave off the imperious claims of instrumental reason and to restore to human experience (individual and collective) the integrity and profundity it had presumably lost to a modernity of mechanized and mass proportions. It was precisely because Kuki shared both the experience and the critical perception of what had proved to be a transnational historical moment that he felt such a strong affinity for the dissident voices raised in the West. Paradoxically, the theoretical idiom of *"Iki" no kozo* bore witness, however unwittingly, to the interval of a heterogeneous modernity that irrevocably severed contemporary Japan from the pre-Meiji past.

It is, however, noteworthy that these dissenting voices in Europe's philosophical modernity were not without Eurocentric resonances—resonances that routinely excluded or diminished the "non-West" under the guise of a universalizing vocabulary. Wilhelm Dilthey, major architect of cultural hermeneutics, committed himself in theory to a project of world-historical proportions; in practice, his interests ended at the borders of Western civilization. Interpretation, he claimed, was meant to reconstruct life-forms that were *somewhat, but not too,* alien. In other words, hermeneutics had been devised to reclaim a carefully chosen past (Tradition) from which an increasingly egalitarian present threatened to become estranged—not to confront stark differences between past and present, between the educated bourgeoisie and the masses, or between Europe and its others. At the

5. Karatani Kojin, "One Spirit, Two Nineteenth Centuries," *South Atlantic Quarterly* 87, no. 3 (Summer 1988): 627.

same time, one might also argue that Dilthey's expansive discursive ambitions reflected, however faintly, a continuing imperialist project on the part of the West to extend its control, material or ideological, to the far reaches of the globe.

This tension between sweeping universalist claims and culturally circumscribed interests was perhaps even more striking in the case of Heidegger. The apparent universality of *Dasein*, the protagonist of that massive philosophical narrative, *Being and Time*, was belied by Heidegger's insistence that the problematic of *Dasein* enjoyed an exclusive relation with the German language and its linguistic-philosophical past. In his reminiscences of conversations with Kuki, recorded in "A Dialogue on Language" (1953) some thirty years after Kuki's extended stay in Europe, Heidegger reiterated his view that Asia lay outside the pale of philosophy. When his Japanese interlocutor noted the compelling quality that European aesthetics had for Kuki's generation, Heidegger responded as follows:

> Here you are touching on a controversial question which I often discussed with Count Kuki—the question whether it is necessary and rightful for Eastasians to chase after the European conceptual systems.[6]

Heidegger did not think to include Kuki's response in the "Dialogue."

Many of the writers and theorists who visited Europe discovered that this covert principle of cultural exclusion operated more overtly in the racial perceptions that distorted European images of its cultural others. Since the beginning of Meiji (1868), Japanese travelers had documented virulent strains of racism in Europe and America, whether directed toward themselves or others. Although Kuki himself left no diaries or memoirs of his European years, we do have one description of him in Herman Glockner's *Heidelberger Bilderbuch*, a description at once favorable and racially telling. Here, Glockner reproduces the words of his mentor, Heinrich Richert, fresh from his first exoticized impression of Kuki:

> Today I made arrangements to give a private tutorial to a Japanese. He is a rich samurai from the Land of Enchantment and he has asked me to read Kant's *Critique of Pure Reason* with him. A gentleman

6. Martin Heidegger, "A Dialogue on Language," in *On the Way to Language*, trans. Peter D. Hertz (New York: Harper & Row, 1971), 3. Heidegger mistakenly referred to Kuki as *Count*; Kuki had inherited the title of *baron* from his father Ryuichi.

of exceptional aristocratic bearing, he gives a completely different impression from other Japanese. He is tall and slender with an oval face. The nose is almost European. His hands are extraordinarily delicate and graceful. His name is Baron Kuki; he tells me it means nine devils in German.[7]

An "honorary European," Kuki's exceptional status in Rickert's eyes only serves to prove the rule of racism. In the 1930s, when Kuki published his philosophical treatise on contingence, he repeatedly illustrated notions of exteriority and exceptionality with the image of a single Japanese in Europe, perceived as yellow because the *essential* attribute was white.

Confronted with such principles of exclusion, Kuki tempered his commitment to the various critical discourses emerging from Europe with a measure of cultural self-defense.[8] Drawing on the philosophical resources he had assembled during his European encounters, Kuki discovered in *iki* an existential disposition free from Western obsessions with identity and certainty, untainted by a rationality of ends. Submitted to the rigors of a structural analysis, *iki* represented a synthesis of three attributes only seemingly at odds with one another: *bitai* (erotic allure); *ikuji* (fearless pride), the legacy of a *bushido* ethos; and *akirame* (resignation), the corollary of a Buddhist worldview. "The secret of erotic allure," Kuki explained, "is to continuously decrease the distance [between oneself and the other] while never allowing that distance to be completely annihilated" (*KSZ*, 1:17). Allure lasts only as long as it remains in the realm of possibility; once realized, it is destined to disappear. The two attributes of pride and resignation—which Kuki traced back to the Edo pleasure quarters—guaranteed that the prospects for perpetuating possibility as possibility became absolute. Pride strengthened one's resolve to maintain possibility indefinitely, while resignation enabled one to forgo fulfillment. In this unlikely alliance of opposites, Kuki discerned a logic unheard-of in the West—"affirmation through negation" and "a commitment to freedom forced by fate." The alluring aesthetic of *iki* evaded the rule of noncontradiction, escaped the logic of identity, and

7. Ishimatsu Keizo, "Heidelberg no Kuki Shuzo," *Kuki Shuzo zenshu geppo* 2 (1980): 4.
8. Although the rest of Asia is virtually absent from Kuki's 1930 aesthetics of ethnic opposition, it is important to note that Japan was simultaneously engaged in subjecting Asia to the same principles of devaluation and exclusion of which it was still a victim. Ironically, the exceptionality of spirit that Kuki claimed for Japan in *"Iki" no kozo* would soon become a pretext for Japan's domination of Asia and the spilling of Asian blood.

defied the limits of the syllogism. Emptied of instrumentality, *iki* offered the prospect of seductiveness for its own sake and replaced the serious labor of love with "disinterested free play."[9]

It seems, then, somewhat of a paradox that the same discursive resources that had enabled Kuki to discover a mode of being beyond the reach of Western metaphysics also encouraged him to subordinate that very mode of being to an absolute logic of ethnic identity and cultural closure. In the final lines of *"Iki" no kozo*, he wrote, "Only when we have grasped the essential meaning of *"iki"* as the self-expression of the being of our ethnos [*minzoku sonzai*] have we attained a complete understanding" (*KSZ*, 1:81). Emptied of its historical and social specificity, *iki* became the chosen signifier of Japan, gathering into its interpretive folds attributes deemed representative of Japanese culture. In this manner, a single word was assigned the task of representing the identity of an inimitable collective subject against the claims of Western universalism. Ultimately, Kuki reenlisted the passion that the style of *iki* had disavowed, this time in the service of national culture. "There is nothing for us," he wrote, "but to persevere in our impassioned *eros* for our culture of *bushido* idealism and Buddhist rejection of reality" (*KSZ*, 1:81).

At this point, one might ask what was sacrificed in such a theoretical transaction between cultures encountering one another within the discursive contours of colonialism. I would suggest, at the very least, that Kuki forfeited the concrete historicity of the popular culture of Bunka-Bunsei (roughly equivalent to the first half of the nineteenth century) where the aesthetic style of *iki* came into its own. *"Iki" no kozo* summons up not the urban topography of Edo's low-lying plebian quarters but rather the eternal landscape of the Japanese spirit. Any historiographical intervention pertains as much to its own present as it does to a moment in the past, and Kuki's particular intervention was no exception. *"Iki" no kozo* exacted high costs not only in the fledgling discipline of Edo historiography but, as we shall see, also in the field of contemporary history.

9. It is interesting to note that Kuki described the aesthetic and moral disposition of *iki* in a manner worthy of Kant's *Third Critique*, replicating most of the significant moments of aesthetic judgment. With this remarkable displacement of European aesthetics, Kuki intimated that Japan was the privileged site of an aesthetic mode of existence. I have addressed this issue more extensively in "The Allure of Difference: '*Iki*' no kozo and the Construction of the Japanese Spirit," (Ph.D. diss., University of Chicago, 1989, 218–23).

An Aristocracy of Taste in an Age of Mass Culture

Kuki's recourse to European discursive strategies reflected other convergences between Japan and the West as well, convergences more specific than a generic apprehension of modernity. At the end of the nineteenth century, Europe confronted the prospect of a disintegrating tradition and a trend toward social leveling that threatened (or promised) a society of drastically different proportions. The humanistic endeavors inaugurated during that era—in particular, the *Kulturwissenschaften* (cultural studies) and cultural hermeneutics—offered refuge in a conception of "culture as truth" and guaranteed a restoration of continuity with a chosen past as well as the privileges that accrued to the guardians of that past. Invented under the impending eclipse, not only of cultural differences but also of caste differences, cultural hermeneutics sought their recuperation in the form of new ethnic and national identities. This was an elitist enterprise,[10] and, as Marxist critic Tosaka Jun pointed out in the 1930s, one that encouraged its practitioners to withdraw from the scene of contemporary social processes into aestheticized reminiscence and subjective interiority.[11]

In Japan, the strategies derived from this European enterprise were first enlisted in a defense of culture during the 1920s, Japan's decade of modernism. This was the era when the effects of modernization, initiated by the Meiji transformation and Japan's realignment with the West, penetrated deep into the grain of everyday life. In a transfigured cityscape of streetcars and high buildings, cafés and dancehalls, new social constituencies rose up from below to become active participants in what was dubbed in

10. Philip Wiley, in his study of the neo-Kantian movement in Germany, suggests that the discourse on culture and cultivation might be read as "the moral and aesthetic defense of a privileged but increasingly beleaguered caste" in flight from the failure of bourgeois liberal politics. See *Back to Kant* (Detroit: Wayne State University Press, 1978), 15–17.

11. See Tosaka Jun's critical genealogy of Western hermeneutics from its classical inception to its Heideggerian phenomenological revision in *Nihon ideologii-ron*, vol. 2 of *Tosaka Jun zenshu* (Tokyo: Keiso Shobo, 1966), 235–49. For other critical analyses of the hermeneutic enterprise by Japanese theorists of the 1930s, see Miki Kiyoshi's "Kaishakugaku to shujigaku" (Hermeneutics and rhetoric), in *Gendai Nihon shiso taikei*, vol. 33 (Tokyo: Chikuma Shobo, 1939), 380–91, and "Shakai kagaku no hoho-ron" (Methodology of the social sciences), in *Miki Kiyoshi zenshu*, vol. 6 (Tokyo: Iwanami Shoten, 1967), 423–53. For more recent critiques by Western theorists, see Jürgen Habermas's *Knowledge and Human Interests*, trans. Jeremy J. Shapiro (Boston: Beacon Press, 1971), 140–86. See also the introduction to Michel Foucault's *Archaeology of Knowledge*, trans. A. M. Sheridan Smith (New York: Harper Colophon, 1972).

English "modern life." As if to lure these urban masses into visibility, culture called on mechanized technologies to accelerate and multiply its representations—in motion pictures, phonograph records, one-yen books, and the rhythms of jazz.[12] In response to the defenders of "authentic culture," it was duly noted that commodification and mechanization (along with those less tangible forms of production with which it is bound) had long since penetrated even the most privileged domains of culture—academe and the arts.[13] These more salient aspects of contemporary culture, however, slip into concealment between the lines of *"Iki" no kozo.*[14]

When Kuki returned to Japan at the close of the decade (1929), Tokyo was preparing to celebrate (with imperial fanfare) the completion of its modern reconstruction from the ruins of the Great Kanto Earthquake of 1923. No doubt the scene that greeted his homecoming resembled the capitals of Europe more than he might have imagined from his distanced vantage point in Paris. Among contemporary observers, there were those who welcomed this modern transformation as a cultural revolution with the potential to empower new social classes. Kuki, however, saw it not as a liberating transcultural modernity, nor as acceptable cultural borrowing, but rather as a sign of the invasive presence of the West. In an essay from the mid-thirties, he recalled his first impression upon returning to Japan in 1929:

> When I walked around the city, wherever I looked, English words were everywhere, on all the billboards. One had the impression that this was a colony, like Singapore or Colombo. Even the newspapers were full of foreign words, and somehow it made me feel ashamed. (*KSZ*, 5:91)

In this new urban landscape, Kuki read the signs of cultural colonization, signs that threatened to level all cultural differences at the expense of an indigenous past.

12. For a tantalizing glimpse of mass culture in the 1920s, see Maeda Ai's brief pictorial review, "Tokyo 1925," *Gendai shiso* vol. 7, no. 8 (Tokyo: Seidosha, 1979): 72–80.
13. See in particular Nakai Masakazu's assessment of the "culture critics" both in Europe and Japan in his 1932 essay "Shisoteki kiki ni okeru geijutsu narabini sono doko" (The tendencies of art at a moment of ideological crisis) in *Nakai Shoichi zenshu*, 4 vols. (Tokyo: Bijutsu Shuppansha, 1965), 2:46–48.
14. For groundbreaking research on mass culture in Taisho and early Showa Japan, see Miriam Silverberg's "Constructing a New Cultural History of Prewar Japan" in this issue; and "The Modern Girl as Militant" in *Recreating Japanese Women, 1600–1945*, ed. Gail Bernstein (Berkeley: University of California Press, 1990).

At the conclusion of *"Iki" no kozo*, Kuki would make a plea to his readers to overcome a temporary lapse in collective memory and *recall* Japan's spiritual culture. Kuki would have it that he spoke in the voice of "Japan." His was a polemic against the trespassing of the West into the domain of an "authentic" Japanese culture. Nevertheless, like the cultural criticism of his European counterparts, Kuki's defense of culture masked a resistance of the few to the rising tide of mass culture, hence his sympathy for the dandy, that purveyor of aristocratic style whom Baudelaire pitted against the undistinguished crowds of mid-nineteenth century Paris. Yet, while Kuki shared Baudelaire's appreciation for the dandy's "aristocratic superiority of mind," his "love of distinction in all things," he neglected the French poet's incisive analysis of the new social relations against which the dandy appeared in high relief. In the prose vignettes of *Le Peintre de la vie moderne*, Baudelaire located his narcissistic rebel in a period of transition when "democracy is not yet all powerful and aristocracy is only just beginning to totter and fall."[15] Displaced by an era in which social distinctions were crumbling, the dandy established a new kind of aristocracy based on style. He protested the division of labor and the industriousness of a society yielding to bourgeois domination by parading his leisure on the streets of modernizing cities. Revealing, too, is the fact that Kuki chose as his privileged signifier of Japan *iki,* the tribute paid to those select individuals who successfully distinguished themselves through mastery of a demanding code of etiquette, style, and discernment.[16] In the last analysis, the anxiety of contamination that pervades *"Iki" no kozo* is as much an anxiety over the *internal* specter of mass culture (and allied possibilities of mass politics) as it is an anxiety over the *external* presence of the West.

15. Charles Baudelaire, *The Painter of Victorian Life: A Study of Constantin Guys*, ed. C. Geoffrey Holme, trans. P. G. Konody (New York: William Edwin Rudge, 1930), 127–32. In the endnotes of *"Iki" no kozo*, Kuki acknowledged the resurgence of a discourse on dandyism in Europe of the 1910s and 1920s (see *"Iki" no kozo*, 1:82, n. 25). It is perhaps fitting that a Europe undergoing the equalizing transfigurations of mass-produced, mass culture should revive a discourse eulogizing an aristocracy of spirit and advocating the distinction of "rare goods" in the developing stages of a commodity culture.
16. Interestingly, in Kuki's interpretation, *iki* (a style intimately linked to the popular culture of Edo commoners) distances itself from merchant/artisan culture and everyday practices in favor of association with a samurai elite and an aestheticized existence in the archives. Whereas *iki* once defined finely articulated differences *within* Japanese culture, in *"Iki" no kozo*, it defines the difference *between* Japan and the West.

The Liability of Form

The contradictions that shadow *"Iki" no kozo* become palpable in a linguistic fissure running through the text. The title itself already suggests an unlikely alliance between two disparate languages: *Iki,* a word with its roots in the popular culture of late Edo, expresses an appreciation of style in a colloquial, even performative, mode; *kozo,* or structure, a weighty analytic term of more recent origin, suggests the continuing dialogue of Japanese intellectuals with Western knowledge.[17] One insightful commentator describes the text as a "magnetic field of language," where a thoroughly mastered philosophical terminology is charged with "capturing alive the language of everyday life."[18] (I would add only the proviso that in Japan of the late 1920s, the language of Edo culture was rapidly losing ground in the vocabulary of everyday life.) Kuki himself attributed this linguistic fissure to an "unbridgeable gap" separating conceptual language from a lived reality that could only be experienced in the recesses of ethnic subjectivity.

Most critical assessments of *"Iki" no kozo* view the text as a resourceful synthesis of Western methods and Japanese subject matter. In the common parlance, "a certain unique Japanese thing" (often conjured up in images of density and opacity) is submitted to the bright illumination of rigorous (Western) philosophical thought. Depending on the perspective of the critic, this so-called synthesis is deemed either a positive accomplishment or a violation. In the preface to *Nihon no shiso* (Japanese thought), Maruyama Masao, postwar historian and ardent believer in the efficacy of rational fictions, commended *"Iki" no kozo* for its structural clarity:

> *"Iki" no kozo* is undoubtedly the most successful example of a three-dimensional elucidation of the internal structure of a concept integral to the way of life of a particular era."[19]

17. Tada Michitaro suggests that this combination of "pure Japanese" with a "difficult, western-style analytic term" became the fashion for book titles in the 1960s. He speculates that Kuki's prescience in this matter accounts for the belated popularity of *"Iki" no kozo.* See Tada Michitaro and Yasuda Takeshi, *" 'Iki' no kozo" o yomu* (Tokyo: Asahi Shimbunsha, 1979), 6.
18. Sugimoto Hidetaro, "Tetsugakuteki zuan," *Kuki Shuzo zenshu geppo* 9 (1981): 1–3.
19. Maruyama Masao, *Nihon no shiso* (Tokyo: Iwanami Shoten, 1961), 4. In this introduction to a series of critical essays on modern Japanese culture and thought, Maruyama deplores the poverty of intellectual history in Japan. The rare praise he accorded *"Iki" no kozo* was, however, conditional. Although he credited Kuki with clarity of exposition, *"Iki" no kozo* did not meet his expectations for a more comprehensive historical analysis that would situate a concept both synchronically and diachronically.

Maruyama's reference to three-dimensionality refers no doubt to the geo-metric figure that appears in the pages of *"Iki" no kozo*, a figure in which Kuki schematically represented a Japanese system of taste.[20] Nonetheless, connoisseurs of Edo culture, as well as those less sanguine about the un-conditional benefits of rationality, have expressed doubts about the merits of Kuki's "geometry of taste" and, more generally, about the merits of a meth-odological approach derived from the West. What such doubts often imply is that Western methods, far from innocent, violate the "Japaneseness" of the subject in question. Long after his discussions with Kuki in the late 1920s, Heidegger, in "The Dialogue on Language," would raise very similar ques-tions concerning the "ethics" of *"Iki" no kozo*. Had Kuki not in fact already succumbed to the temptation of the West when he spoke of *iki* as "sensuous radiance through whose lively delight there breaks the radiance of some-thing suprasensuous?"[21] Heidegger strongly suggested that Kuki's attempt to "say the essential nature of Eastasian art" was already betrayed by the discriminating language of European aesthetics.[22] Interestingly, Heidegger failed to touch on another temptation to which Kuki doubtlessly yielded— the temptation to invest his description of *iki* with Heidegger's own desire for the ineffable beyond of Western metaphysics.[23]

More recently, Karatani Kojin, an attentive reader of both Kuki and Heidegger, has pointed out another and more disturbing side to this en-counter between German and Japanese philosophers. Not without sympa-thy for Heidegger's (and Kuki's) nostalgia for something beyond the hege-

20. For a reproduction of the geometrical figure, see *KSZ*, 1:37, and an unnumbered, final special volume:11–13. One might view Kuki's project to capture an elusive sense of style in the rigid structural precision of a schemata as an attempt to lend durability (and nation-ality) to a fading cultural phenomenon. Derrida's insight into the structuralist passion is of some interest here: "It is during the epochs of historical dislocation, when we are expelled from the *site* [of Being]," he writes, "that this structuralist passion, which is simultaneously a frenzy of experimentation and a proliferation of schematizations, develops for itself" (see Derrida, "Force and Signification," in *Writing and Difference* [Chicago: University of Chicago Press, 1978], 6).

21. Heidegger, "A Dialogue on Language," 14.

22. Tezuka Tomio, the model for the "Japanese" in Heidegger's "Dialogue," now well ad-vised of the reifying trap of metaphysics, amends Kuki's definition of *iki* in a direction that follows Heidegger beyond oppositions between subject and object into the mysteries of being: "*Iki* is the breath of stillness of luminous delight . . . the pure delight of the beckon-ing stillness. The breath of stillness that makes this beckoning delight come into its own is the reign under which that delight is made to come" (see Heidegger, "A Dialogue on Language," 44–45).

23. See Peter Dale's unsparing critique of this encounter in *The Myth of Japanese Uniqueness* (London & Sydney: Croom Helm, 1986), 68–70.

monic reach of modernity, Karatani suggests that Kuki was seeking "the forgotten 'being' of the modern world in the aesthetic way of life of the nineteenth century."[24] Kuki recognized in *iki,* he explains, the possibility of a world of pure surface devoid of all meaning and interiority—in other words, a prescient vision of a postmodern world delivered from a metaphysics of depth (the reigning piety of the West, if we are to believe Roland Barthes). Yet, proposed Karatani, even as Kuki discovered the distinctiveness of Edo, he had already buried it beneath epistemological categories derived from the West. Thus far, Karatani appears to be spelling out Heidegger's vague apprehension that the methodological language of Kuki's inquiry had fateful consequences for its content. Here, Karatani parts company with Heidegger to implicate the German philosopher along with Kuki in a peculiarly modern conspiracy: Heidegger's concern for "Being," observes Karatani, was never far from his faith in the historical mission of a German *Folk,* and Kuki merely retraced Heidegger's itinerary when he deployed a "hermeneutics of ethnic being" to identify the eccentricities of Edo culture as the dwelling place of the Japanese spirit. Both philosophers, charges Karatani, imposed a "despotic system" on the cultural or spiritual disposition they hoped to rescue from the ravages of modernity. In both cases, that "despotic system" harbored ideological potential for imperialism and nationalistic fanaticism.[25]

What Karatani's critique suggests is that the notion of synthesis between method (the West) and matter (Japan) does not adequately describe the transaction conducted in *"Iki" no kozo.* Rather, the concept of an essential Japanese object, of Japaneseness, proves to be the discursive effect of a method with a content all its own. In other words, the form of Kuki's inquiry conferred a meaning that was in no way ideologically neutral. By the late 1930s, Kuki had enlisted the tripartite structure of *iki* in the service of an ultranationalist imperial state. *Bitai* (erotic allure) had been replaced by a less provocative *shizen* (nature), rendered in the reactionary terminology of Nativist Shinto; this, combined with Buddhist resignation and Bushido pride (thoroughly Confucianized), now unambiguously added up to the *kokutai* or unique national essence symbolized by the Divine Regalia (jewel, mirror, and sword).[26]

24. Karatani, "One Spirit," 623.
25. Karatani Kojin, "Edo no seishin," *Gendai shiso,* vol. 14, no. 10 (Sept. 1986): 8–10; and Karatani, "One Spirit," 621–23.
26. Kuki Shuzo, "Nihonteki seikaku" (The Japanese character), in *KSZ,* 3:272–92. See also Karatani's remarks in "One Spirit," 622–23.

Why did *"Iki" no kozo* lend itself so easily to appropriation by an ultra-nationalist ideology? With Karatani's initial insight as a point of departure, I would propose that at least part of the answer lies in the form of Kuki's inquiry. What Kuki discovered deeply embedded in the German romantic and hermeneutic traditions (and widely circulating in Europe's interwar philosophical discourse) was a logic of organicism placed at the disposal of the state. He articulated that logic in the opening lines of *"Iki" no kozo*:

> The relation between meaning and language on the one hand and the conscious being of an ethnos on the other is not one in which the former aggregates to construct the latter; rather it is the living being of the ethnos which creates meaning and language. The relation between the two terms is not a mechanical one in which the parts precede the whole, but an organic one in which the whole determines the parts. (*KSZ*, 1:8)

Following this line of reasoning, any cultural phenomenon (the part) that finds expression in language—*iki* in this case—fulfills a single mission: the self-revelation of an ethnos (the whole) to itself. Lacoue-Labarthe, who has provided us with a careful reading of fascist strains in Heidegger, points out that this essential organicity is infra-political, even infra-social. In other words, it dispenses with questions of political power and social practices to return to anachronistic notions of a pre-political community—in German, the *Volkstum,* and in Japanese, *minzoku*. Following Lacoue-Labarthe's argument, this is a naturally determined community that can only be accomplished and revealed to that community through its *works*—specifically, art, philosophy, and language (the community's language). It is in this aesthetic surplus that the community "deciphers," presents, and recognizes itself.[27] What such logic implies is the "aestheticization of the political"—a project that Benjamin (who had the extreme example of the Italian Futurists in mind) identified as the distinguishing mark of fascism.[28] In the late 1930s, when Japan was deeply mired in imperialist aggression on the Chinese mainland,

27. Philosopher Jean-Luc Nancy calls the extreme expression of this logic *immanentism,* "a condition in which it is 'the aim of the community of beings in essence to produce their own essence as their work (*oeuvre*), and moreover to produce precisely this essence *as community*'" (from Lacoue-Labarthe's discussion of Nancy's *La Communauté désoeuvrée* [Paris: Christian Bourgois, 1986], in *Heidegger, Art and Politics* [Cambridge: Basil Blackwell, 1990], 70).
28. See for example Walter Benjamin's "The Work of Art in an Age of Mechanical Reproduction," in *Illuminations* (New York: Schocken Books, 1969), 241–42.

Kuki was able to claim that a victory over China would bear witness to the philosophical and aesthetic credentials of the Japanese army:

> By vanquishing China, we Japanese must teach them in a decisive manner the spirit of Japanese philosophy. It is our cultural-historical mission to lend spiritual succor to the renewal of their mother country by imprinting our idealistic philosophy in the form of *bushido* in the innermost recesses of their bodies.[29]

Finally, it was Japan's cultural superiority, culture in the narrow sense of aesthetic and spiritual values, that would be revealed on the battlefields of Asia.

The Labyrinth

In a 1931 lecture on Heideggerian philosophy, Kuki described the hermeneutic endeavor in mythic terms:

> At the time when Theseus was about to enter the Labyrinth, he was given a spool of string by Ariadne. He attached one end of the string to the entrance of the cave, and was thus able to find his way out again. In the same manner, we attach the end of the string that guides all philosophical questioning. (*KSZ*, 10:10)

Ostensibly, Kuki used the mythic metaphor to demonstrate Heidegger's conviction that philosophical inquiry must take human existence both as its point of departure and as its destination. I would suggest an additional, if unacknowledged, signification for the mythic Labyrinth. For a moment, imagine Kuki in the role of Theseus, lured into the winding passages of European discourse by the promise of knowledge and power. Once inside the familiar, but not wholly hospitable, passages of the Labyrinth, did he perhaps suffer the anxiety that return might no longer be possible? Was it the unspoken apprehension of an impossible return that engendered the fantasy of deliverance from the Labyrinth? Kuki did in fact believe that he had returned to his imagined point of departure—a self-possessed Japan untainted by its cultural Other. Nevertheless, we might entertain the metaphoric possibility that Kuki never found his way out of the Labyrinth. Rather, he constructed an imaginary site called Japan within the insular passageways of European philosophical discourse.

---

29. See Kuki Shuzo, "Jikyoku no kanso" (Thoughts on the current state of affairs)," *KSZ*, 5:38.

Return to the West / Return to the East: Watsuji Tetsuro's Anthropology and Discussions of Authenticity

Naoki Sakai

Since the publication of *The Study of the Human Being in Pascal* by Miki Kiyoshi in 1924, the question of the human being as *'ningen'*, or the 'being-between', has been repeatedly asked by Japanese writers who were engaged in philosophical debates both inside the academia of national colleges and universities and, outside it, in intellectual journalism, which was rapidly growing with the increasing number of subscribers to newly founded intellectual journals like *Shiso*, *Kaizo*, and *Riso*. *The Study of the Human Being in Pascal* probably marks the first serious and systematic

This essay contains presentations delivered at two conferences in March 1990 at the State University of New York at Binghamton and at Cornell University. Some parts were also presented at the Association for Asian Studies Annual Meeting in April 1990 and at the symposium "Representation of the Other: Japan and the World," held in May and June 1990 at the University of California Humanities Research Institute. This essay is comprised of chapters two and three of *Return to the West/Return to the East: Watsuji Tetsuro's Anthropology and the Emperor System (Seiyo eno Kaiki/Toyo eno kaiki—Watsuji Tetsuro no ningengaku to ten'nosei)*, which was published in a Japanese translation in *Shiso*, 797 (Tokyo: Iwanami Shoten, November 1990). I would like to express my gratitude to the discussants of my papers, Professor Christopher Fynsk (at Binghamton) and Professor Dominick LaCapra (at Cornell), for their valuable comments.

attempt in Japan to introduce Heideggerian Dasein analysis, which Miki Kiyoshi had familiarized himself with while he studied with Heidegger in Germany in the early phase of the Weimar era. In this monumental work, Miki conducted the existential analysis of the human being, or *Ningen Sonzai*, in terms of Heideggerian Dasein as 'state-of-mind'[1] and argued that the human being should be understood as 'being-between', or 'being-thrown-between', an essentially unstable middle entity, or *Chukansha*, suspended between infinity and void. Here, already, one of the concerns that dominated discussions of the human being in the late 1920s and 1930s was clearly delineated: The human being is comprehended to be unsure of itself and is an entity who inquires about itself and relates to itself not through necessities but through possibilities. Miki Kiyoshi continued to ask the question of the human being, first in the context of Marxism, in his attempt to synthesize hermeneutics and Marxism, and, second, after the collapse of Marxism in the mid-thirties, in his exploration of the historical being, or *Rekishi-teki Sonzai*. Perhaps with the exception of Lukács, no contemporary European thinkers were more extensively and intensely read by Japanese intellectuals than Heidegger during this period. Many, including Tanabe Hajime, Kuki Shuzo, and Nishitani Keiji, were very interested in the problem of the human being through their reading of Heidegger. Watsuji Tetsuro was among these intellectuals. Partly in contradiction to Miki, he attempted to modify Heideggerian hermeneutics into a philosophical anthropology as ethics with a comprehension of social praxis that is different from Heidegger's. I believe it is appropriate to argue that, in this respect, the variety of readings of Heidegger reflected the intellectual situation of Japan from the late 1920s through the late 1930s; a different reading of Heidegger's works indicated a different political possibility, and conflicts among the interpretations of Heidegger were closely related to the issue of praxis.

In reading Watsuji's texts, I do not want to follow the culturalist scheme of questioning, which tends to reduce philosophical problems raised by Japanese or any foreign intellectuals to the matter of cultural difference: Many specialists of Japanese thought in Japan and North America, as well as in Europe, are still inclined to let their inquiry be guided by such questions as "Did Japanese scholars who were Oriental understand Western philosophy correctly?" and "How did the Oriental tradition distort their

---

1. See Martin Heidegger, *Being and Time*, trans. J. Macquarrie and E. Robinson (New York: Harper and Row, 1962), part 1, chap. 29, 172–79; hereafter cited in my text as *Being and Time*. Miki's argument, however, seems to be based on a much earlier version of Dasein analysis than that found in *Being and Time*.

understanding of Western philosophy?" The fact of being brought up in the so-called West might help one to be more familiar with Western philosophy, which is, nonetheless, diverse and heterogeneous. It is very difficult to find the grounds to claim that the fact of one's birth guarantees one's "correct" understanding of Western philosophy. Furthermore, the arbitrariness of the identity "the West" must be thoroughly scrutinized. Of course, the same can be said about "Japan" and "the East." I do not want to read Watsuji Tetsuro within the framework of culturalism, in which, as I will illustrate, Watsuji himself was trapped; I would not try to reduce Watsuji's philosophical discourse to an example of the Japanese national character. Instead, I will show the practical and political significance of what the culturalist might call "distortion" and "misunderstanding" peculiar to the national culture in Watsuji's reading of Heidegger, rather than judge Watsuji in terms of "correct" and "incorrect" opposition, although I do admit that simple distortion or misunderstanding is not only possible but also frequent in the comprehension of thought. Sometimes "incorrect" comprehension can be caused by the failure on the part of the reader to take into account regional, class, political, historical, and other heterogeneities. But the diversity of those factors cannot be uniformly and exhaustively attributed to national character and nationality. We must be critical of the many sorts of social stereotyping underlying cultural essentialism, which has been increasingly favored in the name of respect for local particularity.

Watsuji's project in philosophical anthropology as ethics was first outlined in a 1931 publication entitled *Rinrigaku* (Ethics).[2] In this book, the central question of ethics is defined as that of the human being, and it is argued that the question of the human being cannot be addressed merely as the question of what the object designated in this questioning is, since the

---

2. *Rinrigaku* (Ethics) was published as part of the series called *Tetsugaku koza* (Tokyo: Iwanami Shoten, 1931). Watsuji published *Rinrigaku* many times throughout his life, each time making radical modifications to the previous version. I have not yet obtained all of the original versions of *Rinrigaku*. I have only the 1931 version of *Rinrigaku* (Ethics) in the original; the postwar reproduction of the 1934 version of *Ningen no gaku to shiteno rinrigaku* (Ethics as the study of human being); the postwar reproduction of the 1937 version of *Rinrigaku (jo)* or (Ethics [I]); the postwar reproduction of the 1942 version of *Rinrigaku (chu)* or (Ethics [II]), which contains the list of parts rewritten in the postwar publication; and the 1949 version of *Rinrigaku (ge)* or (Ethics [III]). Hereafter, each version is designated in my text by the year of publication. General references to Watsuji's works are cited in my text as *Ethics*. Except for the first 1931 version, Watsuji's works cited in my text are in his collected works, *Watsuji Tetsuro zenshu* (Tokyo: Iwanami Shoten, 1961–1963), which is hereafter cited as *Z*, with volume and page numbers.

study of the human being cannot be subsumed under the study of nature. The opposition between the human being and nature, operating at his insistence upon the irreducibility of the human being into nature, derives from the distinction, somewhat reminiscent of neo-Kantianism, between the two mutually heterogeneous domains of scientific investigation, the human sciences and the natural sciences. Watsuji attributed to Marx this distinction, which was fundamental to the initial formation of his idea of human science, *Ningen no gaku*, as ethics.

Interestingly enough, the itinerary of the argument by Watsuji, who earned credentials as an anti-Marxist liberal, shows how much he owed to *The German Ideology* in the initial formulation of the question of the human being:

> As it is well known, Marx rejected eighteenth-century materialism, because that materialism neglected the moment of historical and social activities in the human being. "The chief defect of all previous materialism is that things, reality, sensuousness are conceived only in *the form of the object, or of intuition (chokkan),* and are never grasped as *sensuous and human activity,* that is, as praxis. This is to say that [the old materialism] never grasps such reality subjectively (shutai-teki ni)." A Thing (Taisho) as nature is grasped as an object, that is, as what is posited as something opposed [to the epistemological subject]. In contrast, Marx insists on grasping reality subjectively (shutai-teki ni) as praxis.[3]

Here Marx's conception of the human being is presented as introducing a new understanding of the sensuous and human reality. Thus, Watsuji claimed that Marx rejected materialisms that treated the human being as a natural object and, instead, emphasized the subjective being, or *Shutai-teki Sonzai*, of the human being as practical activity. While congratulating Marx on the basic conception of human essence as 'an ensemble of social relations' upon which, as we will see, he would build his *Ethics*, Watsuji gave the first determination of the central issue—the human being, or *Ningen*, as the subjective being, or *Shutai-teki Sonzai*—and subsequently charac-

3. *Rinrigaku* (1931), 4; Watsuji's emphasis. The quote is ascribed to Miki Kiyoshi's translation of *The German Ideology* (Tokyo: Iwanami Shoten, 1928 [?]). (Also found in *The German Ideology* [Moscow: Progress Publishers, 1964], 618.) In this translation, Miki Kiyoshi explicitly identified the use of the term 'subject' ('shutai'). Elsewhere, I have explained the variety of Japanese renderings of the term 'subject' and their philosophical implications.

terized the path his inquiry would have to take as a philosophy of praxis. His philosophical anthropology was thus identified as a philosophy of praxis about the subjective being of Man.

Two points should be noted. First, Watsuji followed Marx, particularly in the first "Thesis on Feuerbach," to the extent that the practical and subjective activities of the human being are affirmed. However, when it comes to what we know as the critique of humanism—of which there are many readings today, of course—Watsuji shifted away from Marx's argument. This is even more evident when we examine the other and later versions of his *Ethics*, in which fewer and fewer references are made to Marxist literature in general, until many of the traces of his theoretical struggle with Marxism are erased in the postwar versions. As I hope will become clear when I examine Watsuji's discussions of the authentic self in the 1937 and 1942 versions of his *Ethics*, the repression of his theoretical deficit toward Marx, and eventually toward what was perceived to be the West as a whole, will be shown to be an essential component in the constitution of cultural identity in his and others' culturalist discourse. In Watsuji's anthropology, his uneasiness with certain philosophies and social thoughts is immediately molded into the dichotomies: the West versus the East, and the West versus Japan. Indeed, one is fully entitled to feel ill at ease with some existing ideas, and without the moment of uneasiness, any critical reevaluation of them would hardly be possible. The trouble is that disagreement with the existing modes of thought is explained away solely in terms of the Orient's or Japan's cultural differences. The concept of culture is appealed to as an excuse not to think through the uneasiness one feels with an existing view. This is a feature exclusive not to Watsuji but to culturalism in general. It goes without saying that the same structure, with the terms reversed, exists in cultural essentialism in North America and Europe, which, most often, just like Watsuji's works on cultural typology do, testifies to a certain repression of anxiety that almost inevitably arises from the encounter with any heterogeneous other.

Second, we should note the term 'praxis' in Watsuji's discourse. Despite his emphasis on the sensuous and on human activity, he did not see much of a problem in allying the sort of praxis thematically dealt with in *The German Ideology* with the basically Kantian notion of praxis. Consequently, although Watsuji coined one of the main philosophemes in his *Ethics*, '*koi-teki jissen renkan*', or 'practical relationality in [social] action', after Heidegger's conception of 'equipment',[4] almost no attention is paid to

4. For the term 'equipment', see Heidegger, *Being and Time*, 97.

social relations, which are mediated by equipment. It seems that Watsuji's undue insistence on the irreducibility of his human science or 'the study of the human being' to natural science led to the sanctification of Man, totally independent of 'nature' and free of any contamination by 'material-ism'. Surely his philosophy cannot be characterized as hostile to carnality, as is unequivocally evidenced by his enthusiastic endorsement of sexual affection and his adamant denunciation of puritanism,[5] because of which he has often been portrayed as the liberal and cosmopolitan thinker of modern Japan. Nevertheless, there is a peculiar spiritualism operating in Watsuji's discourse. What one might refer to as 'the materiality of the social' is deliber-ately excluded in his *Ethics*, and, as I will reiterate later, his conception of the social relation cannot afford to entertain the possibility of overdetermination in that relation at all.

The term '*shutai*', or 'subject', itself was thus posited as the central philosopheme around which topics related to praxis, on the one hand, and the determination of particular social relations, on the other hand, would be woven together in Watsuji's study of the human being. Here, however, a glance at the history of the term 'subject' in modern Japanese language seems to be necessary.

This particular rendering of the word 'subject' in Japanese is incon-ceivable beyond the context of what was then called *Jikaku Sonzairon*, or the ontology of self-awareness.[6] To my knowledge, no equivalent of 'subject'

5. See "The community of two people and sexual love," in sec. 2, chap. 3, of *Rinrigaku (jo)* (Ethics [I]) (1937), Z–10, 336–82. In this part, probably, Watsuji is most 'modern' and 'liberal'. After examining sociological and ethnographic publications (by G. Simmel, E. Durkheim, B. Bauch, B. Malinowski, T. Hobhouse, J. K. Folsom, T. Toda, L. H. Morgan, etc.), he argued that the prevailing view of family in primitive societies by Social Darwin-ists like Spencer and Morgan was based on the confusion of sexual relation and kinship, and that, in creating social relations, the sexual relation was the foundation of intimacy and was primary in relation to kinship. From this viewpoint, Watsuji claimed that, in spite of the diversity of familial forms at the level of kinship, the monogamic sexual relation was universal and that the primary definition of community had to be defined in terms of the sexual union of one man and one woman. The romantic view of marriage was internalized in Watsuji's ethics to this extent.
6. Tentatively, I render the term *Jikaku* as self-awareness. Apperception, self-conscious-ness, and self-recognition are also possible as its English equivalents, since *Jikaku* could be equated to the uses of equivalent terms by Kant, Fichte, Hegel, Bergson, Nishida Kitaro, and Heidegger. The Japanese compound *Jikaku* itself, which was also a common word in colloquial conversation, was registered and has been discussed extensively as a philosophical term since the turn of the century. One aspect of *Jikaku* that cannot be ignored is that it is concerned with the unity of the self but that its unity is primarily given

played any major role in the intellectual world in Japan prior to the importation of European philosophical vocabulary during the Meiji period, although the problems that later received rearticulation in relation to 'subject' had certainly been addressed in pre-Meiji Japan, for instance, in Buddhist discourses of various periods. In the process of translating the term 'subject', *'sujet', 'Subjekt',* and so forth, questions internal to the conceptions of 'subject' in modern philosophy, questions that demanded a philosophical, and not philological or linguistic, response were inevitably raised.

As this issue has been seriously questioned, for example, in the context of the critique of ontology in Europe, Japan, and elsewhere for the last several decades, the translation of the term 'subject' must have had to do with the peculiarity of a convention in which the subject in the sense of the nominative case (*shukaku*) was assumed to be identical to the subject (*shugo*) of a proposition. And in a proposition, the subject is linked to the predicate by the copula, thereby entering the register of the being. The situation is further complicated by the fact that the word 'subject' is frequently used to signify an individual who speaks or acts. Subject is often used for both that which is thought or the subject in the sense of theme (*shudai*) and the one who thinks.

The problem of *'Jikaku sonzai'* or the 'being-aware-of-self', was put forth in relation to the topic of modern subjectivity in Japan when the question about the subject thinking or perceiving itself as a theme was asked. Already in this questioning itself, one can detect some uncertainty as to the status of the verb *to think,* for two different ways to posit the subject in relation to this verb are available. One is confined to the formation of knowledge, so that the subject of thinking is exclusively epistemological, and this sort of subject was rendered as *shukan.* In contrast, the other is linked to the issue of action and subsequently to praxis in general, and, as thinking was taken to be an act (as in 'thinking act'), the verb *to think* was included in the group of verbs, such as *to do, to make, to act,* and *to speak.* The consequence is that the subject of thinking is taken to be the subject of action. In this case, the term was translated as *shutai.* What distinguishes the subject as *shutai* from the subject as *shukan,* or the epistemological subject, is primarily the practical nature of *shutai,* because of which the subject as *shutai* cannot be accommodated within the subjective-objective

---

as the unity of the will. This is most clearly manifested in Nishida Kitaro's works of the late 1910s and early 1920s, in which Nishida sought for the conception of apperception, not in cognition but in the modality of possibility.

opposition. For this reason, Watsuji could argue that, insofar as the subjective (*shutai-teki*) being of Man is concerned, it should not be grasped as an object opposed to the epistemological subject (*shukan*).

The distinction between *shutai* and *shukan* has been proven very precarious as is attested to by the frequency of the cases in which these two terms are used interchangeably in Japanese philosophy. Watsuji, who tried to stabilize the distinction by basing it on the opposition of the human sciences and the natural sciences, was, nevertheless, no exception on that score. He appealed to the Kantian exposition in order to explicate the social nature of the human being with which he claimed natural science could not deal and for which the term *shutai,* not *shukan,* was necessary.

The social nature of the human being, that is, the fact that the human being is primarily the subject as *shutai* was deduced from the empirico-transcendental dual structure of the human being. Following Kant's argument about the concepts of transcendental personality and person, Watsuji argued that the social nature of the human being lay in its character:

> The human being finds himself in his object. The ground for such a possibility should be in the fact that the human being is [at the same time] 'I' and 'you' in himself. When the human being finds an object, he finds in it his 'I' that has been externalized into 'you'. We must agree [with Heidegger] that the primordial scene of 'going out', that is, the scene of *ex-sistere,* of transcendence, has been found in the human being. (*Rinrigaku* [1931], 7)

Thus, Watsuji superimposed the Kantian empirico-transcendental double onto the Heideggerian ontico-ontological double. Since this superimposition was a possibility that Heidegger himself had entertained,[7] let me sketch the path of Watsuji's argument. Starting with the determination of subject in terms of the 'I think', which should be able to accompany all 'my' representations, Watsuji stresses the formal character of the transcendental subject[8] as stated by Kant:

7. It goes without saying that the entire project of *Ningen no gaku to shiteno rinrigaku* (Ethics as the study of the human being) is overshadowed by Heidegger's *Kant and the Problem of Metaphysics*, although actual references to Heidegger's book on Kant do not appear until the 1937 version of Watsuji's *Ethics*. Already in 1932, however, Tanabe Hajime's essay "Zushiki 'jikan' kara zushiki 'sekai' e" (From the schema 'time' to the schema 'world'), in *Tetsugaku kenkyu*, vol. 200, 1932, attempted a radical critique and appropriation of Heidegger's book on Kant in order to offer an idea of spatialized schematism.
8. See Watsuji's article "Jinkaku to jinruisei," originally published in *Tetsugaku kenkyu*

We can assign no other basis for this teaching [about the nature of our thinking being] than the simple, and in itself completely empty, representation 'I'; and we cannot even say that this is a concept, but only that it is a bare consciousness which accompanies all concepts. Through this I or he or it (the thing) which thinks, nothing further is represented than a transcendental subject of the thoughts $= X$. It is known only through the thoughts which are its predicates, and of it, apart from them, we cannot have any concept whatsoever, but can only revolve in a perpetual circle, since any judgment upon it has always already made use of its representation. And the reason why this inconvenience is inseparably bound up with it, is that consciousness in itself is not a representation distinguishing a particular object, but a form of representation in general, that is, of representation in so far as it is to be entitled knowledge; for it is only of knowledge that I can say that I am thereby thinking something.[9]

Following Kant's paralogisms of pure reason, Watsuji demonstrates the fundamental mistake involved in the application of categories to the 'vehicle of those categories', to the transcendental subject, in order to show that the transcendental subject, or transcendental personality, the *determining subject* in the application of categories to manifolds of senses, can never be *determined* to be an object to which categories are applied. Therefore, the transcendental 'I', or transcendental personality, must be *mu*, or *nothingness*, insofar as it is sought for as an object (*taisho to shitewa mu*). It is noteworthy that *mu,* or nothingness, which would repeatedly be appealed to in the wartime and postwar culturalist discourse as if, from the outset, it had been the mystical concept issued from some profound Oriental religious consciousness, was first given as a philosophical term in the reading of Kant.[10] In contrast to the transcendental personality, which can never be

---

from 1931 until 1932, and as a monograph in 1938. In this essay, I refer to the 1938 version, which was reproduced in *Z–9*, 317–476.

9. Immanuel Kant, *Critique of Pure Reason*, trans. Norman Kemp Smith (New York: St. Martin's Press, 1929), 331–32, (B404).

10. In fact, Watsuji simply borrowed this use of *mu* from Nishida Kitaro. But Nishida, too, formulated this term in his reading of Kant with regard to the problem of consciousness—in the context of the critique of consciousness and, in particular, of Husserlian phenomenology. However, in spite of the identity of the term *mu*, Nishida and Watsuji employ this philosopheme in very different contexts, and the essentializing or substantializing tendency of Watsuji is very obvious also in this case. As I will show, despite his etymological examination of the Chinese and Japanese words for 'being', Watsuji could never dislodge himself from the ontology of subjectivity, or what Nishida called '*Ronri-teki shugoshugi*'

a being, the person is the thinking being to which the category of substance is applied. Therefore, person is partly a being (*yu*) as opposed to person-ality (*mu*). Yet, person and personality are always combined in the human being as *jikaku sonzai,* or the 'being-aware-of-self'.

> The 'I', who is conscious of the objectified 'I' according to the form of inner sense, that is, according to the 'I' in itself, is nothing but the I of the 'I think', i.e., the subjective ego. Furthermore, the 'I think' is empty without any content, and is the 'transcendental personality', but it is never a 'person'. Therefore, person is neither simply identical to the 'I' as an object nor to the subjective 'I' (shukan ga). (*Jinrui to jinkakusei*, in Z–9, 332–33)[11]

Watsuji attempts to legitimate the use of *shutai* by showing that what is at issue is something that cannot be construed within the scope of *shu-kan*. Precisely because of the limitation inherent in the conception of the epistemological subject, neither the social nature of the human being nor the 'being-aware-of-self' of *Ningen* can be addressed in terms of the clas-sical epistemological subjectivity. To pose the social nature of the human being as an authentic question indispensable to the study of the human being requires something like a 'schematism' about the combination of per-sonality and person, a schematism by means of which to think the internal relationship between '*homo noumenon*' and '*homo phaenomenon*'.[12] From Watsuji's viewpoint, however, Kant's formula was understood to point out both a clue to the possible way to articulate the social nature of human being within his anthropology philosophically and the limit of Kantian critical philosophy that must be overcome in order to give an adequate account of the 'being-with' of the human being (*ningen sonzai no kyodotai*) at the same time.

In *Critique of Pure Reason*, the duality of personality and person is given in the 'self-consciousness in time'. Hence,

---

(logical subjectivism); neither could Heidegger. For Nishida's notion of '*Ronri-teki shugo-shigi*', see *Mu no jikaku-teki gentei* (The apperceptional determination of *mu*), in vol. 6 of *Nishida Kitaro zenshu* (Tokyo: Iwanami Shoten, 1965).

11. For a more detailed discussion of this topic, see Sakabe Megumi, *Perusona no shi-gaku* (Tokyo: Iwanami Shoten, 1989), 121–46.

12. The issue of 'schematism' here seems to be concerned with the question of spatiality as opposed to that of temporality, which was asked by many around that time. Undeni-ably, it was connected to Heidegger's book on Kant. Watsuji, together with Tanabe Hajime and others, saw in Heidegger's discussion an unjustifiable privileging of temporality over spatiality.

> In the whole time in which I am conscious of myself, I am conscious of this time as belonging to the unity of myself; and it comes to the same whether I say that this whole time is in me, as an individual unity, or that I am to be found as numerically identical in all this time.[13]

The 'I' in which time is, is the 'I' of apperception, while the ego in time is the objectified 'I'. For the 'I' of apperception, it is impossible to say that it is in time, while, insofar as the 'I' is objectified, it must be in time, since any entity outside time cannot be an object of experience. These two 'I''s are not identical, but they are synthesized in the person through the schematism of time. "Insofar as the objectified ego is concerned, the ego is in time. Since time is in the ego that is not objectified, however, it is in the stage (*bamen*) of time that the ego, which is *mu,* or nothingness, insofar as it is sought after as an object, objectifies itself" (*Jinrui to jinakakusei*, in Z–9, 334). Watsuji then claims that the dual structure of the human being should be understood in a manner similar to the way Kant demonstrates the duality of empirico-transcendental subjectivity in schematism. Here again, however, he draws attention to the practical nature of *ningen* by pointing out that, while transcendental personality does not relate itself to a subject other than the one to which it is 'numerically identical', the human being is essentially with the others and, therefore, necessarily communal 'being-with': as far as the human being is concerned, the subject must be *shutai,* not *shukan,* since *shukan* relates only to itself and lacks in the moment of communality with other subjects. In thus addressing the social nature of the human being in relation to schematism, Watsuji believes he has explained the inadequacy of the Kantian framework in which the duality of the transcendental 'I' and the empirical 'I' is persuasively laid out, but the 'being-with' of person is ignored.[14] He insists that, while in the theoretical employment of reason, the transcendental subject is indeterminable and unknowable (hence, the subject is *shukan*), the transcendental subject is

---

13. Kant, *Critique of Pure Reason*, 341, (A362).

14. Later, Watsuji also accused Heidegger of an individualistic tendency and of a negligence of the 'being-with'. In view of Heidegger's notion of the 'being-with', I find it very difficult to apprehend Watsuji's critique. Watsuji summarized the Heideggerian argument in terms of individualism. Watsuji failed, however, to take into consideration the wide variety of positions the term *individualism* could possibly connote, and he neglected the fact that it was impossible to ascribe to Heidegger a naïve form of individualism in which the self of an individual person was granted the status of an enduring substance. As I will show, it seems to me that this blindness would have prevented Watsuji from perceiving how akin, in its social and political consequences, his anthropology was to the kind of individualism he detested and objected to so much.

given immediately and concretely (as *shutai*) in its practical employment. (Thus, by ascribing the uncertainty of the 'I' only to the theoretical employment of reason, thereby trivializing it, Watsuji refused to acknowledge the abyssal nature of the 'I'; he resisted the cognizance that the 'I' is groundless, a cognizance without which the resoluteness of Dasein in its authenticity in Heidegger, for instance, would be incomprehensible. At this stage, Watsuji refused to deal with the issue of either 'historicality' or 'co-historizing'. I will come back to this problem later.) Furthermore, from the outset, the transcendental subject as *shutai* is given as 'being-with'. The human being understands its social relationality with others, and this understanding is essentially a practical one that is anterior to theoretical understanding. "The human being exists in such a way that it produces communal life which is mutually understood [by one and the other] prior to consciousness" (*Rinrigaku* [1931], 9). Rephrasing Marx, then, Watsuji argues that, because of the inner structure of the human being, human consciousness is preordained by man's social being. Now his study of Man acquired a specific direction by which the being of Man should be investigated: the dual structure of the *ningen,* or 'being-between'.

In his analysis of the concept 'human being', Watsuji proved himself to be an earnest disciple of Heidegger again. An etymological method was applied to the Japanese and Chinese terms concerning *ningen* in order to reveal the social nature of *ningen*. First, as I have already mentioned, the compound *ningen,* which consists of two characters *nin* (*hito*) and *gen* (*aida*) is submitted to etymological analysis.[15] *Nin* (or *hito*) and *gen* (or *aida*), respectively, mean a person recognized from the third person's perspective or people in general (English *one,* French *on,* or German *Man*), and space between or relationality. Hence, Watsuji says, the term *ningen* already implies the space between people that simultaneously separates and relates one person and another. In addition, *hito,* the specifically Japanese pronunciation for the first character of the compound *ningen,* contains the viewpoint of another person, in that *hito* can never be used directly to

15. Many Japanese terms are made up of Chinese compounds that can be dissembled into unit characters. The phonetic units associated with Chinese characters do not remain identical when the characters are pronounced independently or in combination with other characters. Furthermore, depending on the syntactical and semantic context in which a particular character is placed, the same grapheme may correspond to different phonetic units. Semantically, the Chinese character may be taken to be univocal in Japanese uses. Phonetically, however, it is, in principle, multi-vocal. The pronunciations in the brackets are other phonetic choices for the same characters.

designate the self. *Hito* is used for the German *Man* (*they*, in the English translation of Heidegger) to show the averageness of 'they-self' in some of the Japanese translations of *Being and Time*. It either signifies the Other or others in general who are opposed to 'me' or designates 'myself', seen from the other's viewpoint. Therefore, *nin* of *ningen* should be understood to imply the mediation of the Other in the human being. Yet, it is misleading to regard the human being merely as a composite of individuals mutually mediating one another because the second character, *gen,* of *ningen* shows that the mediation of the Other in the human being is essentially spatial in character. By virtue of its openness as space, *ningen* cannot be confined to a one-to-one relation between two identities. *Gen,* or *aida,* is associated with the world (*yo*) of people (*seken*), the world of the social space (*yo no naka*) in which people are thrown (although Watsuji would no doubt evade such an expression as this because of the theological implications of the term 'thrownness'). Together, the compound *nin* + *gen* should signify that the human being is a being that is in the world of people and that is always mediated by the Other. The 'being-between' of *ningen* was thus analyzed in order to disclose two moments in the social being of Man: the 'being-with', determined as the mutual mediation by each other, and the belonging to society, as an essential mode of the being-in-the-world.

What justifies Watsuji's move to equate the world (*yo*) with society? I cannot find any reasoning on his part to explain on what grounds society can be conceived of as a whole. Are we witnessing an obstinate tendency in Watsuji to substantialize social relations here, as Sakabe Megumi noted it to be?[16] Watsuji said:

16. See Sakabe Megumi, *Watsuji Tetsuro* (Tokyo: Iwanami Shoten, 1986), particularly chap. 2, 53–94. Sakabe also notes the undeniably humanistic tendency of Watsuji's philosophy, which seems to derive partly from his theoretical laxity. "Although Watsuji was under the influence of Nishida philosophy in the formative stage of his ethics, he narrowly delimited Nishida's 'plane of transcendental predicate' or the 'choraic place of *mu*' as the 'human being'. And he heedlessly construed the field of the 'human being' according not to the mutually penetrating—connotative, analogical, chiasmic—logic of the 'weak structure' but to the extensive logic of the 'strong structure' in which totality is conceived of as the sum of mutually exclusive individuals" (94). Sakabe suggests the direction in which the critique of Watsuji's anthropology is to be carried out: "Let me briefly talk about an ideal format for ethics or philosophy. A sort of Systems Theory (indicated by such terms as 'reduction' and 'constitution') that was adopted in *Ethics as the Study of the Human Being* and *Ethics* must be supplemented by historical destruction—or one might say 'deconstruction'—" (237).

> However, how is it possible for *ningen,* which means the totality of the human being (in other words, *seken*), to mean the individual human being at the same time? It is thanks to the dialectic of whole and part. The part is possible only within the whole, and it is in the part that the whole manifests itself. (*Rinrigaku* [1934], in *Z–9*, 19)

The human being is construed as the dual structure of subjectivity, in which the subject *shutai* is at the same time an individual and specific subjective position and the totality according to which the fixity of that subjective position is determined. The concept of totality serves two different ends. First, it enables one to conceive of community[17] as an organic and systematic whole in which one's subjective position is given. Second, totality serves to guarantee that the fixity of a subjective position be immanent in the person, anterior to his or her conscious recognition of it. Accordingly, the human being exists as the particular relationality of one subjective position to another, on the one hand, and as the coherent whole of systematicity among those subjective positions, on the other hand. Furthermore, the understanding of relationality is mutual. It takes the form of "I am conscious of you," but:

> In this case, the act of *seeing you* is already prescribed by your act of seeing, and the act of *loving you* by *your act* of loving. Hence, *my consciousness of you is interwoven with your consciousness of me*. As distinct from the intentionality of consciousness, we call this 'aidagara'. (*Rinrigaku* [1937], in *Z–10*, 73; Watsuji's emphasis)

Aidagara is not mutual in the sense that two intentionalities of consciousness coincide with each other from opposite directions. It is more of a chiasm. Two consciousnesses are mutually prescribed by one another; in the relationality of subjective positions, each consciousness is permeated by the other (*Rinrigaku* [1937], in *Z–10*, 73). For this reason, Watsuji argues that the 'being-between', or human being, is also the relationality of subjective positions (*aidagara*), and that, even if one may not be conscious of it, the human being cannot exist outside the relationality as such. Yet, is it possible to do justice to the chiasmic aspect of sociality within Watsuji's anthropology of subjectivity? Does Watsuji's ethics not have to exclude

17. Watsuji differentiated many communities: the same individual simultaneously belongs to the family, to the neighborhood, and to the nation-state. However, these communities are hierarchically organized, with the state encompassing all the other smaller communities.

the very possibility of conceptualizing chiasm in order that the whole of community be conceived of as systematicity?

Just as the consciousness of an empirical subject is always accompanied by the 'I think', Watsuji says, any consciousness of a particular relationality in which the individual is placed must be preceded by the individual's 'being-between'. The relationality of subjective positions is an a priori condition for the human being (*aidagara sonzai*).

> Even in the expressions of relationality (*aidagara*) such as gesture or behavior, the relationality of subjective positions is already anterior. The relationality can be deployed in its expression, but it is never brought into existence by being expressed. . . . Hence, the expression of a certain relationality is the objectification of an already existing relationality. The presence of many different forms in expression simply means that relationality is *articulated* [*wake*] in many different ways. In other words, what has already *been comprehended* [*wakatte*] about relationality *a priori* is objectified in each instance of expression. (*Rinrigaku* [1931], 91–92; Watsuji's emphasis, brackets mine) [18]

Relationality *has always been comprehended* prior to the objectification of it because the subjective (*shutai-teki*) relationality of the human being is *mu,* or nothingness. "The 'articulation of relationality [*koto wake*]' is potentially comprehended prior to speech. And in speech, it discloses itself [*arawa*] as 'being—' [*de aru*]" (*Rinrigaku* [1931], 92). The anteriority of relationality is explicated in reference to the mode in which relationality exists. If it discloses itself in social expression, how does it exist prior to disclosure? This issue is closely related to the Japanese verb *aru,* Watsuji declares.

Another Heideggerian move. Here, Watsuji relates the 'articulation of relationality' to the issue of ontology, the subjectivity of the human being as articulated in the relationality of subjective positions to the etymological analysis of the verb *aru,* which means 'to be something' (copula) or 'to exist'. He first points out the difference between the term *sonzai* (being), an equivalent to *ningen,* and the German *Sein,* so as to exemplify the grammatical limitation of European languages, which Western ontology has taken for granted. The compound *sonzai* is never confused with a copula in

---

18. *Wake* (and *wakatte*) is to divide, to distinguish, and so on (*wakatte*, from *wakaru*, is to comprehend, to agree: *Wake* and *wakaru* are supposed to share the same etymological root). Therefore, I translate it as to articulate here.

the languages of the Far East, says Watsuji. Instead of the onto-theological determination of 'being', he proposes his analysis of a Japanese verb *ari* or *aru* as an equivalent to the copula and shows that this verb can clearly indicate two distinguished uses among the various corresponding European terms to the English 'being'. When it is used as a copula, the verb *aru* takes a particle *de* to form *de aru,* while it takes another particle *ga* to form *ga aru* when it is used in the sense of existentia (*Rinrigaku* [1931], 84–90; also [1934], in *Z–9*, 28–34). Following Heidegger's argument on *'ousia',* Watsuji relates *ga aru* to the character *yu,* meaning 'there is' or 'to exist', and establishes a passage from '*ga aru*' to '*motsu*' ('to own or 'to have') since the Chinese character *yu* equates existence to possession. Thus, he asserts, the question of the meaning of being in the sense of *existentia* can be communicated to that of having. Since property can be ascribed only to the human being, one who has it is always the human being. In this regard, every being is being owned or had by the human being. Any statement that affirms the existence of a thing necessarily connotes the fact that the thing is in the possession of the human being. It follows that ultimately, for Watsuji, every ontological question should be an anthropological and, subsequently, an anthropocentric question. The project of the study of the human being as 'being-between' asserts itself as an anthropocentric anthropology, as a typical humanism.

That anthropocentrism now reproduces the dual structure of subjectivity can be seen when one reflexively applies his equation of 'to be' and 'to have' to the being of the human being: If the statement "there is a thing" can be equated to the human being's having it, that the human being has itself or owns itself should be inferred from the statement "there is a human being." This is to say that the existence of a particular human being is already in the possession of the systematicity governing the relations among subjective positions within the totality: *Shutai* owns itself. For this reason, the subject as *shutai* discloses its proper self in praxis, whereas in knowledge, the subject does not reveal itself to intuition. The authentic self derives from the fact that the subject is always proper to the designated position in, as well as the property of, systematicity as totality. This is the primary setting within which Watsuji's ethics was further articulated.

For Watsuji, conscience, which deters the individuality of the human being from taking its arbitrary path, is equated to the voice of the totality. The totality in 'me' declares, "Thou shall not." The conflict with the totality immanent in the individual presents itself as a supposedly dialectic interaction between the individual and the totality (here, I am extremely suspicious of

Watsuji's appropriation of the term 'dialectic'). The individual is defined as follows:

> The act of retention which unifies a variety of other acts has been taken to be essentially most individual. But, only because one presumes individual consciousness, can it be taken to be individual. The act of retention itself does not belong to the individual. The same can be said about the unity of the act or the agent of the act. (*Rinrigaku* [1937], in Z–10, 83)

Of course, many acts that are too frequently predicated on the subject as the individual need not be related to the individual at all. As is often the case with individualism, the concept of the individual is kept artificially ambiguous, and the extremely dubious convention of substituting the subject for the individual as its equivalent is allowed to pass unnoticed in most cases. For Watsuji, too, the concept of the individual is far from self-evident.

> He [Max Scheler] said that the absolute solitude is the *inevitable negative essential relation among the finite persons*. A person can be individual not because he is the center of the act but because he negates communality. The essence of individuality is the negation of communality. (*Rinrigaku* [1937], in Z–10, 84; Watsuji's emphasis)

> What is communal in essence can manifest itself *in the mode of the absence of communality*. This is individuality. Therefore, individuality cannot exist independently. *Its essence is negation and emptiness* [*sunyata*]. (*Rinrigaku* [1937], in Z–10, 83; Watsuji's emphasis)

Since communality (*kyodo-sei*) presumes the relationality of subjective positions, individuality happens only when a person fails to identify himself/herself with the designated subjective position. Hence, it is impossible to construe individuality in positive terms: It can only be described as a series of negations. Watsuji does not seem to assume, however, that individuality is the inevitable consequence of human finitude. It can only be thought of as a deviation from what the person immanently is. Thus, individuality is comprehended primarily as a transgression of the existing relationality according to which one's duties are defined in accordance with one's subjective position. It follows that, whereas individuality negates the relationality of subjective positions, individuality affirms and endorses the relationality through the negation of it, just as the transgression, insofar as it is the transgression from the already existing norm, affirms and sanctifies it. Consequently, in Watsuji's ethics, individuality has to be viewed as a rebellion, or as the guise of a rebellion, that is always launched in anticipation of a prearranged resolution: It is a moment of deviation, but it always assumes the return to normalcy. Hence, Watsuji attempts to reduce the whole issue of individuality to what Lacan calls the demand of love on the part of the individual (one might call the individual *sekishi*, or baby, in this instance) toward the totality (which one might consider associating with the emperor[19]), but this demand is expected to be responded to when the individual returns—through confession perhaps—to his or her authentic self. Thus, this particular conceptualization of individuality makes any contest or rebellion against the totality a sinful act that could be redeemed by confession or return.[20] Watsuji's ethics then provides a very clear view of the ethical imperative. It is a call of totality to urge a person to return to his or her authentic self.

Therefore, what constitutes the ethical is the negation of individuality, the negation of negation, which brings a person back to what totality inside that person dictates. It is a return to the subjective position of the authentic self that can be anticipated and understood by others, since the mutual understanding among the people of a given communality is warranted by the very relationality of subjective positions (*aidagara*).

> One who rebels against one's origin by deviating from a certain communality wishes to return to one's origin by negating the rebellion. And this return takes place through the realization of some communality. The movement of this return is a human action which signifies the sublation [*shiyo*] of individual personality, the realization of social communion [*jinrin-teki goitsu*], and the return to the original source of the self. Therefore, this is approved of [*yoshi to serareru*] not only by those people who participate in that communality but also by the profound essence of the self. That is 'good' [*yoshi*]. Accordingly, it is not on the basis of 'good' [*yoshi*] feeling but rather because an action indicates the return to the origin that the value of good is constituted. It follows that one can argue that it necessarily rejects low

19. It is well known that the relation of the emperor to his subject was very frequently presented in terms of "one who looks after the baby" and the "baby who is looked after" in the prewar Japanese State.
20. It seems undeniable that the issue of individuality in Watsuji's ethics was closely connected to the problematics of *tenko*, or political conversion. Needless to say, the confession was the public format in which the *tenko* of a political prisoner arrested under the Public Security Maintenance Law was announced.

value for high value. The highest value is absolute totality, aspiration [in English in the original] towards which is called 'good'. This is why one's subjugation to the authority of the whole—abandonment of individual independence, and love, devotion, or sacrifice—has always been regarded as 'good'. This is illustrated by the fact that, in simple everyday language, the state in which social communion [*jinrin-teki goitsu*] is achieved is called '*naka yoshi*' [on good terms]. (*Rinrigaku* [1937], in *Z*–10, 141–42)

Watsuji proposes a kind of ethics whose central guiding principle is to be 'on good terms' with others: It is a kind of ethics that permits one to neglect other social and ethical concerns in order to remain on good terms with others.

One should also be reminded that Watsuji's ethics clearly and systematically delineated what Louis Althusser would describe thirty years later as the practical nature of ideology in which "we 'live, move, and have our being.'"[21] Here, to be sure, I am not impressed by Watsuji's farsightedness: I am astonished at the high accuracy with which Watsuji's ethics conforms to Althusser's description of ideology in which, in fact, ethics is included. Watsuji's anthropology is decorated with the so-called Oriental cultural costumes, but it can effectively be analyzed by the critique of ideology that originated in Western Europe. The call of totality to urge a person to return to his or her authentic self in Watsuji's anthropology can be explained as a detailed exposition of Althusser's famous definition of ideology that ideology "hails or interpellates concrete individuals as concrete subjects, by the category of the subject";[22] and, as we will see, his philosophy of praxis is an authentic humanism that determines Man as a subject, or *shutai,* owned by the totality, that is, the State.

21. Louis Althusser, *Ideology and the Ideological State Apparatuses*, in *Lenin and Philosophy and Other Essays*, trans. Ben Brewster (New York: Monthly Review Press, 1971), 171.

22. Althusser, *Lenin and Philosophy and Other Essays*, 173. This issue of subjectivity played an important role in Watsuji's postwar discussion of the emperor system. See my essay, "The Invention of the Past Emperor System," in *Modernity and the Japanese Emperor System*, ed. N. Sakai and T. Fujitani (forthcoming from M. E. Sharpe). Indeed, it does not directly follow that the Subject criticized by Althusser is the essence of the emperor system. Watsuji's anthropology poses itself primarily as the State ethics, in which the Subject is equated to the State, and the State can by no means be equated to the emperor system.

. . . .

For Watsuji, therefore, the ethical is a return, a restoration of what a person originally is; but it is not only a return to the original moment in time: The return to the authentic self cannot be construed exclusively in terms of temporality.

> Space is the juxtaposability of subjects, the externality of one sub-
> ject to another. Insofar as it is grasped directly and abstractly, it does
> not contain determining differentiations. So it is simply continuous,
> and the self and the other are not differentiated in it. Such subjective
> externality that is at the same time differential and nondifferential cor-
> responds to what we have been discussing in terms of 'the spatiality
> of the human being'.
>
> As it is understood to mean the subject (*shutai*), the structure of
> [Hegelian] Spirit has both temporality and spatiality. Heidegger has
> already pointed out its temporal nature [of the Spirit]. According to
> him, the negation of negation, which is the essence of the Spirit,
> cannot be understood without reference to temporality. It is accord-
> ing to temporality that we understand the significance of the term
> 'return' in the statement "Idea returns to itself through negation."
> On our part, however, we must go further and ask whether or not
> the return is possible only temporally. What, after all, makes the re-
> turn (Rückkehr, zurückgehen) possible is partition, separation. And
> partition and separation are *originally (kongen-teki niwa) grounded
> on the spatiality of the subject (shutai).* (*Rinrigaku* [1937], in *Z*–10,
> 243–44; Watsuji's emphasis)

As his work *Fudo* (*Climate and Culture*)[23] amply indicates, the totality to which a person belongs is circumscribed in terms not only of historical, political, and sociological factors but also of climatic, geographic, and ethno-graphic specificities. It would be an injustice merely to extract the geo-cultural sense of space from Watsuji's discussion on the spatiality of the human being. But, given the distribution of his statements in his other works, it would be equally misleading to deny that the totality here means a par-

---

23. Watsuji, *Fudo*, in *Z*–8, 1–256; English translation: *Climate and Culture*, trans. Geoffrey Bownas (Japanese Ministry of Education, 1961). This work was first published as a series of articles for the monthly *Shiso*, 1927–1935, then published as a monograph in 1935 by Iwanami Shoten. This is, perhaps, the best example of Watsuji's attempt to 'spatialize' Heideggerian hermeneutics.

ticular geographical place, and the return invariably implies a move in the geographic space. Such a determination of the return immediately evokes the geopolitical and cultural distinction between the West and the East, particularly between "pastoral Europe" and "monsoon Asia," to use the basic categories coined in Watsuji's cultural typology in *Climate and Culture*. Therefore, the return to the specific totality could imply the departure from another specific totality if the identities of these totalities are defined exclusively in geographic terms: An ethical choice could be made to represent an alternative between geopolitical and cultural areas in Watsuji's discourse. In this regard, one might naturally observe that geo-cultural categories are highly charged with ethical value. In a sense, geo-cultural categories begin to serve as ethical categories to the extent that the ethnic-national identity is taken to be the ground of science. At one point during the war, Watsuji went so far as to advocate that sciences, including physics, must be delimited by ethnic-nationality (*minzoku*).[24] The international collaboration of scholarship is possible when each scientist works as a representative of his or her nation. Only through nationalism, Watsuji argues, can internationalism become possible. Therefore, those who do not belong to the nation and who do not work on the basis of the identity of *minzoku* in fact make internationalism impossible.

Imitating the restorationist move in the West toward Eurocentricity, which was to a great extent motivated by an anxiety concerning the putative

24. Watsuji's understanding of internationalism goes as follows: "It is senseless to think of scientists as individuals disregarding their role for the nation. . . . Those who most militantly attack the national delimitation of scholarship are Jewish scholars. But, in their attack, they most vehemently express their own national limits. The particularity of the Jews, unlike any other nations, consists in their ability to leave their own land and, therefore, to exist *dispersed* among other national groups. In other words, the ethnic-national (*minzoku-teki*) being of the Jews lies in the fact of being among other national groups. In this respect, the Jews are not *exclusionistic;* but, precisely because of this, they are especially *exclusionistic*. What is referred to as the transnational cooperation of scholarship is synonymous with Jewish national cooperation" (originally in *Rinrigaku* [1942], in *Z*–10, 557; Watsuji's emphasis). (Here, *minzoku,* which I rendered nation or ethnic-national, can also be race and the German *Volk* in some cases.) It goes without saying that Watsuji's comprehension of the Jews is not only naïve but also a fairly straightforward manifestation of stereotyping that underlies cultural essentialism. This kind of stereotyping can also easily be detected in Watsuji's description of the Asian, notably the Chinese, in his *Fudo* (*Z*–8, 121–34, 242–56) or *Climate and Culture*, 119–33. Yet, it should be noted that this concept of *minzoku* serves as a cornerstone for Watsuji's idea of global scientific cooperation.

loss of the West's superiority over the non-West in the 1930s and which found its cumulative expression in the obsessive emphasis on the idea of the distinctiveness of the West and on the separatist distinction of "We the West" from the rest of the world, Watsuji seemed to produce an equally ethnocentric move toward the East. The impulse to imitate Heidegger and European philosophy now resulted in a desire to react to the West, a desire for symmetry between the West and the East, and eventually for the ethical absolutization of the East in the face of the restorationist declarations by Heidegger, Husserl, and others.[25] No doubt this is a reactive return to the authentic self, but when the subject is construed in spatial terms, the demand of symmetry in the name of equality among civilizations and nations seems to trigger this return to the East in the face of the return to the West in the West. After all, is all return to the original self reactive? Is it not exactly the other side of mimetic identification?[26] Then, for Watsuji, what is the totality to which one is urged to return?

25. On this account, to my knowledge, and to this day, Jacques Derrida's *Introduction to "Origin of Geometry"* remains the most politically and philosophically penetrating critique of such a restorationist logic.

26. See Phillippe Lacoue-Labarthe, *Typography*, trans. Christopher Fynsk (Cambridge: Harvard University Press, 1989); Mikkel Borch-Jacobsen, *The Freudian Subject*, trans. Catherine Porter (Stanford: Stanford University Press, 1988); and, as an essay that bridges these two books, Phillippe Lacoue-Labarthe, " 'Le dernier philosophe' Oedipe comme figure," in *L'imitation des modernes* (Paris: Galilée, 1986), 203–27. There are innumerable cases of the violent manifestation of mimetic identification—the most famous of which include the cases of Takamura Kotaro (poet and sculptor), Miyoshi Tatsuji (poet and French literature specialist), and Hagiwara Sakutaro (poet)—in which the admirers of European culture turned into its detesters overnight. Although his transition came much more gradually, Watsuji should be classified in this group of the admirers of European culture who had repressed their critique of various aspects of European society until the last moment. During the war, Watsuji devoted many pages to the description and denunciation of the Western, particularly Anglo-American, racism that cannot simply be dismissed even today (see, for example, *Nihon no shindo*, in *Z*–14, 295–312, and *Amerika no kokuminsei*, in *Z*–17). His critique, however, was enunciated with the understanding of his own situation, in which there was absolutely no possibility of reaching the intended audience of his critique. Given these conditions, I can see little critical effect in Watsuji's critique of Western racism. In the absence of those to whom his critical words should be addressed, such a critique merely functions as a declaration of exclusionistic loyalty to the community on the part of the author; it would amount to an act of communal self-indulgence. At the same time, we must also take into consideration that, even prior to the war, there were scarcely means of communication whereby the critique of the aspects of the Western societies, including their racism against the Asians and others, could be conveyed to the very audience who ought to listen to such a critique. The existing international power

In his study of the human being, totality is not immediately equated to an existing community. A socio-moral community (*jinrin-teki kyodotai*) may be family, corporation, neighborhood community, or the state, but they are all finite totalities in contrast to the absolute totality, the ultimate principle of the absolute negativity as emptiness, or *sunyata,* to which the ethical is attributed in the last instance (*Rinrigaku* [1937], in *Z–*10, 126). A person may live simultaneously in different finite totalities. Therefore, one's subjective position is determined in its multiplicity. In this regard, in spite of his hostility to individualism, which he regards as a modernist fallacy, he endorses the wide variety of choices on the basis of the division of labor.[27] Nevertheless, the absolute totality is not transcendent with regard to its accessibility to a person, since absolute negativity can be found in the person's belonging to a specific and existing finite totality. After all, the highest and most encompassing of finite totality should be found in the nation-state, where its communality consists not of associations but of individual citizens, so that the individual citizen participates directly in the whole (*Rinrigaku* [1937], in *Z–*10, 156). Therefore, in the nation-state, the relationship between the individual and the totality, the relationship determining the ethical in the subject, must be most clearly revealed.

> Regardless of whether the totality at issue be family, friends, corporation, or the state, it is pointless to talk about individual impulse, individual will, or individual action outside the context of separation and independence from such a totality. . . . The independence of the individual can be sublated in the negation of negation, and, without exception, this is achieved by belonging to some particular socio-moral totality. (*Rinrigaku* [1937], in *Z–*10, 127)

Watsuji presumes that all the deviation from a rebellion against socio-moral totality can necessarily be reduced to individuality. After all, for him, individuality is nothing but mere selfishness. The negation of the socio-moral totality, therefore, cannot imply the transformation of that totality or its re-

---

structure, including the configuration of international mass media, did not allow for a critical voice coming from the non-West to question the self-legitimating discourse in Western Europe, in which the image of the West was constituted. The West constructed its identity primarily as a closure and did not hesitate to use its political and military superiority in order to sustain that closure.

27. This explains his generally positive attitude toward Durkheim in his *Rinrigaku* (1937). This side of his ethics will be emphasized—by Watsuji himself—in his postwar writings on the emperor system.

form: It is preordained that the negation of the totality is ascribable to individual impulse so that it can be recuperated by the totality through moral acts, such as political conversion (tenko) and confession. In Watsuji's conception of negation, there is no moment that alters the very relationship of the individual and the whole: It is negation in the static opposition affirmation—negation. His use of the term 'dialectic' sounds odd, partly for this reason.

> The individual dissolves into that socio-moral totality. Again, it does not matter whether it be family, friends, corporation, or the state. After all, it is pointless to talk about trans-individual will, total will, or dutiful act unless in one's assimilative identification with the totality. It is precisely in this realization of a finite totality that the absolute negativity returns to itself. (Rinrigaku [1937], in Z–10, 127)

Among the existing finite totalities, the nation, which has realized itself in the institution of the state, is most important and sacred because of its sovereignty expressed in the legal institution. It is into this finite totality that the individualistic individual is urged to dissolve through his assimilative identification with it. Furthermore, as Takahashi Tetsuya has argued extensively,[28] Watsuji defines the nation (minzoku) as a cultural community "delimited by the communality of blood and soil" (Rinrigaku [1942], in Z–10, 585). The identity of this community can be formed by its closure and exclusionism: In principle, a cultural community can be 'an open society', but the formation of its identity requires closure (Rinrigaku [1942], in Z–10, 585).

The same argument about national particularism, which is most systematically developed in Climate and Culture, is also deployed here. Watsuji does not, however, seem aware at all that, in order to juxtapose one national characteristic with another, he has to take up a transcendent viewpoint, a bird's-eye view, flying high above the ground where one encounters another. In spite of his dependence on Kant and his abhorrence of unmediated universalism, Watsuji does not recognize that the characterization of an Other's particularity is simply impossible unless his own ethnocentric universalism is accepted. Here we are not concerned with the observation of other national cultures on the basis of the exoticism of international tourism. Watsuji does not seem comprehensive about cultural and social incom-

28. Takahashi Tetsuya, "Kaiki no ho to kyodotai," Gendai shiso 17, no. 9 (Tokyo: Seitosha, September, 1989). Takahashi persuasively shows linkages between Watsuji and Heidegger. Also see Christopher Fynsk, Heidegger, Thought and Historicity (Ithaca: Cornell University Press, 1986).

mensurability. It is by no accident that Watsuji's respect of other national characters would result in certain racial stereotyping in the end. As an authentic culturalist, Watsuji continues to argue that the cultural community forms the substance of the state,[29] but let me not jump to an easy condemnation of Watsuji. Before making any concluding remarks about the totalizing tendency of Watsuji's humanism, the issue is to envision the probable consequences of what is signified by the return to the authentic self and how the dissolving into totality actually takes place.

It is rather amazing that, in Watsuji's conception of the relationality of subjective positions, no conflict results from the simultaneous overlapping of totalities. Not the slightest possibility of indeterminacy is expected when a person is said to belong to anything, from the community of a married couple at the minimum level, up to the nation-state at the maximum level. If ultimately the ethical value judgment is characterized by the return to the authentic self, what would ensue in the situation where one must identify with contradictory subjective positions simultaneously? Or are those finite totalities synthesized in such an organic way that a smaller totality may be assimilated into a larger one, just as an organ is assimilated into a larger system in a living organism (*Rinrigaku* [1942], in *Z–11*, 593)? Is the possibility of overdetermination in the relationality of subjective positions entertained at all in Watsuji's ethics? Obviously not. In this sense, Watsuji's Man does not have the unconscious. Thus, his anthropology uncritically inherits another feature of humanism; that is, of modern constructive subjectivism.

Authenticity is prescribed in terms of the totality's immediate immanence in the person, so that the person's authentic self is given as conforming to the systematicity governing the relationality of subjective positions from the onset. A preestablished harmony is always already implied in the concept of authenticity. As a corollary, one might as well infer that, unlike Heidegger's authenticity, Watsuji's retains no ec-static or pro-jective—not to mention de-centering—character. Perhaps it is because Watsuji conceives of the dual structure of the subject mainly in spatial terms: The subject goes outside of itself, but spatially toward the other person already retained in the relationality (*aidagara*) and not temporally toward the future. As a result, the subject can return to its authentic self through the mutual understanding secured by the very notion of the relationality between the self and the other. Not surprisingly, Watsuji's critique of Heidegger goes as follows:

29. Originally in *Rinrigaku* (1942). In the postwar edition, this part was rewritten. See Appendix *Z–11*, 422.

> [Heidegger's] Dasein is, in this sense, 'beyond itself' (*über sich hinaus*). Yet, Dasein is not concerned with other beings than itself, and is concerned with the possibility of being proper to itself. . . . Dasein is always the end in itself. (*Rinrigaku* [1937], in *Z*–10, 226–27)

Dasein returns to itself through its authentic possibilities, but the being that discloses the totality through the project toward its own death is merely an individual being; according to Watsuji, it is never a human being. Hence, "Heidegger dealt with the death of an individual as the phenomenon of human death, ignoring [the social manifestations of human death such as] deathbed, wake, funeral" (*Rinrigaku* [1937], in *Z*–10, 233), and so on. In passing, let me note that he ignores unnatural death, whose image is not fixed within the network of social customs; he ignores the violent kind of death.

> What Heidegger called authenticity is inauthenticity. Only when such inauthenticity is negated in the merger of the self and the other (*jitafuji*), that is, when the 'self' is forgotten, can authenticity be realized. Retrospectively one may call the totality of the human being thus realized the 'authentic self'. But, in this case, the authentic self is more like Kant's trans-individual subject than Heidegger's individual self which becomes totality through death. (*Rinrigaku* [1937], in *Z*–10, 237)

Now Watsuji is thinking in the rather regressive language of culturalism in which the following formula is accepted to be a truism: *the individualistic West = being* versus *the collectivist East = emptiness or nothingness*. From this standpoint, Watsuji seems to reject Heidegger's argument about 'temporality and historicality' and ventures to announce that Heidegger did not address the issue of 'being-with' at all. Is he completely blind to the question of historicality and to the implications of the famous passages (section 74, "The basic constitution of historicality," *Being and Time*)[30] about the 'being-with' in the destiny of community and Dasein's resoluteness to its own death, passages about the themes that would repeatedly be discussed by Japanese writers in the late 1930s and early 1940s?

Perhaps what Watsuji said about Heidegger's authenticity equally applies to Watsuji's authenticity from Heidegger's viewpoint. This is to say that what is authentic for Watsuji is inauthentic for Heidegger and that the

---

30. See sec. 74, "The Basic Constitution of Historicality" (division 2, chap. 5), *Being and Time*.

reverse is also the case. For the relationality of subjective positions (*aida-gara*) suggests an affinity with Heidegger's 'Man' or 'they' rather than the authentic potentiality-for-Being. Watsuji seems to seek the ground for his ethics in the averageness of 'they', which Heidegger describes in the following:

> The Self of everyday Dasein is the they-self, which we distinguish from the authentic Self—that is, from the Self which has been taken hold of in its own way [*eigens ergriffenen*]. As they-self, the particular Dasein has been dispersed into the 'they', and must first find itself. This dispersal characterizes the 'subject' of that kind of Being which we know as concernful absorption in the world we encounter as closest to us. . . . Proximally, factical Dasein is in the with-world, which is discovered in an average way. Proximally, it is not 'I', in the sense of my own Self, that 'am', but rather the Others, whose way is that of the 'they'. In terms of the 'they', and as 'they', I am 'given' proximally to 'myself' [*mir 'selbst'*]. Proximally Dasein is 'they', and for the most part it remains so. (*Being and Time*, 167; translators' brackets)

Then, it may appear that Heidegger's statement that "Authentic Being-towards-death—that is to say, the finitude of temporality—is the hidden basis of Dasein's historicality" simply does not apply to Watsuji's ethics. If this is the case, resoluteness toward death would not be the essential moment in the return to the authentic self in *shutai,* since the social, as Watsuji conceives of it, seems devoid of uncertainty. This point is made most explicit by the example of his analysis of the trust as a moment of the subjectivity.

Watsuji ascribes trust to the relationality of subjective positions, so trust is primarily an expression of the already existing relationality, that is, of the totality as *shutai*. As a matter of fact, trust is not defined as a moment in generating a new social relation, but it is assumed that it can be known only in its absence. Just as individuality is the negation of totality in his ethics, so trust is a derivative effect of the totality that is always already there. What is deliberately eliminated from Watsuji's conceptualization of trust is its aleatory and adventurous aspect. In due course, he argues against Nicholai Hartmann that trust occurs only where social positions are guaranteed by the relationality of subjective positions and that it should be taken not as the basis of society but as its consequence. Therefore, trust is directed to the systematicity guaranteeing the mutual understanding of subjective

positions rather than to a particular person. According to Watsuji, therefore, one is not supposed to trust another person, but one is supposed to
trust socio-moral totalities like the corporation and the State. In principle,
trust cannot be extended to those whose subjective positions are uncertain
within the network of given social relations. Watsuji's ethics declares: "You
cannot trust strangers." It is evident to me that such a conception of trust
does not allow for the conception of sociality that cannot be integrated into
the *restricted economy* of totality. Furthermore, as Watsuji conceives of the
chiasm of 'you' and 'I' only in terms of symmetrical exchange, he cannot
allow for a surplus in the social. If the sociality means the impossibility of
symmetrical mutuality—or transference—between the self and the Other,
the possibility of sociality as such must be in contradiction to Watsuji's trust.

It is often said that, in contrast to the Heideggerian Dasein analysis, Watsuji's ethics is much more attentive to, and even perceptive of, the
sociality of the human being. My reading is diametrically opposed to that.
What is absent in Watsuji's humanism is the very concern for sociality. Even
as a common word, sociality connotes much more than the relationality
of subjective positions. Normally we do not ascribe sociality to a person
who can only operate within prearranged social relations, such as parent-
child and employer-employee. Sociality is understood to mean the ability to
leave behind the sort of trust warranted by the already existent relations, to
'go out in the world' and to establish new relations with strangers. By the
same token, it should be evident that one's relation to the other must of
necessity contain the possibility of betrayal and contingency, without which
trust would be empty. Only within the element of uncertainty does trust
make sense. I trust a person precisely because I recognize him or her as
one who is potentially capable of betraying me. Here, trust is one's resoluteness to confront the possibility of betrayal; it is a decision to expose
oneself to the possibility of absolute contingency. Even when the relation
appears secured by the institution of a certain *aidagara* or relationality of
subjective positions, uncertainty can never be eliminated. This is to say that
chiasm with others can never be reduced to a transparent mutuality of intersubjectivity. The inner construction of Watsuji's argument of ethics, which
should be summarized as a sort of Systems Theory, did not allow but for
him to misconstrue the very experience of chiasm. Therefore, his claim that
trust is always preconditioned by the relationality of subjective positions
must mean disavowal—disavowal in the psychoanalytical sense, too—of
the moment of uncertainty that, because uncertainty is always interwoven
in every social relation, necessitates one or another form of *alea* in order
to be engaged in any relation with others. Moreover, it is not because of a

rebellious attitude toward the totality, or of an individualistic impulse, or of individuality as an expression of selfishness that uncertainty arises. Uncertainty is inherent in every *aidagara;* uncertainty is inevitable in every social encounter, as Emmanuel Levinas often emphasizes by his phrase 'transcendence of the Other'. Therefore, in order to preserve room for sociality in our discourse, totality should never be conceptualized as systematicity as in Systems Theory; the simultaneity of the social must never be collapsed upon the synchrony of their relationalities that is obtained through transcendental analysis or phenomenological reduction.[31]

It follows that the repression of uncertainty in the relationality of subjective positions amounts to a refusal of the otherness of the Other, of respect for the Other, and, after all, of sociality itself. For example, in her relation to me, my wife's subjective position is 'comprehended and articulated' (*wakatte*) as such, but she is not merely my wife. The situation does not change much even if other relationalities are taken into account. In her relation to a shop owner, she occupies the subjective position of *customer;* in her relation to the teacher of her child, she is *a parent;* in her relation to her junior staff in the office where she works, she is regarded as *boss*. Her subjective position is further articulated as the number of 'practical relationalities in social action' (*jissen-teki koi renkan*) in which she is involved increases. No matter how many predicates one may wish to attribute to her, she cannot exhaustively be defined as the subject of those predicates. She always exceeds the subject; she always retains some surplus over her subjective determination. Thus, she can never be identified with a subject, and, precisely because she cannot be exhaustively identified with any subject, there can be sociality between her and me. Needless to say, the same applies in my relation to myself. Not only am I an Other to myself (Watsuji was fully aware of this sort of Otherness, which can easily be contained by the scheme of *shutai,* or subjectivity), but I am also Other to the dual structure of subjectivity. This is to say that my relation to my self always bears a surplus that is irreducible to the dual structure of the whole and the individual. Thus, I am never reduced to an identity, an individual who identifies with the whole. I am not a unity fashioned after the unicity of the whole. In short, I am not an *individuum*.[32]

31. For the simultaneity of the historico-social, see William Haver, *The Body of This Death: Alterity in Nishida-Philosophy and Post-Marxism*, Ph.D. diss., University of Chicago, 1987.
32. See Jean-Luc Nancy, "La Communauté désoeuvrée," in *Aléa*, 4 (Paris: Christian Bourgois, February 1983): 11–49.

And if the putative systematicity of totality as the human being is always threatened by sociality, the return to the authentic self would require a much more violent decisiveness toward an ecstatic leap into communality, something like the Heideggerian resoluteness, without which the very sense of communal belonging, that our original selves are always already understood and embraced in the subject, would be lost. In order to believe that one is able to return to the authentic self or to keep one's nostalgic sense of belonging insulated from sociality,[33] one would have to take a blind leap into what might be called the destiny of the community. At this stage, Watsuji Tetsuro had to face the problem of one's own death, of the kind of death that is not the death of the average 'they' fixed within the network of social relationalities and customs; he could no longer avoid the problems of unnatural, violent death.

Until the publication of the 1937 version of his *Ethics*, Watsuji's anthropology bore a fundamental shortcoming as a typical theodicy for the modern Japanese State. In spite of its conservative character, particularly in comparison to Heidegger's, Watsuji's philosophy lacked one essential insight into the mechanism of the modern State formation and its reproduction, that is, the insight into the relationship between national community and death.

It is well known that the modern nation-state invents such political and cultural technologies as national history, national flag, national literature, national education, and the imaginary unity of national language, and thereby projects the image of a homogenized and universalized national community. Among those features particular to the modern nation-state is the idea of universal conscription. While this idea dictates that all of the adult male population—in some cases, the female population, as well—over a certain age be submitted to military service, it determines national community in a specific fashion: All the legitimate members of this community are defined as potential soldiers.

As has been asserted by Carl Schmitt and others, the national community acquires the most explicit self-determination in the extremity of war. Then, the national community is unequivocally determined by the

33. This is exactly the case with the Japanese romantics (*Nihon Roman-ha*) and particularly their postwar remnant, Mishima Yukio. For him, death was primarily this mechanism of insulation. It is no accident that the aggressive resoluteness to his own death and nostalgic yearning for integration into the aestheticized image of a people were united in his literary discourse. See "Death in Midsummer," in *Death in Midsummer and Other Stories*, trans. Edward G. Seidensticker (New York: New Directions, 1966), 1–29.

constitution of its membership: One's belonging to the nation is immediately facilitated by one's willingness to join the act of killing a group of people designated as the enemy. Of course, the possibility of killing is always accompanied by the possibility of being killed. Therefore, the possibility of belonging to a national community by killing may also be accompanied by the possibility of belonging to that community by being killed. It is noteworthy that the verb 'to belong' has gained some transitive, as well as transitory, quality in this context. In this regard, neither belonging to the national community nor identification with it designates some static state of affairs, but both designate a *historical* process that one is urged to act on. Historicality cannot be excluded from the issue of belonging to the national community, since belonging, in fact, is always a matter of becoming and acting: Belonging is a sort of historizing. Thus, the idea of universal conscription teaches the masses that they can belong to their nation through the possibility of their own death. Until recently, the nation-state could not shed its determination as the community of death.

The history of modern Japan is nothing but a history in which a national community was formed as the community of 'unnatural' death. Under the Tokugawa regime (1600–1868), only the administrative class of samurai, some 5 percent of the population, possessed the right to kill and be killed for the sake of the polity. Through many reforms in the late nineteenth century, that right and/or duty was extended to about half of the adult population, and, finally, during the 1930s and early 1940s, it was given to the entire population. Literally, total war became possible. It is all too obvious that the antihistorical stance of Watsuji's anthropology proved to be a fatal shortcoming insofar as it claimed to be the theodicy for the prewar Japanese State; historicality had to be regained in order for his anthropology to continue to serve as the State ethics.[34]

In an attempt to identify oneself with the national community through one's own death, one would have to be "brought back to [one's] ownmost potentiality-for-Being-[one's]-Self" (*Being and Time*, 354) in order to die one's own death as a co-historizing in Being-with-Others.[35] Here, since one dies alone, one is relentlessly individualized" (*Being and Time*, 354). "The unwavering precision with which Dasein is thus essentially individualized down to its ownmost potentiality-for-Being, discloses the anticipation of

34. As to Watsuji's explanation of the State ethics, see *Z–11*, 425–30, and *Benshoho-teki shingaku to kokka no rinri* (Dialectic theology and the ethics of the state), in *Z–9*, 443–60.
35. As to co-historizing and Being-with-Others, see *Being and Time*, 436–38.

death as the possibility which is *non-relational"* (*Being and Time*, 354; Heidegger's emphasis)—non-relational, that is, outside *aidagara*. Then, one would have to face "the lostness of the 'they'." This is to say that one would then be expelled from the world of the 'they' warranted by *aidagara* or the relationality of subjective positions, for when one is "resolute, [one] takes over authentically in its existence the fact that [one] is the null basis of one's own nullity" (*Being and Time*, 354). But for this recognition about the aloneness of one's own death and the groundlessness of one's existence that are disclosed by anticipatory resoluteness toward death, the theodicy for the State would never be able to acquire the coercive force with which to command the nation to "die for its country."

In order to serve to legitimate the membership of the national community sanctioned by the State, Watsuji's anthropology should have recuperated all its shortcomings. This is exactly what I found in the second volume of *Ethics*, which was published in 1942. First, historicality and the destiny of the nation:

> We have said that there cannot be a human totality higher than the state, but have never implied that there is not the ultimate absolute totality thanks to which the totality of the state continues to be a totality. Each state and the relations among the states express the way this absolute totality exists, and cannot be apprehended without reference to this origin. From this, however, we cannot conclude that the totality encompassing many states has been formed in human being. These states are moments in the human being, but human being is a fluid scene in which they cannot be unified into one. Such human being may be called 'World History' after Hegel, provided that it is not merely the 'history' of the world but also the historical 'world'. (*Rinrigaku* [1942], in *Z–10*, 432)

Second, the people's self-sacrifice to the state:

> The state is the absolute force for the individual, and demands unconditional devotion from the individual. The individual can return to his/her own ultimate totality through his/her devotion to the state. Therefore, it is said that duty to the state means loyalty (*chugi*) according to which one devotes everything one owns in order to serve the sovereignty of the state. (*Rinrigaku* [1942], in *Z–10*, 434)

• • • •

Many have attempted to distinguish Watsuji's anthropology from Heidegger's philosophical project by stressing the former's concern with 'being-with' and a certain resemblance of his concept *aidagara* to intersubjectivity. Yet, as far as the appropriation of an individual's death by the State is concerned, both Heidegger and Watsuji seem to have come to an almost identical conclusion.

Jean-Luc Nancy, who is primarily concerned with the indivisibility of the individual, showed that Heideggerian individualism led to the blind submission of the individual to totality through the logic of communalist identification.[36] Watsuji Tetsuro, who was a disciple of Heidegger and believed himself to be most rigorously opposed to the individualism of his mentor (Watsuji being primarily concerned with the singularity of the individual), followed the same path also through the logic of communalist identification. It seems to me that, unless one *desists* from this logic of communalist identification, one could easily be taken into a violent jingoistic sentiment.

What has been pursued in my reading of Watsuji's *Ethics* is a peculiar reversal of his logic, a reversal that somewhat resembles what Adorno called the 'cult of death': Watsuji argues that because of the totality immanent in each of the people, they volunteer to devote and sacrifice themselves to the totality. If the existence of the systematicity of the totality and its immanence in the people is seriously questioned, however, the only answer would be that because the individual member of the people sacrifices and 'dissolves his or her individuality' into the whole for the World History, the totality can manifest its existence. At the limit, such a logic could easily produce an argument that the sense of totality is given because people die for it, and that the resoluteness toward one's own death sustains the existence of such a totality.

There is no doubt that during the fifteen-year war (1931–1945), 'dissolving into the whole' immediately suggested the physical erasure of the self, or *kyoshi,* which could mean one's own death. The phrase "*ichioku gyokusai*" ("the total suicidal death of one hundred million," another version of "the final solution") was propagated all over Japanese territories toward the end of the fifteen-year war, and, in view of the manner in which Watsuji conceptualized the authenticity in his ethics, it was no coincidence that the final moment of total suicidal death was imagined as the aesthetic experience of ultimate communion. The death was appropriated into an experience in which one dissolved and got integrated into the nation: Death was

36. See Nancy, "La Communauté désoeuvrée."

transformed into the imagined experience of togetherness and comraderie; the resoluteness to one's own death was translated into the resoluteness toward the identification with the totality. The death was consequently aestheticized so that it could mediate and assimilate one's personal identity into national identity. Finally, the nation was turned into the community of destiny (*unmei kyodotai*) toward death. To use Watsuji's vocabulary, the absolute negativity (= absolute totality) was internalized into the finite totality of a nation-state. In this sense, the absolute totality lost its transcendence and infinity, and became 'expressible'. And Watsuji's ethics of '*nakayoshi*' (being on good terms) transformed itself into the ethics of '*ichioku gyokusai*' (the total suicidal death of one hundred million).

Has modern patriotism ever been free from this logic of communal death?

The Invention of English Literature in Japan

Masao Miyoshi

English is a huge business in Japan today. Practically everyone in this country of 120 million people goes to high school where English is taught several hours weekly for as many as six years; nearly half of all high school graduates go on to colleges and universities which, as of now, continue to require English.[1] What all this means is both a massive dose of English for everyone and an immense pool of English faculty and instructional resources, that is to say, a thriving multibillion-dollar industry. Nearly everybody is exposed to so much school-taught English for so long that this alien language practically serves as a second language for the Japanese. Under such circumstances, it is intriguing indeed to find the studies in Japan of English literature and the English language to be so idiosyncratically coordinated and so markedly divergent from what is understood to be English studies outside of the country. Although this discussion is concerned mainly with the specific nature of the study of English literature in Japan, it seems

---

1. I was told that the Ministry of Education is in the process of discontinuing the collegiate English requirement together with the general education curriculum (*kyoyo-bu*). At the time of this writing, I have not been able to confirm this news or uncover any details of the proposal. (See, however, *Asahi shinbun,* August 28, 1991, and July 25, 1992.)

both necessary and profitable to consider the wider context within which the discipline has evolved and is practiced.

General English Education

Let me begin with a brief survey of institutions involved in English studies in Japan today, focusing on how they operate rather than on how they are officially and bureaucratically organized. There are three main institutional English programs: 1) high-school English, in conjunction with the cram-school (*jukenjuku* or *yobiko*) version, which is largely targeted to the collegiate entrance examination; 2) academic studies in English literature (including the collegiate general education English); and 3) "conversation" school (*kaiwa gakko*) and business English. Although they all seek to teach/study English, they remain discrete with hardly any interchange among them.[2]

First, high school English, together with cram school English, is modular and formulaic, just as basic foreign language teaching tends to be everywhere. From the long history of collegiate exams, a list of certain sentence constructions has been compiled, and the students are expected to master them for they are the likeliest questions to be asked on the exams. Thus, they memorize "No sooner . . . than . . . ," or "It is . . . that . . . ," filling the blank spaces with appropriate words.[3] Likewise, a standard vo-

2. This paradigm of English studies is itself revealing in several ways. First, the instructive structure cannot presume any exposure to or familiarity with English life. In the United States and Europe, foreign language teaching usually emanated either from the immigrants from the region in which the language is spoken or from those returning from missionary or colonial assignments to such a region. Either way, their knowledge and information were organized into a curriculum. Second, the English-speaking people who first helped the Japanese learn the language were missionaries or business-related personnel who were there to convert, "democratize," or otherwise "civilize" the Japanese. Thus, they enjoyed a higher status among their students than did teachers in more ordinary circumstances. Third, more recently, conversation teachers from the United States and Britain are largely adventurous, young people in search of the strong yen. They often have no particular job qualifications except the ability to speak English, which may correlate with the low status of spoken English in Japan. Either way, the relative influence of the teacher-student relationship needs to be further studied. Equal interchange between the Japanese and the English speakers is not in evidence even now.
3. Ito Kazuo, one of the most successful English teachers in today's *yobiko* world, published *Ei-bunpo kyoshitsu* (Kenkyusha, 1979), in which he structurally lists phrase-clause-sentence constructions in a precise grammatical order. It assumes school grammar to be thoroughly logical, rational, and thus explainable. Brilliant in its own way, the book finally has little to do with English as it is used by English-speakers.

cabulary and a set of grammar questions have been developed, and such specimens are learned by heart. The rigor of memorization, it goes without saying, is merciless. At times a teacher offers a canonic text, such as one of Hawthorne's short stories or a Keats poem, but the text for the occasion is tamed and standardized in the sense that it is dissected into component sentence and phrase units. Reorganization of such modular units back into an integral text or speech act is hardly ever anticipated. Thus, when a high school graduate passes the difficult college entrance exam in English, the competence falls within the agreed-upon territory of "exam English" (*juken eigo*), which has very little to do with English as it is spoken in the United States, England, or any other place where English is commonly spoken. This does not mean the language is not understood, because it obviously is. The point, however, is the particular object and mode of understanding that results from the curricula as organized in Japan. I will discuss this further later on, but let me just point out here that the successful college entrant is unlikely to be able to speak or write easily understood English.

Since most students consider what they learn at their schools inadequate for the tough entrance exams, they spend after-school hours at "cram schools," where English and math are the most urgent subjects. The cram school is a profit-driven institution once considered irregular or even sleazy. Because of the democratic and demographic trends that make admission to a prestigious college formidably competitive, however, high-performance cram schools are quickly rising in social esteem as well as commercial value. Nowadays there are even hard entrance examinations for the *yobiko* themselves. As cram schools display spectacular success rates (55 percent are admitted to Tokyo U., 60 percent to Kyoto U., etc.), they come to enjoy prestige, and with the prestige comes influence. It is no overstatement to say that one of the clues to the state of formal English instruction in Japan lies in the practice at cram schools. The learning process is single-mindedly channeled to winning in the competition, thus radically turning English acquisition into a means to a specific career strategy. The critical and cultural speculations that might at times accompany the knowledge of a foreign language are not only irrelevant, but they may, if ever contemplated, even be a distraction.[4]

4. There are relatively few books that discuss the educational and cultural meaning of college entrance exams in the entrance exam–obsessed country. (The competition begins, incidentally, at the kindergarten level. A reputable kindergarten will enable its graduates to enter an elementary school that will make smooth the transfer to a junior high, which in turn. . . .) Kuroha Ryoichi's *Nyugakushiken,* Nikkei Shinsho 285 (Nihon Keizai Singunsha, 1978), offers a concise explanation of the notorious "exam hell" (*juken jigoku*).

As to the second category of institutional English programs, let a few words suffice here, since I will be elaborating on it below. The high school graduates who continue to the college level are faced with more of the same practice. They will read, that is, parse and translate, the canonic work word by word, sentence by sentence. Equivalency is always assumed between the two languages, with the tacit understanding that the balancing of the two sets of vocabulary is all there is to English studies. The controlling idea is thus "accuracy": once an idea is "accurately" transferred from one language context to another, the job is done. Spoken English, which presupposes greater movement within the system of English itself, is relegated to trivial status. Reading is all-important in the world of university English. English in this sense is very much like Latin, or more exactly, *kanbun,* Chinese texts read and pronounced as Japanese.

In fact, throughout the typical student's career in English, the training is predominantly in written documents. Thus, some students feel that they must supplement this written learning with oral practice, and to satisfy this need they enroll at "conversation" schools set up for that purpose. Unfortunately, conversation schools remain by and large commercial enterprises under little academic supervision. Although the number of students who attend such schools is small, it is rapidly increasing. These institutions devoted to lessons in oral English have several interesting features. First, the "conversation" taught in such schools is also formulaic. "How are you, Mr. Smith?" "Fine, thank you, Mr. Tanaka. And how are you?" Thus goes the "conversation," and the minute the teacher—who is often an American or English baccalaureate or undergraduate, and not necessarily in English—tries to conduct an unstructured talk, the effort is met with embarrassed silence. At these schools the student also expects to be taught the substance of conversation, topics and opinions, feelings and attitudes, as well as the sound and shape of English.[5] Second, proper pronunciation is inef-

5. The Japanese reluctance to express feelings and opinions is often described as "shyness," a word that nearly always fails as an explanation. There may be altogether different circumstances. One sometimes forgets that the public exchange of words in the pre-Meiji days was far more formalized than it is now or than it was then elsewhere. English is likely to have been regarded as an "official" language, since a private encounter with an English-speaker was infrequent. This accounts for the publication of numerous *kaiwa-sho* (conversation books) in the very early days of English studies in Japan (1850s–1870s) and since. These books offer formulas for brief speeches designed to be chosen and used at various official occasions; examples are the "afterdinner speech" and the "wedding toast." See Sogo Masaaki, *Nihon Eigaku no akebono: Bakumatsu-Meiji no Eigogaku* (Sotakusha, 1990), chapters 5–9.

fectually attended to. If the notorious confusion of liquids, *l*s and *r*s, is very much talked about, for instance, the rest—from vocalic values to specific consonants, not to mention accent and intonation—receive less emphasis, usually because of the oversized enrollment. Still, those who attend the conversation schools at least hear "real" English sounds,[6] which is not at all the case in most regular schools, where teachers have learned the sounds from their teachers, who learned from their teachers, who . . . for several generations with little exposure to non-Japanese English. Third, however undisciplined they may be, it may well be in such conversation- and business-oriented institutions that Japan's encounter with the outside English world can finally commence. Here, at least, the exchange is unmediated by the long accumulation of the naturalized English, which seems far too autonomous, introspective, and uncommunicable.

These three institutions are discrete, with very little in common. They are staffed by different kinds of instructors trained in different curricula with very little exchange among them. Likewise, they have different clienteles: the high school/college axis, together with the cram school, is more or less limited to the young population at large, whereas the conversation school offers a sort of continuing education mainly directed to youngish adults both in and out of business. Spoken English does not receive respect in the mainstream institutions, where the English phonemes are in fact taught through written phonetic signs (the International Phonetic Alphabet, or IPA) that stand in for pronounced sounds. At times one encounters a Japanese scholar with extensive and accurate knowledge of IPA representations who is at the same time neither willing nor able to sound them out. Thus, oral *Ei-kaiwa* (English conversation) is out, while literate forms of *Ei-go* (English reading), *Ei-bunpo* (English grammar), and *Ei-sakubun* (English composition) constitute the principal field of study. Of course, oral and literate categories can be combined, but they rarely are. At the center are the college and university English departments which, as the clearinghouse of literary and linguistic researches, ought to guide the whole English-learning industry. Do they? If so, how do they guide it?

6. Many Japanese believe even now that British English (which they often call "King's English") is far superior ("more authentic and genuine") to American English. Moreover, there is an aesthetic difference between the two, according to them: The British version is elegant and beautiful, whereas the more plebian American tongue is vulgar and blurry. Such a phonetic judgment is of course a part of the larger cultural belief that Americans are uncultured and materialistic, while Britons are intellectual and well-mannered. This feeling, a legacy of the imperialist era, is carried over into the standard distinction between English and American literatures as well.

The Beginnings of Studies in
English Literature

Japan's mid-nineteenth-century encounter with the outside world was largely involuntary. To the extent that it could not be resisted, the rendezvous was one-sided; it was, in fact, nearly an invasion. The recognition of this helplessness led Japan to both adore and reject the West at the same time. When studies of English were at last acknowledged to be a necessity by the Tokugawa government in 1856, the program was first placed at the Institute for Research on the Barbarian Books (Bansho Shirabe Dokoro). After many protests from Western diplomats, the name was changed seven years later to Kaiseisho, or the Institute for Open Development. Using shipwrecked sailors, interpreters in Dutch, and Chinese books on the geography and language of the West, the institute tutored the young samurai gathered from all parts of Japan. It was a government school from the beginning, and after it grew to be the University of Tokyo, it was placed under the jurisdiction of the Ministry of Education. English studies, in short, arose in response to the needs of the state.[7]

Earlier, the teachers were recruited from foreigners attracted to the typical colonial situation and the generous compensations. All courses, regardless of the subject, were taught in English, and every student had to study English (language and literature) as well. The tenure of the faculty was temporary. At the same time, they were left alone in their conduct of courses by the ministry. The reasons for the foreign teachers' freedom were several. First, the need to learn from the West was so urgent for both the Tokugawa and Meiji governments that they were in no position to interfere. Second, general thought control was relatively relaxed in the earliest years of the Meiji era, although the government tightened its hold soon thereafter. Third, the educational bureaucrats were determined to emulate Britain and eagerly sought to find or create parity and equivalence between the two nations. Thus, although the government was ever on guard against the dangers of alien teachings, the acceptance and importation of much of alien thought and customs was considered desirable and inevitable.

This climate did not last long, however. The Meiji oligarchy was sufficiently alarmed by the rising oppositionist movement, and the Imperial

7. Earlier, however, "Dutch learning" had existed in defiance of Tokugawa prohibition. By the end of the Tokugawa rule, the authorities knew that any suppression of "Western studies" was not only futile but counterproductive.

Precept on Education was issued in 1890 to set the course of the Ministry of Education and all the institutions under its jurisdiction along the line
of emperorism, which enabled wide-ranging control and centralization. The
Sino-Japanese War of 1894–95 intensified the wariness of the state officials. Japan was well on its way to Asian domination. The Ministry gradually
phased out the system of foreign teachers as it sought to tighten its rein
over the faculty and curricula and to reduce the costs of education. Japanese faculty trained abroad were to replace the foreign teachers and it was
under such circumstances that Lafcadio Hearn's contract was not renewed
and Natsume Soseki (who later became Japan's best-known novelist) filled
the vacancy around the turn of the century. Thereafter, foreign teachers
became supplementary luxuries, not fundamental players, in Japan's educational structure. This could be considered the first step in nationalizing
education, the teaching of English literature in particular.[8] Of course, the
disappearance of the English-speaking faculty meant the silencing of foreign sounds as well as alien opinions. "De-oralization" of English in Japan
could be said to have commenced at this point.

Easy to recognize but hard to comprehend fully is the remoteness of
the Japanese and English languages from one another. In the late 1850s
and early 1860s, the need for word-books, or inter-language dictionaries,
was quite urgent. The two sets of vocabulary were far from parallel, however; too often, objects and ideas in one society were absent in the other.
The invention of equivalences was thus the first critical step in an arduous
process of translating English words into Japanese.

The assumption of equivalence between two languages at least implies equivalence between the two cultures. The relations between Japan
and England were overwhelmingly characterized by differences rather than
similarities, however, and such an idea of equivalence was hard to accept
and nearly impossible to realize in the practice of translation. Nevertheless,
the Japanese felt that it was strategically vital and politically crucial to insist
on equivalence and symmetry. The idea of cultural comparability was in-
extricable from the basic quid pro quo principle of international diplomacy.
The fact that an English text could be translated into Japanese, and vice
versa, was seen at least partially as an act of demonstrating Japan's cultural compatibility with Britain at a time when the British Empire ruled the

8. Inoue Tetsujiro, the Dean of the School of Letters then, later recalled the circumstances
in *Kaikyu-roku,* 252–54, quoted in *Nihon no eigaku hyaku-nen,* vol. 1, p. 66.

world. Further, the Japanese aspiration to stand side by side with the British may well have been more than just a quest for cultural legitimacy. Its own imperial agenda did not lag long behind its confrontation with the Western threats in the mid-nineteenth century: Japan was to be the Britain of at least the Far East.

The difficulty in actually translating from English to Japanese was immense. When John Stuart Mill's *On Liberty* was translated in 1871, the translator had to diverge from the tract into a summary of Mill's life, as he was unable to naturalize the exotic political text. Shakespeare's plays were "translated" into *kabuki* productions in the 1870s via Charles and Mary Lamb's *Tales,* a rendition of the plays designed for children. Thus, it was a remarkable feat that by Soseki's time, merely a generation later, Shakespeare's texts had been "Japanized" together with many canonic works including eighteenth-century, Romantic, and Victorian poems and novels. Whether or not such textual transformations into Japanese were "accurate" requires a different study in a different context. What matters here is that the task was carried out and that it contributed to the formation of a bourgeois culture, and along with it, "literature."

The Japanese word for literature, *bungaku,* had been in use for many centuries. Earlier it had meant "studies" in general, or "textual commentaries," and not 1) literary productions, a category of aesthetic writing and performance considered distinct from others such as rituals, ceremonies, science, religion, history, and philosophy; or 2) organized studies thereof, an institutionalized discipline. This newer formulation arose in the West at the end of the eighteenth century. Historically, it was implicated in the development of national/regional consciousness at the time when Christianity was losing its hold on Europe and secularization was on the rise. Literature emerged as nationalism began to require the unifying myth for a nation-state for governance, especially at the time when Europe encountered the non-West in its program of colonial expansion. English literature, for example, was organized by colonial administrators in India earlier than in England, according to a recent study, as Britain faced the need to explain itself to the Indian subjects.[9] Literature was also useful as the ruling class was confronted with the proletariat displaced by the expansion of industrial capitalism. Together with "culture," an even more diffuse idea, literature was to provide a sense of agreement and community among the dispa-

9. See Gauri Viswanathan, *Masks of Conquest* (New York: Columbia University Press, 1989).

rate groups of a nation. The Meiji enlightenment leaders found a similar need for "literature" in Japanese society and used the word *bungaku* in the new sense that had spread by Soseki's time among writers and scholars. In short, by 1900 literature seems to have taken root in Japan with all its problematic contours intact.

People knew what was meant by several compound words of *bungaku: bungakusha* (men of letters), *bungaku-shumi* (arty taste), *bungaku seinen* (arty adolescent), and *bungakkai* (literary world). The specific application of the word—what belonged to literature and what didn't—however, was far from clear. The line between literature and history, or between literature and popular conventions, for instance, was blurred. It took decades to reach the vaguest agreement as to the circumference of literary work and performance.

Even less understood was the newly institutionalized discipline of literary studies, *bungaku* in the second sense. Even in the West, where literature has a longer history, the definition of literature has never been resolved, as those in academia well know vis-à-vis the conflicts among old New Criticism, new New Criticism, criticisms of difference, cultural studies, and "conventional" scholarship. The situation in nineteenth-century Japan was certainly no better.[10] As a matter of fact, the general uncertainty surrounding the nature of literature as a discipline was manifest in its academic organization itself. The University of Tokyo in the second half of the nineteenth century was in a constant flux. It changed its name and structure practically every year. In 1877 it established the School of Letters (*Bungakubu*), together with the School of Science and the School of Law, but the School of Letters was not a purely "literary" school. It comprised departments of philosophy, history, and political economy in the First Division (*Dai-ikka*) and a Department of Japanese and Chinese Literatures in the Second Division (*Dai-nika*). Courses in the English language and English literature were taught in all the departments in both divisions, but English literature as a discipline was not formed into a separate institutional unit until

---

10. Tsubouchi Shoyo wrote *Shosetsu shinzui* (The essence of the novel) in 1885. Though this work was really only a compilation of ideas and arguments from various English magazines, encyclopedia articles, and textbooks, as well as Edo writings, Tsubouchi's urgent need to explore the nature of the novel as it relates to other literary and artistic forms, in short, the genealogy of literature, is perfectly understandable. It was an effort to discover a place for "literature" in a gradually "modernizing" Japanese society. In the book, he only rarely uses the term *bungaku,* employing mainly *bungei* (art of writing) or *bijutsu* (fine arts).

1887.[11] When Soseki entered the university in 1890 and graduated from the Department of English three years later, the program had been pretty much established as a curriculum. What then did Soseki study, and how did he feel about his studies?

Natsume Soseki as an English Scholar

By the time Natsume Soseki succeeded Lafcadio Hearn as a lecturer in the English department at the Imperial University of Tokyo in 1903, most of the problems with English studies in Japan had already surfaced. The linguistic distance between the two languages, the uncertainties surrounding the discipline of literature, and the weight of nationalism that hung heavy on the studies of foreign literature at the height of imperialism—these issues confronted scholars at every stage in the newly evolving discipline of English literature in Japan, though they were only infrequently articulated.

There had been a succession of British and American teachers for nearly thirty years at the university. None of them before Lafcadio Hearn's arrival in 1892 was a distinguished scholar, and they automatically introduced in their courses the canon of English literature that was being established in their own home countries.[12] Thus, Soseki learned English literature from one James Main Dixon, a graduate of St. Andrew's at Edinburgh, who later taught at the University of Washington and the University of Southern California. Soseki recalled his teacher afterward before an audience of college students:

> [Dixon] told me to recite a poem or a sentence, or to write in English. He scolded me when I mispronounced a word or omitted an article. He asked in exams when Wordsworth was born or died, or how many Shakespearean folios were extant, and told us to list Scott's works

11. The history of the name and organization of the [Imperial] University of Tokyo is extremely complex, and it is difficult to summarize the logic of the changes. It is clear, however, that the binarism of the Japanese/Chinese as stagnant (*koro*), endangered, and deserving protection and the Western as attractive to the useful (*yuyo*) human resources was acutely felt. See then President Kato Hiroyuki's report to the Ministry of Education quoted in *Tokyo Teikoku Daigaku gojunen-shi,* vol. 1 (Tokyo Teikoku Daigaku, 1932), 685–87. See also *Kigen 2600-nen hoshuku kinen: Gakujutsu taikan* (Tokyo Teikoku Daigaku, 1940).
12. The one exception was Ernest Fenollosa, who taught at the university between 1878 and 1886. Fenollosa, however, mainly taught philosophy, not literature. See *Nihon no Ei-gaku hyaku-nen* 4 vols. (Kenkyusha, 1968–69).

chronologically. You young people would know whether these facts could enable us to understand what English literature is. No one had any idea from this what even literature could mean, not to say English literature.[13]

Most teachers seem to have simply recycled what they had learned at their colleges, dutifully covering the eras and genres, filling mechanically the dates and facts of biographical and other events, and drilling in prosody and rhetoric. They gave little thought to what memorizing dates and names meant. There were a few among the foreign teachers who had been trained in philology in Germany, and they no doubt taught the most recent grammatic and scientific theories. They were not, nor could they have been, distracted by the idea of a possible difference between English literature in Japan and English literature in Britain or the United States. Nor were they concerned with what literature could mean in the context of Japanese society then. What was good in their home countries was of course good enough for their Japanese students. Facts were unchallengeable as long as they were facts. Whether such "universalism" and "positivism" deserve commendation or condemnation, the Japanese students were expected to swallow the teachings whole, without being told what it was that they were ingesting. There were very few students like Soseki who kept their nagging doubts alive.

Soseki's career in the English field lasted well beyond his student days. For over a decade he tried to accept the discipline as it was then practiced. As a student, he wrote on Whitman's poetry or the Romantic ideas of nature. After graduating from the university, he went on to teach and then in 1900 was ordered by the Ministry of Education to study in England for the purpose of learning English literature firsthand so that he might transplant it upon his return. Thus began the most miserable two years of his life. He attended W. P. Ker's lectures at London University, and finding them too elementary, had tutorials with W. J. Craig. Craig, however, was too preoccupied with his Arden Shakespeare Edition and, besides, could not take a Japanese scholar of English very seriously. Soseki had no one to talk to and was desperately lonely. He persisted nevertheless in pondering what literary studies meant and, what was more important for him, what it could mean for a Japanese to study English literature. He read, wrote, and collected books in nearly total isolation until he had a severe nervous breakdown.

13. "*Watakushi no kojin shugi*" (My individualism), *Soseki zenshu,* vol. 11 (Iwanami Shoten, 1985), 440–41.

The notes he kept in London were later organized into three essays, two of which are theoretical attempts to discover "universal literary forms" that would enable every scholar to approach literary works regardless of national borders. While *Theory of Form in English Literature* (*Eibungaku kei-shiki ron,* 1903) and *Theory of Literature* (*Bungaku ron,* 1907) are obvious failures, they nonetheless clearly display serious misgivings with academic criticism and scholarship as well as a determination to examine the validity of (foreign) literary studies to its logical end. *Literary Criticism* (*Bungaku hyoron,* 1909), on the other hand, is a more conventional literary history of eighteenth-century English literature.[14] This book is impressive in its range of information and shrewdness of judgment. Remarkable documents as they all are, Soseki's dissatisfaction with himself as a critic and a scholar is undisguised. He may not be accurate in calling his own works "corpses of failed attempts, or worse, corpses of deformed children,"[15] but his verdict on his own critical procedures as lacking in "clarity," "originality," and "meth-odology" emanating from a "confused mind"[16] will have to be accepted. A Japanese scholar of English literature, as Soseki saw it, had to either imi-tate what an English scholar had already said or make do with casual and arbitrary impressions, and thus he/she could not have the confidence of being a genuine scholar. The possibility of a Japanese scholar shaping a new opinion from his/her own perspective never seems to have occurred to Soseki. "If you want to be a scholar," he advised, "you should choose a universal subject. English literature will be a thankless task: in Japan or in England, you'll never be able to hold up your head. It's a good lesson for a presumptuous man like me. Study physics."[17] He gave up English soon thereafter and devoted himself to writing fiction. In fiction he could at least feel he was "true to himself" (*jiko honi*).[18]

Around the turn of the century, on the other hand, three Japanese published books in English that would represent Japanese culture and society from their own viewpoints. Uchimura Kanzo's *How I Became a Christian: Out of My Diary* (1895); Niitobe Inazo's *Bushido: The Soul of Japan* (1899), and Okakura Kakuzo's *The Ideals of Japan* (1903), *The*

14. For a brief discussion of these "theoretical" books, see my *Accomplices of Silence: The Modern Japanese Novel* (Berkeley: University of California Press, 1974), 58–61.
15. *Soseki zenshu,* vol. 11, 446.
16. *Bungaku hyoron,* "Jogen" (Preface), *Soseki zenshu,* vol. 10, 37.
17. Letter, September 12, 1901, *Soseki zenshu,* vol. 14, 188.
18. "*Watakushi no kojin shugi*" (My individualism), *Soseki zenshu,* vol. 11 (Iwanami Sho-ten, 1985), 443–46.

Awakening of Japan (1904), and *The Book of Tea* (1906) are all essentialist books pleading for the uniqueness of Japanese culture. Although their aspiration for situating Japanese culture among the ranks of world civilizations in its own terms is perfectly understandable, their placement of Japan in Asia as its leader is—even in the light of the turbulent years between the Sino-Japanese and Russo-Japanese Wars—dangerously prophetic of its disastrous adventures half a century later. It is notable, however, that by writing these texts in the language of the dominant other, the three men were seeking to make Japan available to the indifferent outside world and thereby to lessen Japan's marginality. Had they received a proper response from the Western intellectuals in a dialogue that would help them place Japanese culture and society in the world, the course of the modern Japan might have been different. They were, however, more or less ignored except by a very few such as Ernest Fenollosa who, though an "Orientalist," took an active interest in Japanese literature. Also, the sort of energy that had propelled these three ran out, and the disappearance of foreign teachers exacerbated the trend. The number of works in English by Japanese writers has been minimal ever since, and Japan's isolation has deepened.

The critical issues Soseki confronted were never vigorously discussed, but rather were deliberately avoided, and institutionalization of English literature continued on. *Eigo Seinen* (literally, English-Language Youths, translated as *The Rising Generation*) was launched in 1898 to serve—despite its ghastly title—as the central organizing paper of the English establishment of Japan to this day. A massive number of translation projects began to render most canonic texts of Britain and the United States available at a brisk pace. The founding fathers of English studies in Japan established their patriarchy in the 1920s, compiling dictionaries and publishing historical surveys and biographical accounts. A sizeable series of annotated texts were published in the 1920s as well, some of which still serve as the standard texts for students. Such productions lasted until the early 1940s when the intensifying Fifteen-Year War silenced the students of enemy literature for several years.

Recent Studies

With the U.S. occupation after World War II, English studies revived and newer Anglo-American names were energetically introduced for several decades. Nevertheless, during the century and a quarter of English studies, the scholarly orientation has been remarkably consistent. Works and writers were usually mediated and contextualized by the totalizing historical narrative of English (and American) literature. Such history was segmented into *literary* histories and biographies. Theoretical studies of any kind were rarely attempted, and the long-tested interpretation and appreciation via annotations, impressions, and comments were substituted for scholarly investigations. What has prevailed then, is the ongoing doctrine of equivalence, which by emphasizing identification minimizes the significance of difference. The problems of English literature as they are faced in England are transplanted to become the problems of the Japanese study of English literature. There is nearly total indifference to the Japanese context in which such naturalization of alien perspectives must continually occur. Thus, Shakespeare studies by L. C. Knights and Frank Kermode—authoritarian and ethnocentric as they are—are accepted by Japan's scholars as authentic and, therefore, authoritative. In fact, it seems the more ethnically exclusive a critic is, the greater the respect proffered him/her. Take the nearly universal and unabated worship of T. S. Eliot in Japan. His Eurocentricity and Anglo-Catholicism are not only tolerated but in fact revered as the unassailable truth, as if the colonial attraction to the metropolitan and imperial center were the desirable and inevitable gesture of a cultured sophisticate. Eliot's *Idea of a Christian Society* and *Notes Toward the Definition of Culture* are taken at face value as *the* textbooks for understanding culture. Thus, Aimé Cesaire, George Lamming, and Ngugi, who might propose to them alternative arts and views, are by and large unread by the non-Western Japanese. Edward Said's *Orientalism* has been read principally as a part of the Middle East discourse and is viewed as having little to do with Japan or cultural understanding generally.

Younger scholars continue to take note of new theoretical developments in Europe and the United States. New names are again becoming familiar to the Japanese scholars and students. As ever before, new works —by Derrida, Foucault, feminists, Jameson and Frankfurt theorists, Eagleton, and lately, so-called New Historicists—are being introduced and translated. Although enthusiasm with the new in the West is considerably less visible now than it was in the late 1940s through the 1960s, the English studies business seems far from bankrupt. Thus, the April 1991 issue of *Eigo seinen* (*The Rising Generation*) is devoted to "Rereadings of Literary History." One scholar writes about the Marxist perspective, efficiently and intelligently summarizing Jameson, Eagleton, and Benedict Anderson and touching on some other issues such as the *Tempest* criticism in recent days. Another discusses "New Historicism" as he criticizes Stephen Greenblatt and his company (Louis Montrose, Don Wayne, and Catherine Gallagher are on his list). Still another scholar introduces feminist criticism, briefly mentioning Lilian Robinson, Showalter, Gubar and Gilbert, Toril Moi, Irigaray, and many others. Although the writing is not acute or insightful, it does well the job of listing active names. All are indeed good introductory essays, useful to curious beginners. What is absent in all of the articles, however, is any indication of the awareness of the meaning of these critics and theorists in the context of both English studies in Japan and Japanese society/culture itself. Whatever New Historicism may mean in the United States (is it the white man's—or the humanist's—last hope?), can it mean the same thing in Japan? Do these critics in Japan also believe in the hermetic autonomy of history that will enclose (or foreclose) the possibility of resistance and opposition? How does the Japanese scholar situate New Historicism in Japan's own social and historical context? Shouldn't there be a new generation of Sosekis? There is no indication of new Sosekis gnawed by similar doubts. Instead, there is only the old acceptance of the authority of the West—even when a Western critic questions the authority of the West![19] Despite the newness of the names now being cited in Japan, it is the continuity and persistence of the old habit, rather than the freshness and originality of an unfamiliar evolution, that are striking at present.

The most authoritative survey of English studies in Japan is a collection of essays by leading scholars in the field that examines the 100 years since 1868 (*Nihon no Eigaku hyaku-nen*). As is to be expected of works by Japanese scholars nowadays, it is comprehensive and informative. What is most striking about the publication, however, is the nearly

19. Most books being published now continue to talk about English/American authors and works as if the Anglo-American authors and the Japanese scholars were positioned together in the same space. It is never clear who the intended readers of these studies could be. I spent some time in December 1990 at the University of Tokyo and Gakushuin University browsing through their B.A. and M.A. theses in English literature, which read almost without exception as if the authors had tried their best to sound English/American/neutral. The resulting theses were no more than simplified encyclopedia entries, totally clichéd and inane. Incidentally, Professor Kishi Tetsuo of Kyoto University voices a view vis-à-vis the International Shakespeare Congress in Tokyo that there can and should be Japanese readings of Shakespeare, in *Asahi shinbun,* August 1991. Commenting on the same Congress, Stephen Greenblatt remarks, "The most exciting papers at the World Shakespeare Congress in the summer of 1991 were by Japanese Shakespeare scholars explaining the relation between Shakespeare and Noh, Kyogen, and Bunraku" ("The MLA on Trial," *Profession 92* [New York: MLA, 1992], 40). I hope Greenblatt will soon be able to elaborate on the grounds for his enthusiasm.

complete absence in it of historically interpretive speculation. Japan's contact with the West in the nineteenth century was a moment of heightened self-consciousness of Japan in the world, as has been discussed above. The writers and students of the time were alerted to the difference of the self from the other, and this shock of discovery brought all habits of thought into an unprecedented crisis. The Japanese accepted the challenge to undertake monumental reforms and adaptations in a struggle against perceived colonial subjugation. Understanding English was a part of this program. Their task was carried out, and they survived the crisis. Yet the centenary project neither interprets nor evaluates the historical development as a whole or individual scholars and their works specifically. As if in fear of possibly desecrating the memories of their ancestors, they refrain from the job of criticism and merely celebrate in reverence. A critical analysis of the mid-nineteenth-century crisis is yet to be undertaken.

More recently, the Pacific War placed English studies in a singular circumstance. Scholars were, according to an article in the 100-year history, "devoted" to the literature of England,[20] and yet were prohibited from pursuing it further by the leaders of their country. The author of the article says that research and teaching were entirely suspended, although speculation continued in agonized silence throughout the wartime crisis. After the summer of 1945, they reflected on the war experience, and tried to make sense of English studies in Japan. The article is a deeply personal account of the war experience, and it contains the potential for important questions. What is remarkable about the article, however, is that there is no intellectual engagement in it concerning the question of Japan in the world, the Japanese imperialist ambition interlocked with Western hegemonism, of which the studies of English in Japan have been a part. It remains mum even about the nature of the particular difficulties faced by the scholars of English. Did they approve of the war? Did they oppose and resist? If they did not, why not? If they did, how? If they were bewildered and disabled, where did this paralysis and impotence come from? Power and literature, literature and culture, politics and culture, economy and academia—such issues are simply ignored in the ongoing studies of English, as the author of the article and other scholars reflect on the critical war years in peaceful retrospection. Even now, several decades after the so-called postwar period, at this safe distance of time, there has been no significant statement

20. Hirai Masao, "Showa no Eibungaku kenkyu," *Nihon no Eigaku hyakunen,* vol. 3, 79.

concerning the crisis of scholarship as it was implicated in the devastating militarism of domination, aggression, and suppression. All the familiar repetitions of modular annotations, timely introductions, arbitrary impressions, and self-serving reminiscences ("I met Northrop Frye" and "when I had my last talk with Samuel Beckett") fill the intellectual vacuity of academia. However accurate, clever, or sensitive, such undertakings are trivial, or worse. Instead of modular segmentations and random fragmentations, all critical notes need to be aligned. English and Chinese literatures, literature and arts, culture and politics, economy and academia, the state and intellectuals—all must be reconnected and reexamined.

The situation of literary scholarship in other parts of the world might not be much better.[21] Cynicism and quietism are certainly not limited to Japan. Nevertheless, questions *are* being raised by a few nearly everywhere in the world as to the efficacy of the nation-state as the form of governance or as a space for study, or as to literature as a discrete discipline, or even concerning "culture" as a viable concept. National literature as it existed in the late nineteenth century, or even as late as the 1960s, is now very much in doubt in a good many places. For "literature" to be alive, it may require a different organization in a different context. Shouldn't the problem be unambiguously acknowledged and confronted in Japan as well, so that the vigor of critical speculation can be restored?[22] There are scholars outside of Japan who are eager to hear from their Japanese colleagues how they read, interpret, organize, and re-organize English—or any other— literature.

21. Studies of Japanese, both in language and literature, are far more advanced in the United States than in any other part of the world, yet the spread of familiarity as well as scholarship between Japan and the United States is hardly in balance. The United States is a central reference point in the minds of an overwhelming majority of Japanese; the reverse cannot be claimed for Americans.

22. See the Epilogue, as well as chapter 9, of my *Off Center: Power and Culture Relations between Japan and the United States* (Cambridge: Harvard University Press, 1991).

The Discursive Space of Modern Japan

Kojin Karatani
Translated by Seiji M. Lippit

Periodization

The word *Showa* and discourse concerning the Showa period suddenly began to proliferate in the summer of 1987, when news of the emperor's illness spread. By the beginning of 1989, after so many recountings of "the End of Showa," Showa ended. Once it had ended, it became apparent that a "Showa period" had existed, and its historical review could begin. What are the implications of periodizing history according to era names?

Since the Meiji period (1868–1912), Japanese era names have functioned as "one reign, one name," but prior to Meiji, they were changed frequently. The reasons for change included favorable omens and natural disasters; in addition, some changes were tied to specific years in the sexagenarian cycle, according to divination theory. In other words, the change of

In preparing the translation of this article, I consulted Sandra Buckley's translation of an earlier version of Karatani's essay "1970 = Showa 45," *Polygraph* 2, no. 3 (1989). —Trans.

era names was magical, or ritualistic, and was aimed at the rebirth, through death, of an era/world (*yo*). This function has not changed with "one reign, one name." The periods Meiji, Taisho, and Showa themselves organize eras (worlds) that possess a beginning and an end. However, these divisions are merely internal to the nation and often give rise to illusions.

For example, we are in the habit of saying Meiji literature, or Taisho literature, which thereby evokes a certain coherent image. The same applies to the Edo period: The terms *Genroku* and *Bunka-Bunsei* produce a similar sense of comprehension. This type of understanding, however, confines us within a strange illusion, which becomes clear if we simply think in terms of the Christian calendar. I became aware of this when teaching Meiji literature at Yale in 1975. For example, modern literature in Japan comes into being during the Meiji 20s through 30s, but it never occurred to me before that this period is what is called the "fin de siècle" in the West, or that the Taisho period (1912–1926) corresponds to World War I (Taisho 3) and the Russian Revolution (Taisho 6). Although I was well aware of these facts, I never considered them. This example underscores the extent to which divisions according to era names such as Meiji, Taisho, or Showa make one forget relations to the exterior and construct a single, autonomous, discursive space.

Simply doing away with periodization by era names and thinking in terms of the Christian calendar would not resolve this problem. One cannot account for Meiji literature according to the concepts of the nineteenth and twentieth centuries only—there is something there that disappears when the proper name *Meiji* is removed. This is not to say, however, that there exists a topology unique to Japan, or any internally confined time and space. In fact, what this proper name maintains is a relation to the exterior that does not allow for internal cohesion. Moreover, the image of what is "Meijiesque" or "Taishoesque" does not strictly correspond to the life of the emperor. The terms *Meijiesque* and *Taishoesque,* insofar as they symbolize certain relational structures, do in fact exist, and to dispose of them would also be to discard such relational structures.

It is significant that the Christian calendar, while it appears to represent simply a linear chronology, itself contains narrative divisions that are given significance, from the outset, by the narrative of Christianity. Furthermore, the divisions of a hundred years or a thousand years maintain a specific ritual significance. If the calendar were merely a linear chronology, the fin de siècle would probably not occur. Moreover, the calendar projects not only a fin de siècle significance onto events; it gives birth, in fact, to the very phenomenon of the fin de siècle. Even were this not the case, the fact that we view history according to hundred-year divisions, such as the eighteenth, nineteenth, or twentieth centuries, already gives birth to narrative punctuation. There is no essential difference between that and speaking of Meiji literature. In other words, when we think in terms of the Christian calendar, we are confined within a system of thought that views local history as universal, and this "universality" makes us forget the type of discursive space to which we belong.

Of course, the Christian calendar is indispensable; it is, however, something on the order of the metric system, and any Christian significance must be abstracted from it. It is indispensable in order to make explicit the fact that each nation's "era/world" is only a communal, illusory space, and that a plurality of worlds (eras/worlds) exists simultaneously, maintaining relations with one another, and further, that all periodization is arbitrary. The "universal" world can signify only the interrelational structure of these multiple worlds.

. . . .

Earlier, I mentioned that periodization according to era names produces an illusion; we must be aware, however, that any division has the potential to produce such illusions. The divisions of prewar and postwar, for example, are widely used. Certainly, World War II is one point of demarcation, and the events of 1989, which revealed the end of the postwar U.S.-Soviet duality, constitute another. These divisions, however, do not account for everything, nor are they the most important. Japan indeed changed after losing the war, but many areas also remained unchanged. Even among the most obvious transformations, there are those that were set in motion before and during the war. Do we then simply discard such divisions?

Periodization is indispensable for history. To mark off a period, that is, to assign a beginning and an end, is to comprehend the significance of events. One can say that the discipline of history is, to a large extent, fought out through the question of periodization, for periodization itself changes the significance of events. For example, there is the concept of the Middle Ages. A mediocre German historian first began using this term in the eighteenth century, and historians ever since have been battling over the question of how far the Middle Ages extend. Some argue that they extend as far as the eighteenth century—that even Newton, for example, was a man of the Middle Ages—while others argue that modernity began in twelfth-century

Europe. Yet they don't go so far as to discard the period of the Middle Ages itself.

Today, one talks of division as episteme (Foucault) or paradigm (Kuhn). There is also a school of history (the Annales School) that, like Yanagida Kunio in *The History of Meiji and Taisho*, attempts to view history as a domain without clear demarcations. Things remain essentially unchanged, however. What is put forth under the name of *paradigm* is the production of discontinuous divisions within a science that is taught as systematic or textbook knowledge, and what is called *episteme* establishes discontinuous shifts as breaks woven by discursive events, as opposed to the transcendental Subject or Idea. The Annales School examines the transformations and intermingling of differential areas rather than the obvious political and historical divisions, but this, too, simply puts forth another demarcation, according to which the traditional division/conferral of meaning is altered.

Larger demarcations, however, such as before or after the New Stone Age, are also possible. According to which perspective is taken —years, decades, centuries, millennia—the nature of periodization itself changes. Furthermore, the object, as well as the significance, of history changes. The question, however, is not which division is predominant. Lévi-Strauss writes that "history is a discontinuous set composed of domains of history."[1] In other words, history is but one method, and a distinct object for it does not exist. Therefore, it is important to be aware of the level, or domain, from which one speaks. It is important to realize that any periodization, insofar as it assigns a beginning and an end (telos), cannot escape a certain teleological arrangement.

Meiji and Showa

As I mentioned earlier, *Meiji* and *Taisho* do not strictly correspond to the lives of the emperors and are unrelated to the emperors personally. The emperor is indeed only a symbol. The same can be said for *Showa*. Wittgenstein states that the meaning of words lies in their usage. That is, in order to understand the meaning of the word *Showa,* we need to look at how it is used. What everyone forgot en masse after Showa ended is that at least until 1987, *Showa* was virtually unused by historians. Until that time,

1. Claude Lévi-Strauss, *The Savage Mind* (Chicago: University of Chicago Press, 1966), 259–60.

many books and articles were written with *Showa* in their title (e.g., *History of Showa*, *Showa Literature*), but these generally refer to the prewar period. The term *postwar* is applied to the period after Showa 20. Similarly, since 1965, the word *postwar* itself has seldom been used. It was around 1965 that people began speaking of the end of postwar literature; conjointly, the term *Showa* lost its significance as a historical division.

For example, phrases such as "early Showa" and the "Showa 10s" are popular, but this type of phrasing is possible only until the Showa 30s. I have seldom heard the phrase "Showa 40s," because the expression "the 1960s" overlaps with the Showa 30s, and after that it is normal to speak of the 1970s or 1980s. Between the Showa 30s and the 1960s, there is not only a gap of five years but a significant difference in nuance as well. In contrast to the latter, which is viewed within an international perspective, the former drags with it the context of Japan since the Meiji period. It was perhaps only in the Showa 30s that both were able to coexist. In that sense, one can say that Showa ended around Showa 40 (1965), as I will elaborate later. In other words, this usage of the word demonstrates its meaning more correctly than any strict prescription.

For example, the New Left movement of around 1970 came into being according to a consciousness of worldwide simultaneity. Looking back from that perspective, the political struggle that erupted around the revision of the U.S.-Japan Security Treaty (the AMPO struggle) in 1960 appears to have been only the beginning of that movement. However, the AMPO struggle of Showa 35 differs fundamentally from the New Left movement. The AMPO struggle was an intensive reexamination of the various questions that had persisted since Meiji. It was only much later, however, that I was able to understand this; at the time, at eighteen, I didn't think of these matters at all. I didn't grasp the perspective of the critic Takeuchi Yoshimi, who tried to place the AMPO struggle within the context of Japan since Meiji, nor did I understand why the historian Hashikawa Bunzo related the struggle to the questions of nationalism and modernization raised by the prewar Japanese Romantic School. What I was able to extract from them was only the fact that Japan's "premodernity" still lingered after the war or, perhaps, was being revived. At the same time, I didn't understand Mishima Yukio's right-wing transformation in the late 1960s—or rather, the fact that Mishima hadn't changed but had merely taken this struggle of 1960 as an opportunity to remove the "mask" he had worn after the war.

While the issues that Takeuchi Yoshimi put forth were problems of pre-Showa 20, they were also problems of pre-Meiji 20; the philosophi-

Table 1 Meiji and Showa

Meiji	Showa
(10 Seinan War)	(11 February 26 Incident)
22 Promulgation of Constitution	21 Promulgation of New Constitution
27 Sino-Japanese War	26 Peace Conference, U.S.-Japan Security Treaty
37 Russo-Japanese War	35 AMPO Struggle / New U.S.-Japan Security Treaty
	39 Tokyo Olympics
43 Annexation of Korea, High Treason Incident	43 Student Movement
44 Revision of Treaties	44 Return of Okinawa
45 General Nogi's Suicide	45 Mishima Yukio's Suicide

cal problems of pre-Showa 20 were, in a sense, a re-presentation of the questions of pre-Meiji 20. For example, the February 26 incident of Showa 11 is re-presented as a Showa Restoration that inherits the spirit of Saigo Takamori of Meiji 10 and realizes the Meiji Restoration to its fullest extent. Parallelism that is invisible under the Christian calendar becomes apparent in Table 1, which compares post–Meiji 20 with post–Showa 20. These startling correspondences are all situated in the process of Japan's transformation into a nation-state of Western-power status: the establishment of the modern nation-state, the achievement of economic development, and the revision of unequal treaties. Of course, this parallelism was not born only from within Japan. It signifies that the interrelational structure that situates Japan with the West and within Asia has not fundamentally changed. To put it differently, we can view what is Meijiesque or Showaesque as the discursive spaces exposed by this relational structure. In turn, the discursive space of the Taisho period resembles that of 1970 because of the combination of a sense of achievement and an autonomous internalization, which has repressed this relational structure.

The Discursive Space of Modern Japan

In the late 1950s, Takeuchi Yoshimi attempted to reevaluate the infamous wartime conference known as "Overcoming Modernity" (*Kindai no Chokoku*). This represents a different undertaking from, for example, a contemporary evaluation of the "deconstruction of modernity" in Nishida Kitaro that disregards its political context. In fact, Takeuchi investigated the "Overcoming Modernity" debate within the very domains that we would rather avoid today:

> "Overcoming Modernity" was, as it were, the condensation of the aporia of modern Japanese history. With the outbreak of total war, and faced with the philosophical problem of analyzing the idea of eternal war, the oppositional relations situated within the fundamental axis of tradition—restoration and revolution, emperor-worship and expulsion of foreigners, isolation and open country, nationalism and modernization, East and West—exploded, at a single stroke, as a problem: this was the "Overcoming Modernity" debate. Thus the presentation of the problem at this juncture was justified and was able to draw the interest of intellectuals. Yet the *dual nature of the war* was not dissected, in that it was not understood as aporia, and for that reason a philosophical subject with the capacity to reverse the meaning of Yasuda's destructive force did not emerge. Consequently, this aporia dissipated into thin air, and "Overcoming Modernity" became merely an analytic version of state military discourse. And the dissolution of the aporia prepared the philosophical groundwork for the postwar collapse and colonization of Japan.[2]

"The dual nature of the war" signifies that the war was simultaneously a war of aggression against Asia *and* a war to liberate Asia from the Western powers. To put it another way, it was at the same time the Pacific War and the Greater East Asia War.

The very "dissection" of this duality is dangerous, however, for the two can never be separated: One cannot affirm the one while negating the

2. Takeuchi Yoshimi, "Kindai no chokoku" (Overcoming modernity), in vol. 8 of *Takeuchi Yoshimi zenshu* (Tokyo: Chikuma Shobo, 1980), 64–65; Karatani's emphasis.

other. Takeuchi's logic is also extremely risky, and this is already apparent in his earlier work on nationalism:

> If nationalism is desired at all costs, what is to be done? Since it is impossible to evade the peril of ultra-nationalism and maintain only nationalism, the sole path lies, rather, in drawing out a genuine nationalism from within ultra-nationalism. That is, to draw out revolution from within counter-revolution.[3]

The evaluation of "Overcoming Modernity"—that is, the evaluation of the Kyoto School and the Japanese Romantic School—functions according to precisely the same logic, a logic that is nearly religious: It is only by passing through evil that salvation is possible.

Modern Japan, however, is situated within a structure that compels this type of risky logic; this is demonstrated dynamically in the two decades following the Meiji Restoration. I will present this structure according to two axes. The first consists of National Rights and People's Rights. These represent two tendencies that intersect with the Meiji Restoration; insofar as the Meiji Restoration was a revolution, it belonged to People's Rights, and insofar as it aimed to establish a sovereign nation against the Western powers, it belonged to National Rights. The fact that these two split, producing the Popular Rights movement, and that the National Rights advocates attained victory by imposing the constitution and parliamentary system *from above,* is well known. Considered in isolation, this opposition appears to represent a struggle between good and evil.

The other axis consists of the West and Asia. The revolutionaries of the Meiji Restoration believed that the revolution and independence of Japan could be maintained only by revolution in Asia, and above all, in China. This is similar to Trotsky and Che Guevara thinking that the success of their revolutions depended on revolution in Europe and Central America, respectively. The export of revolution was indeed the defense of revolution. In Meiji, the liberation of Asian countries from the imperialist control of the Western powers (i.e., the export of the Meiji Revolution) signified the defense of Japan itself. This was represented, above all, in the figure of Saigo Takamori. Saigo was purged by Okubo Toshimichi and others—the "one-nation nationalists," as it were—and was eventually killed during the Seinan War. This, too, appears to be a struggle between good and evil.

---

3. Takeuchi Yoshimi, "Nationalism to shakai kakumei" (Nationalism and social revolution), in vol. 7 of *Takeuchi Yoshimi zenshu* (Tokyo: Chikuma Shobo, 1981), 19–20.

296 Japan in the World

Yet in actuality, the two axes mentioned above intermix. For example, Takeuchi Yoshimi refers to the Seinan War as the Second Restoration. Yet from another perspective, this war signifies the absolute destruction of the old feudal powers, since Saigo's troops consisted only of warriors, and did not contain any element of People's Rights. It amounts to nothing more than the rebellion of the discontented, old warrior families. It is more accurate to say that Saigo became a symbol following his death, as Takeuchi himself states: "Whether to view Saigo as a counter-revolutionary or as the symbol of eternal revolution is a problem that will not be resolved easily. Yet it is difficult to define Asianism outside the context of this problem."[4]

The Meiji government that had rejected Saigo's plan to deploy troops to Korea enacted the same plan after Saigo's death, no longer as the export of revolution, however, but according to the same consciousness as Western imperialism. What is important is this type of reversal and conversion (tenko). For example, many supporters of the Popular Rights movement were Asianists, who aimed at revolution and the liberation of Asia. This is the opposite of Fukuzawa Yukichi's De-Asianism (datsu-A ron). As the example of Genyosha (Dark Ocean Society) typifies, however, the conversion from People's Rights to National Rights in the late Meiji 10s necessitated the transformation of Asianism into imperialism.

This type of reversal recurs in Showa. Conversion cannot be thought of in terms of only one axis, and similarly, the perspective of Japan versus the West alone cannot capture this dynamic. Figure 1 organizes this intermingling.

As I have stated repeatedly, the classifications shown in Figure 1 are not static. For example, there were conversions from IV Marxism to III Asianism (Yasuda Yojuro), and from III Asianism to II Imperialism. Furthermore, conversions from I to II, exemplified by Fukuzawa Yukichi, occurred rather frequently. In considering the question of conversion, we cannot exclude the phenomenon of postwar conversions, which included those from II to I or IV, and from III to I or IV. In actuality, these four quadrants are traversed around and around.

In all likelihood, we will not be able to escape this structure in the future. Postwar "space" consists of a domain that has discarded Asia; it is, in other words, the right-hand section of the diagram. Whether as invasion or liberation, the prohibition against interfering in Asia has dominated the

4. Takeuchi Yoshimi, "Nihon no Asiashugi" (Japanese Asianism), in vol. 8 of *Takeuchi Yoshimi zenshu* (Tokyo: Chikuma Shobo, 1980), 156.

Figure 1   Japanese Discursive Space

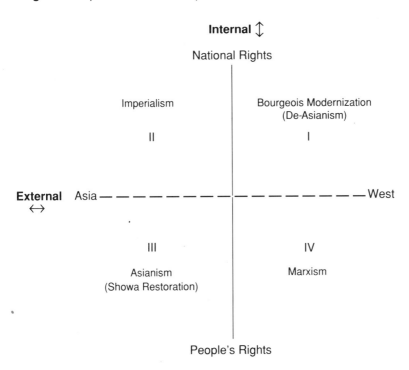

Note: Marxism is placed in quadrant IV because, for Marxism, Asia is nothing more than the underdeveloped nation, in general.

postwar discursive space. This is true on the level of consciousness, despite the fact that Japan has actually achieved an economic domination of Asia unparalleled before the war.

It was this type of discursive space that Takeuchi criticized:

> I believe that the aggressive aspect of the Greater East Asia War cannot be denied by any argument. But, by detesting the aggression so much, to reject as well the notion of Asian solidarity that was exposed through the form of aggression, is like throwing out the baby with the bathwater. For the Japanese would never be able to restore their lost sense of objectives.[5]

5. Takeuchi Yoshimi, "Nihonjin no Asia-kan" (Japanese views of Asia), in vol. 5 of *Takeuchi Yoshimi zenshu* (Tokyo: Chikuma Shobo, 1981), 119.

Takeuchi did not make such statements in the 1960s to encourage sympathy for Asia. According to his reasoning, the stagnation of Asia (particularly of China) was caused by the resistance to Western civilization. On the other hand, Japan was successful in its "modernization" because there was no resistance. There was no desire to protect the self, or rather, there was no self to protect in the first place. Takeuchi's Asianism thus reexamines the very question of Japanese identity.

After 1970, however, the type of criticism that Takeuchi wrote is itself canceled out. For example, in the context of the economic development of the 1970s, the fact that a self did not exist was highly valued. It is precisely because of this fact that Japan was able to become a cutting-edge super-Western consumer and information society. Indeed, there was no self (subject) or identity, but there was a predicative identity with the capacity to assimilate anything without incurring any shock or giving rise to any confusion. This is what Nishida Kitaro read as "predicative logic," or "the logic of place," in which he identified the essence of the emperor system. In this sense, after 1970, when Showa and Meiji were forgotten and Japan began to exist within a worldwide simultaneity, it is precisely the emperor as zero-degree sign that began to function structurally.

Things Taishoesque

Clearly, the fact that *Showa* fell out of use after 1970 does not signify that the Japanese had distanced themselves from a local perspective tied to the emperor and adopted an international perspective. Rather, as I mentioned previously, it signifies that the Japanese were confined within a dimension that eradicates everything outside of the first quadrant of the diagram. To a certain extent, this is a phenomenon that came into being during Taisho.

Just as Showa ended, for all practical purposes, in Showa 39 (Tokyo Olympics), Meiji ended in Meiji 37 (Russo-Japanese War). Thus, Natsume Soseki, who began writing fiction after the Russo-Japanese War, appeared to the dominant literary circles as a person from the previous age; Soseki himself was aware of this. For the naturalists, members of the White Birch School, or the "Taisho humanists," the type of qualitative differences and tensions among the East, West, and Japan that troubled such Meiji intellectuals as Soseki did not exist, except as quantitative differences, or as differences in scale. Marxism emerged in Japan as an extension of this situation—the Marxist perspective was based on a consciousness of worldwide simultaneity and homogeneity. In this manner, Marxists analyzed Japanese history prior to the Meiji Restoration within a universal perspective (but one that was actually based on a Eurocentric model).

In the period leading to the Russo-Japanese War, a consciousness of worldwide simultaneity did not exist, because this was precisely what was being confronted. The war had a simultaneous effect on countries in Asia and around the world that were under colonization by the West. Things were different following the Russo-Japanese War. For example, in the case of World War I, although Japan was a participant, the tension of simultaneity was lacking; it was only a distant event on another shore. Japan profited from this war and did not experience the disastrous effect that it had on Europe. Furthermore, Japan behaved like a Western imperialist power toward Asia. Yet, proportionately, the consciousness of worldwide simultaneity and of racial perspective strengthened, and at the same time, "things Japanese" began to be emphasized. In the realm of literature, this is demonstrated by the dominance of the *watakushi shosetsu* (I-novel).

"Things Taishoesque" emerged from a consciousness of autonomy, as tension between Japan and the West began to ease following the Russo-Japanese War, and Japan proclaimed its separation from Asia. The same applies to the 1970s; in general, it is in this type of period that discourse on Japan and on Japanese culture begin to proliferate. It should be noted that Fukuzawa Yukichi's *De-Asianism* and Okakura Tenshin's *Ideals of the East* were written amidst the tension that existed before this consciousness of autonomy was established. Both, however, take on a different meaning following the Taisho period.

For example, Natsume Soseki's *Theory of Literature* is premised on the difference between *Eastern literature* and *Western literature*. That is precisely why he attempted to objectify them both, "scientifically," and according to the same foundation (i.e., according to the material/social level of language). Yet, in this case, he speaks of Eastern literature and not of Japanese literature. Following the Taisho period, these two were completely reversed; as Japan and the West began to be seen on the same level, the differences between them were emphasized. *The West* became only an image, as did *the East*.

Okakura Tenshin aims at the rejuvenation of the Asian countries collapsing under Western colonialism in *Ideals of the East* (1903), which he wrote in English before the Russo-Japanese War:

Asia is one. The Himalayas divide, only to accentuate, two mighty civilisations, the Chinese with its communism of Confucius, and the Indian with its individualism of the Vedas. But not even the snowy barriers can interrupt for one moment that broad expanse of love for the Ultimate and Universal, which is the common thought-inheritance of every Asiatic race, enabling them to produce all the great religions of the world, and distinguishing them from those maritime peoples of the Mediterranean and the Baltic, who love to dwell on the Particular, and to search out the means, not the end, of life.[6]

The counterattack against the West is carried out not through Western-style military force or material power but through "love" and art. The East (Asia) is not merely an image determined by the West, nor does it have a common identity by virtue of the shared fate of colonization. Rather, it maintains a certain practical identity. Okakura considers the historical intercourse throughout Asia, and afterwards, he explains Japan's privileged position:

> The unique blessing of unbroken sovereignty, the proud self-reliance of an unconquered race, and the insular isolation which protected ancestral ideas and instincts at the cost of expansion, made Japan the real repository of the trust of Asiatic thought and culture. . . . Thus Japan is a museum of Asiatic civilisation; and yet more than a museum, because the singular genius of the race leads it to dwell on all phases of the ideals of the past, in that spirit of living Advaitism which welcomes the new without losing the old. . . . The history of Japanese art becomes thus the history of Asiatic ideals— the beach where each successive wave of Eastern thought has left its sand-ripple as it beat against the national consciousness.[7]

Japan's privileged position derives from its accidental capacity to preserve, as a "repository," the product of Asian intercourse. Okakura's works, like those of Uchimura Kanzo, were written in English for an exclusively Western audience; in other words, they were not intended to inspire the Japanese. Takeuchi Yoshimi writes about Okakura: "In this position, Okakura is more an apostle of transcendental value alienated from the Japanese nation. The Japanese nation would not listen to his appeal, and so he had to take his appeal to the world. And here, Okakura's beauty/spirit/ Asia maintains a position similar to the notion of faith in Uchimura Kanzo."[8]

Uchimura and Okakura were not unpatriotic, but their patriotism was

6. Kakuzo Okakura, *The Ideals of the East* (London: John Murray, 1903), 1.
7. Okakura, *Ideals of the East*, 5–8.
8. Takeuchi Yoshimi, "Okakura Tenshin," in vol. 8 of *Takeuchi Yoshimi zenshu* (Tokyo: Chikuma Shobo, 1980), 173.

revealed only to Westerners and was not directed internally. Within Japan, Uchimura's God and Okakura's beauty/spirit/Asia existed as an absolute, transcendent exteriority. The Taisho discursive space came into being with the eradication of the transcendent otherness and exteriority maintained by Uchimura Kanzo and Okakura Tenshin. Thus, many members of the White Birch School, as well as many naturalists—in other words, many of the Taisho writers—were first disciples, then apostates, of Uchimura. It was not only the discarding of Christianity but the eradication of absolute otherness that specified things Taishoesque. The Taisho discursive space emerged as an affirmation of "Japanese nature," and the eradication of the West and Asia as Other.

In turn, this was erased in one violent sweep by the Marxist movement. What early Showa Marxism (Fukumotoism) produced was precisely an absolute otherness, a consciousness of the absoluteness of relations existing beyond individual consciousness. It was not religion, but it gave birth to religious questions never before raised by any religion in Japan. It was there that conversion first became an issue, and it was in fact only through Marxism, and the experience of conversion from it, that existential and religious questions were raised in Japan.

"Things Showaesque" cannot be entirely separated from Marxism, for the latter does not simply represent a universalist ideology but also forcibly emphasizes the absoluteness of relations to the exterior. The literary critic Kobayashi Hideo was aware of this:

> When an ideology is imbued with a universal aspect, resisting every distinct interpretation advanced by individual writers, we encounter "socialized thought" in its primary form. Our young writers could not help being intoxicated on this strange new substance. . . . Never before had writers labored to create, relying so on ideas and theories; again, never before had writers so completely ignored their actual, physical lives. It is not just that they had forgotten how to embody or to internalize an idea. Rather, being intoxicated on a system of thought too bloodless to allow any real internalization or embodiment, the Marxist literary movement had no essential significance apart from its intoxicating effect.[9]

Kobayashi Hideo wrote this in 1935, after the Marxist movement had already been destroyed, and during the "literary renaissance" that revived Tai-

9. Kobayashi Hideo, "Fiction of the Self," trans. Paul Anderer (Stanford: Stanford University Press, forthcoming).

shoesque writers. However, Kobayashi was able to make this assertion precisely because, in some sense, his own criticism also introduced a kind of absolute otherness. In other words, things Showaesque are clearly established as a rejection of Taishoesque autonomy (which does not contradict its cosmopolitanism).

The Taishoesque merits examination because, as I have already suggested, it resembles the post-1970 discursive space in Japan. The following typically demonstrate the Taisho period: a self-complacency that can introduce anything from the outside without actually maintaining a conception of the exterior; or, conversely, a delusionary, insular mentality that thinks of itself as worldwide, even though it is entirely local; or further, the self-deception of being unaware of "invasion," even while Japan is in fact advancing mercilessly throughout the world.

For example, near the end of Meiji, in 1910, Japan annexed Korea, not, of course, according to what Okakura Tenshin refers to as Eastern "love" but by Western-style military force. Okakura died a few years later. His "ideals" had already been shattered during his lifetime. Yet his assertions were also actualized in a strange way, for the Japanese annexation of Korea was viewed not as a Western-style colonization but rather as an attempt to transform Koreans into Japanese through "love." This was the height of self-deception. Japanese colonial domination is detested even today precisely because of this "love." Although the discursive space of the Taisho period is thus established at the point where Koreans are incorporated into the Japanese empire, it exists as if this event never occurred. For this reason, Taishoesque humanism is questionable.

The meaning of Okakura's writing is reversed when it is read as something directed internally. The privileging of Japan is taken from it quite literally. In his short story "The Laughter of the Gods," Akutagawa Ryunosuke writes that any kind of thought, whether it be from China, India, or the West, is necessarily transformed by the gods (*kami*) of this island country.[10] Although it takes on a negative form, this is an assertion of Japan's uniqueness.

The same can be said for the founder of Japanese anthropology, Yanagida Kunio. Murai Osamu points out that Yanagida was deeply involved in the Korean annexation as a bureaucrat and consequently ignored and omitted Korea in his scholarship. Instead, he turned to the Southern Islands. The Southern Islands, however, were not a different exterior but

10. Akutagawa Ryunosuke, "Kamigami no bisho" (Laughter of the gods), in vol. 4 of *Akutagawa Ryunosuke zenshu* (Tokyo: Chikuma Shobo, 1987), 386–88.

rather a kind of motherland (although, in fact, Okinawa was traversed by international intercourse). This constitutes the search for identity in the interior and amounts to the rejection of the Other. Japanese folklore itself came into existence with the colonization of Korea.

Transformations in Emperor Theory

Yanagida Kunio located the ancient origins of the imperial ceremonies in village ceremonies. Of course, Yanagida was trying thereby not to belittle the emperor system but rather to make it more familiar to the masses. Whatever his intentions, however, it should be noted that in the context of the Meiji period, this was an exceptional way of thinking. The anthropological analysis of the emperor system does not signify simply the development of a scientific thought.

The national socialist Kita Ikki, who was executed as the leader of the 1936 coup d'état proclaiming the "Showa Restoration," claimed that the pre-Meiji emperor was no different from an "aboriginal chieftain." In truth, as I stated previously, era names prior to Meiji constituted a magical function to control nature. "One reign, one name" negated this in order to establish the emperor as the sovereign of a modern nation-state. For Kita Ikki, the Meiji emperor was a constitutional monarch who existed as an institution; in other words, the emperor himself and his ceremonial essence were essentially irrelevant. We find a similar conception in Hegel: "It is wrong therefore to demand objective qualities in a monarch; he has only to say 'yes' and dot the 'i,' because the throne should be such that the significant thing in its holder is not his particular make-up."[11]

Prior to the Russo-Japanese War, the emperor was considered a German-style emperor by the Japanese, including Kita Ikki. However, what Yanagida produced in the Taisho period was a perspective that viewed the Japanese emperor as an aboriginal chieftain. This cannot be separated from the fact that during this period, international tension, or rather, the emperor as a symbol of this tension, began to weaken. People are conscious of the emperor when they are also conscious of international tension, and when the emperor is forgotten, it is because tension with the outside has eased. The same applies to the Edo period. During the period of isolation, the emperor may as well have not existed; he existed only for the

11. Georg Wilhelm Friedrich Hegel, *Hegel's Philosophy of Right*, trans. T. M. Knox (Oxford: Oxford University Press, 1967), 289.

Mito School or for the National Scholars. When a national crisis emerged at the end of the Tokugawa era, however, the emperor was called forth as sovereign in order to secure the sovereignty of the Japanese nation-state.

However much he was dressed in the clothes of antiquity, the emperor after Meiji was the sovereign of a modern nation-state. The revolutionaries of the Meiji Restoration concentrated all authority in the emperor in order to eradicate the plural, feudalistic configuration of power. Just as in Europe, this was an unavoidable process in the establishment of the modern nation-state. By making the emperor sovereign, Japan was able to become a modern nation-state. Sovereignty, however, is not only internal to a nation; it maintains an external relation as well. Whether it is emperor sovereignty or people's sovereignty, we become conscious of the issue of *sovereignty* only in the context of relations to the exterior.

Hegel criticizes the separate treatment of domestic and external sovereignty. According to his thinking, external sovereignty, which emerges with "the relation of one state to another," appears as "something external" and as "a happening and an entanglement with chance events coming from without"; but in fact this "negative relation" is "that moment in the state which is most supremely its own," and belongs to the essence of sovereignty.[12] In other words, any discourse on the nation-state that is not premised on the existence of other nation-states is merely a discourse on community (*kyodotai-ron*).

In the Taisho period, however, the emperor was considered something entirely domestic; this amounted to nothing other than viewing the emperor system in terms of discourse on community. We should note that Yanagida called his folklore studies "Neo-National Studies" (*shin-kokugaku*). Of course, Yanagida was not a narrow-minded nationalist; he tried to think scientifically and universally. What is important is that the "universalism" of the Taisho period is linked, in this manner, to internalization and the emphasis on Japanese uniqueness.

Similarly, during the 1970s, cultural anthropology, and the historians who introduced it, began to theorize the emperor system; these arguments, however, are ahistorical and lack a political perspective. In essence, they represent the aboriginal chieftain argument. There are, for example, scholars, like Yamaguchi Masao, who point out the similarity between the emperor system and African sovereignty, and scholars, like Ueno Chizuko, who point out the sovereignty of Oceania. These arguments are presented

12. Hegel, *Philosophy of Right*, 209.

as attempts to dismantle the emperor system by thinking of it in more funda-mental terms, but as I pointed out earlier, even Kita Ikki was already aware of this. Furthermore, it is questionable whether these sovereignty theories can account for even the Nara and Heian period emperors, much less the modern emperor system.

For example, despite the fact that the Japanese political system prior to the Russo-Japanese War was a constitutional monarchy, it was not the Diet that ruled but, rather, the elder statesmen (i.e., Restoration leaders from the Choshu clan). The Meiji constitution gave the power of supreme com-mand over the army and navy to the emperor, because the elder statesmen, while accepting the parliamentary system, attempted to secure a power that existed beyond the Diet. In the Taisho period, such theories as Minobe Tatsukichi's "emperor as organ," which argued that insofar as the emperor followed the decisions of the Diet, the army and navy were also under its control, were able to gain currency precisely because it was a relatively calm period, both internationally and domestically. In the Showa period, however, this constitution became the basis for the autonomy of the army and navy, placing them beyond the control of the Diet. The military sought to justify its arbitrary action, which had economic depression as its back-ground, by seeking the deification of the emperor. This was entirely different from the notion of "the emperor system that lives among the people," and it arose within the context of international tension. In a similar fashion, the English people believed, until the nineteenth century, that their king had healing powers, but this had absolutely no relation to the British Empire.

It is true that in thinking through the question of emperor-system fascism, we cannot ignore its mythological structure. In the seventies, how-ever, all political and economic historicity was ignored. To ignore this, and to attempt to discover the origins of the emperor system in the past or among the people, appears to be more fundamental; in reality, however, it is not. Rather, that in itself is historical; it is noteworthy that this type of discourse on the emperor system arose in the Edo period (National Studies) and in the Taisho period (Neo-National Studies). It relies on a one-nation (one-community) model. Consequently, it appears scientific, for structural theory is premised on a closed system. Even when this system introduces the Other, or the outside, these already belong within the communal system, as part of it.

What are called "exterior" and the "Other" in cultural anthropology do not in fact maintain any exteriority or otherness. Rather, they are indis-pensable to the community and are thus part of it. For example, the historian

Amino Yoshihiko attempted to find the basis for overturning the emperor system in outcast groups, yet ended up finding the emperor system there, because outcast groups are not external to the system; the community system is precisely that which includes them. Amino, who had previously written on the Mongol Invasion and had seen in that international crisis the transformation of the ancient system, was subsequently caught in the trap of structural theory.

To discover plurality and otherness on the inside does not amount to escaping interiority. Yanagida called his folklore the "study of introspection," but this, too, was simply introspection within the community. In the same way, today's anthropological and semiological discourse is nothing more than sollipsistic introspection, and that, in itself, functions as the ideology of Neo-National Studies.

There are other, more "fundamental," strategies that fall under the name of relativizing the emperor system and tracing it back to a previous state of plurality; these result, as with Yanagida, in a move to the Southern Islands. Some, like Yoshimoto Ryumei, have literally turned to the Southern Islands, while others, like Umehara Takeshi, have looked to Jomon or Ainu culture. Whether toward the south or toward the east, and whether to affirm or negate the emperor system, this type of "introspection" has produced no effect. It is similar to the fact that the widespread discourse on Japan and the Japanese of the 1970s produced nothing, and it is the very historicity of the space that has popularized this kind of discourse that we must examine.

The Death of General Nogi

The weakening of the consciousness of Showa and of the emperor following Showa 40 (i.e., after the Tokyo Olympics) is similar to the rising sense of achievement and internalization that followed the Russo-Japanese War. As I stated earlier, this internalization and cosmopolitanism are not contradictory—even as Japan internationalized and maintained a consciousness of worldwide simultaneity, the "outside" was lost. It appears that in order for the transformation of discursive space to become clearly fixed in consciousness, some symbolic event must occur. Marx says that we need tragedy in order to part cheerfully with the past, and one can say that Mishima Yukio's death in 1970 was such an event.

We are used to speaking of this period as the 1960s, yet if we consider the questions of the late sixties in terms of the Showa 40s, a different aspect begins to appear. Within the former perspective, this is the high point of the New Left, which in turn is usually situated within a worldwide simultaneity. The New Left movement has been read as a critique of modern Western rationalism; if we look at this period from another perspective however, that of the discursive space of modern Japan, it can be read as the return, if only temporarily, of the left-hand side of the coordinate space that had been repressed after the war (see Figure 1). For example, Maoism (the Cultural Revolution) was, as Yasuda Yojuro understood, a kind of pan-Asianism. In addition, the critique of modern, Western rationalism in this period resembles the "overcoming modernity" debate of before the war. Hence, the closeness that Mishima Yukio felt for the New Left was not, in fact, without basis.

We were surprised by Mishima's suicide in 1970. Yet, if he had committed harakiri (ritual suicide) in *Showa 45*, there would have been no cause for surprise. Mishima himself must have been aware of this. We are used to reading Mishima's action as a re-presentation of the February 26 rebellion, but we should recall instead the *junshi* (following one's lord in death) of General Nogi in Meiji 45. General Nogi's suicide, through its very anachronism, also shocked the people of the time. *Junshi,* in relation to an emperor who is the head of a constitutional monarchy, is unthinkable. General Nogi adopted a relation of loyalty as to a feudal lord. It is natural that Akutagawa Ryunosuke and Shiga Naoya, who were raised in the modern nation-state of post-Meiji 20, mocked Nogi's anachronistic action.

The event shocked Mori Ogai and moved him to write *The Last Testament of Okitsu Yogaemon*. Thereafter, Ogai shifted to historical fiction dealing with samurai and people of the feudal world. *Feudal* here signifies the existence of a relation of absolute loyalty to one's direct lord but not to any higher authority. Consequently, a feudal system, in contrast to the modern nation-state with its centralized authority, is overrun by the revolts of multiple powers. The characters that Ogai describes in *The Abe Family* are willing, because of their loyalty to their lord, to commit treason against the clan. These feudal people maintained an independence that is missing in the individual of the modern nation-state, who is constituted as subject by being entirely subject to one sovereign. In truth, it was not this type of modern individual who supported the Popular Rights movement of Meiji 10 but rather the feudal person, with his conceit and sense of independence. Yet, as the Seinan War of 1878 demonstrates, they were unavoidably led to a civil war aiming to negate national sovereignty.

The instruction in Ogai's will to be buried as "Iwami Native Mori Rintaro" does not signify a nostalgic return to his birthplace but contains within it the negation of the institution of the modern Meiji nation-state, which he himself supported and helped construct. What captivated Ogai was not the antiquated quality of the feudal person but his sense of independence and plurality, which had been lost in the modern "interiority" of the Taisho period.

Natsume Soseki was also shocked by this incident and was led to write *Kokoro*. In this novel, Sensei says:

> Then, at the height of the summer, Emperor Meiji passed away. I felt as though the *spirit of the Meiji era had begun with the Emperor and had ended with him*. I was overcome with the feeling that I and the others, who had been brought up in that era, were now left behind to live as *anachronisms*. I told my wife so. She laughed and refused to take me seriously. Then she said a curious thing, albeit in jest: "Well then, *junshi* is the solution to your problem.
>
> I had almost forgotten that there was such a word as "*junshi*." It is not a word that one uses normally, and I suppose it had been banished to some remote corner of my memory. I turned to my wife, who had reminded me of its existence, and said: "I will commit *junshi* if you like; but in my case, it will be through loyalty to the spirit of the Meiji era." My remark was meant as a *joke;* but I did feel that the *antiquated word* had come to hold a new meaning for me.
>
> A month passed. On the night of the Imperial Funeral I sat in my study and listened to the booming of the cannon. To me, it sounded like the last lament for the passing of an age. Later, I realized that it might also have been a salute to General Nogi. Holding the extra edition in my hand, I blurted out to my wife: "*Junshi! Junshi!*"
>
> I read in the paper the words General Nogi had written before killing himself. I learned that ever since the Seinan War, when he lost his banner to the enemy, he had been wanting to redeem his honor through death. I found myself automatically counting the years that the general had lived, always with death at the back of his mind. The Seinan War, as you know, took place *in the tenth year of Meiji*. He must therefore have lived for thirty-five years, waiting for the proper time to die. I asked myself: "When did he suffer greater agony—during those thirty-five years, or the moment when the sword entered his bowels?"
>
> It was two or three days later that I decided at last to commit suicide. Perhaps you will not understand clearly why I am about to die, no more than I can fully understand why General Nogi killed himself. *You and I belong to different eras, and so we think differently.* There is nothing we can do to bridge the gap between us. Of course, it may

be more correct to say that we are different simply because we are two separate human beings.[13]

The passage contains subtleties that do not lend themselves to summary, so I have included the full quotation. By this time, *junshi* is already an "antiquated word" that can only be a "joke" (and, until Mishima Yukio actually died, I considered what he was saying to be a joke). Furthermore, although what Sensei calls "the spirit of Meiji" may not be limited to "the tenth year of Meiji," it undoubtedly represents something prior to Meiji 20.

Sensei clearly feels guilt at having betrayed his friend K, yet he also understands that K did not necessarily die out of failed love or his friend's betrayal. This triangular relationship maintains an entirely different aspect. K was a stoic idealist: "Having grown up under the influence of Buddhist doctrines, he seemed to regard respect for material comfort as some kind of immorality. Also, having read stories of great priests and Christian saints who were long since dead, he was wont to regard the body and soul as entities which had to be forced asunder. Indeed, he seemed at times to think that mistreatment of the body was necessary for the glorification of the soul" (*Kokoro*, 176).

In this light, K appears merely an eccentric and idealistic youth. Yet, this extreme type seems to be specific to certain periods; take, for example, Kitamura Tokoku, who turned to Christianity, or Nishida Kitaro, who turned to Zen. In the face of the rapidly forming bourgeois nation-state, they both took refuge in "interiority" after losing their respective political battles. That is, after the possibilities of the Meiji Restoration were closed off, they tried to position themselves against all worldly things. They were also necessarily defeated by worldly/natural things. Tokoku committed suicide, and Nishida endured humiliation to enter the special course at the Imperial University. K can be considered a similar type.

Therein lies the reason that Sensei respects K and follows in his wake. There is also ill will directed against his unapproachable model, and this is hidden in the goodwill, whereby Sensei says, "In an attempt to make him more human, I tried to encourage him to spend as much time as possible with the two ladies" (*Kokoro*, 180). This represents a temptation to make K submit to the worldly/natural things that he has refused. K dies not because of his friend's betrayal but because of the consciousness of his impotence and hollowness—of his inability to achieve the independence of his inner self. Consequently, we should say that within the problem of

13. Natsume Soseki, *Kokoro*, trans. Edwin McClellan (Chicago: Gateway Editions, 1957), 245–46; Karatani's emphasis. This work is hereafter cited in my text as *Kokoro*.

the triangular relationship lies a political question. Both Sensei and K were guilty of betrayal: the betrayal of the multiplicity of possibilities that existed prior to the rapidly consolidating modern nation-state of the Meiji 20s. The same can be said for Soseki himself.

Soseki believed English literature to be something on the order of Chinese literature. At first he thought: "I would have no regrets, if that were the case, in devoting my entire life to its study," but "in the back of my mind, as I graduated, I had a sense of wastefulness, as though I had been deceived by English literature."[14] The "Chinese literature" to which Soseki was willing to devote his life differed from the Southern School Chinese painting or the Chinese poetry to which he turned in his later years. It had been something connected to Asia, and to People's Rights, and it symbolized the multiple possibilities contained within the Meiji revolution. What Soseki referred to as the "spirit of Meiji" was not the spirit of the entire age of Meiji, which he detested. He felt no sympathy for General Nogi's thinking. Rather, what Nogi's suicide recalled for Soseki was the repressed and forgotten revolution represented by Saigo Takamori, who died as rebel leader of the Seinan War in which Nogi had taken part on the side of the government.

For Soseki, Chinese literature configured the universe of East Asia, just as Latin had for Europe, and its loss meant not only the loss of a specific Japanese identity but of "universality." Soseki, however, differed from Okakura Tenshin, who opposed the universality of Asia ("Asia is one") to the universality of the West. In contrast to Okakura, who retrieved an imaginary universality from within a poetic and aestheticist fantasy, Soseki did not seek universality in either the West or the East. Consequently, he unavoidably became theoretical.

Soseki began writing fiction after the Russo-Japanese War, when the Japanese had completely swept Asia from their consciousness and were attempting to place themselves alongside the great Western powers. His fiction represents a conscious resistance against the exclusive standard of the already established modern novel. This can be seen even in the type of satire represented by his first work, *I Am a Cat*; Soseki inscribed in this work all the genres that had been suppressed by the nineteenth-century modern novel. In other words, he did not convert from a theorist to a novelist; his creative activity was itself a critical practice. Yet, Soseki was viewed as simply behind the times by the young, cosmopolitan writers and critics of this period.

14. Natsume Soseki, "Bungakuron" (Theory of literature), in vol. 25 of *Nihon kindai bungaku taikei*, ed. Uchida Michio (Tokyo: Kadokawa Shoten, 1969), 473.

The Death of Mishima Yukio

Soseki, who was born in the third year of Keio (1867), may have identified his own life with the reign of Emperor Meiji—hence Sensei's statement about "beginning and ending with the Emperor." The same may be said of Mishima Yukio, who was born in the last year of Taisho. In a sense, Mishima ended Showa by ending his own life.

Although Soseki wrote *Kokoro*, he was not about to commit suicide himself. On his deathbed, he is reported to have said, "I cannot afford to die." This does not mean that Soseki was afraid of death. Soseki refused to create a sense of self-closure on his existence and to dramatize his life. He did not leave any testament comparable to Mori Ogai's "Iwami Native Mori Rintaro." He *simply* dropped dead; however, to *simply* die is not to render one's life meaningless.

Soseki was able to write the tragedy *Kokoro* precisely because he was not the type of person to make his own life into a tragedy. The spirit of Meiji is tragic because it is something that cannot be retrieved. Yet, the spirit of Showa is different, for like the Showa Restoration, it constantly traces and re-presents/evokes the spirit of Meiji—meaning, of course, the possibilities of pre-Meiji 20.

The critic Yasuda Yojuro, of the prewar Japanese Romantic School, wrote in 1969: "The fundamental spirit of the Great Asian Revolution was the intention to succeed the Meiji Restoration. Furthermore, it was the succession of the spirit of the great Saigo Takamori. This feeling (*kokoro*) was also alive in the Greater East Asia War."[15] As I mentioned earlier, Yasuda identified, from this perspective, a similar succession in the Red Guards of the Cultural Revolution. Yet, for him, "the intention to succeed" signifies that the object to be succeeded is already nonexistent. As Yasuda himself writes:

> In truth, the period of a void in both literature and thought was appearing in early Showa. . . . Further, early Showa was the post-World War I era. And underlying *Cogito*, to the extent that we thought and understood ourselves to be Husserlian, was something like a will to withstand the postwar degeneration, and a movement toward a Japanese reflection. This experience has served as a kind of lesson in terms of the resolve following the Greater East Asian War. Our generation, therefore, is not simply a prewar school, nor, obvi-

15. Yasuda Yojuro, "Nihon Romanha no jidai" (The age of the Japanese Romantic School), in vol. 36 of *Yasuda Yojuro zenshu* (Tokyo: Kodansha, 1988), 82.

ously, a war-time school. From a world historical viewpoint, we were a post–World War I school.[16]

Yasuda understands this "void" positively, as irony. To put it another way, it is *seriously frivolous*. The spirit of Meiji to which Yasuda succeeds has no content—but to denigrate content, to remain empty, is precisely what defines Romantic irony. Instead of saying "contradiction," Yasuda says "irony." "Contradiction" constructs a problem and then works toward its solution. For Yasuda, it is such solemnity that is contemptible; what constitutes irony is scorn for contradiction and scorn for problems. This irony distinguishes Yasuda not only from the Left, but from the Right as well, and it was this absolute irresponsibility and vacuity that attracted people of the generation of Hashikawa Bunzo and Mishima Yukio.

Yasuda differs from those who attempted to reenact the Meiji Restoration. He was certainly aware, however, that the spirit of Meiji could be re-presented precisely because it was nonexistent. To borrow the words of Marx, the "spirit of Meiji" was tragedy, and the "spirit of Showa" that repeated it was farce.

Of course, the Meiji Restoration itself was a re-presentation; it was an "Imperial Restoration." Just as in the case of the French Revolution, ancient designs were mobilized in the Meiji Restoration. Consequently, as Yasuda says, the spirit of Meiji is linked to the teachings of the medieval poet/emperor Gotoba. There were, however, tasks worthy of realization in the Meiji Restoration, just as there were with Kita Ikki and the Showa Restoration, but none existed—and none could exist—within the Japanese Romantic School.

In *The Bridges of Japan* (1936), Yasuda claims that he merely wishes to "explicate the thought" of Okakura Tenshin.[17] Yasuda begins with an account of world intercourse in antiquity and praises the "sad and lonely bridges of Japan," which contrast with the bridges of the West and China. Of course, he does not, like a "Japanist" (*Nihonshugisha*), proclaim a strong Japan or a military Japan. Again, like Okakura, he rejects the Westernization of culture. Furthermore, he rejects "things warrior-like," as well as the view of Japanese history distorted by samurai. Throughout, he recounts "an indulgence in the gentle arts of peace."

After the Russo-Japanese War, Okakura wrote, in *The Book of Tea*: "The average Westerner . . . was wont to regard Japan as barbarous while

16. Yasuda, "The Age of the Japanese Romantic School," 12, 114.
17. Yasuda Yojuro, "Nihon no hashi" (The bridges of Japan), in vol. 4 of *Yasuda Yojuro zenshu* (Tokyo: Kodansha, 1986), 163.

she indulged in the gentle arts of peace; he calls her civilised since she began to commit wholesale slaughter on Manchurian battlefields. . . . Fain would we remain barbarians, if our claim to civilisation were to be based on the gruesome glory of war. Fain would we await the time when due respect shall be paid to our art and ideals."[18] There is a certain Romantic irony contained here; it is, however, of a different order than the play of German Romantic irony, and it maintains a certain historical practicality.

The reason that Yasuda appears to say the same thing as Okakura, but in reality does not, lies in the fact that Japan actually did "commit wholesale slaughter on Manchurian battlefields." Yasuda identifies a "new worldview" in Manchukuo. It is unthinkable that Yasuda, who had been a Marxist, was unable to make the determination that Manchukuo represented nothing other than Japan's imperial domination, yet he necessarily and consciously negates it. According to Socrates, irony is "the pretence of ignorance," and Yasuda was precisely pretending ignorance. In this sense, Japanese Romantic School irony is based on the negation of reality and a faith in an unreal beauty. In the terms of Kawabata Yasunari's *Snow Country*, which Yasuda lauded, it is the perception of the beauty of a "sad, lonely Japan" (represented by the character Komako) beyond the tunnel. Yasuda's aestheticism, however, which appears at first glance to be apolitical, and even antiwar, was in fact able to realize the distinguishing feature of fascism: the "aestheticization of politics."

For Yasuda, it was not only that the Showa Restoration contained nothing to be realized, but that it constituted a struggle against the very concept of realization, a struggle to discard all thinking since the Meiji Enlightenment. When Mishima Yukio, who had been a young member of the Japanese Romantic School, attempted to reenact the Showa Restoration in Showa 45, it was literally a farce, a fact that Mishima did not attempt to conceal. In the same way, the last character to be reincarnated (repeated) in *The Sea of Fertility* is an imitation; *The Sea of Fertility* ends in a "sea of emptiness."

In this manner, Mishima, by re-evoking the spirit of Showa, put an end to it. Borrowing the words of Marx, this non-tragic farce existed so that we could part cheerfully from Showa. There is probably no spectacle more ridiculous than the Right and conservatives attempting to appropriate Mishima's death. His action was entirely ironic: What he attempted to realize was the destruction of the very thought that aims at realizing something. It is not that the Japanese culture he aimed to defend had nothing in it, but,

18. Kakuzo Okakura, *The Book of Tea* (New York: Dover Publications, 1964), 2–3.

rather, it was this very nothingness in the culture that he aimed to defend.

Near the end of *The Decay of the Angel*, the last volume in the *Sea of Fertility* tetralogy, the woman questions the protagonist Toru: "Kiyoaki Matsugae was caught by unpredictable love, Isao Iinuma by destiny, Ying Chan by the flesh. And you? By a baseless sense of being different, perhaps?"[19] Having been made to realize that he is a counterfeit, lacking in necessity, Toru plans to commit suicide in order to prove that he is genuine, but he fails. One can say that in this work, Mishima used the narrative framework of metempsychosis to capture the history of modern Japan. In this context, what does it mean that the protagonist of the final volume is a counterfeit?

According to Mishima's way of thinking, the emperor should have died in Showa 20, even as his supporters predicted at the time. He would have thereby become a god. But with his renunciation of divinity, the emperor lived on as a symbol of postwar national unity. Mishima scorned this emperor personally. The reincarnated emperor after the war was nothing more than a counterfeit, but it was no different from Mishima's self-contempt at having survived what should have been the "Final War." For Mishima, in order for an object to attain a genuine, absolute beauty (divinity), it must be burned, like Kinkakuji (the Temple of the Golden Pavilion). Mishima's suicide signifies, as well, the killing of the postwar emperor.

The Recurrence of Showa

The reason that 1970 constitutes a watershed year is not because of Mishima's spectacular death. For example, as symbolized by the Red Army Incident, the New Left movement collapsed in the early seventies and, as expressed through the foreign currency market and the oil shocks, the structure of the postwar world order began to crumble. Situated within the U.S.-Soviet binary structure and using it unilaterally as it developed, Japan emerged in the eighties as an economic giant. Yet in terms of consciousness, it remained entirely confined to interiority. Every kind of information from the outside had been transmitted and consumed, but the "outside" did not exist. In terms of discursive space, Japan was confined within quadrant I (see Figure 1).

It was only after 1985 that the Japanese began to feel international

19. Mishima Yukio, *The Decay of the Angel*, trans. Edward Seidensticker (New York: Vintage Books, 1974), 206.

tension, and, at the same time, the problems of "Showa" and the emperor were revived. It was not only because the end of Showa neared but also because Japan found itself once more in the midst of international tension that the Showa Emperor became a historical problem. This arose not from within Japan, but through exterior relations with Asia and the West. At this point, the discourse on the emperor from the late seventies necessarily lost its luster.

It goes without saying that Showa continued even after Mishima ended the spirit of Showa. It continued for eighteen years. In the late seventies, the emperor, like the failed suicide Yasunaga Toru, aged quietly. Faced with the emperor's longevity, supporters and detractors alike were at a loss, because it was a question not of "spirit" but of biological fact. One can say that the very existence of the emperor caused the meaning of Showa to fade.

Yet, in terms of the chronology presented in Table 1, this period, after the end of Meiji, bypassed the Taisho period and, in fact, corresponds to Showa 5 (1930). In other words, because Showa lasted for such a long time, it revolved around once more to "Showa." Moreover, as the end of the U.S.-Soviet dichotomy in 1989 and the revival of Japan and Germany made explicit, the world is clearly beginning to resemble the 1930s, or early Showa. The "new world order" of Nishida Kitaro (i.e., the creation of world-wide political and economic blocks) is rapidly progressing. This situation developed in the eighties, with similar phenomena arising in all different contexts, but with the exception of Japan, all continuity with the past had been broken, and all wartime leaders were dead. Thus, with a gesture of negation toward the past, the same past could, in fact, be revived (e.g., "European unification" was previously realized by the Nazis).

In Japan, however, this was impossible, for the emperor lived on. The personal misfortune of the emperor was not confined to the time of defeat. It also lay in the fact that Japan's revival—commanding, in effect, a "Greater East Asia Co-Prosperity Sphere" and drawing the scrutiny and caution of the countries of the world—was symbolized by the emperor. The same emperor had continued his metempsychosis as symbol. The forgotten Showa is once more brought to consciousness not only because it has ended but also because we are now in the process of confronting something Showa-esque. In terms of the earlier diagram (Figure 1), we are confronting the entire coordinate space, and we must reexamine, once again, the whole of this discursive space of modern Japanese history.

Theory's Imaginal Other:
American Encounters with South Korea and Japan

Rob Wilson

So he [the Korean] did suffer with the blues, in the old days, and repression was unbearable to him! Even for an Asiatic.
—Henri Michaux, *A Barbarian in Asia*

1

Negotiating the postmodern terrain of the 1990s, it may now be the case that "Korea," like "Japan," must be warily inflected in quotation marks. Haunted by the American political imaginary, that is to say, "Korea" gets produced and projected as a cultural sign and occidental distortion from within some redemptive master narrative of global modernization. Or, worse yet, as Edward Said contends in a critique of the most textually self-scrupulous or "postparadigm" anthropology, this conflicted nation-state can be articulated only from within unequal structurations of capital/symbolic capital under the gaze of Empire.[1] In terms of cultural capital and geo-political clout, "Korea" by no means equals "Japan," whatever the share of orientalism blandly obtaining. With the trauma of "Vietnam" re-coded into family melodrama and uplifting sagas of self-redemption, the divided and American-policed terrain of South/North Korea still troubles the con-sumerist bliss of the suburban shopping mall like the return of the Cold War repressed.[2]

Estranging Western logic or selfhood in exotic otherness can posit little cure from such skewed narratives of geopolitical encounter as "dia-logue" or "travel," although such strategies in defamiliarization may disturb a certain discursive inertia. While visiting imperial Japan and colonized Korea in the early 1930s as the self-ironical "barbarian in Asia," the French surrealist poet Henri Michaux, for example, had presciently intuited that "the Japanese [culture] has been modern for ten centuries" not only for the preci-sion and geometry of their uncluttered architecture and art but also for their uncanny ability to imitate, mimic, and assimilate "things Western" into their

---

1. "Panic theory" sites afflicting the language games of normative science are articulated in Arthur Kroker, "The Games of Foucault," *Canadian Journal of Political and Social Theory* 11 (1987): 1–10; no less trenchantly, deconstructive readings of "Japan" perme-ate the special issue of *South Atlantic Quarterly* 87 (1988) entitled "Postmodernism and Japan," edited by Masao Miyoshi and H. D. Harootunian, for example, Stephen Melville's "Picturing Japan: Reflections on the Workshop," 639. Said's post-Orientalism critique is entitled "Representing the Colonized: Anthropology's Interlocutors," *Critical Inquiry* 15 (1989): 205–25. The concept of "misrepresentation" used throughout would implicate American writers in deconstructive dynamics of cross-cultural dialogue occurring in the postmodern era. As Brook Thomas generalizes the case for politicized textuality, "Consti-tuted by both a temporal and spatial gap, representation is structurally dependent on mis-representation. Since by [poststructuralist] definition representation can never be full, all acts of representation produce an 'other' that is marginalized or excluded"; see Thomas's "The New Historicism and Other Old-Fashioned Topics," in *The New Historicism*, ed. Harold Veeser (New York: Routledge, 1989), 184. On the related, yet undertheorized, issue of American misrepresentation ("underrepresentation") of Korean and Japanese immigrants to the United States, see Won Moo Hurh, "The '1.5 Generation': A Paragon of Korean-American Pluralism," *Korean Culture* 11 (Spring 1990): 21–31.
2. On the geopolitical function of American representations of Vietnam in postmodern genres, see John Carlos Rowe, " 'Bringing It All Back Home': American Recyclings of the Vietnam War," in *The Violence of Representation: Literature and the History of Violence*, ed. Nancy Armstrong and Leonard Tennenhouse (New York: Routledge, 1989), 197–218, and "Eye-Witness: Documentary Styles in the American Representations of Vietnam," *Cultural Critique* 3 (1986): 126–50.

own techno-poetics.[3] If such is the case, this allows the Japanese to be considered the first culture that we could nominate, after Lyotard's imperative of capitalist culture discarding forms and collaging narratives, "postmodern" before they were ever even "premodern."[4] As Michaux shrewdly claimed when confronting this Asian will to modernity, "The cinema, the phonograph, and the train are the real missionaries from the West" (*BA*, 70).

Nevertheless, "Korea" resists such an easy assimilation into this deconstructive paradigm of "Japan" as a postmodern condition of "infantile capitalism";[5] that is, national sublation into one hypercommunicative and brand-name glutted "empire of signs" encapsulating the imaginal presence, if not the collective worship, of a half-Zen, half-imperial nothingness that serves so well the dynamics of the commodity form.[6] Lest we forget, "South" and "North" must be affixed as differential prefixes to "Korea," tying any poststructural flights of "satellited reference" down to the dialectics of twentieth-century history that have divided this pre-Perry "Hermit Kingdom" into a tormented landscape of belligerence and self-division: half-Capitalist, half-Communist, bipolarized by the Cold War "language game" whose power struggles and outcomes are weightier than the difference of textual terms.

Resisting specular or simulacrous analysis, "[South] Korea" yet

3. Henri Michaux, *A Barbarian in Asia*, trans. Sylvia Beach (New York: New Directions, 1949 [first published in France by Gallimard in 1933]), 160–61; hereafter cited in my text as *BA*. Japan's nineteenth-century absorption of "things Western" is registered in Yukichi Fukuzawa, *Autobiography*, trans. Eiichi Kiyooka (New York: Schocken, 1972). Fukuzawa presciently notes the geopolitical changes in 1859: "As certain as day, English was to be the most useful language of the future. I realized that a man would have to be able to read and converse in English to be recognized as a scholar in Western subjects for the coming time" (98).

4. See Jean-François Lyotard, "Answering the Question: What Is Postmodernism?" in *The Postmodern Condition: A Report on Knowledge*, trans. Geoff Bennington and Brian Massumi [and Regis Durand] (Minneapolis: University of Minnesota Press, 1984), 71–82, on the "aesthetic of the sublime" becoming the aesthetic of consumption.

5. See Asada Akira, "Infantile Capitalism and Japan's Postmodernism," *South Atlantic Quarterly* 87 (1988): 629–34.

6. See Nishida Kitaro, "The Logic of the Place of Nothingness and the Religious Worldview," in *Last Writings*, trans. David A. Dilworth (Honolulu: University of Hawaii Press, 1987), 47–123; this theory of "overcoming the modern" through cultivating *mu no basho* (the place of nothingness) is related to the growth of postmodern capitalism in Japan in Asada Akira, "Infantile Capitalism"; also see Karatani Kojin, "One Spirit, Two Nineteenth Centuries," *South Atlantic Quarterly* 87 (1988): 615–28, for indigenous and post-Marxist strands theorizing Japan as a pre-Barthesian "place of absence."

seems to emerge and abide as a nation-state that appears more atavistic, pungent, thingy, and street-fighting raw; it is a land that is furiously modern-izing and "democratizing" by daily moving from rice farming through heavy construction to megachips on an American-Japanese ("Ameripan") model that would estrange itself from both First World superpowers (America and Japan) through positing and preserving some *Korean* essence, charac-ter, or national identity immune to symbolic domination. By all accounts, this twentieth-century history is a troubled one, especially since the libera-tion and emergence of separate Korean regimes from 1945 to 1947, and the Korean War ended unresolved in 1953 with the Korean peninsula a smoldering ruin of Cold War ideology. Regressive differentiation of the two countries now threatens to give way to advanced eclecticism, dialectical emergence to sublime submergence: However refigured and historicized from a postmodern perspective, "Korea" remains a beleaguered sign.

Still, the skewed assumption lingers in various genres that (as Marx noted of subaltern classes in *The Eighteenth Brumaire of Louis Bonaparte*) if "they cannot represent themselves, they must be represented"—as flow-ing silks, lofty pagodas, ancient gates, shaman drums, old men in white silks like Confucian holdovers, dog soup and snake dinners, kimchi wagons—as anything but theory-read students of Seoul advocating a rational critique of Third World dependency and a logic of liberation, that so-called dead narrative from the text-glutted, world-weary bastions of the postmodern condition. What can only be called a grandly orientalist rhetoric of Korean misrepresentation/underrepresentation still grinds on in diverse genres, as I will detail, despite much needed disturbances from emerging counter-languages and creolized poetics of "ethnographic surrealism" or "surreal ethnography."[7]

---

7. See James Clifford, "On Ethnographic Surrealism," in *The Predicament of Culture: Twentieth-Century Ethnography, Literature, and Art* (Cambridge: Harvard University Press, 1988), 117–51, on the growth of French ethnology (e.g., Michel Leiris and Georges Bataille) that builds on defamiliarizing tactics of French surrealism, the common goal being "to see culture and its norms—beauty, truth, reality—as artificial arrangements, susceptible to detached analysis and comparison with other possible dispositions." Al-though Michaux is not mentioned, he clearly grows out of this climate of surreal ethnog-raphy: Michaux himself admitted in a new preface to *Un Barbare en Asie* in 1967 that his surreal travelogue had imperiously bypassed the real for the imaginary, challenging his own set of poetic representations by wondering aloud "N'vais-je rien vu, vraiment?"—see Laurie Edson, *Henri Michaux and the Poetics of Movement* (Saratoga, Calif.: Anma Libri, 1985), 52; and on introspective dimensions of such hyper-literary travel into "strong

320 Japan in the World

Holding vulgarly political urgencies at bay, postmodern culture is fast becoming a promiscuously global collage of cultures, codes, rites, styles, voices, and narratives shorn of affect, history, situation, identity, and depth; indeed this "hysterical sublime" of self-dispossession and temporal bewilderment has come to resemble the unconscious behavior of that *No* actor Michaux encountered in Osaka during the 1930s who was playing a drunkard and evoking a self-ironic patchwork of gestures and signs:

> One day I saw an actor who was miming drunkenness. It was quite a while before I realized it. He had made up his part by taking from one drunkard this, from another that, from such a one the break-down of his speech, from another of his gestures, or his fumbling acts, or his lapses of memory; and so with these scraps he had made himself a harlequin's costume for drunkenness that had no connection with any possible drunkard, no center, no truth, and had been constituted as if by a man who did not know what drunkenness was, and would be unable to picture it to his inner self. And yet that seems unbelievable in Japan, which is so full of drunkards. I must say it was amusing. (*BA*, 157)

As a sign of inventive bricolage, this Japanese play-drunkard can be decoded as a Barthesian onion-of-styles without a center or truth-claim; as culture, furthermore, this drunkard mimics a heterogeneous compound of creolized elements that postmodern ethnographers would see resisting *any* narrative of Western homogenization into McDonald's family of man.[8] Yet this intertextual play of semiotic bliss took place, of course, within a network of Japanese domination and the production of a pan-Asiatic empire

---

exoticism," see Malcolm Bowie, *Henri Michaux: A Study of His Literary Works* (Oxford: Clarendon Press, 1973), 61–65, who argues that "there is a sense in which he [Michaux] inhabits the world the Surrealists merely longed for" (24).

8. As Clifford argues in "The Pure Products Go Crazy" (claiming of William Carlos Williams that, as "participant observer" of modernism's fascination with the indigenous, anti-Puritan, and native, "In this expanded sense a poet like Williams is an ethnographer"), "modern ethnographic histories are perhaps condemned to oscillate between two metanarratives: one of homogenization, the other of emergence; one of loss, the other of invention," *The Predicament of Culture*, 17. Clifford, as American utopian of "new worlds" and "new forms" done over in a postmodern or heteroglossic mode, is pro-surreal, pro-creole, propagating "several hybrid and subversive forms of cultural representation, forms that prefigure an inventive future." On related issues of geopolitical displacement, liberal disillusionment, and cross-cultural semiotics, see James Clifford and Vivek Dhareshwar, eds., "Travelling Theories/Travelling Theorists," special issue of *Inscriptions* 5 (1989).

that was giving these Koreans, as Michaux noted (see epigraph above), a profound case of the twentieth-century political blues ("le 'caffard' ").

Taking a rhetorical turn that aims to estrange the normative into the allegorical and to deform objective description into poly-vocal collage, American ethnography in the 1980s had begun to shift its inherited narratives away from scientistic closure and ideal totalization of other cultures as "the beautiful" toward representing the "unnameable" of other cultures through a " 'writing at the limit' [or "poetic sublime"], where we seek to push against limits imposed by conventions of syntax, meaning and genre"— to quote Stephen A. Tyler's anti-empiricist manifesto from *Writing Culture* agitating for states of postrealist "evocation"—that deracinated term of de-historicized purity so dear to symbolist poets such as Mallarmé and Poe.[9] Or, as Michaux remarked of his own antirealist literary travelogue, *Un Barbare en Asie*, in a new preface in 1967 undermining truth-claims to ethnographic representation, he had created a "Voyage réel entre deux imaginaires."[10] Two cultural and political imaginaries ("East"/"West") are thereby radically collaged by Michaux into the transactional space (real) of the poem-as-journey.

Ethnography's "end of description" and seemingly schizoid flight from functionalist totalizations and the illusions of de-politicized empiricism reflect a wide-spread tremor of the postmodern condition in which master narratives of Western enlightenment and emancipation break down, free themselves from claims to history and mastery, turn fictive, and thereby undermine their own claims to truth-status. Yet this avant-gardist death (or hyper-production) of narrative may be symptomatic less of generic (or paradigm) exhaustion and more of a larger social crisis of mimetic contagion: the imposition of commodity logic and sublime irreality on a blandly global scale that makes critique or resistance doomed to capitulation, or at best to

9. See Stephen A. Tyler, "Post-Modern Ethnography: From Document of the Occult to Occult Document," in *Writing Culture: The Poetics and Politics of Ethnography*, ed. James Clifford and George E. Marcus (Berkeley: University of California Press, 1986), 136–40; and "Ethnography, Intertextuality, and the End of Description," in *The Unspeakable: Discourse, Dialogue, and Rhetoric in the Postmodern World* (Madison: University of Wisconsin Press, 1987), chap. 3.

10. Henri Michaux, *Un Barbare en Asie* (Paris: Gallimard, 1967), 14. For related poetic and ethnographic experiments in textual deformation, see Trinh T. Minh-ha, "The Language of Nativism: Anthropology as a Scientific Conversation," in *Woman, Native, Other: Writing Postcoloniality and Feminism* (Bloomington: Indiana University Press, 1989), 119–26.

recapitulation of Late Capital's processes, whether as theory (for example, the cachet afforded "cognitive mapping") or as contestational art (witness the hermeneutic industry of poetic pluralism now emerging in the 1990s to integrate "Language Poetry" into the postmodern).[11]

2

If American ethnography, radically textualized and re-coded, has been re-functioned into a self-conscious genre of cultural description in which the Western articulation of cross-cultural otherness at the boundaries of scientistic language or vested interest turns back into a defamiliarization and critique of one's own cultural positioning, this news of "traveling theory" as poeticized/politicized representation has yet to reach other contemporary genres:[12] The examples I will invoke regarding the discursive and geopolitically situated production of (mis)representations of South Korea are (A) Fulbright-sponsored anthropological research into the makeup of

11. Immune to deformation, this remains the post-Marxist reading of Fredric Jameson as argued in "Postmodernism, or the Cultural Logic of Late Capitalism," *New Left Review* 145 (1984): 53–91, and "Third-World Literature in the Era of Multinational Capitalism," *Social Text* 15 (1986): 65–88, wherein Jameson writes of nationalistically self-defensive cultures such as China (and South Korea): "One important distinction would seem to impose itself at the outset, namely that none of these cultures can be conceived as anthropologically independent or autonomous, rather, they are all in various distinct ways locked in a life-and-death struggle with first-world cultural imperialism—a cultural struggle that is itself a reflexion of the economic situation of such areas in their penetration by various stages of capital, or as it is sometimes euphemistically termed, modernization." Contrasting the neo-Nietzschean assault on totalizing theories of history and language systems (Lyotard and Baudrillard) with the post-Marxism of Jameson and Terry Eagleton, Christopher Sharrett sees a Western crisis in "narrative closure" resulting: "For Jameson, the most important tendency of postmodernism is the ultimate reification of alienation as accepted state of being since the subject is cut off from any historical sense—lacking an understanding of causality, and asked to accept that utopian or radical options are naive or outdated." See Sharrett's "Postmodern Narrative Cinema: Aeneas on a Stroll," *Canadian Journal of Political and Social Theory* 12 (1988): 78–104.

12. For a dialectical approach to this "crisis of representation" afflicting Anglo-American anthropology, if not social science in general, see George E. Marcus and Michael M. J. Fischer, *Anthropology as Cultural Critique: An Experimental Moment in the Human Sciences* (Chicago: University of Chicago Press, 1986). For a discourse textualizing, narrating, and empowering cross-cultural interactions as "intertextual" and geopolitically situated, see James Der Derian and Michael J. Shapiro, eds., *International/Intertextual Relations: Postmodern Readings of World Politics* (Lexington, Mass.: D. C. Heath, 1989).

Korean universities where countergovernment dissent is centered; (B) P. J.
O'Rourke's gonzo journalism for *Rolling Stone* on street demonstrations
before the 1988 Olympics staged in Seoul; and (C) NBC's coverage of the
Olympics. Throughout, and finally, I will invoke Michaux's poetic travelogue
as a counterexample of wild theory to emulate, wherein the whole model
of bipolar opposition into superior/inferior, us/them, and civilized/barbaric
has been so radically disturbed that the poet/ethnographer self can only
flee from the cross-representational glut of history, translation, and culture
into some meditative state of image evacuation, a "space within." This, of
course, remains the most invidiously literary ("poetic") strategy of all, trying to claim some kind of ideological immunity from within the transpolitical
space of the poem.

Supported by a modest research grant from the Korean-American
Educational Commission in 1984, Fredric Marc Roberts and Chun Kyung-
soo, an American and a Korean anthropologist, coauthored what they call
"a primarily descriptive" analysis of Seoul National University (the premier
university in South Korea) as a subculture of "fictive kinship" and an enclave of antigovernment ferment; their essay is entitled, tellingly enough,
"The Natives are Restless: Anthropological Research on a Korean University."[13] Reporting on the "intensely inbred" and "personalistic" makeup of
the SNU anthropology department, in lieu of harder "quantitative data" and
"systematic interviewing" still under way, Roberts and Chun would cast scientific light on these Korean "students' privileged roles as critics of liberal
society and opponents of the government" (NR, 74). This analysis is done
largely from the American's politically transcendental stance of "being in a
whirlwind without being part of it" (NR, 68). Beyond such radically innocent
claims of de-historicized neutrality, however, their goal was more avowedly

13. Fredric Marc Roberts and Chun Kyung-soo, "The Natives are Restless: Anthropological Research on a Korean University," *Korea Fulbright Forum* 1 (1984): 67–92; hereafter
cited in my text as NR. The ethnography of Korean culture practiced, for example, by
Kim Harvey and Laurel Kendall is more other-voiced and de-centered in a project wherein
Western science is initiated by female shamans and (partly) surrenders the narrative authority of Western objectivity to the first-person singular of "Yongsu's mother": see the
fiction-like experiment, for example, of Laurel Kendall, *The Life and Hard Times of a
Korean Shaman: Of Tales and the Telling of Tales* (Honolulu: University of Hawaii Press,
1988). My own contribution toward rendering a more heteroglossic, "poetic ethnography"
of Korea is *Waking In Seoul* (Honolulu: University of Hawaii Press, 1988); and "Poetic
Encounters with the Blues Singers of Asia" [with photographs by Drayton Hamilton],
EastWest 7 (1987): 32–40. See also footnote 24.

pragmatic: to help foreign scholars, especially Americans, "orient them-selves" [*sic*] within such a teaching situation filled with "restless natives" who seem to have carried 1960s protests into a permanent revolution in the 1980s. What could these unruly Korean students have against such goodwilled and scrupulously conducted ethnographic "research"?

In many respects, I must admit that Roberts and Chun helpfully illu-minate a "Two Culture" and "Two Curricula" system in which SNU students read forbidden or forgotten books of radical theory ("including neo-Marxist and dependency theory analysis") and their Korean professors try to ignore or refute them. As I know from my own two-year Fulbright experience in President Chun Doo-won's Seoul, SNU remains a tormented place in which to teach or to carry on the goals of normative knowledge. Try teaching Emer-sonian transcendence in a room filled with tear gas. Yet these anthropolo-gists of university culture use a grandly dispassionate tone and detached attitude that are well in keeping with the antitheory tactics and narrative ironies claiming to neutralize and objectify this ethnographic "description" from the generous, wizened perspective of the apolitical West. Distancing the Korean students' claim at SNU to share "'true' ideologies and theories" (NR, 89), Roberts and Chun can only point out the indigenous simplifica-tions and contradictions afflicting such a blatantly unempirical and politi-cized project: "the present generation of S.N.U. students includes those who see years in the United States or Western Europe as a period of brain-washing into Western forms of thought, a kind of intellectual imperialism. Among many students, there is a strong feeling that Korean social science must undergo a process of indigenization, so it can develop its own unique approaches to the problems of Korea" (NR, 89–90).

As Roberts and Chun remark, however, with an occidental canni-ness immune to such naïve theories of social truth and threats of indige-nous anthropology "currently" politicizing history and still in vogue in the discourse-backward Third World, "Ironically, the very critical approaches to Korean society that these students currently take on are often themselves products of the West (e.g., neo-Marxism, dependency theory, etc.)" (NR, 90). Needless to say, these Korean students' time would be better spent doing quantitative research or studying, as disciplinary antidote to such *worldly* passion, "the extensive critical literature" around these theories (NR, 82) rather than applying "dependency theory" to understand Korean-American relations. Blatantly and by more subtle allegiances of narrative value and bipolar ascription of protagonist/antagonist roles, such social science "de-scription" helps to articulate and disseminate what Gayatri Spivak has called—less piously—American "crisis management" in the Third World.[14] If belligerent South Korean natives grow restless from heady Western theory and the lure of totalization at SNU, the discipline officiates, like a good-willed Henry James narrator, intervening from within, yet somehow above, the representational fray. Such American innocence barely puts the self or disciplinary science at risk or play: In effect, the narrative viewpoint of Roberts and Chun would lift selfhood out of the sociological torments and unresolved conflicts of Cold War history into the discourse of hard science.

By vulgar contrast, in February of 1988, *Rolling Stone* (once seemingly an outlet in the late 1960s for vernacular critiques and counterculture rock but now gleefully a tool of mass marketing and supply) published P. J. O'Rourke's "Seoul Brothers," recording a participant/observer narrative on the Korean presidential election under the politically cynical heading "IRRATIONAL AFFAIRS." That the postmodern politics and low-blow humor of this gonzo journalism are by now thoroughly reactionary should come as no surprise to O'Rourke's jaded, doped, and commodified audience; that the language could be so blatantly orientalist and racist seemed, in its ill-spirited assumptions, somehow a tactic reeking of the crudest semiotics of Empire.

As O'Rourke's hyper-cool, yet thrill-seeking, piece infamously opens, "When the kid in the front row at the rally bit off the tip of his little finger and wrote, KIM DAE JUNG, in blood on his fancy white ski jacket—I think that was the first time I ever really felt like a foreign correspondent. I mean, here was something really fucking *foreign*."[15] O'Rourke's arrogantly American

14. See Sarah Harasym, "Practical Politics of the Open End: An Interview with Gayatri Spivak," *Canadian Journal of Political and Social Theory* 12 (1988): 51–69: "What they [Third World students studying in America] read is ideological stuff in journals and newspapers written by people who are not aware of this fully. On the other hand, the fact that all of these foreign students are at universities is eminently visible, and the fact that they will go back and themselves perhaps work to keep this crisis management intact is an added bonus" (54).
15. P. J. O'Rourke, "Seoul Brothers," *Rolling Stone*, 11 Feb. 1988, 93–117; hereafter cited in my text as *RS*. For a willfully imperialist view of other cultures from the Republican tourist point of view, see P. J. O'Rourke, *Holidays in Hell* (New York: Atlantic Monthly Press, 1988), and Ihab Hassan, *Selves At Risk: Patterns of Quest in Contemporary American Letters* (Madison: University of Wisconsin Press, 1990). Wallowing in resentment at postmodern reconfigurations of the globe, the latter offers an amusing theory of why such writers ("travelers") like O'Rourke (and himself) are hated abroad as "neocolonial" opportunists (see 70–77).
Hunter S. Thompson, using that steady stream of verbal shock tactics and street-smart

political cynicism and sense of cultural repugnance toward the nonwhite, nonindividuated natives soon register a thoroughgoing reduction of these demonstrating Koreans from foreign, to subhuman, to robotic undifferentiation: "And as I was looking at this multitude [at a political rally], and I was thinking, 'Oh, no, they really all do look alike'—the same Blackgama hair, the same high-boned pie-plate face, the same tea-stain complexion, the same sharp-focused look in one-million anthracite eyes." Amid such a stone-like, Stone Age people—"anthracite eyes"?—though O'Rourke is squeezed and heaved when riot police emerge to break up what (understandably) soon became an anti-Chun, anti-imperialist demonstration, he claims he was, "most of all, overwhelmed by the amazing stink of kimchi, the garlic and hot-pepper sauerkraut that's breakfast lunch and dinner in Korea" (RS, 93). For O'Rourke's sardonic narrator, the will to politics is reduced to spectacle, behavior to style, and style to a catalog of racial, cultural, and dietary inferiorities: A whole people and historical process are summed up in a stream of reductive epithets reeking not only of ignorance but of white, neocolonial venom smugly insulated from such emancipatory struggles. Far from being exceptional, however, isn't O'Rourke tapping into some deeply nationalist vein of cultural venom and a neo-Roman style of geopolitical crisis management?

Korean demonstrators are derided as "jeerleaders," protesting mothers are part of a "mommy riot," riot police inflict parental "tough love" on "rock-hard Korean bodies"—*stone* is used to figure the dominant, dehumanizing metaphor—yet our First World journalist craves more action, more bloodshed, and cultural spectacles for the folks back in L.A. and is disappointed: "The voting was just what every journalist dreads, quiet and well organized. There were no Salvadoran shoot-'em-ups, no Haitian baton-

------

hyperbole for which his brand of *Rolling Stone* "gonzo journalism" is noted, describes Korean-Americans in Hawaii with hatefully orientalist attributes and totalizing sentiments that have little basis in reality: "The Korean community in Honolulu is not ready, yet, for the melting pot. They are feared by the *haoles* [whites], despised by the Japs and Chinese, scorned by Hawaiians and occasionally hunted for sport by gangs of drunken Samoans, who consider them vermin, like wharf rats and stray dogs" (see *The Curse of Lono* [with Ralph Steadman] [New York: Bantam, 1983], 36). Having lived in Honolulu for over ten years, I can attest that such a description is way off, both in overall sentiment and in the very language and metaphors used—"Japs"?, "gangs" of Samoans?, "wharf rats and stray dogs" in Honolulu? For American ethnography's use of new journalist devices of composite construction and quasi-fictive narration, see *Anthropology as Cultural Critique*, 75–76.

twirler machete attacks, no puddles of Chicago sleaze running out from under the voting booths" (*RS*, 98). Just "a Punch-and-Judy show" (*RS*, 101) with demonstrating students, beaten into unconsciousness, lying with "a bad, bloodless look" on their faces. (That *Rolling Stone* apologized to the Korean-American Coalition and to L.A. city councilman Michael Woo for this ill-conceived "satire" does not excuse this pseudoliberal journal for deploying the blatant orientalism of their own headlines, demeaning photographs, and cynical subtitles.)

Nowadays, these restless *natives* of radical otherness, so to speak, are contesting their facile and de-historicized "translation" into such reductive English and mediated Americanese, into *Rolling Stone* and NBC icons of the primitive, foreign, or weird. Now, in such uneven translations into Eurocentric language games, the weaker historical subject can contend against the stronger representational power by recognizing what is at stake in such symbolic dominations, using "counterpunches," such as the Korean news media's parading of U.S. athletes stealing and rudely cavorting to counter NBC's image of the boxing fiasco as a way of summarizing the latent anarchy and fraternal belligerence of Korean culture.[16]

As Lee Kyung-won soon asked about NBC's Olympic coverage, which unwittingly had brought anti-American sentiment to a new peak throughout South Korea, "But is it too much of asking to add one bilingual and bicultural reporter to its reportorial team?" (*Korea Herald*, November 30, 1988). Or, as William Oscar Johnson summarized in *Sports Illustrated* (October 10, 1988), "NBC, which many Koreans seemed to consider interchangeable with U.S.A., had become the villain of the Games. The network was described by a variety of citizens—from high school students to

16. On this problematic of language imbalances ("translation" into the hegemonic structures of "World English") reflecting, deforming, and allegorizing larger geopolitical struggles and relationships, see Talal Asad, "The Concept of Cultural Translation in British Social Anthropology," *Writing Culture*, 141–64. I have discussed this beleaguered "power struggle" between Korean and American journalists with a Korean media expert, Yon-yi Sohn, back studying journalism ("and cultural imperialism") in the States. In the wake of the Olympic coverage and other uneasy symbolic shifts, for example, even the progovernment *Korean Herald* can now report (in an editorial of 4 December 1988): "Until a few years ago, South Korea was, perhaps, one of the few countries on earth where no shouts of 'Yankee-go-home' were heard. Today, anti-American rhetoric has become virtually a normal slogan for vociferous activists." For a historicized analysis of this phenomenon, in the context of an emerging South Korean shift toward a mimicry of postindustrial Japan, see Jinwung Kim, "Recent Anti-Americanism in South Korea," *Asian Survey*, 39 (1989): 749–63.

a peddler of dried squid—as a mean-minded, arrogant behemoth that had insulted them with its portrayal of South Koreans and their games." Clearly, the natives of postmodern culture are growing increasingly restless under the stereotypical, facile, dehumanizing gaze of the "mega-media," which, instead of talking to Korean journalists or Korean students about their political situation and culture, glibly summarizes it with a visit to a shopping market or a snake-soup shop, where the American reporters can jest at the broken English and quaint customs of the scurrying, half-comprehending natives. Such representations are monological, uninformed, and unconsciously imperialist in their assumption that American standards and customs should pervade far crannies of the globe: "American Express: Don't Leave Home without It" might serve as the slogan of this bland assumption that imperial sameness should and will pervade this liberally Americanizing zone of postmodern interpellation into hard labor and shopping-mall bliss.

Granted, by poststructural definition of any context-situated sign, no one culture can ever fully articulate the differential system and interiority of another culture; still, in an era of postmodern textuality, there can and should be more sensitivity to what Bakhtin called dialogical "outsidedness," more openness to cross-cultural differences, nuances, tones, ceremonies, literacies, rites, signs, and customs that constitute the ethnographic-poetic real. The West, too, must see itself from the point of view of the East, as de-centering and insufferable as such judgments may feel. Cultural "outsidedness" is more than just an appeal to dialogue and language games of poetic justice; it entails a formal transformation from within First World discourse, genuinely being effected and translated ("re-coded") by the alien languages, values, and viewpoints emerging from outside any mimetically closed or would-be dominant system.

3

For Henri Michaux, as surreal "barbarian" from the culture capital of the world, Paris, travel (using the travelogue as poetic-ethnographic genre) enacted a form of self-divesture, a way of abandoning habits and smug values, with the culturally coded "I" fleeing from its past into a perpetually new present that is always outside itself, always other (beholding, praying to, invoking the other). Asian peoples were for him "the last resistants" to Western monotony; everywhere in *A Barbarian in Asia*, Michaux exulted in excess, difference, and made poetic propaganda "for an endless variety of civilizations" (*BA*, v) by which to counter the idea of only one (monologue).

His "orientalism" is vulgarly explicit, ironic, and exaggerated enough to be-come what I would call, tonally, a "mock orientalism," such as when he claims that political domination is hard "even for an Asiatic."

Each culture, for Michaux, comprises a syncretic personality com-posed "of a thousand different elements"; each culture in Asia comprises a sensuous style (*BA*, vi) and confronts the barbaric outsider as a landscape not of humanistic sameness but of utter estrangement halting predictable codes. Going beyond Marxist analysis and Christian pieties, Michaux con-tends that a miner's strike should be supplemented, and is, by "a miner's civilization." He journeys into cultural coexistence: "To avoid war—construct peace." That is, to avoid the monologue of pan-Western or pan-Asiatic imperialism, both political and cultural, one should construct estranging dialogues and multiple styles, instigate interrogations of oriental and occi-dental, so-called civilized and so-called barbaric. Rather than a conversion experience into the commodity form or technocratic empowerment, there should be a risk-taking conversion through otherness, outsidedness, the living of cultural and national difference: If "Western philosophies make one's hair fall out and shorten one's life," Asian philosophies have aimed at magic and longevity, creating mantras of life-giving power that the West needs to hear before it is too late (*BA*, 9).

Fed up with hegemonic closures of the West, finally, Michaux per-forms a kind of magical, Buddhist-like deconstruction upon his whole jour-ney from barbaric irony into civilized otherness and deracinated worship: Culture is seen as impure and agglutinative, a "horrid mixture" of prejudice and religion wherever he looks. Hence, his narrator oddly mimes not Jesus or Emerson but Buddha, as Michaux retires from cultural landscapes into the sublimity of the transhistorical self, boasting of an interior vastness or geography within—is not this "the supernatural" he asks, this pre- or post-cultural emptiness (*BA*, 185)? Ironically, he adds a postscript from Buddha, evacuating the hold of history as so much textual illusion: "What is civiliza-tion? A blind alley. No, Confucius is not great. No, Tsi Hoang Ti is not great, nor Guatama Buddha, but since then nothing better has been done" (*BA*, 185). Ironically, voiding the ethnographic journey into cultural outsidedness, Michaux closes by giving his voice over to the sovereign imagination of Buddha, miming the self-absorbed language of the pre- (or post-?) modern East: " 'Pay no attention to another's way of thinking. Hold fast in your own island. GLUED TO CONTEMPLATION' " (*BA*, 186). Textual encounter with the blues singers of Asia gives way to encounter with the ground of sing-ing and imagining, dissolving Western ego into Eastern self, narration into celebration, if not magic. "Kill the Buddha of semiotic glut" is his implicit cry, voiding party politics into wild poetics and science into silence.

Granted, my own analysis of these various genres of cross-cultural representation (poetic travelogue, anthropological description, gonzo journalism, and TV reportage) between America and South Korea has been, at times, suffused with a modernist nostalgia for the narrative of emancipation and resonant with postmodernist hope for a discursive space of utopian transformation. Surely "Korea" or any emerging nation-state remains more than a "social text" for American self-examination or critique, more than an embattled exemplum of modernization/postmodernization. Yet, my assumption remains that such a radically innocent American stance of posthistory and postpolitics must not lose touch with those ongoing critiques and projects voiced from outside (as well as from within) this jaded language of dead narrative and semiotic glut.[17] A thousand points of post-socialist light need not refract into the steady-state blindness of ideological conversion or immunity from disciplinary critique.

17. On contestations of "America" from within the cultural hegemony of liberalism, see Ramón Saldívar, *Chicano Narrative: The Dialectics of Difference* (Madison: University of Wisconsin Press, 1990). For a discussion of American/Japanese postmodern culture as "posthistorical," in dialectical terms proposed by Alexandre Kojeve, see Alan Wolfe, "Suicide and the Japanese Postmodern: A Postnarrative Paradigm?" *South Atlantic Quarterly* 87 (1988): 571–89. On Asian and American re-codings of post–Cold War history, also see the trenchant analysis of this "post" offered by Arif Dirlik, "Postsocialism?: Reflections on 'Socialism with Chinese Characteristics,' " *Bulletin of Concerned Asian Scholars* 21 (1989): 33–44. That is, Korean/American cross-representations must be situated, as they emerge, within a geopolitical dialogue of Late Capitalism/Postsocialism as much as within the banalities of First World/Third World encounters.

A related problematic of "(mis)representing Korea" must emerge in any more broadly theorized analysis I might attempt: in the de-essentializing wake of poststructuralist and "postsocialist" configurations of global politics throughout post–Mao Asia and post–Berlin Wall Europe, for example, how can we theorize and represent "North Korea" as such? Hasn't my own analysis, in insidiously representative *American* fashion, misrepresented "North Korea" and its socialist project by, in effect, silencing the counter claims of Kim Il-Sung to represent the "self-reliant Korea" of, by, and for the people of the land? Ironically enough, even the Soviet Union, these end-of-ideology days, seems to be ignoring, bypassing, and mocking the hermetic claims of the "Great Leader" to represent "Korea" to the liberal totality of the postmodern world. "Korea" is over as unitary sign.

4

Theory's radical desire for otherness within the force fields of global modernization/postmodernization now functions, by and large, to imagine some egress from everyday structures of high-capitalist hegemony, knowing full well that this will-to-theory is itself constituted within Western disciplines of knowledge and the dynamics of self-interpellation and liberal control. Immune to threats of historical closure or terrors of nihilistic futility, nonetheless, symbolic enclaves of cultural collage and radical difference will continue to emerge and proliferate in the 1990s to stake out the signs and practices of imperial resistance.

So situated, however, the whole project of cross-cultural theorizing may begin to seem, in certain Western articulations, specular—textually tired, if not defunct. However vanguard the claims for such revisionary power in totalization, still, the question of cross-cultural theory at this moment of "traveling theory" often comes down to registering a very real predicament of self/other speculation, if not to confronting a state of sublime blockage in which theory seems morally inappropriate or historically undone. I would phrase this question of theorizing the comparative interactions and geopolitically situated speculations such as those obtaining between postmodern USA and Japan or USA and South Korea in the following terms: To what extent is it possible—or even desirable—to represent a non-Western culture from within the syntax, terms, and narratives, or the policies and protocols of Western culture?

However self-reflexive cultural theory becomes about its own situatedness, its own management within geopolitical structures and institutions of symbolic domination, can such power-affiliated theory produce anything but another imaginal/utopic construct of this non-Western culture? Can we merely aspire to the condition of Henri Michaux, hence exit the situation of cultural glut into mescaline, hermeneutic excess and the poetics of interior silence? If such discourse seems locked within its own cherished idealizations, the narrative of textual redemption drones on. Furthermore, however compellingly represented, how "non-Western" or autonomous is this other country or remote cultural formation? Consider a distinctive cultural apparatus such as modern Japanese film, for example, which emerges after (if not before) World War II within some kind of implicit (coded) or explicit (censored) dialogue with icons of American liberal subjectivity.

Is "sublime Japan" or "beautiful Korea" just a Western projection of exotic immensity, heterogeneous riches, unrecuperable difference; in short, is an unimaginable post-Kantian otherness better left untheorized, unsayable, and unsaid? Fearful of cross-cultural misrepresentation, is the postmodern future threatened with various versions of linguistic solipsism or the semiotic warfare of re-essentialized nationalism?[18]

Can such comparative speculations, positing semiotic enigmas of affinity, likeness, and *sameness* (as in Roland Barthes's semiotically imperial *L'Empire des signes*), or, on the other hand, imagining enclaves of dialogue, difference, remoteness, and staunch *unlikeness* (as in Noel Burch's fascinated re-coding of Japanese film techniques in *To the Distant Observer*) break with Western tactics enforcing symbolic domination?[19] Can the most self-reflexively radical cross-cultural poetics (as in Henri Michaux's *A Barbarian in Asia* or American avant-garde ethnography) exonerate the maker from strategies of imperial appropriation and disciplinary design? Are we just fated to produce/reproduce glitzy optical illusions of sameness/difference as a way to install/deconstruct Western models of specular subjectivity, or liberal selfhood, in effect enforcing further entrenchments of theory's mastery and control?

Understanding entails representing the cultural other; and "representing otherness" necessarily involves both a theorizing and a historicizing of this other: that is, representation entails an attempt to posit a total field of otherness and difference and yet to articulate the times and spaces in which this cultural difference can emerge. Yet the very notion of "representation," for all practical purposes within paradigms of poststructural textuality, might as well be re-coded into the blatantly guiltier and specular term "misrepresentation," thereby suggesting a shared predicament of narrative construction that, however principled, experimental, or goodwilled, seems fated to the mutual construction of fictive otherness. For "represen-

18. The predicament whether any First World intellectual can "represent" (speak for) the subaltern subject, neither of whom can, without self-division and ideological misrecognition, convey his/her own class interests within the "international division of labor" and discourse is explored with maximal lucidity in Gayatri Spivak, "Can the Subaltern Speak?" in *Marxism and the Interpretation of Culture*, ed. Cary Nelson and Lawrence Grossberg (Urbana: University of Illinois Press, 1988), 271–317. The question becomes: What follows from such a hyper-textualized politics of "representation"?
19. For opposing theorizations of a non-Western culture by Western semioticians, see Roland Barthes, *L'Empire des signes* (Geneva: Editions Skira, 1970), and Noel Burch, *To the Distant Observer: Form and Meaning in the Japanese Cinema* (Berkeley: University of California Press, 1979).

tation" further carries within its claims the charges and burdens not only of deconstructive textuality but of political situatedness, that is, the sense of representing powers, purposes, and designs beyond intentional choice or communal willing. (To cite an American usage of this double sense of "representation" as textualized affiliation, Emerson's characters are "representative men," and what each represents is some aspect not only of the over-soul and of transcendental egotism, as is proclaimed, but of emerging national power and expansionist willing.)

So theorized, such "(mis)representations" of cross-cultural otherness can emerge to voice constructs of geopolitical poetics with often dimly perceived or misrecognized projects and agendas accruing cultural capital for discipline and self. Beyond the quest for agonistic individuation and marketplace sublimity, these anxious textualizations function, in effect, as symbolic strategies and discursive practices, furthermore, to create non-Western alternative models of subjectivity and new regimes of rationality as well as to disseminate counter-hegemonic modes of cultural production.

A certain *mise en abyme* recursiveness sets in, and the project of cross-cultural imagining seems doomed to world-weary repetition and post-structural angst involving a set of time-honored tropes and paradoxical terms: Theory projects a world elsewhere that serves, often unconsciously, a set of Western projects and agendas, functions and dispositions produced and situated nowhere but at home. Lacking some pragmatic sense of theory as emancipatory instrument or dialogical tool, there seems no egress from these recursive structures of domination and empowerment, these double discourses encoding liberty and coercion, these "misrepresentations" in which the traveling theorist produces himself/herself and the other/same as real.

A position of dialectical deconstruction toward such cross-cultural imaginings, however, assumes that whatever construct of otherness has been historically and provisionally articulated from within a position of power/knowledge can and should be thoroughly deconstructed, interrogated, beleaguered, and layed bare as an optical illusion and regime of Western truth. The agendas and projects of such truth-claims need to be historicized to show exactly how they emerge, propagate, circulate, function, and recur to enact a strategy of disciplinary subjection. Once this Western or First World construct of cultural otherness has been subjected to tactics of deconstruction, however, the next move is a countermove: a re-positing and re-presenting eventuating in another construct/paradigm of otherness or outsidedness, a historical construct of power/knowledge that can, should, and will itself be deconstructed in time. So situated, theory becomes a pragmatic instrument participating in and provoking the reified imaginals of historical change. Or, in the words of William James articulating theory's cash-value dynamism and consequentiality, *"Theories thus become instruments, not answers to enigmas, in which we can rest."* [20]

The larger question of textual misrepresentation, as I have outlined in several genres, still distorts, warps, and pressures the cross-cultural interactions and political dynamics obtaining between America and South Korea. These allied misrepresentations have taken place at least since the Korean War ended unresolved in 1953. As a function of Cold War oppositionality, this language of bipolarity had to be invented, propagated, and maintained in a once-unified country and culture.

Whatever the rhetoric of liberty and populist pluralism that was used to disseminate and liberally cloak its historical origin, the invention of "South Korea" by the United States in 1945 had much to do with a right-wing stabilizing of land in the power elite (who had for the most part survived under Japanese colonization) and everything to do with repressing the emergence of "people's collectives" seeking land reforms from Seoul, like those in the Communist North. In other words, with the 38th parallel and the DMZ, "Korea" was reinvented as a Cold War bastion of unresolved and belligerent polarities between two powerful worldviews and alternative hegemonies, with America holding the economic cards and calling the democratic shots in the South, despite long-standing claims from the grass-roots level for a redistribution of land, power, wealth, and choice. These historical origins called for, and have resulted in, much American forgetting.

Whereas the Vietnam War can be said to have undergone an obsessive practice of symbolic mourning during the 1970s and 1980s, with such works as *Born on the Fourth of July* (film) and *Dog Soldier* (novel) serving as just two illustrations of this melodramatic reworking of traumatic materials emerging from the political unconscious, it remains the case that, as Bruce Cumings concedes in *The Origins of the Korean War*, "in the United

20. William James, "What Pragmatism Means," in *The Writings of William James: A Comprehensive Edition*, ed. John J. McDermott (Chicago: University of Chicago Press, 1977), 380. On redemptive uses of "prophetic pragmatism" as a libertarian tradition, see Cornel West, *The American Evasion of Philosophy: A Genealogy of Pragmatism* (Madison: University of Wisconsin Press, 1989); the disciplinary hold of pragmatic idealism on any such redemptive moves is measured, less sanguinely, in Rob Wilson, "Literary Vocation as Occupational Idealism: The Example of Emerson's 'American Scholar,'" *Cultural Critique* 15 (1990): 83–114.

States in spite of three decades of intense involvement with Korean affairs, the country remains for the most part an unknown nation."[21] If Asia is a territory of vast misrepresentation subject to recurring tropes of Western orientalism, Korea remains more simply an enclave of sublime forgetting.

Can any seriously engaged writer or scholar, whether historian or poet, anthropologist or tourist, political strategist or journalist, nowadays claim a stance of neutrality or objectivity, or assume some cloak of textual immunity from distortion when treating ("representing") these Cold War materials of South Korea from the perspective of the political and economic victor? In other words, confronting the return of the Cold War repressed to a level of symbolic reengagement, by working "North/South Korea" up into language, can any writer do anything but misrepresent, misrecognize, mystify, liberalize, and thereby further entrench the American presence and purpose in inventing and differentiating the Republic of South Korea from its communist rival to the North?

Despite this once-hermit country's tormented engagement as a geographical bargaining chip in the Cold War struggle between America and the Soviet Union for postwar hegemony, and even notwithstanding the spectacles of modernity of the 1988 Olympics held in Seoul, North/South "Korea" still comprises for postmodern Americans a forbidding and forgotten landscape of belligerency wherein, as Cumings and John Halliday now document, an "unknown war" once took place. (Indeed, the way American discourse uses "Korea" to refer to South Korea alone effectively elides the ongoing claims of the Democratic People's Republic of North Korea to be known as "Korea" at all.)

Why this American case of collective repression, this anxious forgetting of modern history, and how will these traumatic Cold War materials return from Asia to haunt and disfigure the Adamic proclamations of the American psyche in the 1990s as we seemingly enter the end of history/ideology on the winds of consumer-driven freedom? Assuming the perspectival damages and dangers of special-case pleading and First World distortion, perhaps the only credible stance to take toward producing/representing Korea is the ethically qualified and politically situated claim enacted by Bruce Cumings. "While I can never fully appreciate the Korean experience," Cumings admits, in summarizing his history of the liberation and

21. Bruce Cumings, *The Origins of the Korean War: Liberation and the Emergence of Separate Regimes, 1945–1947* (Princeton: Princeton University Press, 1981), xxviii. Also see Jon Halliday and Bruce Cumings, *Korea: The Unknown War* (New York: Viking, 1988).

emergence of separate Korean regimes from 1945 to 1947, "my perspective as an outsider and the freer atmosphere in which I work may have some compensation."[22] Without theorizing larger consequences of geopolitical change, an immediate compensation becomes the cross-cultural meaning that accrues as both Koreans and Americans move beyond erasing or distorting history and toward theorizing a more thoroughly archived understanding of Cold War politics. However subjected to the tropes and terms of unconscious orientalism, the American scholar here must labor to undo a vast and dangerous forgetting of Cold War history.

If postwar American or Japanese postmodernists can quite happily forget Korea forty-five years later and Vietnam twenty years later, Koreans *cannot* forget the United States, which, even today, is drawn into policing, modeling, funding, and negotiating the divided Cold War dialectics of North and South some forty-five years after the country was liberated from Japanese colonization. For Koreans, the United States remains the country that has defined, fascinated, and haunted the DMZ-existence of South Korea from 1945 to the present, when even East and West Germany have unexpectedly dismantled the Berlin Wall and moved toward constituting a post–Cold War reunion and the Soviet Union has dissolved.

Caught up and self-divided in the global politics of Russia/China and Japan/USA, the nation-state of "Korea" remains one of the last icons of dialectical polarization and Cold War torment still haunting the postmodern world. Korea still functions, for the most part, as an imaginary vacancy without much glitz or glamour for the First World. The students of SNU necessarily practice guerilla politics/poetics in the streets to get some mass-media attention, as if the master narrative of Americanization might change.

Surely, as European traveling theorist numero uno, Immanuel Kant never visited Tokyo or Seoul. Nevertheless, although Kant may have disqualified pre-Meiji Japan from the higher domains of Western sublimity and thereby installed the Japanese into an eternal landscape of "the beautiful," the small, and the cute, still, his theory of higher aesthetics amusingly droned on to project its transpolitical management of the sublime globe: "In love, the German and the Englishman have a pretty good stomach, a bit fine in sentiment, but of a hale and hearty taste. The Italian is in this respect moody, the Spaniard fantastic, the Frenchman inclined to enjoy forbidden fruit."[23] Cultural representation of national styles served a project of domi-

22. Bruce Cumings, *The Origins of the Korean War*, xxvii.
23. Immanuel Kant, "The Sense of the Beautiful and the Sublime" [1764], in *Immanuel*

nation through circulating modes of reflection, taste, and the will to theorize and substantiate German grandeur.

Trapped in the postmodern predicament of re-essentializing nationalism and positing cultural otherness as a symbolic defense against global homogenization, the American scholar nevertheless has to supplement his/her disciplinary Emersonianism and stance of liberal goodwill toward America's global sublimity with critical doses of Michaux and ethnographic poetics, I would suggest, to move beyond dominations of cultural capital and imaginal constructions of "Korea" and "Japan" dispersed at the borders of the field. Crossing nation-state boundaries and enforcing uncontested constructs of power/knowledge, symbolic representations of otherness can masquerade more invidious forms of material domination, and if these transactions can be resisted at the level of signs, then the often unconscious labors of producing and managing a postindustrial Empire of Sublimity will have been interrupted ever so slightly.[24]

Kant's Moral and Political Writings, ed. Carl J. Friedrich (New York: Modern Library, 1949), 11. On the ideology of the sublime as a political totality and imaginal construct of post-Hegelian nation-states, see Slavoj Žižek, *The Sublime Object of Ideology* (London: Verso, 1989), and Rob Wilson, *American Sublime: The Genealogy of a Poetic Genre* (Madison: University of Wisconsin Press, 1991).

24. For a related discussion of these issues, see Rob Wilson, "(Post)Modernizing South Korea: An Essay on the Korean American Interface," *Chaminade Literary Review* 3 (1990): 129–47; and S. E. Solberg, "Perceptions and Distortions: Stephens' and Wilson's 'Korea,'" and Rob Wilson, "Poison and Truth: S. E. Solberg's 'Korea,'" *Korean Culture* 12 (1991): 4–30, a special issue on Western views of Korea.

The Difficulty of Being Radical: The Discipline of Film Studies and the Postcolonial World Order

Mitsuhiro Yoshimoto

Discourse on the Other

Dilemmas of Western Film Scholars?

Writing about national cinemas used to be an easy task: Film critics believed all they had to do was to construct a linear historical narrative describing a development of a cinema within a particular national boundary whose unity and coherence seemed to be beyond all doubt. Yet, this apparent obviousness of national cinema scholarship is now in great danger, since, on the one hand, we are no longer so sure about the coherence of the nation-state and, on the other hand, the idea of history has also become far from self-evident. As the question of authorship in the cinema was re-problematized by poststructuralist film theory, the notion of national cinema has been similarly put to an intense, critical scrutiny.

The problematic of national cinema scholarship becomes further complicated when we deal with non-Western national cinemas; these pose an additional problem with regard to the production of knowledge. It is often argued that any attempt to write about non-Western national cinemas should be accountable for all the complicated questions concerning the discourse on the Other. Writing about non-Western national cinemas has been situated in such a way that it is inescapable from the question, "Can we ever know the Other as the truly Other?"[1] What is required by the hermeneutics of the Other sought out in non-Western national cinema scholarship is neither a simple identification with the Other nor an easy assimilation of the Other into the self. Instead, it is a construction of a new position of knowledge through a careful negotiation between the self and the Other.

To further explore this problematic of non-Western film scholarship, let us focus on the study of Japanese cinema. Not surprisingly, the axiomatics of the discursive mode of Japanese film scholarship has also been constructed on the opposition between the self and the Other or between Western theory and Japanese culture. This opposition in Japanese film studies creates a certain epistemological difficulty, which Peter Lehman summarizes as follows:

> Japan raises unique problems for Western film scholars. The situation can be summarized, perhaps a little too cynically, as follows: Western film scholars are accusing each other of being Western film scholars. Or to put it a bit more accurately, Western film scholars are accusing each other of being Western in their approach to Japanese film. Is this a genuine dilemma with possible solutions or is it a pseudo-issue which obscures the real issues? Is it productive for us as modern Western film scholars to pursue this quest for the proper Japanese response?[2]

As this passage suggests, there are many writings or meta-discourses on how to study the Japanese cinema properly, and by problematizing dilemmas of Western scholars of Japanese film, Lehman himself contributes to this thriving meta-discourse industry. More specifically, Lehman intervenes in critical exchanges between David Bordwell/Kristin Thompson and Joseph Anderson/Paul Willemen.

One of the points of dispute in this controversy is whether we should

---

1. Zhang Longxi, "The Myth of the Other: China in the Eyes of the West," *Critical Inquiry* 15, no. 1 (Autumn 1988): 127.
2. Peter Lehman, "The Mysterious Orient, the Crystal Clear Orient, the Non-Existent Orient: Dilemmas of Western Scholars of Japanese Film," *Journal of Film and Video* 39, no. 1 (Winter 1987): 5.

call Ozu Yasujiro a modernist filmmaker. It starts with Bordwell and Thompson's claim that since the narrative mode of Ozu's films systematically defies the rules established by the classical Hollywood cinema, Ozu should be regarded as a modernist director. Paul Willemen criticizes Bordwell and Thompson by saying that to call Ozu a modernist is not so much different from European modernist artists' questionable appropriation of African tribal sculpture in the early twentieth century. Bordwell responds that Willemen's critique does not hold, since African sculptors never saw modernists' art work, but Ozu was thoroughly familiar with the Hollywood cinema. Lehman intervenes in this skirmish and takes side with Willemen. According to Lehman, Bordwell dismisses too easily the similarities between traditional Japanese art and Ozu's films, both of which, as Joseph Anderson points out, construct discontinuous, non-narrative space. Furthermore, Lehman quotes Willemen to claim that Bordwell has completely misunderstood the meaning of modernism:

> Ozu's films cannot be claimed as modernist, since the point about modernism is precisely that it is a *critique* of, not a neutral alternative to, dominant aesthetic practices.[3]

Lehman's critique of Bordwell and Thompson is well taken. We should all join Lehman and be "baffled as to why Bordwell and Thompson ever characterized Ozu as a modernist in the first place."[4] At the same time, we should also be appalled by Willemen's and Lehman's Eurocentric view of modernism, which does not consider what modernism possibly means for the non-West. A seemingly innocent question of Ozu's modernity, in fact, cannot be answered unless we carefully take into account the specificities of Japanese cinema, social formations, and history. Such a problematic in Japanese or non-Western cinema scholarship will finally lead to many more fundamental questions concerning the definitions of a nation and of a cinema.

The Subject of Cross-Cultural Analysis

The possibility of studying a non-Western national cinema without erasing its own specificities has been recently attempted in the emerging

3. Lehman, "The Mysterious Orient," 8. Lehman quotes this passage from Paul Willemen, "Notes on Subjectivity: On Reading Edward Branigan's 'Subjectivity under Siege,'" *Screen* 18, no. 1 (1978): 56.
4. Lehman, "The Mysterious Orient," 8.

field of Chinese film studies. E. Ann Kaplan's essay on the Chinese cinema shows great sensitivity toward the issue of cultural specificities and the difficulty of what she calls "cross-cultural analysis."[5] As Kaplan points out, "Cross-cultural analysis . . . is difficult—fraught with danger," since "[w]e are forced to read works produced by the Other through the constraints of our own frameworks/theories/ideologies" (CCA, 42). Yet, despite its inherent danger, according to Kaplan, it is still worth attempting cross-cultural analysis, because "theorists outside the producing culture might uncover different strands of the multiple meanings than critics of the originating culture just because they bring different frameworks/theories/ideologies to the texts" (CCA, 42). The question is whether cross-cultural analysis can really contribute to a cultural exchange between two different cultures on an equal basis, to the understanding of the Other without making it fit to the underlying assumptions of the analyst's own culture, or simply, to a non-dominating way of knowing and understanding the Other.

The major feature of Kaplan's essay is its nonlinearity. It contains so many questions, self-reflexive remarks, and qualifications; that is, the tone of the essay is, as Kaplan says, "tentative":

> So, on the one hand, we have Chinese film scholars turning to American and European film theories to see what might be useful for them, in their writing on both American film and their own cinema; on the other hand, we have some American scholars writing tentative essays on Chinese films. (Those scholars, like Chris Berry, who have lived in China and know the culture and the language are obviously no longer "tentative.") We have, then, a sort of informal film-culture exchange of a rather unusual kind, precisely because of its relative informality. (CCA, 40)

Kaplan's essay on the Chinese cinema is tentative because she has not lived in China and does not know the Chinese language and culture. Yet, according to Kaplan, this tentativeness of informal discourse can become formal knowledge if one goes to and lives in China and becomes an expert in things Chinese. Thus, there is nothing *unusual* about this "informal film-culture exchange": On the contrary, the model of cross-cultural exchange presented here is a classic example of what Gayatri Spivak calls the "arro-

---

5. E. Ann Kaplan, "Problematizing Cross-Cultural Analysis: The Case of Women in the Recent Chinese Cinema," *Wide Angle* 11, no. 2 (1989): 40–50; hereafter cited in my text as CCA.

gance of the radical European humanist conscience, which will consolidate it*self* by imagining the other, or, as Sartre puts it, 'redo in himself the other's project,' through the collection of information."[6]

As we will see in a moment, the mapping of critical discourses on the Chinese cinema by Kaplan is remarkably similar to the polarized scholarship on the Japanese cinema. While either the Western or native expert on a national cinema provides specific information about the cultural background of that cinema, the Western theorist constructs a theoretical framework that gives rise to new insight on the aspects of the national cinema never noticed by area studies experts before. The only difference is that the position of the theorist has become less certain vis-à-vis the non-Western culture, so that any theoretical analysis of the Other can no longer escape a certain sense of hesitation that is hard to find in actual writings on the Japanese cinema.

This sense of hesitation about Western intellectuals' own critical position on and distance from the non-Western culture is widespread in the postmodern West, and compared to the extreme logical consequences reached by postmodern critical ethnography, Kaplan's self-reflexive essay does not go far enough. By pushing to the limit the self-examination of knowledge production in relation to the Other, postmodern critical ethnography has radically put into question not only the position of the analyzing subject, equipped with the latest knowledge of theory and critical methodologies, but also those of the expert subject and the "radical European [or American] humanist conscience" that claim to know the Other based on the authenticity of experience and self-claimed deep understanding of the Other's culture.

In his essay on the Japanese cinema, Scott Nygren attempts to re-articulate the terms of cross-cultural exchange between Japan and the West from a "postmodern perspective." Nygren argues that postmodernism puts into question a linear, evolutionary model of history constructed by a paradigm of modernism, so that "a discontinuous and reversible model of history now seems more productive in conceptualizing cross-cultural relationships."[7] Instead of accepting the traditional view that modern Japanese

6. Gayatri Chakravorty Spivak, "Theory in the Margin: Coetzee's *Foe* Reading Defoe's *Crusoe/Roxana*," in *Consequences of Theory*, ed. Jonathan Arac and Barbara Johnson (Baltimore: Johns Hopkins University Press, 1991), 155. The passage quoted continues as follows: "Much of our literary critical globalism or Third Worldism cannot even qualify to the conscientiousness of this arrogance."
7. Scott Nygren, "Reconsidering Modernism: Japanese Film and the Postmodernist Context," *Wide Angle* 11, no. 3 (1989): 7.

history is a history of mere imitation and assimilation of the West, Nygren proposes an alternative relation between the West and Japan, characterized by a mutual cross-cultural exchange: Traditional Japanese culture gave inspiration to Western modernists as much as Western humanism had a deconstructive impact on feudal aspects of Japanese society. Nygren thus posits a chiasmatic correspondence between Japan and the West on the one hand and between tradition and modernism on the other:

> This paper will argue that classical Hollywood conventions often valorized (although misleadingly) under the name "realism" served to reinforce dominant cultural ideology in the West, while functioning to deconstruct dominant values in Japan. . . . Although the influence of Japanese traditional culture on the formation of Western modernism is well known, in many respects the situation in Japan was the reverse: it was Western tradition, not Western modernism, that played a key role in the formation of what we call "Japanese modernism."[8]

What Nygren attempts to find in this reversed specularity is an "alternative access to a postmodern situation":

> If postmodernism is conceived in the West as a non-progressivist freeplay of traditionalist and modernist signification without progressivist determinism, is it possible to discuss a postmodernist reconfiguration of Japanese culture where Western values of humanism and anti-humanism seem reversed in their relation to tradition and the modern? Can Asian societies in general be theorized in terms of an alternative access to a postmodernist situation?[9]

Yet, this particular model of cross-cultural exchange between the West and Japan, in light of the postmodernism articulated in the passages above, begs the basic facts of West/non-West relations.

There is no need for us to remind ourselves that the West and the non-West do not voluntarily engage in cross-cultural exchange. The relation between the two has always taken the form of political, economic, and cultural domination of the non-West by the West. Not surprisingly, the emergence of modern Japanese literature and film more or less coincides with the age of high imperialism and nationalism. Yet, nowhere in the text do we find questions concerning the ineluctable relations existing among modernism, imperialism, and nationalism (or nativism). Is it the case that by

8. Nygren, "Reconsidering Modernism," 8.
9. Nygren, "Reconsidering Modernism," 7.

providing Japan with Western tradition, which is said "to deconstruct dominant values in Japan," Western imperialism had some empowering effect on Japan? I don't think this is what is argued in the essay; yet at the same time, it is hard not to deduce this disturbing conclusion from the essay's logic, either.[10]

The notions of cross-cultural analysis and cross-cultural exchange are ideologically dubious for the following reasons. First, as we will see in a moment, it contributes to the concealment of the questionable, complicit division of national cinema scholarship between history and theory. Second, it also contributes to the myth of a specular relation between Western theory and non-Western practice. In film studies, there are many examples of arguments perpetuating this myth. We have just discussed two examples above. Another powerful instance can also be found in the field of Japanese film studies. In *To the Distant Observer: Form and Meaning in the Japanese Cinema*, which still remains the most provocative study on the Japanese cinema in any language, Noel Burch calls for the "possibility of an immense productive relationship which could and should be developed between contemporary European theory and Japanese practice." "And," continues Burch, "Marxism had always regarded such mutually informative relationships between theory and practice as essential to its growth."[11] Inspired by Roland Barthes's "study" of "Japan," *Empire of Signs*, Burch constructs a utopia called "Japan," in which Western critical theory materializes its critical insight in concrete artistic practices. Japan as the Other is then conceived as mere supplement, safely contained within the epistemological limit of the West.

Examples of this discursive mode are not confined within Japanese film scholarship. Julianne Burton presents a similar view in her article on Third World cinema and First World theory, "Marginal Cinemas and Main-

10. In her essay on the writing of history, Janet Abu-Lughod cautions us that "with each higher level of generality, there are reduced options for reconceptualization. That is why I believe it is absolutely essential, if we are to get away from Eurocentric views of the universe, to 'pick our respondents' carefully and broadly." See "On the Remaking of History: How to Reinvent the Past," in *Remaking History*, ed. Barbara Kruger and Phil Mariani (Seattle: Bay Press, 1989), 118. Those who write on Japan as non-specialists necessarily have to depend on the works by specialists, which are already interpretations of the primary materials. There is nothing wrong with this dependency itself; the problem is that they often choose wrong authorities to support their argument.

11. Noel Burch, *To the Distant Observer: Form and Meaning in the Japanese Cinema* (Berkeley: University of California Press, 1979), 13; hereafter cited in my text as *JC*.

stream Critical Theory."[12] While Burch tries to establish a complimentary relation between Western theory and Japanese practice, Burton attempts to appropriate Third World cinema within the sphere of Western critical discourse by designating the former "marginal" and the latter "mainstream." In Burton's scheme, critics of Third World cinema should be enlightened by the insights of Western critical theory, particularly by the "theory of mediation," and Western critical theory in turn should be modified so that it can accommodate and appropriate Third World films and the specific contexts surrounding them. This sounds good as far as it goes. But who in the end benefits by this cross-cultural exchange? Who dictates the terms of this transaction between the West and the Third World?[13] Burton's critique of Third World filmmakers and critics is dependent on her misuse of the concept of mediation. She does not use this crucial concept to articulate the relation between Third World film practices and various subtexts of film production and consumption. Rather, Burton has recourse to the concept of mediation to insert Western theorists into the position of subject, which, by criticizing the naïveté of Third World practitioners who believe in "unmediated" transparency of meaning, plays the role of "mediator" between Western high theory and Third World practice not only for the First World audience of Third World film but also for Third World people as the uninitiated.

In his essay on the Third Cinema debate, Homi Bhabha argues that critical theory's appropriation of the Other as a good object of knowledge is an epistemological colonization of the non-West:

> Montesquieu's Turkish Despot, Barthes' Japan, Kristeva's China, Derrida's Nambikwara Indians, Lyotard's Cashinahua "pagans" are part of this strategy of containment where the Other text is forever the exegetical horizon of difference, never the active agent of articulation. The Other is cited, quoted, framed, illuminated, encased in the shot/reverse-shot strategy of a serial enlightenment. Narrative and the *cultural* politics of difference become the closed circle of in-

12. Julianne Burton, "Marginal Cinemas and Mainstream Critical Theory," *Screen* 26, nos. 3–4 (May–August 1985): 2–21.
13. For an extensive critique of Julianne Burton's argument, see Teshome H. Gabriel, "Colonialism and 'Law and Order' Criticism," *Screen* 27, nos. 3–4 (May–August 1986): 140–47. See also Scott Cooper, "The Study of Third Cinema in the United States: A Reaffirmation," in *Questions of Third Cinema*, ed. Jim Pines and Paul Willemen (London: BFI, 1989): 218–22.

terpretation. The Other loses its power to signify, to negate, to initiate its "desire," to split its "sign" of identity, to establish its own institutional and oppositional discourse. However impeccably the content of an "other" culture may be known, however anti-ethnocentrically it is represented, it is its *location* as the "closure" of grand theories, the demand that, in analytic terms, it be always the "good" object of knowledge, the docile body of difference, that reproduces a relation of domination and is the most serious indictment of the institutional powers of critical theory.[14]

Interestingly, the title of Bhabha's essay is "The Commitment to Theory," not "The Indictment of Theory," although what Bhabha argues is diametrically opposite to Burton's project. This false resemblance between the two, or the double nature of theory in relation to the Other, is precisely a sign of the complexity of the problem we must deal with. What is to be done is neither a simple celebration nor condemnation of critical theory; instead, what is at stake is the precise location of theory in critical discourse on/of/by the non-West. This problematic of theory will be discussed more fully in the following sections, but for a moment, I would like to come back to my third point about the notion of cross-cultural exchange (or analysis). By designating only one direction of subject-object relation, this popular notion elides the issue of power/knowledge. While Western critics as subject can analyze a non-Western text as object, non-Western critics are not allowed to occupy the position of subject to analyze a Western text as object. When non-Western critics study English literature or French cinema, it is not called cross-cultural analysis. Whatever they say is interpreted and judged only within the context of Western discourses. The cross-cultural analysis, which is predicated on the masking of power relations in the production of knowledge, is a newer version of legitimating cultural colonization of the non-West by the West.

A binarism of self/Other, which underlies the project of cross-cultural analysis, is a trap. It abstracts the role of power in the production of knowledge, and depoliticizes the structure of domination found in West/non-West opposition. The studies of non-Western national cinemas based on the axiomatics of self/Other opposition cannot but reproduce the hegemonic ideology of Western neocolonialism. It can produce knowledge on non-Western national cinemas only for those who can put themselves into the position of

---

14. Homi K. Bhabha, "The Commitment to Theory," in *Questions of Third Cinema*, 124.

the subject (i.e., Western theorists). Discourse on the Other and its corollary, cross-cultural analysis, not only fix the non-West as the object to be appropriated but also transform serious political issues into bad philosophical questions. For instance, as we have already observed, Peter Lehman's critique of Bordwell, Thompson, Heath, and so forth is right on target; however, the dilemmas of Western scholars of Japanese film on which he speculates are also false dilemmas created by the mistaken assumptions and premises of meta-discourses on Japanese film criticism. Being dependent on the framework of self/Other dichotomy, Lehman misses what is fundamentally at stake: The structural dilemma created by discourse on the Other is in fact only a disguise for a legitimation of Western subjectivity supported by another fundamental opposition underlying Japanese film scholarship.

History and Theory

Two Types of Japanese Film Scholarship
In *Cinema: A Critical Dictionary*, edited by Richard Roud, there are seven entries on Japanese directors; of these seven, three essays (on Mizoguchi, Naruse, and Ozu) are written by Donald Richie, while Noel Burch contributes two essays (on Kurosawa and Oshima).[15] This division of labor in Roud's volume mirrors the two different types of Japanese film scholarship: On the one hand, the Japanese film and area studies specialists tend to take up the historical study of Japanese cinema, since they possess a good command of the Japanese language and are familiar with Japanese culture but not with the theoretical advancement made in film studies; on the other hand, film critics well versed in theory but not in the Japanese language write on Japanese cinema from "theoretical perspectives."

The critic who represents area studies specialists is Donald Richie, whose *Japanese Film: Art and Industry*,[16] cowritten with Joseph Anderson, is a combination of conventional, linear narrative sketching the development of the Japanese film industry and a compilation of chronologically arranged, short commentaries on hundreds of films. If, as the blurb by David Bordwell on the back cover of the book says, *The Japanese Film* is really "the definitive study in any Western language of the Japanese cinema," it is

15. Richard Roud, ed., *Cinema: A Critical Dictionary*, 2 vols. (London: Martin Secker and Warburg, 1980).
16. Joseph L. Anderson and Donald Richie, *The Japanese Film: Art and Industry*, expanded ed. (Princeton: Princeton University Press, 1982).

presumably because Richie and Anderson know the language and culture, or simply Japan. The fact that Richie freely draws on his firsthand knowledge of directors like Ozu and Kurosawa also seemingly gives a sense of authenticity to his other important books on those directors and secures his position as the authority of the Japanese cinema. What Richie embodies in Japanese film scholarship is the figure of cultural expert. What is appreciated and valued is the authenticity of the personal experience of the (anthropologist) expert "who was actually there."

In contrast to the empiricism of Donald Richie, the strength of a theoretical study is said to lie in the analyst's mediated detachment from the object of study. The importance of Noel Burch's work on the Japanese cinema is derived precisely from this sense of detachment as a result of his unfamiliarity with the mass of native Japanese discourses. By radically decontextualizing the Japanese cinema, Burch has succeeded in displacing the Japanese cinema from the margin to the forefront of contemporary film scholarship and, however indirectly, has contributed to the critique of ethnocentrism in the institution of film studies.

Thus, the real division in Japanese film scholarship is created not by the West/Japan dichotomy but by the opposition between theory and history. What is at stake is not simply the shortcomings of either theoretical work (Burch) or historical study (Richie) but the unproblematic division between history and theory itself. Generally speaking, both sides are quite respectful of each other and do not meddle in the affairs of the other group. Far from creating antagonism, the split within Japanese film studies has reached a curious equilibrium, a peaceful coexistence of theorists with area studies specialists. It is this mutually complicit relation between theory and history that should be questioned and re-articulated. Put another way, we need to reexamine how the differentiation of empirical history from abstract theory creates an illusion that different critical approaches could democratically coexist side by side without any interference. What is at stake in the end is not a specific problem debated in the field of Japanese film studies but the question of how Japanese film studies is constructed as an academic sub-discipline.[17]

17. For instance, see David Desser, *Eros Plus Massacre: An Introduction to the Japanese New Wave Cinema* (Bloomington: Indiana University Press, 1988), 2–3. Desser argues that his purpose is to "situate the New Wave within a particular historical, political, and cultural context" without challenging the already existing other modes of critical discourse. Yet contextualization should not be mere supplement to theoretical abstrac-

The Classical Hollywood Cinema and a New Tribal Art

The theoretical mode of Japanese film studies derives its impetus from the rigorous theorization of the narrational mode of Hollywood cinema and a renewed interest in possible radical alternatives. One of the major accomplishments of film studies is the deconstruction of the sense of continuity and the impression of reality created by the Hollywood cinema. It has been shown that that sense of continuity becomes possible precisely because of, for instance, numerous discontinuities whose existence is concealed by a series of alternations and repetitions constructing symmetrical structures. In theoretical studies of the Japanese cinema, the indigenous mode of Japanese film practice, based on structural principles of traditional art—privileging of surface over depth, presentation instead of representation, organization of nonlinear, non-narrative signifiers, and so on—is said to be inherently radical and thus puts into question the representational mode of the classical Hollywood cinema. From this particular theoretical perspective, Burch rewrites the history of the Japanese cinema in order to present the Japanese cinema as a prime example of an alternative to the institutional mode of representation.

Understandably, this theoretical tyranny of Burch's argument is not unchallenged. David Desser is one of those who question Burch's formalist position; however, by accepting formalist reification of a form/content division, he presents a confused counterproposal. According to Desser, "since traditional Japanese art is already formally subversive, a genuinely radical, political Japanese art must move beyond the merely formally subversive; it must also move beyond the kind of radical content apparent in the prewar tendency films or the postwar humanistic, left-wing cinema of the 1950s."[18] To the extent that he asserts the formal subversiveness of traditional Japanese art, Desser writes within the framework constructed by Noel Burch, and his criticism is not really a criticism but a revision within a formalist framework. The questions I would like to ask are much more simple and fundamental: What does traditional Japanese art subvert? Is it, as Burch argues, the representational mode of the classical Hollywood cinema? What does traditional Japanese art have to do with the Hollywood cinema?

---

tion or formalism. If it is merely supplemental, then, that mode of contextualization is nothing more than vulgar historicism. When it takes the form of a radical questioning, contextualization becomes a critical practice of *mediation,* which demolishes the edifice of democratic pluralism.

18. Desser, *Eros Plus Massacre*, 24.

The classical Hollywood cinema has certainly played a crucial role in the formation of any national cinema that had access to it, yet it can never have complete control over how a particular national cinema is constructed. A national cinema as the culture industry exists in a complex web of economic, ideological, and social relations, and the classical Hollywood cinema constitutes only one element of those relations. As Judith Mayne correctly points out, the excessive emphasis on the classical Hollywood cinema as the norm has a constrictive effect on the attempt to study and/or search for an "alternative" cinema:

> The classical Hollywood cinema has become the norm against which all other alternative practices are measured. Films which do not engage the classical Hollywood cinema are by and large relegated to irrelevance. Frequently, the very notion of an "alternative" is posed in the narrow terms of an either-or: either one is within classical discourse and therefore complicit, or one is critical of and/or resistant to it and therefore outside of it.[19]

Nobody can question the dominance of the Hollywood cinema in the world film market. However, this does not automatically mean that the Hollywood cinema has been dominant trans-historically or trans-culturally. We need to put the Hollywood cinema in specific historical contexts; instead of talking about the Hollywood cinema as the norm, we must examine the specific and historically changing relations between the Hollywood cinema and other national cinemas.[20]

Other questions concern a special position accorded to the Japanese cinema in non-Western national cinema scholarship. Why has the Japanese cinema become so important in the battle against the institutional mode of representation? Why can the Japanese cinema be so easily incorporated into theoretical discourses of Anglo-American film studies, while theory seems to become problematic in the analysis of, say, the Chinese cinema? Why suddenly has the possibility of cross-cultural analysis become an issue in the analysis of the Chinese cinema, while it has never been an issue in studies of the Japanese cinema, except in various meta-discourses that appeared mostly in the form of review essays?

19. Judith Mayne, *Kino and the Woman Question* (Columbus: Ohio State University Press, 1989), 3.
20. For the specific place of Hollywood in the postwar Japanese cultural system, see my forthcoming "The Aporia of Modernity: The Japanese Cinema and the 1960s," (Ph.D. diss., University of California, San Diego).

One way of approaching these questions is to go back to the issues of modernism, the avant-garde, and the Japanese cinema to which I briefly refer in the beginning of this essay. For Bordwell and Thompson, Ozu is a modernist filmmaker in a class with Dreyer, Bresson, Godard, and the like. For Burch, the prewar Japanese cinema as a unified whole is comparable to European avant-garde cinemas. Despite the difference in their claim and the register of concepts used in their argument, Burch and Bordwell/Thompson participate in the same critical project. In both cases, the logic used to legitimate their claims is dependent on the observable formal features commonly found in two groups of objects that are drastically different in other aspects. To this extent, Burch, Bordwell, and Thompson's argument seems to be a variation of the discourse of art history claiming the existence of affinity between modern and tribal artifacts. This formalist logic is criticized by James Clifford as wishful thinking by Western critics.

> Actually the tribal and modern artifacts are similar only in that they do not feature the pictorial illusionism or sculptural naturalism that came to dominate Western European art after the Renaissance. Abstraction and conceptualism are, of course, pervasive in the arts of the non-Western World. To say that they share with modernism a rejection of certain naturalist projects is not to show anything like an affinity. . . .
>   The affinity of the tribal and the modern is, in this logic, an important optical illusion—the measure of a *common differentness* from artistic modes that dominated in the West from the Renaissance to the late nineteenth century.[21]

But what Burch and Bordwell/Thompson argue is more "radical" than a kind of colonial discourse questioned by Clifford. For what they find is not just affinity but identity between the Western avant-garde and the Japanese cinema or Ozu and Western modernist filmmakers. For their projects, a mere affinity or optical illusion is not enough, so that, for instance, according to Burch, instead of merely resembling avant-garde practices, the Japanese cinema should be an avant-garde art. Burch's purpose is to find an autonomous group of film practices that is not analogous to but identical with what he calls avant-garde.

By the recent Japanese film scholarship, the Japanese cinema is construed as a new tribal art. At the same time, the emphasis on iden-

21. James Clifford, *The Predicament of Culture: Twentieth-Century Ethnography, Literature, and Art* (Cambridge: Harvard University Press, 1988), 192.

tity instead of affinity also makes it the avant-garde in the guise of a tribal art. For this reason, Burch and others choose to study Japanese but not Chinese, Indian, or any other non-Western national cinemas. The double identity of the cinema—tribal *and* avant-garde—requires them to choose the cinema of a nation that is perceived to be sufficiently different from, but have some common elements with, Western capitalist nations. Japan fulfills their utopian dream. On the one hand, Japan is exotic; according to Burch, "Japan offer[s] traits which seem even more remote from our own, Western ways of thinking and doing, more remote than comparable traits of other Far-Eastern societies" (*JC*, 89). On the other hand, an exotic Japan is similar enough to the West, since "these traits also lend themselves to *a Marxist critique of modern Western history in many of its aspects*" (*JC*, 89). Burch sublates the contradiction of Japan and the Japanese cinema by situating them "with regard both to the dominant ideological profile of Western Europe and the Americas, and to those practices, scientific, literary and artistic, which instantiate the Marxist critique of that dominance" (*JC*, 89). What makes Burch's sublation possible is Japan's ambivalent geopolitical position: economically part of the First World but culturally part of the Third World. The dialectic of the traditional art form and Western influences that Burch finds in the history of the Japanese cinema is homologous with the schizophrenic division of Japan's relations to other nations.

Conclusion

The genealogy of film studies shows that it started as a contestation against the academicism in the 1960s and remained in the forefront of the changing humanities and a redrawing of disciplinary boundaries. In the name of the avant-garde and subversion, however, film studies has consolidated itself as a respectable academic discipline whose discursive organization is not very different from such a traditional discipline as literary studies. One of the concrete examples of this irony can be observed in the division of labor in national cinema studies, which uncannily mirrors the geopolitical configuration and division of a contemporary postcolonial world order. The opposition between the classical Hollywood cinema and the alternative modes of film practices is created with a good intention of avant-garde radicalism; however, the kind of politics articulated in this binarism is a different matter entirely. In the peculiar division of national cinema studies, American, European, Japanese, and other non-Western cinemas are studied to promote distinctively different critical and political agendas. Therefore, we need to carefully reexamine whether, by engaging ourselves in national cinema studies, we are mechanically reproducing, instead of analyzing, the ideological picture of a postcolonial world situation constructed by Western postindustrial nations. More precisely, we must question whether, in the name of critical opposition to Hollywood, we are, on the contrary, contributing to the hegemony of and the accumulation of cultural capital by the United States.

How can we stop fashioning the discipline of film studies into a mirror of postcolonial world geopolitics? Can the neocolonial logic of film studies be corrected by going back to that perennial epistemological question, "Can we ever know the Other as the truly Other?" The problem here is not that this question is too complicated to be sufficiently answered by any response; that is, the problem is not the impossibility of the answer but the formulation of this particular question itself. By construing the Other as the sole bearer of difference, this seemingly sincere question does nothing but conceal the fundamentally problematic nature of the identity of the self.

The so-called imperialist misrepresentation or appropriation of the Other is an oxymoron. The Other cannot be misrepresented, since it is always already a misrepresentation. Imperialism starts to show its effect not when it domesticates the Other but the moment it posits the difference of the Other against the identity of the self. This fundamental imperialism of the self/Other dichotomy can never be corrected by the hermeneutics of the Other or cross-cultural exchange; on the contrary, the latter reinforces the imperialist logic under the guise of liberal humanism, or what Spivak calls "neocolonial anticolonialism."

Let us debunk once and for all the imperialist logic of questions based on the self/Other dichotomy. Let us go back to that spirit of true radicalism that once made film studies such an exciting space for critical thinking.

Index

Contributors

Eqbal Ahmad is professor of international relations and Middle Eastern studies at Hampshire College in Amherst, Massachusetts, where he teaches in the fall semesters. He lives in New York City and Islamabad, Pakistan, and writes a weekly column for several Third World newspapers. He is a Writing Fellow (1991–1993) of the MacArthur Foundation's Program in Peace and International Security, and managing editor of *Race and Class*.

Perry Anderson teaches at UCLA and is a member of the editorial board of *New Left Review*. Among his books are *Passages from Antiquity to Feudalism* (1974), *Lineages of the Absolute State* (1974), *Considerations on Western Marxism* (1976), and *In the Tracks of Historical Materialism* (1984).

Bruce Cumings is professor of international history at the University of Chicago and the author of a two-volume study, *The Origins of the Korean War*.

Arif Dirlik is professor of history at Duke University. His works include *Anarchism in the Chinese Revolution* (1991), *Schools into Fields and Factories: Anarchists, the Guomindang and the Labor University in Shanghai, 1927–1932* (with Ming K. Chan, 1991), *The Origins of Chinese Communism* (1989), *Revolution and History: The Origins of Marxist Historiography in China, 1919–1937* (1978), and *Marxism and the Chinese Experience: Issues in Contemporary Chinese Socialism* (co-edited with Maurice Meisner, 1989).

H. D. Harootunian teaches in the departments of history and East Asian languages and civilizations at the University of Chicago. His most recent work on Japanese nativism is entitled *Things Seen and Unseen* (University of Chicago Press, 1988).

Kazuo Ishiguro, an English-educated novelist, is author of *The Remains of the Day*, for which he received the 1989 Booker Prize. His earlier publications include *A Pale View of Hills* (1982) and *An Artist of the Floating World* (1986), for which he was awarded, respectively, the Royal Society of Literature Prize and the Whitbread Book of the Year Award.

Fredric Jameson is the director of the Graduate Program in Literature and the Center for Critical Theory at Duke University. He has published numerous books on Marxism, literary theory, poststructuralism, and postmodernism. His books include *Marxism and Form, The Prison House of Language, The Political Unconscious, The Ideologies of Theory: Essays 1971–1986,* and *Fables of Aggression.* He also co-edits, with Stanley Fish, the series Post-Contemporary Interventions.

Kojin Karatani is a professor of literature at Hosei University and the author of *Marx: The Center of Possibilities, The Origins of Modern Japanese Literature,* and, most recently, *Research I & II,* among numerous other publications. He has been a visiting professor at both Yale and Columbia Universities.

Oe Kenzaburo is a leading contemporary novelist in Japan. Among his better-known works are *Man'ei gannen no futtoboru* (A football game in the first year of Man'ei) (1973) (translated as *The Silent Cry,* 1974), *Do jidai gemu* (Contemporary games) (1979), and *Atarashii hito yo mezameyo* (Wake up to a new life) (1983).

Seiji M. Lippit is pursuing a doctorate in Japanese literature at Columbia University.

Masao Miyoshi is professor of English and comparative literature and the director of the Program in Japanese Studies at the University of California, San Diego. His most recent publication is *Off Center: Power and Culture Relations Between Japan and the United States* (Harvard University Press, 1991).

Tetsuo Najita is Robert S. Ingersoll Distinguished Service Professor at the University of Chicago. He is the outgoing president of the Association of Asian Studies and the author of *Visions of Virtue,* which has recently been translated into Japanese and issued by Iwanami.

Leslie Pincus is assistant professor of Japanese literature at UCLA. She is completing a book entitled *The Allure of Difference: Kuki Shuzo and the Construction of the Japanese Spirit.* Her current research explores the links between aesthetics and ideology in interwar Japan.

Naoki Sakai teaches Asian studies at Cornell. He is the author of *Voices of the Past: The Status of Language in Eighteenth–Century Japanese Discourse* (Cornell University Press, 1991).

Miriam Silverberg is in the history department at UCLA. She is the author of *Changing Song: The Marxist Manifestos of Nakano Shigeharu* (Princeton University Press, 1990) and is writing a cultural history of prewar Japan.

Christena Turner is an anthropologist and assistant professor of sociology at the University of California, San Diego. Her recent work includes "Democratic Consciousness in Japanese Labor Unions" in Ellis Kraus, ed., *Democracy in Japan* (1989) and a forthcoming book, *Making Sense: Consciousness, Commitment, and Action in Japanese Unions.*

Rob Wilson is associate professor of English at the University of Hawaii. He is the author of *American Sublime: The Genealogy of a Poetic Genre* (University of Wisconsin Press, 1991). He has essays forthcoming in *East-West Film Journal*, *Verse*, and *Korean Culture*. He is general editor of the SUNY Series on the Sublime.

Mitsuhiro Yoshimoto is a Ph.D. candidate in comparative literature at the University of California, San Diego. He began teaching in the Department of Asian Languages and Literatures and the Program in Comparative Literature at the University of Iowa in the fall of 1991. His articles on postmodernism, film theory, and Japanese film have appeared in *Public Culture*, *Quarterly Review of Film and Video*, and *East-West Film Journal*.